THE LIFE OF
MARY BAKER G. EDDY

AND THE
HISTORY OF CHRISTIAN SCIENCE

MARY BAKER G. EDDY

From a photograph taken in Concord, N. H., in 1892

THE LIFE OF
MARY BAKER G. EDDY
AND THE
HISTORY OF CHRISTIAN SCIENCE

BY

WILLA CATHER and
GEORGINE MILMINE

Introduction and afterword to the Bison Book Edition
by David Stouck

University of Nebraska Press
Lincoln and London

First Bison Book printing: 1993
Most recent printing indicated by the last digit below:
10   9   8   7   6   5   4   3   2   1

Library of Congress Cataloging-in-Publication Data
Cather, Willa, 1873–1947.
The life of Mary Baker G. Eddy and the history of Christian Science /
by Willa Cather and Georgine Milmine; introduction and afterword by
David Stouck.
p. cm
Originally published: New York: Doubleday, Page & Co., 1909.
ISBN 0-8032-1453-7.—ISBN 0-8032-6349-X (pbk.)
1. Eddy, Mary Baker, 1821–1910. 2. Christian Scientists—United
States—Biography. 3. Christian Science—History—19th century.
4. Christian Science—History—20th century. 5. Christian Science.
I. Milmine, Georgine. II. Title.
BX6995.C35 1992
289.5′092—dc20
[B]
CIP 92-37437

Reprinted from the original 1909 edition published by Doubleday,
Page & Company. The University of Nebraska Press is indebted to the
Leon S. McGoogan Library of Medicine, University of Nebraska Medical Center, Omaha, for supplying a copy of this hard-to-find edition for
reproduction.

∞

NOTE

The following history was first published in serial form in *McClure's Magazine*, 1907-1908. It has since been revised and new material has been added.

G. M.

CONTENTS

Introduction to the Bison Book Edition   XV

CHAPTER   PAGE
  I. Mrs. Eddy's American Ancestors—Mark Baker, and
       Life on the Bow Farm—Schooldays in Til-
       ton—Early Influences—Her First Marriage   3

 II. Mrs. Glover as a Widow in Tilton—Her Interest
       in Mesmerism and Clairvoyance—The Disposal
       of Her Son—Marriage to Daniel Patterson   26

III. Mrs. Patterson First Hears of Dr. Quimby—
       Her Arrival in Portland—Quimby and His
       " Science "   42

 IV. Mrs. Patterson Becomes Quimby's Patient and
       Pupil—Her Defence of Quimby and His The-
       ory—Her Grief at His Death—She Asks Mr.
       Dresser to Take up Quimby's Work   .   .   56

  V. The Quimby Controversy—Mrs. Eddy's Claim that
       Christian Science Was a Divine Revelation to
       Her—The Story of Her Fall on the Ice in
       Lynn and Her Miraculous Recovery   .   .   71

 VI. The Quimby Controversy Continued—Mrs. Eddy's
       Attempts to Discredit Quimby—Her Charge
       that He Was Always a Mesmerist—Quimby's
       Adherents Defend Him   88

CHAPTER   PAGE

VII. Dr. and Mrs. Patterson in Lynn—Their Sep-
       aration—Mrs. Patterson as a Professional Vis-
       itor—She Teaches Hiram Crafts the Quimby
       "Science"—Mrs. Patterson in Amesbury   .   105

VIII. Two Years with the Wentworths in Stoughton—
       Mrs. Patterson Instructs Mrs. Wentworth
       from the Quimby Manuscripts and Prepares
       Her First Book for the Press   .   .   .   121

IX.   Mrs. Glover Goes into Partnership with Richard
       Kennedy—Their Establishment in Lynn—
       Mrs. Glover's First Disciples—Disagreements
       and Lawsuits   134

X.   Mrs. Glover's Influence over Her Students—
       Quimby Discredited—Daniel Harrison Spof-
       ford—Mrs. Glover's Marriage to Asa Gilbert
       Eddy   155

XI.   The First Appearance of *Science and Health*—
       Christian Science as a System of Metaphysics
       —As a Religion—As a Curative Agent   .   .   176

XII. Mrs. Eddy's Belief that She Suffered for the
       Sins of Others—Letters to Students—The
       Origin and Development of Malicious Animal
       Magnetism—A Revival of Witchcraft   .   .   211

XIII. The "Conspiracy to Murder" Case—Arrest of
       Eddy and Arens on a Sensational Charge—
       Hearing in Court—Discharge of the De-
       fendants   245

CHAPTER   PAGE

XIV.   Mrs. Eddy Addresses Boston Audiences—She is
       Tortured by Her Fear of Mesmerism—Or-
       ganisation of " The Church of Christ, Scien-
       tist "—Withdrawal of Eight Leading Mem-
       bers—Mrs. Eddy's Retreat from Lynn   .   262

XV.   The Massachusetts Metaphysical College Organ-
       ised—Death of Asa Gilbert Eddy—Mrs.
       Eddy's Belief that He Was Mentally As-
       sassinated—Entrance of Calvin A. Frye   .   281

XVI.   Mrs. Eddy's Boston Household—A Daily War-
       fare Against Mesmerism—The P. M. Soci-
       ety—An Action Against Arens for In-
       fringement of Copyright   298

XVII. Literary Activities—Mrs. Eddy as an Editor—
       The Rev. Mr. Wiggin Becomes Her Liter-
       ary Assistant—His Private Estimate of
       Mrs. Eddy and Christian Science   .   .   312

XVIII. The Material Prosperity of Church and College
       —Mrs. Eddy Goes to Live in Commonwealth
       Avenue—Discontent of the Students—A
       Rival School of Mental Healing—The
       Schism of 1888   340

XIX.   Mrs. Eddy Rallies Her Forces—Growth of
       Christian Science in the West—The Mak-
       ing of a Healer—The Apotheosis of Mrs.
       Eddy   361

CHAPTER   PAGE

XX. The Adoption of a Son—Mrs. Eddy's Household and the New Favourite—A Crisis in Christian Science—Mrs. Eddy is Driven from Boston by " M.A.M." 379

XXI. The New Policy—Mrs. Eddy Resigns from Pulpit and Journal and Closes Her College —Disorganisation of the Church and Association—Reconstruction on a New Basis— Mrs. Eddy in Absolute Control and Possession 391

XXII. Life at Pleasant View—Mrs. Eddy Produces More Christian Science Literature—Foster Eddy Is Made Publisher of the Text-Book—The Story of His Fall from Favour —Rule of Service 411

XXIII. Josephine Curtis Woodbury and the Romantic School—Birth of the Prince of Peace—Mrs. Eddy Withdraws Her Support—" War in Heaven " 428

XXIV. Mrs. Eddy Adopts the Title of " Mother "— Beginning of the Concord Pilgrimages— Mrs. Eddy Hints at Her Political Influence —The Building of the Mother Church Extension 441

XXV. George Washington Glover—Mrs. Eddy's Son Brings an Action Against Leading Christian Scientists—Withdrawal of the Suit—Mrs. Eddy Moves from Concord, N. H., to Newton, Mass. 453

CONTENTS

CHAPTER   PAGE

XXVI. Training the Vine—How Mrs. Eddy Has Organ-
       ised Her Church—Her Management and
       Discipline—The Church Manual—Recent
       Modifications in Christian Science Practice
       —Membership of the Church—Practical
       Results of Mrs. Eddy's Life-Work .   . 460

Appendix A 486

Appendix B 489

Appendix C 494

Afterword to the Bison Book Edition   497

ILLUSTRATIONS

Mary Baker G. Eddy. From a photograph taken in Concord, N. H., in 1892 . . . . *Frontispiece*

FACING PAGE

Mark Baker, Mrs. Eddy's father 10
Daniel Patterson, Mrs. Eddy's second husband . . 34
The house in North Groton, N. H., where Mrs. Eddy, then Mrs. Daniel Patterson, lived for seven years . 38
Phineas Parkhurst Quimby 48
Mary Baker G. Eddy. From a tintype given to Mrs. Sarah G. Crosby in 1864 62
Facsimile of the second sheet of the first " spirit " letter from Albert Baker, Mrs. Eddy's brother, to Mrs. Sarah Crosby 66
Mary Baker G. Eddy. From a photograph taken in Amesbury, Mass., in 1870 114
Mary Baker G. Eddy. Helping an Amesbury photographer to get a successful picture of a baby . . 114
Title page and part of the first page of the manuscript from which Mrs. Glover taught Mrs. Wentworth the system of mental healing which she ascribed to P. P. Quimby 128
Richard Kennedy. From a photograph taken in Lynn, Mass., in 1871 152
Asa Gilbert Eddy, Mrs. Eddy's third husband . . . 168
Daniel H. Spofford 252
Edward J. Arens 252

ILLUSTRATIONS

FACING
PAGE

Mary Baker G. Eddy.   From a tintype given to Lucy
    Wentworth in Stoughton, Mass., in 1870   .   .   270
Mary Baker G. Eddy.   From a photograph taken in
    Boston in the early eighties   270
Calvin A. Frye.   From a photograph taken about 1882   294
Mary Baker G. Eddy.   Taken about the year 1886,
    while at the head of her college in Boston   .   .   308
Mary Baker G. Eddy.   As she looked in 1870 when she
    first taught Christian Science in Lynn, Mass.   .   308
The Reverend James Henry Wiggin, who was for four
    years Mrs. Eddy's literary adviser   .   .   .   328
Christian Scientists' Picnic at Point of Pines, July 16,
    1885   348
Ebenezer J. Foster Eddy, the adopted son of Mrs. Eddy   384
George Washington Glover, Mrs. Eddy's only child .   .   384
Pleasant View, Mrs. Eddy's home in Concord, N. H.   .   414
The First Church of Christ, Scientist, in Boston.   The
    Mother Church   450

INTRODUCTION

By David Stouck

In 1906 the future American novelist Willa Cather was called to New York to begin work in the editorial offices of *McClure's* magazine. Willa Cather was thirty-two and the author of approximately thirty published stories, most of which were set in pioneer Nebraska, where she had been raised. At that time interest in Christian Science was at its height and Willa Cather's first lengthy assignment at *McClure's* was to edit a manuscript about the charismatic leader of this popular new religion. The materials had been collected by a newspaperwoman named Georgine Milmine and when the series of sensational articles about Mrs. Eddy appeared between January 1907 and June 1908 Georgine Milmine was listed as author. Similarly, when the articles were published in book form by Doubleday in 1909, sole credit for the book was given to Georgine Milmine.

Willa Cather has always been associated with the writing of *The Life of Mary Baker G. Eddy and the History of Christian Science,* but the extent of her involvement with the book has been unclear. Cather's companion, Edith Lewis, wrote in her biography that the manuscript and materials were compiled and brought to S. S. McClure by Georgine Milmine but had to be verified and rewritten.[1] In his biography of S. S. McClure, Peter Lyon reports that the job was given to Willa Cather and asserts that "[a]lthough Miss Cather's name was not put on the final result, her hand is evident in every line; she deserves much of the credit for a remarkable portrait of a remarkable woman."[2] Stewart Hudson records that Witter Bynner wrote in a copy of the book that the material "was put into the painstaking hands of Willa Cather for proper presentation, so that a great part of it is her work."[3]

Cather herself, however, denied any significant part in the Eddy biography. In a 1934 letter to Harold Goddard Rugg, for example, she says she was put in charge of the material supplied by Miss Milmine, but that she only did some cutting and rewriting and could not claim authorship for the book, which she considered in fact poorly written.[4] She had issued an even stronger denial in a letter to Mrs. Genevive Richmond, 8 December 1933, in which she says that her part in the biography was only a matter of coordinating material and in some instances rewriting a few paragraphs for the serial publication. To credit her as the author, she says, would be inaccurate. She only worked at it for serial publication and never saw it in book form.[5]

But Cather's involvement in the Christian Science series was greater than she chose to admit. Two letters first of all make this very clear. In one, written to her father on 17 December 1906, she explains that she will be late for Christmas because she must stay in New York to complete work on the March installment of the Christian Science series. She tells her father that she did not write the first article,[6] but that her work appears beginning with the February issue.[7] The actual extent of that work was revealed when the late L. Brent Bohlke discovered a letter from Cather to Edwin H. Anderson, director of the New York Public Library, in which she says that, except for the first chapter, she has in fact written the whole book![8]

Cather's letter to Anderson, who was a friend from her Pittsburgh years,[9] was written on 24 November 1922 in response to his request for details about the Christian Science articles.[10] Because Willa Cather's will prohibits the publication of her correspondence, this unusually candid letter cannot be directly quoted here. Cather set down in numbered paragraphs her recollection of the matter as it developed. What follows is a paraphrase of the contents of the letter: Cather says that Georgine Milmine had spent years collecting an enormous amount of material concerning Mary Baker Eddy and the history of Christian Science, including newspaper clippings from the 1880s, court records, and early editions of Mrs. Eddy's writings. Miss Milmine[11] knew that she did not have the technical skills to write a biography and so she sold the collection to S. S. McClure who in turn set three or four of his staff to work on the story. Burton J. Hendrick wrote the initial installment about Mrs. Eddy's early years; it was based chiefly on popular myth and the biased recollections of jealous relatives. Cather says she was chosen to take over the series because her work was unprejudiced—she had no quarrel to pick with Christian Science. She found the work good training (it involved traveling around New England authenticating all the materials used), but at the same time it was not the kind of writing she was really interested in or willing to defend. Ironically, she observes, Miss Milmine is named the author of a book of which she didn't write a word. Cather concludes her letter to Anderson by insisting that the information remain confidential and Anderson accordingly locked her letter in a vault at the library, and it was not opened until after both Cather and Anderson had died.

Cather's letter to Edwin Anderson describes the Christian Science project as magazine work and her letter to Genevive Richmond (see note 5) implies she was not involved in any way in turning the articles into book form. However, in Boston, the Mary Baker Eddy Archives and Library of The First Church of Christ, Scientist, possesses the manuscript of the "Milmine" book and Willa Cather's editing is evident on its pages. Cather's handwriting is not only identifiable in edits for the typesetter but in notes on separate pages that continue to query such matters as church membership, the importance of the *Christian Science Journal,* etc.[12] Although in her lifetime she continued to minimize her role in *McClure's* sensational Christian Science series, Willa Cather is indisputably the principal author of *The Life of Mary Baker G. Eddy and the History of Christian Science.*

This being the case, we must ask in what ways it is important to identify and read this book as part of the Cather canon. Certainly, it was her first extended piece of writing (she worked at the series for eighteen months, December 1906 through May 1908), and at 495 pages it would be surpassed in length only by *The Song of the Lark.* It is also one of the few instances of a Cather text for which we have a manuscript. Cather would always dismiss the book as journalism and her biographers and critics agree that the writing is uneven, but for readers and students today it presents an important profile of Cather's developing voice and a glimpse of the range of subjects and styles that would eventually make up her special stock in trade as a novelist. For example, in the discussion of Mrs. Eddy's metaphysics we hear the voice of the rational, scientifically-minded university student earnestly dissecting philosophical issues; while in the account of Mrs. Eddy's business acumen we hear the self-assured, often biting young journalist who takes an amused but scornful view of the theologian who turned her denial of material reality into monetary profit. As the strange drama of Mrs. Eddy's life unfolds in the narrative, we become aware of Willa Cather, the burgeoning novelist with a powerful and sympathetic interest in human psychology. And in her puzzlement over a view of the world as ghostly and immaterial we glimpse perhaps the romantic idealism of such sympathetic but deluded fictional figures as Claude Wheeler and Lucy Gayheart that Cather would eventually create. While some chapters are a mechanical stitching together of the testimonial evidence, affidavits and journal items gathered—the work of a journalist hurrying to meet a deadline—other parts contain some of the finest portrait sketches and reflections on human nature that Willa Cather would ever write.

The central interest of the narrative is in Mary Baker Eddy's unflagging struggle to achieve fame and power and in the psychological roots of her unique personality. The portrait is stark and melodramatic, the details often tawdry. There is the hysterical, overwrought child who as a woman still had to be rocked to sleep in a cradle; the young mother who refused to care for her child; the woman who married three times but spent many vagarious years living off the kindness of strangers; the woman who at age fifty, with another person's ideas, was just beginning to grope her way towards her "brave career" and the religious philosophy that denies the existence of physical life.

Cather spares none of the harsh details of Mrs. Eddy's monomania or her desire for mastery, but she also shows how Mrs.

Eddy could transform people's lives in a wonderful way. She tells us that "[t]he one thing she could not endure was to be like other people," and that this in turn made her an exciting presence in the humdrum villages of nineteenth-century New England:

> She was like a patch of colour in those gray communities. She was never dull, her old hosts say, and never commonplace. She never laid aside her regal air; never entered a room or left it like other people. There was something about her that continually excited and stimulated, and she gave people the feeling that a great deal was happening. (122–23)

The reader of Cather's novels might think here of Marian Forrester in *A Lost Lady* and that impression would be quickly reinforced by another passage:

> Even while she was dependent on precarious hospitality, [Mrs. Eddy] managed to invest her person and her doings with a certain form and ceremony which was not without its effect. . . . She was now a woman of forty-seven; her wardrobe was shabby and scant; she still rouged her cheeks; the brown hue of her hair was crudely artificial . . . Certainly, neither village gossips nor rustic humourists had spared her. But the stage did not exist that was so mean and poor, nor the audience so brutal and unsympathetic, that [Mrs. Eddy] could not, unabashed, play out her part. (120)

Willa Cather's thinking and writing about Mary Baker Eddy probably left its strongest visible imprint on *My Mortal Enemy* and the portrait of Myra Henshawe.[13] Mrs. Eddy's rage for mastery, her selfishness, and her power over biddable young men are all akin to the vindictive fictional heroine, surrounded by her boyish admirers, with a head that would have graced a Roman Emperor but who, we are told, is at the same time not unlike "the saints of the early Church."[14] Something essential in Mrs. Eddy's character, as Willa Cather understood it, is captured in the following description, which would seem to anticipate the character of Myra Henshawe:

> It was when Mrs. Eddy was weaving her spell about a new favourite that she was at her best, and it was then that she most believed in herself. But she could never stop with enchanting, merely. She must altogether absorb the new candidate; he must have nothing left in him which was not from her. . . . [But] she never loved any one so well that she could not, in a moment of irritation, believe him guilty, not only of disloyalty, but of theft, knavery, blackmail, or abominable corruption. . . . All the suspicion, envy, and incontinent distrust which so often blazed in Mrs. Eddy's eyes seemed to have found a concrete and corporeal expression in this thing, Mesmerism. (382, 387)

The latter was Mary Baker Eddy's "mortal enemy," a phrase that Cather could not have used without remembering the central demoniclike role attributed in Mrs. Eddy's metaphysics to "mortal mind." Cather quotes the following passage, for example, from *Science and Health:* "Tumors, ulcers, tubercles, inflammation, pain, deformed joints, are all dream shadows, dark images of mortal thought which will flee before the light" (365).

A study of religion in Willa Cather's fiction must include knowledge of this book. Willa Cather was born and raised in a Baptist family and as a middle-aged woman, with her family, she transferred her membership to the Episcopal Church. In her later novels she reveals detailed knowledge and sympathetic understanding of Roman Catholicism. But in no other piece of writing does Cather tackle so squarely metaphysical issues, especially the problem of evil. Mrs. Eddy denied its existence, called it an illusion of "mortal mind," but in presenting Mrs. Eddy's metaphysics in Chapter 11 Cather argues against what she sees as the illogicality of the system. (This chapter and parts of Chapter 12 are important in revealing Cather's skill in logical reasoning and her knowledge of philosophy.) Although Cather valued immensely the physical world of the senses, especially sight and sound, she knew that it was concomitant with violence, disease, and death. But to deny the existence of physical evil, as for example the woman in the 1909 story "The Profile" denies the reality of her scarred face, is to cut oneself off from normal human contacts.[15]

In her rewriting and interpretation of Scripture Mrs. Eddy adjusted the Lord's Prayer to read "Our Father-Mother God, all Harmonious." What Cather made of a religion that presented the feminine idea of God as higher than the masculine (188), that saw a woman succeeding Christ to reveal the spiritual origin of humankind, is difficult to determine because her presentation of this aspect of Christian Science is determinedly neutral (343–46). However, any study of Cather's feminism should take into account what is implied by the various ways in which she presents this powerful female leader.

Cather's most frequent stance is to focus with amusement on the ironies of Mrs. Eddy's ambitious but inconsistent behavior, especially her preoccupation with financial prosperity while preaching a religion that does not credit the existence of the material world. After describing the illogical course of Mrs. Eddy's arguments and her frequent emotional outbursts, Cather observes wryly that "however incoherent Mrs. Eddy became in other matters, she was never so in business" (217). She narrates how Mrs. Eddy selected her favorite students to pay for the printing, advertising, and marketing of *Science and Health*: "For [Mrs. Eddy], in spite of her reluctance to risk money on it, believed intensely in her book" (177). There are numerous such statements, the biographer's tongue in cheek, and we see a capacity for satirical humor rarely sustained for any length in the main body of Cather's work. She tells us after a description of Mrs. Eddy's rivalry with one of her former students, Josephine Woodbury, that "Mrs. Woodbury published a veiled account of her differences with Mrs. Eddy in a pamphlet modestly entitled *War in Heaven*" (435). Cather is very much the amused observer here of human nature with its many shortcomings. She shows us, for example, how Mrs. Eddy's vanity comes to the fore when editors write laudatory articles about her and she in turn directs all Christian Scientists to subscribe to their publications. Cather reports that one politician, who also ran a political newsletter, was able, after flattering Mrs. Eddy, to drop out of politics altogether because of the increased revenue from his publication.

But almost unquestionably the finest writing in *The Life of Mary Baker G. Eddy* occurs in the character sketches and narratives of those lives that at some point were touched by Mrs. Eddy. Willa Cather's relationship to the materials collected by Georgine Milmine was in places not unlike her relation to the materials she gathered herself for writing *Death Comes for the Archbishop;* that is, she was fashioning literary portraits from information about historical personages, and turning anecdotal facts into compelling narrative.

At times there is a tragic cast to the stories that accrue around the early history of the Christian Science church. There is the story of the Pierre, South Dakota, woman who, zealous in her new faith, allowed two of her children to die without seeking medical assistance. Cather observes that "the martyrdoms of a thousand years have proved what men and women can do and endure under the tyranny of an idea" (327).

In contrast, there is the comic story of Mrs. Eddy's rival within the faith, the romantic and impulsive Josephine Woodbury who, with her students, "lived in a kind of miracle-play of their own; had inspirations and revelations and premonitions; saw portents and mystic meanings in everything; and spoke of God as coming and going, agreeing and disagreeing with them" (429). Their story reaches its climax when Mrs. Woodbury gives birth to a son, said to be the result of an immaculate conception or "mental generation." The child is baptized as "The Prince of Peace," but after a rift within the church is denounced by Mrs. Eddy as "an imp of Satan."

And there is the story of the Brown sisters of Ipswich (234) who, like Dr. Archie's wife in *The Song of the Lark,* are obsessed with cleanliness. Miss Lucretia dies of pneumonia caught from airing out the house on a cold day to eradicate every possible speck of dust. The irony, of course, as Stewart Hudson points out, is that Lucretia Brown frantically pursued dust while her Christian Science faith denied its reality. The stories of such characters contain the same kind of sophisticated ironies as the story of Dona Isabella and the problem of her age in *Death Comes for the Archbishop.*

These portraits stand with the best of Cather's writing. There is an unforgettable vividness in the description of the boyish but shrewd Richard Kennedy, Mrs. Eddy's first business partner and subsequent bitter enemy (135); in the picture of Calvin Frye, the stolid, almost inarticulate bachelor who devoted most of his adult life attending to Mrs. Eddy's financial and personal needs (295); and in the account of Joseph S. Eastman, a converted captain who left behind twenty-one years of terrors at sea for "an adventure of the mind which was vastly stranger" (368). Cather writes with admiration for this man and with sympathy for the cravings of his spirit. She also creates a sharp portrait of Mary Baker Eddy's in-laws, and all their rustic eccentricities (169).

But the most vivid and polished of these portraits is that of the Rev. J. H. Wiggin, a one-time Unitarian minister employed for four years by Mrs. Eddy as her literary adviser (332). Cather's portrait is that of a bulky, genial scholar, an American Dr. Johnson, who loved the table, the theatre, and whose conversation was rich in literary quotations, anecdotes, and humor. Wiggin is one of Cather's worldly priests; his is a fond portrait more than tinged with the author's characteristic nostalgia for the nineteenth-century theatre and the gentlemen who were its patrons. She is especially fascinated by Wiggin's rewriting of *Science and Health;* she compares several passages to show how ideas that in earlier editions were befogged by the writing now were made to stand out clearly. But perhaps most significant is the apparent proximity between this man's views of Mary Baker Eddy and her own. She writes that "[h]e was often aghast at her makeshifts and amused by her persistence, while he delighted in her ingenuity and admired her shrewdness. He could find lines in his favourite *Macbeth* applicable even to Mrs. Eddy, and he seemed always heartily to have wished her well" (336). She quotes from a long letter he wrote to a friend about Christian Science theology:

There is nothing really to understand in "Science and Health" except that *God is all,* and yet there is no God in matter! What they fail to explain is, the origin of the *idea* of matter, or sin. They say it comes from *mortal mind,* and that mortal mind is not divinely created, in fact, has no existence; in fact, that nothing comes of nothing, and

> that matter and disease are like dreams, having no existence. . . .
> No, Swedenborg, and all other such writers, are sealed books to
> [Mrs. Eddy]. She cannot understand such utterances, and never
> could, but dollars and cents she understands thoroughly. (338)

Cather endorses Wiggin's ironic but charitable views explaining that "[w]e have no other picture of [Mrs. Eddy] done by so capable a hand, for no one else among those closely associated with her ever studied her with such an unprejudiced and tempered mind, or judged her from a long and rich experience of books and men, enlightened by a humour as irrepressible as it was kindly" (337). Wiggin's point of view accordingly was Cather's.

The excitement Cather sometimes felt in her subject is revealed at moments in the book's style. While much of the writing is simply competent journalism, a stitching together of the information and documents collected, there are passages where the fiction writer takes over and shapes her story on more novelistic lines, giving the reader a long perspective on Mrs. Eddy's life and career. In these passages we find sentences, such as the last one quoted above, with syntactic features characteristic of Willa Cather's most evocative writing, sentences that begin with unmarked themes and bare noun phrases, then open up to modification, especially to postmodification—participial adverbs, appositives, and absolutes. For example, Cather describes the torment of Mrs. Eddy's early years in such a sentence:

> Her mind was turned in upon itself; she had been absorbed in ills
> which seem to have been largely the result of her own violent na-
> ture—lacking any adequate outlet, and, like disordered machinery,
> beating itself to pieces. (57)

In the series of postmodifiers of the sentence's ending, Cather strikes a deeper chord, evokes something poetic and desperate about her subject, suggestively associating her neurasthenia with nineteenth-century industrialism. Similarly, to record an elusive feeling an old acquaintance has in remembering Mrs. Eddy, Cather uses a clause in adverbial apposition:

> Like all of Mrs. Eddy's old intimates, she speaks of their days of companionship with a certain shade of regret—as if life in the society of this woman was more intense and keen than it ever was afterward. (65)

There are not many of these sentences which attempt to communicate something beyond the reach of a journalist's prose, but when we come across one we hear the voice of the future novelist striving to convey things for which language is finally inadequate.

There are numerous accounts in the book of the spell that Mrs. Eddy's remarkable personality cast over her students, likened in one passage to "the wind stirring the wheatfield" (314). In this same passage Cather describes, in language that looks forward to *Death Comes for the Archbishop,* how Christian Science spread westward in America as part of that age-old and profound human need for religion: "Copies [of the *Christian Science Journal*] found their way to remote villages in Missouri and Arkansas, to lonely places in Nebraska and Colorado, where people had much time for reflection, little excitement, and a great need to believe in miracles" (313).

In most of the book Cather avoids such romantic views and judges Mrs. Eddy and her religion according to the rational standards of scientific thought established by Descartes, Newton, and Locke. She cites the New England historian and popularizer of evolution, John Fiske, who described the physical science of cause and effect as "one of the world's latest and most laborious acquisitions," and she herself affirms it to be "the basis of the health and sanity of modern life" (243). But the radical idealism at the heart of Christian Science was not something ultimately foreign to Cather's Romantic imagination and by the mid 1920s, when writing *The Professor's House,* she would subtly repudiate Fiske when the Professor is advised by his detracters to adopt something of Fiske's more genial style.[16] And contrary to Fiske, Professor St. Peter gives a lecture in which he discredits not the physical world but laboratory science as a way of making life meaningful (68–69). The yearning to live in an "invisible, inviolable world" is the romantic dream of several Cather protagonists, most notably Claude Wheeler in *One of Ours* and Lucy Gayheart.[17] They are viewed finally as deluded by their dreams, alienated from reality, but when such romantic dreams are part of a community of the faithful, as the protagonists experience them in *Death Comes for the Archbishop*, those yearnings are endorsed by the author as the highest reach of human culture. That Cather should have no quarrel with Christian Science is not surprising, given the imaginative path her own career followed.

Finally, this book could be said to hold a special interest for us in the late twentieth century when our critical sensibility is preoccupied with the textual nature of history. Cather's largely disinterested, businesslike approach to her subject frequently foregrounds the research materials from which her narrative has been constructed—affadavits, letters, oral testimonies, journal articles, etc. Much of this material, whether identified as legend or transcribed evidence, remains transparently documentary and allows us to see in turn the writer arranging and interpreting the evidence. An important part of this book then, for our study of Willa Cather, is the performance of the narrator, speaking here in a number of different voices, rehearsing, if you like, the many parts of the future novelist.

NOTES

1. See Edith Lewis, *Willa Cather Living* (New York: Alfred Knopf, 1953; rept. Lincoln: University of Nebraska Press, 1976), 63–64.
2. See Peter Lyon, *Success Story: The Life and Times of S. S. McClure* (New York: Scribner's, 1963), 299. Lyon's account is based on conversation and correspondence with Witter Bynner, who in 1906 was assistant editor at McClure's. See page 415.
3. See Stewart Hudson's "Introduction" to the second edition of *The*

Life of Mary Baker G. Eddy and the History of Christian Science (Grand Rapids: Baker Book House, 1971), xvii.

4. Willa Cather to Harold Goddard Rugg, 10 November 1934, Rugg Collection, Baker Library, Dartmouth College.

5. Willa Cather to Genevive Richmond, 8 December 1933, Mary Baker Eddy Archives and Library, The First Church of Christ, Scientist, Boston. See Robert J. Peel's *Mary Baker Eddy: The Years of Authority* (New York: Holt, Rinehart and Winston, 1977), 472.

6. Burton J. Hendrick of the McClure staff is credited by Cather as the author of the first installment, but Mark Sullivan also played a part in the series, for he describes in *The Education of an American* (New York: Doubleday, Doran & Co., 1938, 202) his work of checking Milmine's facts in some of the remote parts of New Hampshire.

7. Cather does not actually identify the work she is doing by name, but a letter written the same day (17 December 1906) by S. S. McClure to Cather's father, who was then ill, states that "she is involved in a piece of work absolutely vital to the magazine on a series of articles on Christian Science that no one but her seems to be able to do just right." (Letters in Cather family collection)

8. See L. Brent Bohlke, "Willa Cather and *The Life of Mary Baker G. Eddy*," *American Literature* 54 (May 1982), 288–94.

9. See Kathleen D. Byrne and Richard C. Snyder, *Chrysalis: Willa Cather in Pittsburgh, 1896–1906* (Pittsburgh: Historical Society of Western Pennsylvania, 1980), 68–69, 108.

10. Willa Cather to Edwin H. Anderson, 24 November 1922, Anderson Papers, Manuscripts and Archives Division, New York Public Library. Although this letter (and all others) by Cather may not be published, according to the terms of her will, it may be read at the New York Public Library.

11. L. Brent Bohlke, following Cather's biographers E. K. Brown and James Woodress, refers to Georgine Milmine as "Mrs. Milmine" (citation in note 8). She was in fact married, to a Benjamin Welles, but Cather is correct in calling her Miss Milmine because she continued to use her maiden name professionally.

12. Kevin Synnott, Russell Sage College, Troy, New York, examined the "Milmine Collection" in the Mary Baker Eddy Archives and Library and found three different sets of manuscripts related to the biography. The first, dated at New York 1904, consists of 127 half-pages of typescript signed by Georgine Milmine and appears to represent an early attempt on her part to write the biography. The second, a carbon

of a typescript for the book, consists of 414 pages with edits by both Milmine and Cather. The third consists of two copies of partial manuscripts with edits by Georgine Milmine. There are no manuscripts or typescripts for the *McClure's* articles.

13. Stewart Hudson's introduction to the second edition of *The Life of Mary Baker G. Eddy* (Baker House Books) makes some insightful connections between the biography and specific themes and patterns of characterization in Cather's fiction. Hudson notes, for example, the inescapable link between the title *My Mortal Enemy* and Mrs. Eddy's metaphysics of evil and mortal mind.

14. Willa Cather, *My Mortal Enemy* (New York: Random House, 1961), 93.

15. There is an excellent discussion of Christian Science and "The Profile" in Hudson's introduction to the second edition, xx–xxiv.

16. Willa Cather, *The Professor's House* (New York: Alfred Knopf, 1925), 32.

17. For a full treatment of this theme see two articles by Blanche H. Gelfant: "Movement and Melody: The Disembodiment of Lucy Gayheart," *Women Writing in America* (Hanover: University Press of New England, 1984), 117–43; and "'What Was It . . . ?': The Secret of Family Accord in *One of Ours*," *Willa Cather: Family, Community, and History*, ed. John J. Murphy (Provo: Brigham Young University Humanities Publications Center, 1990), 85–102.

THE LIFE OF
MARY BAKER G. EDDY

AND THE
HISTORY OF CHRISTIAN SCIENCE

THE LIFE OF MARY BAKER G. EDDY AND THE HISTORY OF CHRISTIAN SCIENCE

CHAPTER I

MARY A. MORSE BAKER,[1] the future leader of the Christian Science Church, was the sixth and youngest child of Mark and Abigail Baker. She was born July 16, 1821, at the Baker homestead in the township of Bow, near the present city of Concord in New Hampshire. As a family the Bakers were of the rugged farmer type of the period to which they belonged. From the days of John Baker, their earliest American ancestor, who came from East Anglia and obtained a freehold in Charles-town, Mass., in 1634, throughout five generations [2] to Mark Baker, they had worked the unwilling soil of their New England farms, and brought up large families to labour after them. One of their number had engaged in the pre-Revolutionary wars, and in 1758 received a captain's commission from Governor Benning Wentworth of New Hampshire. This was

---

[1] Mrs. Eddy was named in part for her grandmother, Mary Ann Moore (or O'Moor) Baker. She wrote her name as above, using only the initial of her second name.
[2] The five generations were (1) John, (2) Thomas, (3) Thomas, (4) Joseph, (5) Joseph, who was the father of Mark Baker and the grandfather of Mrs. Eddy.

3

Joseph Baker, the grandfather of Mark who married Hannah, the daughter of Captain John Lovewell, hero of " Lovell's Fight," and through her came into possession of the homestead in Bow. According to family tradition this farm, which was given to Hannah Lovewell by her father, was originally a part of " Lovell's Grant," a tract deeded to Captain Lovewell by the government for " gallant military service."

As far back as the memory of any of the present generation of Bakers goes, however, the farm was first occupied by Joseph Baker 2d, and his wife, whose name is recorded by the Baker family both as Mary Ann O'Moor and Marion Moore.[3] Of their large family of children, Mark, born May 2, 1785, was the youngest,[4] and at the death of his father in 1816, he, with an elder brother, James, inherited the farm. Mark's share of the estate included the farmhouse and barns, with the obligation to support his mother. The farm was hill land, rising from the valley of the Merrimac River, and not especially fertile, but as his fathers before him had done, he managed, by toiling early and late, to wring from it a living for himself and his large family. In May, 1807, he had married the daughter of Nathaniel and Phebe Ambrose, neighbours across the Merrimac, in Pembroke, and brought her home to his father's house. Like the Bakers, the Ambrose family were severe Congregationalists, and farmers of the familiar New England type. Deacon Ambrose and his wife were staunch

[3] Mrs. Eddy and at least one other descendant gives the name as Marion Moore, but from statistics copied from the family Bible of this Joseph Baker, and now in possession of his great grand-daughter, it is recorded that Joseph Baker was born November 9, 1741, and died in February, 1816. It gives the name of his wife as Mary Ann O'Moor, who was born December 11, 1743, and died January 26, 1835, and names ten children born to them. See Appendix A.
[4] The Joseph Baker record names ten children, as follows: John, James, David, Jesse, William, Hannah, Joseph, Mary Ann, Philip, and Mark.

supporters of their church, and they had brought up their daughter, Abigail, to be both pious and thrifty. As the wife of Mark Baker she is remembered for her patience and industry. She devoted all her energies to the care of her family, and was faithful in attendance at church. And this simple record, like that of many another heroic New England housewife, is all that is known of Mrs. Eddy's mother.

The dominating influence in the Baker home was Mark, and he made his presence felt in the community as well. His character was naturally strong, and as narrow as his experience and opportunity had been. Born ten years after the American Revolution, he grew up in the atmosphere of sharply-defined opinions and declared principles, peculiar to the times. The country was still comparatively undeveloped and scantily populated, and without the broadening influences made possible by later inventions. His house, in the middle of an isolated farm, was remote from its neighbours; the nearest town was Concord, then a place of two or three thousand inhabitants, and where, except on market days and church days, he almost never went. The hard daily labour of the farm, and the equally hard work which he made of his politics and religion, comprised all his interests. To conquer the resisting land, to drive a good bargain, to order his conduct within the letter of his church law, to hate his enemies and to hold in contempt all who disagreed with him—these were the rules by which he shaped his life. High-tempered, dominating, and narrow, he was not content merely to adhere to his own principles, letting other men live as they would, but sought to impress his convictions upon his neighbours. There are instances of life-long quarrels between

Mark Baker and those who differed from him in business, politics, and religion. A quarrel over a question of business with his brother James resulted in a complete separation of the two families (although they lived as neighbours for years) from 1816 almost to the present time.[5] A charge which he brought against a church brother was arbitrated for several years before church committees; and his local political quarrels during abolition days were frequent and bitter. He lived on the Bow farm from 1785 to 1836, and in Sanbornton Bridge (now Tilton) from 1836 until his death in 1865, and to those who knew him in these two communities he is still a vivid memory. In appearance he was tall and lean, his muscles hardened by labour. His iron jaw and tense gray eye bespoke determination and resistance. The very tap of his stick, as he tramped along the country roads, conveyed a challenge. His voice was terrific in power and volume. The Baker voice is a tradition in New Hampshire, and stories are told in Bow of the Baker brothers at work in distant fields upon their farms, thundering like gods to each other across the hills.

Mark's neighbours called him " Squire " Baker, and the younger folk called him " Uncle." They found him sharp at a bargain, but honest in his dealings, and while he paid his workers the smallest wages, he always sacredly kept his word, and in his narrow way he was a good citizen. He tried his friends by his fierce temper and his intense prejudices, which kept him, in one way and another, in a continual ferment. " A

---

[5] Only a few years ago Mrs. Eddy renewed this family connection by sending for Representative Henry Moore Baker of Concord, a grandson of James Baker, to call upon her at Pleasant View, her home in the same city. Mr. Baker was, until October, 1909, one of the three trustees appointed by Mrs. Eddy in 1907 to take charge of her property interests.

tiger for temper, and always in a row." "You could no more move him than you can move old Kearsarge" (a local mountain). "An ugly disposition, but faithful to his church, and immovable in his politics." These are the comments of his old neighbours in Tilton to-day.

Inevitably, he carried his religion and politics to extremes. In the Congregational church he was an active figure, faithful and punctilious in performing all its requirements. Not only did he fulfil his own church obligations, but he saw that his brethren and sisters fulfilled theirs. He brought charges of backsliding against fellow-members when they failed to attend public worship or communion, and was willingly appointed to visit and "labour" with the delinquents. It seems probable that Mark enjoyed this duty and performed it thoroughly. He had his own church troubles, too. The yellowed books of the Tilton Congregational Church record many a disputation between him and the brethren. A quarrel between Mark Baker and William Hayes was aired before the congregation year after year, but the two were never reconciled. The church did not follow Mark's wishes in the settlement of the differences, and after bringing up the old charges again and again, and receiving no satisfaction, he applied for a letter of dismissal, because he "could not walk in covenant with this church." When his request was refused, he placed himself on record as "feeling aggrieved at the doings of the church on this subject."

A story which has passed into neighbourhood tradition illuminates the man and shows the strength and quality of his religious feeling. One Sunday in his later years he mistook the day and worked as usual about his place. On Monday morning he started for church, but was disturbed at seeing his neighbours at work. As usual he took them to task. " Sister Lang," he said, frowning at a neighbour who was placing out her tubs for washing, " what is the meaning of this on the Lord's Day? " The woman replied that as the day was Monday she was preparing to do the family washing, but Mark commanded her to prepare for church instead, and went on his way. Farther along he stopped again. " Brother Davis," he cried, " what is this commotion in the streets? Why are not the church bells ringing for public worship? " He was again assured that it was Monday; but he was not convinced until he arrived at the church and found the doors closed. He hurried to Elder Curtice, who confirmed his fears. " Is it possible that I have broken the Lord's Day? " exclaimed Uncle Baker in alarm, and he knelt with his pastor and prayed for forgiveness. Back to his home went the old man, the godly part of him purged. But the old Adam remained, and as he strode up the hill he trembled with excitement. A tame crow, a pet of the children of the neighbourhood, hopped on a bush in front of him, cawing loudly. In his perturbed condition, the sight of the bird made Mark angrier than ever, and raising his stick, he struck the crow dead. " Take that," he said in a passion, " for hoppin' about on the Sabbath," and he stormed on up the hill. At home he kept the day strictly as Sunday to atone for his worldliness of the previous day.

In politics he was no less intense. He was a pro-slavery advocate before the war, and an unbending Copperhead during it. He hated Abraham Lincoln above all men. Two luckless young women, selling pictures of Lincoln, once entered his house to induce him to buy, but saved themselves from ejection only by a hasty flight. " I'll never forget what he said about Lincoln," said one of his old neighbours now living. "When the news of Lincoln's assassination reached Sanbornton Bridge, I stopped at Mark Baker's to tell him of it. ' What!' he cried, and throwing down his hoe, he shouted at the top of his voice, ' I'm glad on't!' "

When his politics and religion clashed as they did during the Civil War, the old man was sorely torn. His pastor, Elder Corban Curtice, was a Republican who believed in the righteousness of the war, and Mark, with others of a different political faith, attempted to have the minister removed for " political preaching." Failing in this, some of the oldest members left the church. But Mark Baker remained. He went to church as regularly as ever, and abided by all its rulings as before, but his protest was expressed in a manner altogether characteristic. He sat doggedly through the sermon, his eyes fixed on the elder. The moment the word " rebellion " left the preacher's lips—whether he referred to the rebellion of the States or the rebellion of the angels—Mark Baker sprang to his feet, and, with flashing eyes and clenched fists, strode indignantly out of the church.

These incidents show the calibre of the man who was Mrs. Eddy's father. There is no doubt that he possessed qualities out of the ordinary. With his natural force and strong convictions, and with his rectitude of character, he might have been more than a local figure, but for the insurmountable obstacles of a childishly passionate temper and a deep perversity of mind. He was without imagination and without

sympathy. From fighting for a principle he invariably passed
to fighting for his own way, and he was unable to see that the
one cause was not as righteous as the other. His portrait—
a daguerreotype—shows hardness and endurance and immova-
bility. There is no humility in the heavy lip and square-set
mouth, no aspiration in the shrewd eyes; the high forehead
is merely forbidding.[5] [1-2]

All Mark Baker's children were born in the little farmhouse
in Bow, between 1808 and 1821. There were three sons—
Samuel, Albert, and George Sullivan—and three daughters—
Abigail, Martha, and Mary.[6] The family also included Mark
Baker's mother. According to pioneer custom the early Bakers
had built their house on top of the hill upon which their farm
lay, fully half a mile from the public road, which at that point
follows the course of the Merrimac River in the valley. However
inconvenient and impractical this choice of a site may have been,
it left nothing to be desired in the view. Across the green
valley of woods and fields, through which flows the white-banked
river, one can see from the Baker hill-top the long blue ranges
of the White Mountains. Nearer at hand there are glimpses
of clean white villages, and at the left is the city of Concord.
The nearest house is out of sight at the foot of the hill. In
Mark Baker's day it was occupied by his brother James, with
whom Mark was not in friendly relation.

The house itself is of wood, unpainted, and extremely small

---

[5] [1-2] In his last years he was afflicted with a palsy of the head and hands, and
suffered from facial cancer although it did not cause his death. Of his family,
nearly all have died of cancer in some form. His two eldest daughters and
their three children, and two of his sons, Samuel and George, all died of the
dread disease.

[6] Samuel Dow, born July 8, 1808; Albert, born February 5, 1810; George
Sullivan, born August 7, 1812; Abigail Barnard, born January 15, 1816;
Martha Smith, born January 19, 1819; Mary A. Morse, born July 16, 1821.

From a tintype. Courtesy of Mrs. H. S. Philbrook

MARK BAKER
Mrs. Eddy's father

and plain.   A narrow door in the centre opens directly upon
the stairway.   On the left hand is a little parlour, lighted by
two small-paned windows, and containing a corner fireplace.   A
larger room at the right, used as a granary by the present
owner, was once the kitchen and living-room.   Overhead there
were three or four small sleeping-rooms.   One wonders where
the family of nine bestowed themselves when they were all in
the house at once.   The house has not been occupied for many
years.   The windows are boarded up, and it is desolate and
forsaken.   Yet it is not forgotten, for every summer Christian
Scientists come to visit the spot where their leader was born.
It is a shrine to the devout, who carry away stones and handfuls
of soil and little shrubs, as souvenirs.

  The Baker children were brought up like other farmers' families of that time and place.   The older ones worked about the
farm and in the house, and in the winter when farm work was
" slack " they attended the district school.   Lonely and unstimu-
lating enough the life seems from this distance, but as a matter
of fact it was useful and not uninteresting.   It was before the
days of steam railroads and the thousand modern aids to living,
when every farmer's family was an industrial community in
itself.   All the supplies of the household, as well as food and
clothes, were produced at home.   Each man and woman and girl
and boy of the farms was a craftsman, their daily work requiring physical strength and mental ingenuity and a kind of
moral heroism.   The school supplied their intellectual interests,
the church satisfied their religious emotions, and for social
diversion there were corn-huskings and barn-raisings and quilt-
ing-bees.   The rest was hard labour.

The qualities of Mark Baker were transmitted to his children. They were all high-tempered and headstrong and self-assertive, and they did not lack confidence in themselves in any particular. At home, however, they were trained to obedience and up to the time at least of the birth of his youngest daughter, Mark Baker was master in his own house.   But from the beginning it was evident that special concessions must be made to Mary. She was named for her grandmother, who made a pet of her from the first, and no doubt helped to spoil her as a baby. Mrs. Baker, the mother, often told her friends that Mary, of all her children, was the most difficult to care for, and they were all at their wits' ends to know how to keep her quiet and amused.   As Mary grew older she was sent to district school with her sisters, but only for a few days at a time, for she was subject from infancy to convulsive attacks of a hysterical nature. Because of this affliction she was at last allowed to omit school altogether and to throw off all restraint at home.   The family rules were relaxed where she was concerned, and the chief problem in the Baker house was how to pacify Mary and avoid her nervous " fits."   Even Mark Baker, heretofore invincible, was obliged to give way before the dominance of his infant daughter. His time-honoured observance of the Sabbath, which was a fixed institution at the Baker farm, was abandoned because Mary could not, after a long morning in church, sit still all day in the house with folded hands, listening to the reading of the Bible.   Sundays became a day of torture not only to the hysterical child, but to all the family, for she invariably had one of her bad attacks, and the day ended in excitement and anxiety. These evidences of an abnormal condition of the nerves are im-

portant to any study of Mrs. Eddy and her career. As child
and woman she suffered from this condition, and its existence
explains some phases of her nature and certain of her acts,
which otherwise might be difficult to understand and impossible
to estimate.

Until Mary's fifteenth year the routine of life at the farm
was unbroken except for the departure from home of her two
eldest brothers to start life for themselves, and the death of
her grandmother Baker. In choosing their occupations, Mark
Baker's sons turned away from the farm, new opportunities
having been opened by the expanding industrial and commercial
life of the country. Samuel, the eldest, went to Boston, in
company with a neighbour's son, George Washington Glover,
to learn the trade of a stone mason, as the quarries of New
Hampshire had then been recently opened. Albert, the second
son, had a higher ambition. He prepared himself for college
and entered Dartmouth. He was graduated in 1834, and
immediately went to Hillsborough Center, N. H., to study law
in the office of Franklin Pierce, afterward President of the
United States. Under the influence of Pierce young Baker
entered politics. He served one term as Assemblyman in the
State Legislature, and received the nomination for Representative in Congress; but he died in 1841 before the election. He
was then only thirty-one years old, and his character and
ability seemed to justify the high opinion of his friends, who
regarded him as a coming man.

The death of the elder Mrs. Baker occurred in January, 1835,
and early the following year Mark Baker sold the homestead
and moved his family to a farm near the village of Sanbornton

Bridge (now called Tilton), eighteen miles north of Concord. Sanbornton Bridge was, in 1836, growing into a lively manufacturing village. It already contained public-spirited citizens, and had considerable social life. Altogether it afforded larger opportunities than the Bow farm; and here the interests of the Baker family now centred. Abigail, the eldest daughter, soon married Alexander Hamilton Tilton,[7] the rich man of the village, and settled there. Her husband owned the woollen mill, and accumulated a considerable fortune from the manufacture of the " Tilton tweed," which he put on the market. Mrs. Tilton was extremely handsome and dignified, and her strong character, in which the Baker traits were tempered by a kindliness of spirit and a keen sense of responsibility, made her a leading figure in that little community. She was also capable and adaptable. When her husband died she took charge of his business, and was even more successful in its management than he had been. George Sullivan Baker formed a partnership with his brother-in-law. Martha, the second daughter, married Luther C. Pillsbury, deputy warden of the New Hampshire penitentiary in Concord, but after the death of her husband she returned to live in Sanbornton Bridge. Here, too, Mark Baker and his wife lived out their days, and here Mary Baker passed her girlhood, married, returned as a widow, married again, and once more returned as a deserted wife.

As soon as they were settled on the new farm, Mary was sent to the district school at the Bridge. The schoolhouse stood on the site of the present Tilton Seminary. It was a

[7] At the request of Charles Tilton, who gave the village a town hall, Sanbornton Bridge was renamed Tilton in 1869. Charles Tilton was a nephew of Alexander Hamilton Tilton.

two-story wooden building, painted red.   The district school occupied the lower floor, while the upper room was used for a small private school, where the higher English branches were taught.   After a time these upper classes came to be known as the "academy," and it was here that Dyer H. Sanborn, the author of Sanborn's Grammar, taught for five years at a later date.   Mary was then nearing her fifteenth birthday, and as she had received almost no instruction at Bow, the family hoped that another attempt at school might be more successful.

It is one proof of Mary's remarkable personality that her old associates remember her, even as a child, so clearly.   The Baker family was not one to be readily forgotten in any community, and Mary had all the Baker characteristics, besides a few impressive ones on her own account.   The writer has talked with scores of Mary Baker's contemporaries in the New Hampshire villages where she lived, and in their descriptions of her, their recollections of her conduct, and their estimates of her character, there is a remarkable consistency.   Allowance must always be made, in dealing with the early life of a famous person, for the dishonour of a prophet in his own country.   Such allowance has been made here, and nothing is set down which is not supported by the testimony of many witnesses among her neighbours and relatives and associates.

When Mary attended the district school in Tilton, she is remembered as a pretty and graceful girl, delicately formed, and with extremely small hands and feet.   Her face was too long and her forehead too high to answer the requirements of perfect beauty, but her complexion was clear and of a delicate colour, and her waving brown hair was abundant and always becomingly arranged. Her eyes were large and gray, and when overcharged with expression, as was often the case, they deepened in colour until they seemed to be black. She was always daintily dressed, and even at fifteen succeeded in keeping closer to the fashions than was common in the community or in her own home. But in spite of these advantages Mary was not altogether attractive. Her manners and speech were marred by a peculiar affectation. Her unusual nervous organisation may have accounted for her self-consciousness and her susceptibility to the presence of others, but whatever the cause, Mary always seemed to be " showing off " for the benefit of those about her, and her extremely languishing manners were unkindly commented upon even at a time when languishing manners were fashionable. In speaking she used many words, the longer and more unusual the better, and her pronunciation and application of them were original.

Sarah Jane Bodwell, a daughter of the Congregational minister at Sanbornton Square, " kept " the school then, and finding Mary very backward in her studies in spite of her age and precociousness, she placed her in a class with small children. Mary seemed indifferent about getting into a more advanced class and did not apply herself. Her old schoolmates say that she was indolent and spent her time lolling in her seat or scribbling on her slate, and apparently was incapable of concentrated or continuous thought.

" I remember Mary Baker very well," said one of her classmates now living in Tilton. " She began to come to district school in the early summer of 1836. I recollect her very distinctly because she sat just in front of me, and because she was such a big girl to be in our class. I was only nine, but I helped her with her arithmetic when she needed help. We studied Smith's Grammar and ciphered by ourselves in Adams's New Arithmetic, and when she left school in three or four weeks we had both reached long division. She left on account of sickness.

"I remember what a pretty girl she was, and how nicely she wore her hair. She usually let it hang in ringlets, but one day she appeared at school with her hair 'done up' like a young lady. She told us that style of doing it was called a 'French Twist,' a new fashion which we had never seen before. In spite of her backwardness at books she assumed a very superior air, and by her sentimental posturing she managed to attract the attention of the whole school. She loved to impress us with fine stories about herself and her family. The schoolgirls did not like her, and they made fun of her as schoolgirls will. I knew her for a long time afterward, as we grew up in the same village, but I can't say that Mary changed much with her years."

Mrs. Eddy's own story of her early education should also be considered. In her autobiography, *Retrospection and Introspection,* she says that she was kept out of school much of the time because her father "was taught to believe" that her brain was too large for her body; that her brother Albert taught her Greek, Latin, and Hebrew; and her favourite childhood studies were Natural Philosophy, Logic, and Moral Science. From childhood, too, Mrs. Eddy recalls, she was a verse-maker, and "at ten years of age I was as familiar with Lindley Murray's Grammar as with the Westminster Catechism;

and the latter I had to repeat every Sunday." Mrs. Eddy
has also said that she " graduated from Dyer H. Sanborn's
Academy at Tilton." But at present she makes no pretension
to such scholarly attainments. "After my discovery of Christian Science," she says, " most of the knowledge I had gleaned
from schoolbooks vanished like a dream." Only Lindley Murray
remained, and he in an apotheosized state. "Learning was so
illumined," she writes, " that grammar was eclipsed. Etymology
was divine history, voicing the idea of God in man's origin and
signification. Syntax was spiritual order and unity. Prosody,
the song of angels, and no earthly or inglorious theme."

Mrs. Eddy's schoolmates are not able to reconcile her story
with their own recollections. They declare frankly that they
do not believe Albert Baker taught her Hebrew, Greek, and
Latin. He entered college when Mary was nine, and left home
when she was thirteen. There were, they say, no graduations
from Dyer H. Sanborn's Academy, for the girls and boys left
school when they were old enough to go to work or to marry.
They insist that Mary's education was finished when she reached
long division in the district school.

At church, too, Mary made a vivid impression. Like the
rest of Mark Baker's family, she attended service regularly;
and she took pains with her costume, and the timing of her
arrival, so that members of the congregation have retained a
distinct picture of Mary Baker as she appeared at church.
She always made a ceremonious entrance, coming up the aisle
after the rest of the congregation were seated, and attracting
the general attention by her pretty clothes and ostentatious
manner. No trace of early piety can be found in a first-hand

study of Mrs. Eddy's life, yet in her autobiography she constantly refers to deep religious experiences of her childhood. As her chief recollection of Bow farm days, she relates a peculiar experience, intended to show that, like little Samuel, she received ghostly visitations in early youth. She writes:

> For some twelve months, when I was about eight years old, I repeatedly heard a voice, calling me distinctly by name, three times, in an ascending scale. I thought this was my mother's voice, and sometimes went to her, beseeching her to tell me what she wanted. Her answer was always: "Nothing, child! What do you mean?" Then I would say: "Mother, who *did* call me? I heard somebody call *Mary,* three times!" This continued until I grew discouraged, and my mother was perplexed and anxious.

At another time her cousin, Mehitable Huntoon, heard the voice and told Mary's mother about it. "That night," continues Mrs. Eddy's narrative, " before going to rest, my mother read to me the Scriptural narrative of little Samuel, and bade me, when the voice called again, to reply as he did, ' Speak, Lord; for thy servant heareth.' The voice came; but I did not answer. Afterward I wept, and prayed that God would forgive me, resolving to do, next time, as my mother had bidden me. When the call came again I did answer, in the words of Samuel, but never again to the material senses was that mysterious call repeated."

Mrs. Eddy tells the story of her admission to church membership and of her discussions with the elders, and Christian Scientists draw a parallel between this incident and that of Christ debating at the age of twelve with the wise men in the temple. "At the age of twelve," writes Mrs. Eddy, " I was admitted to the Congregationalist (Trinitarian) Church." She describes her horror of the doctrine of predestination, while she was preparing to enter the church, and how she wept over the necessity of believing that her unregenerate sisters and brothers would be damned.   Peace, however, followed a season of prayer, and when she finally appeared at church for examination on doctrinal points, she flatly refused to accept that of predestination.   She says:

> Distinctly do I recall what followed. I stoutly maintained that I was willing to trust God, and take my chance of spiritual safety with my brothers and sisters,—not one of whom had then made any profession of religion,—even if my credal doubts left me outside the doors. . . . Nevertheless, he (the minister) persisted in the assertion that I *had* been truly regenerated, and asked me to say how I felt when the new light dawned within me. I replied that I could only answer him in the words of the Psalmist: " Search me, O God, and know my heart; try me, and know my thoughts; and see if there be any wicked way in me, and lead me in the way everlasting."
>
> This was so earnestly said, that even the oldest church-members wept. After the meeting was over they came and kissed me. To the astonishment of many, the good clergyman's heart also melted, and he received me into their communion, and my protest along with me.

The official record bearing on this point, taken from the clerk's book of the Tilton Congregational Church, is as follows:

> 1838, July 26, Received into this church, Stephen Grant, Esq., John Gilly and his wife Hannah, Mrs. Susan French, wife of William French, Miss Mary A. M. Baker, by profession, the two former receiving the ordinance of baptism. Greenaugh McQuestion, Scribe.

As Mary Baker was born on July 16, 1821, and as this record is dated " 1838, July 26," she was evidently seventeen, and not twelve, when the event described above took place.

At home Mary was still allowed to have her own way as completely as in her baby days. Indeed, by this time she, as well as her family, had come to consider this privilege a natural right, and she grew constantly more insistent in her demands upon her parents and brother and sisters, who had found by long experience that the only way to live at all with Mary was to give in to all her whims. In a household where personal labour was exacted from each member, Mary spent her days in idleness. Where her sisters dressed plainly, she went clad in fine and dainty raiment, and where implicit obedience was required of the others, Mary ignored, and more often opposed, the wishes of her father; and in the clashes between them, her mother and sisters usually—at least in her younger years—ranged themselves on her side, and against her father. Mary's hysteria was, of course, her most effective argument in securing her way. Like the sword of Damocles, it hung perilously over the household, which constantly surrendered and conceded and made shift with Mary to avert the inevitable climax. Confusion and excitement and agony of mind lest Mary should die was the invariable consequence of her hysterical outbreaks, and the business of the house and farm was at a standstill until the tragedy had passed.

These attacks, which continued until very late in Mrs. Eddy's life, have been described to the writer by many eye-witnesses, some of whom have watched by her bedside and treated her in Christian Science for her affliction. At times the attack resembled convulsions. Mary fell headlong to the floor, writhing and screaming in apparent agony. Again she dropped as if lifeless, and lay limp and motionless, until restored. At other times she became rigid like a cataleptic, and continued for a time in a state of suspended animation. At home the family worked over her, and the doctor was sent for, and Mary invariably recovered rapidly after a few hours; but year after year her relatives fully expected that she would die in one of these spasms. Nothing had the power of exciting Mark Baker like one of Mary's "fits," as they were called. His neighbours in Tilton remember him as he went to fetch Dr. Ladd,[8] how he lashed his horses down the hill, standing upright in his wagon and shouting in his tremendous voice, "Mary is dying!"

Outside the family, Mary's spells did not inspire the same anxiety. The unsympathetic called them "tantrums," after a better acquaintance with her, and declared that she used her nerves to get her own way. In later years Mark Baker came to share this neighbourhood opinion, and on one occasion, after Mary had grown to womanhood, he tested her power of self-control by allowing her to remain on the floor, where she had thrown herself when her will was crossed, and leaving her to herself. An hour later when he opened the door, the room was deserted. Mary had gone upstairs to her room, and nothing was heard from her until she appeared at supper, fully recovered. After that Mary's nerves lost their power over her father to a great extent, and when hard put to it, he sometimes complained to his friends. A neighbour, passing the house one morning, stopped at Mark's gate and inquired why Mary, who was at that moment rushing wildly up and down the second-story piazza, was so excited; to which Mark replied bitterly: "The Bible says Mary Magdalen had seven devils, but our Mary has got ten!"

Unquestionably, Mary's attacks represented, to a great degree, a genuine affliction. Although Dr. Ladd sometimes impatiently diagnosed them as "hysteria mingled with bad temper,"

---

[8] Dr. Nathaniel G. Ladd, the village physician.

he was, without doubt, deeply interested in her case. He dabbled a little in mesmerism and sometimes experimented on Mary, whom he found a sensitive subject. He discovered that he could partly control her movements by mental suggestion. "I can make that girl stop in the street any time merely by willing it," he used to tell his friends, and he often demonstrated that he could do it.

Mesmerism was a new subject in New England in those days, and there was much experimenting and excitement over it. There is no doubt that it formed one of the early influences in Mrs. Eddy's life, and that it left an indelible impression upon her supersensitive organisation. Charles Poyen, a French disciple of Mesmer, had travelled through New England, lecturing and performing marvels of mesmeric power in the same towns in which Mrs. Eddy then lived. In his book, *Animal Magnetism in New England*, which was published in 1837, he gives an account of his experiences there and says: "Animal magnetism indisputably constituted in several parts of New England the most stirring topic of conversation among all classes of society." He called it a "great Truth," "The Power of Mind Over Matter," a "demonstration," a "discovery given by God," and a "science." Whether or not Mary Baker saw or heard Poyen, or read his book, she must have heard of his theories, and must have been familiar with the phrases he used, as they were matter of common household discussion and would appeal strongly to a girl of Mary's temperament. In Christian Science she has given an important place to "Animal Magnetism," and there is a chapter devoted to it in her book, *Science and Health*.

Andrew Jackson Davis,[9] afterward the celebrated Spiritualist, had already begun to astound the public by his remarkable theories of the universe and disease, and by his extraordinary literary feats.   The healing of disease by means outside regular channels was commonly reported, and new religious ideas were developing.   It was a more prolific period than usual for all sorts of mystery and quackery in New England.

Another influence of these early years, which had an effect upon her later career, may be traced to the sect known as Shakers, which had sprung up in that section of New Hampshire.   Their main community was at East Canterbury, N. H., five miles from Tilton, and Mary Baker was familiar with their appearance, their peculiar costume, and their community life. She knew their religious doctrines and spiritual exaltations, and was acquainted with their habits of industry and thrift.   In her girlhood there were still living in the neighbourhood people who remembered Ann Lee,[10] the founder of the sect.   All through Mary's youth the Shakers were much in the courts because of the scandalous charges brought against them, and on one occasion they were defended by Franklin Pierce, in whose office Albert Baker studied law.   Laws directed against their community were constantly presented to the Legislature, and complaints against them were frequently heard.   A famous " exposure " of Shaker methods, written by Mary Dyer, who had been a member of the Canterbury community, was published in Concord in 1847; and the Shakers and their doings formed one of the exciting topics of the times.

[9] Author of *The Great Harmonia*, etc.   See Appendix B.
[10] Fleeing from England in 1774, Ann Lee spent her first few years in America at Concord and the neighbouring towns.

That these happenings made a profound impression on Mary Baker and became irrevocably a part of her susceptible nature is evident; for we find her reverting to and making use of certain phases of Shakerism when, later, she had established a religious system of her own.[11]

When Mary was twenty-two years old she married George Washington Glover, a son of John and Nancy Glover, who were neighbours of the Bakers at Bow. " Wash " Glover, as he was called, was a big, kind-hearted young fellow, who had learned the mason's trade with Mary's brother, Samuel, and he was an expert workman. The families were already connected through the marriage of Samuel Baker to Glover's sister, Eliza. After learning his trade, Glover had gone South, where there was a demand for Northern labour, and it was on one of his visits home that he fell in love with Mary Baker. They were married at Mark Baker's house December 12, 1843, and Glover took his bride back with him to Charleston, S. C. Six months later he was stricken with yellow fever and died in June, 1844, at Wilmington, N. C., where he had gone on business.

His young wife was left in a miserable plight, being far from home, among strangers and without money. Mr. Glover, however, had been a Freemason, and his brothers of that order came to his wife's relief. They buried her husband and paid her railroad fare to New York, where she was met by her brother George and taken back to her father's house. Here, the following September, her son was born, and she named him George Washington, after his father.

---

[11] See Appendix C.

CHAPTER II

MRS. GLOVER had now to face a hard situation. Her brief
married life had ended in adversity, and returning a widow to
her father's house, she was without means of support for
herself or her child, and she had neither the training nor
the disposition to take up an occupation, or to make herself
useful at home. Her sisters and brothers were married and
gone from home, and her parents were growing old and less
able to cope with her turbulent moods. Embarrassing as this
position would have been to most women, Mrs. Glover did not
apparently find it so. She took it for granted that she was
to receive not only the sympathy of her relatives but their
support and constant service, and that they should assume the
care of her child. She divided her time between her father's
house and that of her sister Abby, and her baby was left to her
mother and sister or sent up the valley to a Mrs. Varney, whose
son, John Varney, worked for the Tiltons. Frequently, too,
the child stayed with Mahala Sanborn, a neighbour who had
attended Mrs. Glover at his birth. But wherever he was, it was
not with his mother, who had shown a curious aversion to him
from the beginning. " Mary," said her father, " acts like an

old ewe that won't own its lamb. She won't have the boy near her."

It must be said to the credit of the Baker family that they met Mrs. Glover's demands with a patience and faithfulness that seems remarkable from a family of such impatient and dominating character. They gave her the best room in each house and regulated their domestic affairs with a view to her comfort. When her nerves were in such a state of irritation that the slightest sound annoyed her, Mark Baker spread the road in front of his house with straw and tan bark to deaden the sound of passing waggons. The noise of children disturbed her, so the baby was sent to Mahala Sanborn or to Mrs. Tilton. At her sister's house they tiptoed about the rooms and placed covered bricks against every sill that the doors might close softly. At both houses she was rocked to sleep like a child in the arms of her father or her sister, and then gently carried to bed. Sometimes, at the Tiltons', this task fell to John Varney, the hired man, who like the members of her own family, rocked her to sleep and carried her to bed. To put an end to this practice, Mrs. Tilton ordered a large cradle made for Mrs. Glover. It was built with a balustrade and an extension seat at one end upon which Varney could sit, and by rocking himself as in a chair, also rock the cradle. Another symptom of her pathological condition was her intense desire for swinging. A large swing was hung from hooks in the ceiling of her room at Mrs. Tilton's, and here she was swung hours at a time by her young nephew, Albert Tilton. When Albert tired of the exercise he sometimes hired a substitute, so that " swinging Mrs. Glover " became a popular way of

earning an honest penny among the village boys.   One of these
" boys " has described his experience to the writer.   " Some
days," he said, " Mrs. Glover was so nervous she couldn't have
anybody in the room with her, and then I used to tie a string
to the seat and swing her from outside her bedroom door."
Mark Baker and John Varney were obliged often to carry her
in their arms and walk the floor with her at night to soothe
her excitable nerves, and when everything else failed, Mark
used to send for old " Boston John " Clark to come and quiet
Mrs. Glover by mesmerism.   Clark was a bridge-builder from
one of the villages up the valley who had acquired some reputation as a mesmerist, practising, like Dr. Ladd, upon any subject who was willing, and particularly happy when he discovered a " sensitive " like Mrs. Glover.   He never failed to
soothe her, and after one of his visits, the Baker family enjoyed
a space of quiet from the incessant turmoil of Mary's nerves.
Yet Mrs. Glover was neither helpless nor incapacitated.   She did
not keep to her bed and she was able to go about the village and
to attend to whatever she was interested in.   Her neighbours
remember her at church gatherings and at the sewing circle,
where she went regularly although she did not sew.   It was
one of Mrs. Glover's notions, after her six months in Charleston, to imitate the Southern women in little matters of dress
and manner, and at the sewing circle she sat and gave voluble
descriptions of her life in the South and the favourable impression she had made there, deploring the loss of the daily
horseback ride she had been accustomed to take in South
Carolina.

Twice Mrs. Glover made an effort at self-support.   While

living with Mrs. Tilton she taught a class of children, holding
the sessions in a small building, once used as a shop, on the
Tilton place.   After a few weeks' trial she gave it up.   A little
later she repeated the experiment, but with the same result.
Although Mrs. Glover was later to have a " college " of her
own, and to be its president and sole instructor, teaching was
assuredly not her vocation in these early Tilton days.   Perhaps
a dozen of her Tilton pupils are still living, and they are fond
of relating anecdotes of the days when they went to school
to Mrs. Glover.   They all remember that the teacher required
the class to march around the room singing the following
refrain:

> " We will tell Mrs. Glover
> How much we love her;
> By the light of the moon
> We will come to her." [1]

Mrs. Glover began now to enjoy considerable local fame on
account of her susceptibility to mesmeric influence, and her
clairvoyant powers.   She had developed a habit of falling into
trances.   Often, in the course of a social call, she would close
her eyes and sink into a state of apparent unconsciousness, during which she could describe scenes and events.   The curious
and superstitious began to seek her advice while she was in

---

[1] This song was evidently an adaptation of a popular " round " of that period,
which ran:

> " Go to Jane Glover
> And tell her I love her
> And by the light of the moon
> I will come to her."

A correspondent gives the information that in Crieff, Perthshire, Scotland,
a similar " round " was in popular use previous to the year 1840, the words
of which were:

> " Go to Joan Glover
> And tell her I love her
> And by the light of the moon
> I will come to her."

this trance state. "Boston John" Clark experimented with her, putting her into the mesmeric sleep and attempting to trace lost or stolen articles by means of her clairvoyance. Once she tried to locate a drowned body. These efforts were not attended with any great success, but interest in mesmerism and clairvoyance ran high, and any one who could fall into a trance and describe things was sure to be an object of wonder. John Varney conceived the notion of turning this talent of Mrs. Glover's to practical account. "Boston John" was sent for, and Mrs. Glover, at Varney's suggestion, described the hiding-place of Captain Kidd's treasure, which was then a topic of exciting speculation. She indicated a spot near the city of Lynn, Mass. Varney and his cronies set out for the place and spent several days digging for the treasure, but without success.

A few years later when spiritualism swept over the country, Mrs. Glover took on the symptoms of a "medium." Like the Fox sisters, she heard mysterious rappings at night, she saw "spirits" of the departed standing by her bedside, and she received messages in writing from the dead. There are people living who remember very distinctly the spiritism craze in Tilton, and who witnessed Mrs. Glover's manifestations of mediumship. One elderly woman recalls a night spent with Mrs. Glover when her rest was constantly disturbed by the strange rappings and by Mary's frequent announcements of the "appearance" of different spirits as they came and went.

Mark Baker's house was one of those where spirit séances were held. The whole community was more or less interested and a few went to extremes. One of this number became so excited over the wonderful phenomena of Mrs. Glover's writing mediumship that his mind was temporarily unbalanced. A former Tilton woman, who remembers these events, writes of Mrs. Glover's ability as a writing medium: " This was by no means looked upon as anything discreditable, but only as a matter of great astonishment."

During these years, too, Mrs. Glover tried her hand at writing. She spent many hours in her room " composing poetry," which sometimes appeared in the poet's corners of local newspapers, and there is a tradition that she wrote a love story for *Godey's Lady's Book*. This literary tendency was a valuable asset, which Mrs. Glover made the most of. It gave her a certain prestige in the community, and she was not loth to pose as an " authoress." Perhaps it was this early habit of looking upon herself as a literary authority which led her to take those curious liberties with English which have always been characteristic of her. She drew largely upon the credit of the language, sometimes producing a word or evolving a pronunciation which completely floored her hearers. Some of these words and phrases have passed into local bywords. " When I vociferate so loudly, why do you not respond with greater alacrity? " she sometimes seriously demanded of her attendants. She referred to plain John Varney as " Mr. Ve-owney," and few ordinary words were left unadorned. She sought also to improve upon nature in the matter of her own good looks. Although she had a beautiful complexion, she rouged and powdered, and although she had excellent teeth, she had some of them replaced by false ones, " made entirely of platinum," as Mrs. Glover described them.

On the whole, it is no wonder that Mrs. Glover was not taken seriously in her own town. Artificiality spread over all her acts, and in no relation in life did she impress even her nearest friends or her own family with genuine feeling or sincerity. Indeed, she was bitterly censured in those years for the more active faults of selfish and unfilial conduct and a strange lack of the sense of maternal duty. In 1851 Mrs. Glover had given her son, George, to Mahala Sanborn. The boy, having reached the age of seven, was growing too large to be sent about from one house to another to be looked after. Mrs. Glover's mother had died of typhoid fever in November, 1849, and Mrs. Tilton was growing each year more impatient and weary of Mrs. Glover's conduct. So when Mahala Sanborn married Russell Cheney and was preparing to move away from Tilton, Mrs. Glover begged her to take George to live with her permanently. Mrs. Cheney, who was attached to the boy, at last consented to do so, and George accompanied her and her husband to their new home in North Groton, and was called by their name.

Mark Baker, in the fall of 1850, had married Mrs. Elizabeth Patterson Duncan, a widow of Londonderry, N. H., and moved into the village of Tilton. Mrs. Glover continued to live at home, spending most of her time there now, for her stepmother was of a pliable nature and gentle disposition, and had taken up the task of attending to Mary's wants with a patience equal to that of Mrs. Glover's own mother.

Notwithstanding Mrs. Glover's shortcomings of temper, she could be amiable and attractive enough when she chose. To men she always showed her most winning side, and she had never lacked admirers. One of her suitors at this time was Dr. Daniel Patterson, an itinerant dentist practising in Tilton and the villages thereabouts. Dr. Patterson was large, handsome, and genial. He wore a full beard, dressed in a frock coat and silk hat, and was popular among his patrons. Although he was industrious enough at his business and made a living sufficient for himself, he was not a genius at money-making, and he was not inclined to exert himself much more than was necessary. From his first acquaintance with Mrs. Glover he was determined to marry her. Conscientious Mark Baker, when he heard of Dr. Patterson's intention, visited the dentist and told him of Mary's ill-health and nervous afflictions, but interference only strengthened the doctor's determination, and on June 21, 1853, the wedding took place at Mark Baker's house, although Dr. Patterson was obliged to carry his bride downstairs from her room for the ceremony, and back again when it was over. Mrs. Glover had been very ill and weak that spring and was not yet recovered. After her marriage she spent the days of her convalescence in Tilton with her husband, and then they went to Franklin, a neighbouring village where Dr. Patterson was practising. But Mrs. Patterson's invalidism, from being intermittent, soon became a settled condition. She sent for her cradle while they were living in Franklin, and the older residents still recall the day that Patterson drove into town with a large waggon containing his wife's cradle.

From Franklin they went, in a short time, to North Groton, where the Cheneys and young George Glover were living. North Groton, in the southern fringe of the White Mountains, was very remote and could be reached only by stage. Like all the White Mountain region, it was beautiful in the summer season, but in the winter it was rugged and desolate. The farmhouses were far apart, and the roads were sometimes impassable. Often one would not see a neighbour or a passerby for weeks at a time when the snow was deep; and the winters there were very long. In a lane off the main road, the Pattersons lived in a small frame house, which faced a deep wood. At the right rose the mountains. Back of the house there was a swift mountain brook, and there the dentist had built a small sawmill, which he operated when there was not much dentist work to do, or when his wife's ill-health made it necessary for him to stay closely at home. He also practised homœopathy intermittently, but in the main he worked at his dentistry, driving to the nearby towns to practise, and leaving his wife alone or in the care of their occasional servant. There was only one near neighbour. It is not strange that, under these circumstances, Mrs. Patterson fell into a state of chronic illness and developed ways that were considered peculiar by her friends.

Her neighbours in North Groton tell the old story of her illnesses, her hysteria, her high temper, and her unreasonable demands on her husband. She required him to keep the wooden bridge over the brook covered with sawdust to deaden the sound of footsteps or vehicles, and, according to local tradition, he spent many evenings killing discordant frogs, whose noise disturbed Mrs. Patterson. Other stories sink further toward burlesque. Old inhabitants of North Groton still remember the long drive which a neighbour made for Mrs. Patter-

DANIEL PATTERSON

Mrs. Eddy's second husband

son one stormy winter night. While the doctor was away in Franklin, attending to his practice, Mrs. Patterson fell into a state of depression which ended in hysterics. A neighbour was sent for, and Mrs. Patterson declared she was dying, and that her husband must be brought home at once. To her own family this situation would not have seemed the desperate affair it was to Mrs. Patterson's neighbour. Moved by the entreaties of the dying wife, he set out at night on the thirty-mile drive to Franklin, over roads that were almost impassable from heavy snowdrifts. His horses became exhausted and he stopped at Bristol only long enough to change them for a fresh pair. Arriving at Franklin the next morning he made haste to inform Dr. Patterson of his wife's dying condition. To his astonishment the dentist looked up and remarked, " I think she will live until I finish this job at least," and went on with his work. When they reached North Groton late that day, they found Mrs. Patterson sitting in her chair, serene and cheerful, having apparently forgotten her indisposition of the night before.

Gradually the sympathy of her neighbours was withdrawn from Mrs. Patterson, and in North Groton, as in Tilton, she came to be harshly criticised. Many years afterward, upon the occasion of the dedication of the Christian Science Church in Concord, N. H., July 16, 1904, a North Groton correspondent, under the head, " Time Makes Changes," wrote in the *Plymouth Record*:

With the announcement of the dedication of the Christian Science Church at Concord, the gift of Mary Baker Glover Patterson Eddy, the thoughts of many of the older residents have turned back to the time when Mrs. Eddy, as the wife of Daniel Patterson, lived in this place. These people remember the woman at that time as one who carried herself above her fellows. With no stretch of the imagination they remember her ungovernable temper and hysterical ways, and particularly well do they remember the night ride of one of the citizens who went for her husband to calm her in one of her unreasonable moods. The Mrs. Eddy of to-day is not the Mrs. Patterson of then, for this is a sort of Mr. Hyde and Dr. Jekyll case, and the woman is now credited with many charitable and kindly acts.

Although Mrs. Patterson now lived near her boy, George, she did not see a great deal of him. He had started to go to school, and used sometimes to stop at his mother's house on his way home, but she never cared to have him with her. Instead, and by some perverse law of her nature, she showed a deep affection for the infant son of her neighbour, naming him Mark after her father, and making plans for his education and future. In 1857 Russell Cheney and his wife went West to live, taking George Glover with them. George was now thirteen. He was excited at the prospect of the trip, and after bidding his mother good-bye, he was taken to Tilton a day before the time set for their departure, to say farewell to his Grandfather Baker and his Aunt Tilton.

In *Retrospection and Introspection* Mrs. Eddy gives the following account of her separation from her son:

After returning to the paternal roof, I lost all my husband's property, except what money I had brought with me; and remained with my parents until after my mother's decease.

A few months before my father's second marriage to Mrs. Elizabeth Patterson Duncan, sister of Lieutenant-Governor George W. Patterson, of New York—my little son, about four years of age, was sent away from me, and put under the care of our family nurse, who had married, and resided in the northern part of New Hampshire. I had no training for self-support, and my home I regarded as very precious. The night before my child was taken from me, I knelt by his side throughout the dark hours, hoping for a vision of relief from this trial. The following lines are taken from my poem, "Mother's Darling," written after this separation:

> "Thy smile through tears, as sunshine o'er the sea,
> Awoke new beauty in the surge's roll!
> Oh, life is dead, bereft of all, with thee,—
> Star of my earthly hope, babe of my soul."

My dominant thought in marrying again was to get back my child, but after our marriage his stepfather was not willing he should have a home with me. A plot was consummated for keeping us apart. The family to whose care he was committed, very soon removed to what was then regarded as the Far West.

After his removal a letter was read to my little son informing him that his mother was dead and buried. Without my knowledge he was appointed a guardian, and I was then informed that my son was lost. Every means within my power was employed to find him, but without success. We never met again until he had reached the age of thirty-four, had a wife and two children, and by a strange providence had learned that his mother still lived, and came to see me in Massachusetts.

From Enterprise, Minn., where the Cheneys settled, Mrs. Patterson often had news of her son. Mrs. Cheney and her husband wrote frequently to their relatives and friends in North Groton and Tilton, giving details of their life and of George's progress. Mr. Cyrus Blood of North Groton, one of George Glover's early chums, remembers a visit he paid to Dr. Patterson, during which Mrs. Patterson read a letter from George, in which he told her of leaving the Cheneys and enlisting in the Civil War. This was in 1861 when George was seventeen. "She seemed as well pleased, and as proud," writes Mr. Blood, "as any mother with a boy in the army." The present writer has also read a letter from Mrs. Patterson to P. P. Quimby of Portland, Me., dated July 29, 1865, in which she describes her son as "mortally ill at Enterprise, Minn.," and declares that unless he is better at once she will start for the West "on Monday."

George Glover made an excellent record as a soldier; was wounded at Shiloh and honourably discharged; was appointed United States Marshal of the Dakotas; knocked about the Western states as a prospector and miner, and finally settled at Lead, S. D., where he now carries on his mining enterprises. He has a wife and four children, the eldest of whom is a daughter named Mary Baker Glover, for her grandmother. Mrs. Eddy and her son met for the first time after their long separation, in 1879, Mrs. Eddy having sent a mysterious telegram begging him to come to her immediately. She was then living in Lynn. The Glovers live in a handsome house in Lead which Mrs. Eddy built for her son in 1902. None of the family is a Christian Scientist. Several years ago when Glover's eldest daughter died his neighbours expressed amazement that he had not called upon Mrs. Eddy to cure her. " Why, do you know," replied George, " I never thought of mother! "

In March, 1860, three years after George had gone West with the Cheneys, Dr. and Mrs. Patterson became involved in a dispute with a neighbour and moved away, this time trying Rumney, the next village. At first they boarded with Mrs. John Herbert, a widow at Rumney Station, and later they lived by themselves in a house belonging to John Dearborn in Rumney Village, a mile from the Station. Mrs. Patterson's reputation had preceded her and she was at once a topic of discussion. She went out but seldom, and then propped up with pillows in a carriage. It was said that she suffered from a spinal disease. From the Herbert family and from her husband she required the utmost attention. Dr. Patterson waited upon her constantly when he was at home, carrying her downstairs to

The house in North Groton, N. H., where Mrs. Eddy, then Mrs. Daniel Patterson, lived for seven years

her meals and back again to her room. When he was not at home, she was able to walk about and attend to most of her wants unassisted; but when he returned she relapsed into a state of helplessness.

From the traditions which abound in these villages it is evident that the Pattersons' marriage was an unfortunate one. Dr. Patterson's bluff and rather coarse geniality must greatly have irritated his high-strung and self-centred wife, and there is no doubt that, on his part, he came quickly to see the force of Mark Baker's advice against the marriage. He seems to have responded faithfully to his wife's demands, and to have endured her irascibility with patience. It was probably a relief to both when Dr. Patterson went South, after the Civil War began, in the hope of securing more profitable employment as an army surgeon. He visited the early battlefields, and, straying into the enemies' lines, was taken captive and sent to a Southern prison. In his absence Mrs. Patterson showed that she was capable of a gentler sentiment toward her husband. During his confinement in prison she published (June 20, 1862) the following poem, the last stanza of which is slightly reminiscent of certain lines in Lord Byron's poem to the more celebrated patriot, Bonnivard:

TO A BIRD FLYING SOUTHWARD

By Mary A. Patterson

Alas! sweet bird, of fond ones reft,
Alone in Northern climes thus left,
To seek in vain through airy space
Some fellow-warbler's resting place;
And find upon the hoarse wind's song—
No welcome note is borne along.

Then wildly through the skies of blue,
To spread thy wings of dappled hue,
As if forsooth this frozen zone
Could yield one joy for bliss that's flown;
While sunward as thine eager flight,
That glance is fixed on visions bright.

And grief may nestle in that breast,
Some vulture may have robbed its rest,
But guileless as thou art, sweet thing,
With melting melody thou'lt sing;
The vulture's scream your nerves unstrung,
But, birdie, 'twas a *woman's tongue.*

I, too, would join thy sky-bound flight,
To orange groves and mellow light,
And soar from earth to loftier doom,
And light on flowers with sweet perfume,
And wake a genial, happy lay—
Where hearts are kind and earth so gay.

Oh! to the *captive's* cell I'd sing
A song of hope—and *freedom* bring—
An olive leaf I'd quick let fall,
And lift our country's blackened pall;
Then homeward seek my frigid zone,
More chilling to the heart *alone.*

Lone as a solitary star,[2]
Lone as a vacant sepulchre,
Yet not alone! my Father's call—
Who marks the sparrow in her fall—
Attunes my ear to joys elate,
The joys I'll sing at Heaven's gate.

Rumney, June 20, 1862.

---

[2] Byron's " Prisoner of Chillon," when relating how the bird perched and sang upon the grating of his donjon, exclaims :

" I sometimes deem'd that it might be
My brother's soul come down to me ;
But then at last away it flew,
And then 'twas mortal well I knew,
For he would never thus have flown,
And left me twice so doubly lone,
Lone as the corse within its shroud,
Lone as a solitary cloud,— " etc.

Left alone, and once more penniless, after her husband's imprisonment, Mrs. Patterson again fell back upon her relatives. She wrote to Mrs. Tilton for assistance. Mrs. Tilton went to Rumney, settled Mrs. Patterson's affairs there, and took her back to Tilton.

It is this part of her career that Mrs. Eddy has sought to blot out of existence. She makes no reference to it in her autobiography, and in another place has said that no special account is to be made of the years between 1844 and 1866. These twenty-two lost years—between her twenty-third and forty-sixth birthdays—were, as has been shown, spent in fretful ill-health and discontent. It was a hard life, sordid in many of its experiences, petty in its details, and narrow in its limitations. Yet there is nothing to show that Mrs. Eddy made an effort to improve her hard situation, or to make herself useful to others; and at forty she was known only for her eccentricities.

CHAPTER III

WHILE Dr. and Mrs. Patterson were living in Rumney, it
was announced in the village that a new healer, Phineas Parkhurst Quimby of Portland, Me., would visit Concord, N. H.,
to treat all the sick who would come to him. Stories of the
marvellous cures he was said to perform had spread throughout
New England. Stubborn diseases, which had resisted the skill
of regular physicians, were reported as yielding promptly to
the magic of the Quimby method. This new doctor, so the
story ran, used no medicines, and never failed to heal; and upon
hearing these tales the sick and the suffering—particularly those
who were the victims of long-standing and chronic diseases—
took heart and tried to reach him. Among these was Mrs.
Patterson. Her husband wrote to Dr. Quimby from Rumney
on October 14, 1861, that Mrs. Patterson had been an invalid
from a spinal disease for many years. She had heard of
Quimby's " wonderful cures," and desired him to visit her. If
Dr. Quimby intended to come to Concord, as they had heard,
Dr. Patterson would " carry " his wife to see him. If not,
he would try to get her to Portland.

Dr. Quimby did not visit Concord, and Dr. Patterson
soon went South, but in the following spring (May 9, 1862)
Mrs. Patterson herself wrote to Quimby from Rumney, appeal-

ing to him to help her, and setting forth her truly pathetic situation. She had been better, the letter said, but the shock of hearing that her husband had " been captured by the Southrons " and again prostrated her. She had, she wrote, " full confidence " in Dr. Quimby's " philosophy, as explained in your circular," and she begged him to come to Rumney. She had been ill for six years, she said, and " only you can save me." Hard as the journey to Portland would be, she thought she was sufficiently " excitable," even in her feeble condition, to undertake it.[1]

Although Quimby could not go to Rumney as she requested, Mrs. Patterson clung to the idea of seeing him. After she had returned to her sister's home in Tilton, she talked of Quimby constantly, and begged Mrs. Tilton to send her to Portland for treatment. But Mrs. Tilton would not consent, nor provide money for the trip, as she considered Dr. Quimby a quack and thought the reports of his cures were greatly exaggerated. Instead, she sent Mrs. Patterson to a water cure— Dr. Vail's Hydropathic Institute at Hill, N. H. At the Hill institution Dr. Quimby was just then a topic of eager interest among the patients, and Mrs. Patterson finally resolved to reach Portland. She wrote again to Dr. Quimby from Hill, telling him that although she had been at Dr. Vail's cure for several months, she had not been benefited and would die unless he, Quimby, could help her. " I can sit up but a few minutes at a time," she wrote. " Do you think I can reach you without sinking from the effects of the journey? "

Mrs. Patterson knew that it was useless to appeal again to

[1] This letter, with others from Mrs. Patterson to Dr. Quimby, is in the possession of Quimby's son, George A. Quimby of Belfast, Me.

her sister, and as there was no one else, she used her wits. From time to time she applied to Mrs. Tilton for small sums of money for extra expenses. By hoarding these she soon had enough to pay her fare to Portland, and she, therefore, set out.

Mrs. Patterson arrived at the International Hotel in October, 1862, and with scores of others, who went flocking to Quimby, she was helped up the stairs to his office.

Dr. Quimby now becomes such a potent influence in Mrs. Patterson's life that some understanding of the man and his theories is necessary for any complete comprehension of her subsequent career.

Phineas Parkhurst Quimby was "Doctor" only by courtesy: he had taken no university degree and had studied in no regular school of medicine. He was regarded by the educated public as an amiable humbug or a fanatic, but by hundreds of his patients he was looked upon as a worker of miracles. His methods resembled those of no regular physician then in practice, nor did he imitate the spiritualistic and clairvoyant healers who at that time flourished in New England. He gave no drugs, went into no trances, used no incantations, and did not heal by mesmerism after he had discovered his "science." He professed to make his patients well and happy purely by the benevolent power of mind.

Fantastic as this idea then seemed, Quimby was no ordinary quack. He did not practise on the credulous for money, and his theories represented at least independent thought and patient, life-long study. He was born in New Lebanon, N. H., February 16, 1802, but spent the larger part of his life in Belfast, Me. He was one of seven children, and his father was a poor, hardworking blacksmith. Quimby, therefore, had practically no educational advantages; indeed, he spent actually only six weeks in school. Apprenticed as a boy to a clockmaker, he became an adept at his trade. The Quimby clock is still a domestic institution in New England; hundreds made by Quimby's own hands are still keeping excellent time. Quimby had an ingenious mind and a natural aptitude for mechanics. He invented, among other things, a band-saw much like one in use at the present time, and he was one of the first makers of daguerreotypes. From the first he disclosed one rare mental quality: his keen power of observation and originality of thought forbade his taking anything for granted. He recognised no such thing as accepted knowledge. He developed into a mild-mannered New England Socrates, constantly looking into his own mind, and subjecting to proof all the commonplace beliefs of his friends. He read deeply in philosophy and science, and loved nothing better than to discuss these subjects at length.

In those days a man of Quimby's intellectual type did not lack subjects of interest. In the '30's the first wave of mental science, animal magnetism, and clairvoyance swept over New England. The atmosphere was charged with the occult, the movement ranging all the way from phrenology and mind-reading to German transcendentalism. Quimby's interest was directly stimulated by the visit of Charles Poyen, the well-known French mesmerist, who came to lecture in Belfast. The inquiring clock-maker became absorbed in Poyen's theories, formed his acquaintance, and followed him from town to town. Inevitably, Quimby began experimenting in the subject which so interested him. Discovering that he had mesmeric power, he exercised it upon many of his friends and easily repeated the performance of Poyen and other exhibitors. From becoming their imitator he became their rival, and abandoning his workshop, started out as a professional mesmerist. Among the wonder-workers of the early '40's, " Park " Quimby, as he was popularly called, became pre-eminent. Always considered an original character in his native village, he was now regarded as an outright crank, and was the subject of much amiable jocularity.

In the course of his experiments, Quimby discovered that his most sensitive subject was Lucius Burkmar, a boy about seventeen years old, over whom he had acquired almost unlimited hypnotic control. The two travelled all over New England, performing mesmerics feats that have hardly been duplicated since, everywhere arousing great popular interest, and, in certain quarters, great hostility. Psychic phenomena were then incompletely understood; clergymen preached against mesmerism, or animal magnetism, as the work of the devil,—a revival of ancient witchcraft; while the practical man regarded it as pure fraud. The newspapers frequently vilified Quimby and Burkmar, and they were more than once threatened by mobs.

Then, as now, the public mind associated the occult sciences with the cure of physical disease. Clairvoyants, magnetisers, and mind-readers treated all imaginable ills. When blindfolded, they had the power—according to their advertisements —of looking into the bodies of their patients, examining their inmost organs, indicating the affected parts, and prescribing remedies. Hundreds of men, women, and children, whose cases

" the doctors had given up as hopeless," fervently testified to their power. Thus Quimby and Burkmar inevitably received numerous appeals from the sick. After a few trials, Quimby became convinced that in a mesmeric state Burkmar could diagnose and treat disease. Though absolutely ignorant of medicine and anatomy, Burkmar described minutely the ailments of numerous patients, and prescribed medicines, which, although absurd to a physician, apparently produced favourable results. For three or four years Quimby and Burkmar practised with considerable success. Consumptives, according to popular report, began to get well, the blind saw, and the halt walked.

Quimby then made an important discovery. After careful observation, he concluded that neither Burkmar nor his remedies, in themselves, had the slightest power. Burkmar, he believed, did not himself diagnose the case. He merely reported what the patient, or some one else present in the room, imagined the disease to be. He had, Quimby thought, a clairvoyant or mind-reading faculty, by which he simply reproduced the opinion which the sick had themselves formed. Quimby also discovered that, in instances where improvement actually took place, the drug prescribed had nothing to do with it. Once Burkmar, in the mesmeric state, ordered a concoction too expensive for the patient's purse. Quimby mesmerised him again; and this time he prescribed a cheaper remedy—which served the purpose quite as well. After a few experiences of this kind, Quimby concluded that Burkmar's prescriptions did not produce the cures, but that the patients cured themselves. Burkmar's only service was that he implanted in the sick man's mind an unshakable faith that he would get well. Any other person, or any drug, Quimby declared, which could put the patient in this attitude of mental receptivity and give his own mind a chance to work upon the disease, would accomplish the same result. He made this discovery the basis of an elaborate and original system of mind cure; he dropped mesmerism, dismissed Burkmar, and began to work out his theory. He experimented for several years in Belfast, and, in 1859, opened an office in Portland.

Quimby had the necessary mental and moral qualifications for his work. His personality inspired love and confidence, and his patients even now affectionately recall his kind-heartedness, his benevolence, and his keen perception. Even his opponents in the controversy which has raged over his work and that of Mrs. Eddy, speak well of him. " On his rare humanity and sympathy," says Mrs. Eddy, " one could write a sonnet."

He was a small man, both in stature and in build, quick, sensitive, and nervous in his movements. His large, well-formed head stood straight on erect, energetic shoulders. He had a high, broad forehead, and silken white hair and beard. His eyes, arched with heavy brows, black, deep-set, and penetrating, seemed, as one of his patients has written, " to see all through the falsities of life and far into the depths and into the spirit of things." At times his eyes flashed with good-nature and wit, for Quimby by no means lacked the jovial virtues. If his countenance suggested one quality more than another, it was honesty; whatever the public thought of his ideas, no one who ever saw him face to face doubted the man's absolute sincerity. He demanded the same sympathy which he himself gave. He dealt kindly with honest doubters, but

PHINEAS PARKHURST QUIMBY

would have nothing to do with the scornful. Unless one really wished to be cured, he said, his methods had no virtue. On one occasion, instead of taking his place beside a certain patient, he turned his chair directly around and sat back to back. " That's the way you feel toward me," he declared. His offices were constantly filled with patients, and his mail was enormous. People came to consult him from all over New England and the Far West. He treated " absently " thousands who could not visit him in person.

Mrs. Julius A. Dresser, one of his early patients and converts, thus describes her first meeting with Mr. Quimby:

I found a kindly gentleman who met me with such sympathy and gentleness that I immediately felt at ease. He seemed to know at once the attitude of mind of those who applied to him for help, and adapted himself to them accordingly. His years of study of the human mind, of sickness in all its forms, and of the prevailing religious beliefs, gave him the ability to see through the opinions, doubts, and fears of those who sought his aid, and put him in instant sympathy with their mental attitudes. He seemed to know that I had come to him feeling that he was a last resort, and with little faith in him and his mode of treatment. But, instead of telling me that I was not sick, he sat beside me and explained to me what my sickness was, how I got into the condition, and the way I could have been taken out of it through the right understanding. He seemed to see through the situation from the beginning, and explained the cause and effect so clearly that I could see a little of what he meant. My case was so serious, however, that he did not at first tell me I could be made well. But there was such an effect produced by his explanation, that I felt a new hope within me, and began to get well from that day.

He continued to explain my case from day to day, giving me some idea of his theory and its relation to what I had been taught to believe, and sometimes sat silently with me for a short time. I did not understand much that he said, but I felt the spirit and the life that came with his words; and I found myself gaining steadily. Some of these pithy sayings of his remained constantly in mind, and were very helpful in preparing the way for a better understanding of his thought, such, for instance, as his remark that, "Whatever we believe, that we create," or, "Whatever opinion we put into a thing, that we take out of it."

In all the relations of life, Quimby seems to have been loyal and upright.   Outside of his theory he lived only for his family and was the constant playmate of his children.   His only interest in his patients was to make them well.   He treated all who came, whether they could pay or not.   For several years Quimby kept no accounts and made no definite charges.   The patients, when they saw fit, sent him such remuneration as they wished.   Inevitably, he drew his followers largely from the poor and the desperately ill.   " People," he would say, " send for me and the undertaker at the same time; and the one who gets there first gets the case."

Quimby was thoroughly convinced that he had solved the riddle of life, and that ultimately the whole world would accept his ideas.   His subject possessed him.   He wearied his family almost to desperation with it, and wore out all his friends.   He discussed it at length with any one who would listen.   To put it in writing, to teach it, to transmit it to posterity,—that was his consuming idea.   His only fear was lest he should die before the " Truth " had made a lasting impress.   He wrote about it in the newspapers,—not, however, as extensively as he desired, for the editors seldom printed his articles, regarding them as the veriest rubbish.   He selected, here and there, especially appreciative and intelligent patients, discussed his doctrine with them exhaustively, and enjoined them to teach unbelievers.   His following was not wholly among the ignorant and humble.   Edwin Reed, ex-mayor of Bath, Me., declares that Quimby cured him of total blindness.   He visited him as a young graduate of Bowdoin, had his sight completely restored, spent several months studying the theory, and left with the conviction, which he has never lost, that Quimby was a strong and original thinker. Julius A. Dresser, whose name figures largely in the history of mental healing, early became absorbed in Quimby. For several years he was associated with him, receiving patients and explaining, as a preliminary to their meeting with the doctor, his ideas and methods. In 1863 Dr. Warren F. Evans, a Swedenborgian clergyman, visited Quimby twice professionally. He became a convert, and, in several books well known among students of mental healing, developed the Quimby doctrine. " Quimby," he said, " seemed to reproduce the wonders of Gospel history."

About 1859 Quimby began to put his ideas into permanent form. George A. Quimby thus describes his father's literary methods: [2]

Among his earlier patients in Portland were the Misses Ware, daughters of the late Judge Ashur Ware, of the United States Admiralty Court; and they became much interested in "the Truth," as he called it. But the ideas were so new, and his reasoning was so divergent from the popular conceptions, that they found it difficult to follow him or remember all he said; and they suggested to him the propriety of putting into writing the body of his thoughts.

From that time he began to write out his ideas, which practice he continued until his death, the articles now being in the possession of the writer of this sketch. The original copy he would give to the Misses Ware; and it would be read to him by them, and, if he suggested any alteration, it would be made, after which it would be copied either by the Misses Ware or the writer of this, and then re-read to him, that he might see that all was just as he intended it. Not even the most trivial word or the construction of a sentence would be changed without consulting him. He was given to repetition; and it was with difficulty that he could be induced to have a repeated sentence or phrase stricken out, as he would say, "If that idea is a good one, and true, it will do no harm to have it in two or three times." He believed in the hammering process, and in throwing an idea or truth at the reader till it would be firmly fixed in his mind.

---

[2] Article in the *New England Magazine*, March, 1888.

In six years Quimby produced ten volumes of manuscripts. In them he discussed a variety of subjects, all from the standpoint of his theory.   He wrote copiously on Religion, Disease, Spiritualism, " Scientific Interpretations of Various Parts of the Scriptures," Clairvoyance, " The Process of Sickness," " Relation of God to Man," Music, Science, Error, Truth, Happiness, Wisdom, " The Other World," " Curing the Sick," and dozens of other topics.   He gave all his patients access to these manuscripts, and permitted all who wished to make copies, overjoyed whenever he found one interested enough to do this. He also encouraged his followers to write, themselves, frequently correcting their essays and bringing them into harmony with his own ideas.   Quimby's writings, as a whole, have never been published ; but the present writer has had free and continuous use of them.

From these manuscripts can be deduced a complete and detailed philosophy of life and disease.   They refute the assertion sometimes made, that Quimby was a spiritualist, or that he made the slightest claim to divine revelation.   Certain admirers sometimes compared him with Christ ; but he himself wrote a long dissertation called *A Defence Against Making Myself Equal with Christ*.   He usually calls his discovery the " Science of Health," and " The Science of Health and Happiness " ; once or twice he describes it as " Christian Science." Scores of times he refers to it as the " Science of Christ."   He also repeatedly calls it " The Principle," " The Truth," and " Wisdom."

Though he never identified his doctrine with religion, and never dreamed of founding an ecclesiastical organisation upon it, his impulse at the bottom was religious. He believed that Christ's mission was largely to the sick; that He and His apostles performed cures in a natural manner; and that he had himself rediscovered their method. Jesus Christ, indeed, was Quimby's great inspiration. He distinguished, however, between the Principle Christ and the Man Jesus. This duality, he said, manifested itself likewise in man.

In every individual, according to Quimby, there were two persons. The first was the Truth, Goodness, and Wisdom into which he had been naturally born. In this condition he was the child of God, the embodiment of Divine Love and Divine Principle. This man had no flesh, no bones, and no blood; he did not breathe, eat, or sleep. He could never sin, never become sick, never die. He knew nothing of matter, or of the physical senses; he was simply Spirit, Wisdom, Principle, Truth, Mind, Science. Quimby, above all, loved to call him the " Scientific Man." This first person was, so to speak, encrusted in another man, formed of matter, sense, and all the accumulated " errors " of time. This man had what Quimby called " Knowledge "—that is, the ideas heaped up by the human mind. According to Quimby, this second man held the first, or truly Scientific man, in bondage. The bonds consisted of false human beliefs. The idea, above all, which held him enthralled, was that of Disease. The man of Science knew nothing of sickness. The man of Ignorance, however, consciously and unconsciously, had been impregnated for centuries with this belief. His whole life, from earliest infancy, was encompassed with suggestions of this kind. Parents constantly suggest illness to their children; doctors preach it twenty-four

hours a day; the clergy, the newspapers, books, ordinary conversation,—the whole modern world, thought Quimby, had engaged in a huge conspiracy to familiarise the human mind
with this false concept. This process had been going on for
thousands of years, until finally unhealthy ideas had triumphed
over healthy; beliefs had got the upper hand of truth; knowledge had supplanted wisdom; ignorance had taken the place of
science; matter had superseded mind; Jesus had dethroned
Christ.

Quimby regarded his mission in the world as the reëstablish-
ment of the original and natural harmony. Though his philosophy embraces the whole of life, he used all his energies in
eradicating one of man's many false " beliefs," or " errors,"—
that of Disease. His method was simplicity itself. The medical profession constantly harped on the idea of sickness;
Quimby constantly harped on the idea of health. The doctor
told the patient that disease was inevitable, man's natural inheritance; Quimby told him that disease was merely an " error,"
that it was created, " not by God, but by man," and that health
was the true and scientific state. " The idea that a beneficent
God had anything to do with disease," said Quimby, " is superstition." " Disease," reads another of his manuscripts, " is
false reasoning. True scientific wisdom is health and happiness. False reasoning is sickness and death." Again he says:
" This is my theory: to put man in possession of a science that
will destroy the ideas of the sick, and teach man one living
profession of his own identity, with life free from error and
disease. As man passes through these combinations, they differ
one from another. . . . He is dying and living all the time to

error, till he dies the death of all his opinions and beliefs. Therefore, to be free from death is to be alive in truth; for sin, or error, is death, and science, or wisdom, is eternal life, and this is the Christ." " My philosophy," he says at another time, " will make man free and independent of all creeds and laws of man, and subject him to his own agreement, he being free from the laws of sin, sickness, and death."

Quimby, after dismissing Burkmar in 1845, never used mesmerism or manipulated his patients. Occasionally, after talking for a time, he would dip his hands in water and rub the patient's head. He always asserted that this was not an essential part of the cure. His ideas were so startling, he said, that the average mind could not grasp them, but required some outward indication to bolster up its faith. The cure itself, Quimby always insisted, was purely mental.[3]

---

[3] As far back as 1857, a writer in the Bangor *Jeffersonian* contradicts the statement that Quimby cured mesmerically. " He sits down with his patient," the letter says, " and puts himself *en rapport* with him, which he does without producing the mesmeric sleep. The mind is used to overcome disease. . . . There is no danger from disease when the mind is armed against it. . . . He dissipates from the mind the idea of disease and induces in its place an idea of health. . . . The mind is what it thinks it is and, if it contends against the thought of disease and creates for itself an ideal form of health, that form impresses itself upon the animal spirit and through that upon the body."

CHAPTER IV

MRS. PATTERSON BECOMES QUIMBY'S PATIENT AND PUPIL—HER
DEFENCE OF QUIMBY AND HIS THEORY—HER GRIEF AT HIS
DEATH—SHE ASKS MR. DRESSER TO TAKE UP QUIMBY'S WORK

Upon reaching the hotel in Portland where Dr. Quimby had his offices, Mrs. Patterson was received by Julius A. Dresser and introduced to Dr. Quimby. George A. Quimby, Mrs. Julius A. Dresser, and the Hon. Edwin Reed all remember Mrs. Patterson's appearance at this time. She was so feeble that she had to be assisted up the stairs and into the waiting-room. She had lost the beauty of her earlier years. Her figure was emaciated, her face pale and worn, and her eyes were sunken. After the fashion of the time, her hair hung about her shoulders in loose ringlets, and her shabby dress suggested the hardness and poverty of her life. Yet Mrs. Patterson, as she was introduced to other patients sitting about the waiting-room, made something of an impression.

" Mrs. Patterson was presented to Dr. Quimby," says one of the patients who was present, " as ' the authoress,' and her manner was extremely polite and ingratiating. She wore a poke bonnet and an old-fashioned dress, but my impression was that her costume was intended to be a little odd, as in keeping with her ' literary ' character. She seemed very weak, and we thought she was a consumptive."

Mrs. Patterson almost immediately informed Quimby that she was very poor, and asked his assistance in getting an inexpensive boarding-place. Quimby, by personal intercession, obtained a room for her at reduced rates in Chestnut Street. According to George A. Quimby, Quimby's son and secretary, Mrs. Patterson's first stay in Portland lasted about three weeks. As far as her health was concerned the visit seemed a complete success. Under Quimby's treatment the spinal trouble disappeared and Mrs. Patterson left his office a well woman. But this hardly-achieved visit to Portland meant much more to her than that. For the first time in her life she felt an absorbing interest. Her contact with Quimby and her inquiry into his philosophy seem to have been her first great experience, the first powerful stimulus in a life of unrestraint, disappointment, and failure. Her girlhood had been a fruitless, hysterical revolt against order and discipline. The dulness and meagreness of her life had driven her to strange extravagances in conduct. Neither of her marriages had been happy. Maternity had not softened her nor brought her consolations. Up to this time her masterful will and great force of personality had served to no happy end. Her mind was turned in upon itself; she had been absorbed in ills which seem to have been largely the result of her own violent nature—lacking any adequate outlet, and, like disordered machinery, beating itself to pieces.

Quimby's idea gave her her opportunity, and the vehemence with which she seized upon it attests the emptiness and hunger of her earlier years. All during her stay in Portland she haunted the old man's rooms, asking questions, reading manuscripts, observing his treatment of his patients. Quimby at first took a decided liking to her. " She's a devilish bright woman," he frequently said. Always delighted to explain his theories, in Mrs. Patterson he found a most appreciative listener. Both on this and subsequent visits he permitted her to copy certain of his manuscripts. Undoubtedly he saw in Mrs. Patterson, in her capacity as an " authoress," a woman who could assist him in the matter dearest to his heart,—the popularisation of his doctrines.

Her devotion to her teacher was that of a long-imprisoned nature toward its deliverer. Her greatest desire seems to have been to teach Quimby's philosophy and to exalt him in the eyes of men. Soon after her recovery she wrote the following letter to the Portland *Courier:* [1]

When our Shakespeare decided that " there were more things in this world than were dreamed of in your philosophy," I cannot say of a verity that he had a foreknowledge of P. P. Quimby. And when the school Platonic anatomised the soul and divided it into halves to be reunited by elementary attractions, and heathen philosophers averred that old Chaos in sullen silence brooded o'er the earth until her inimitable form was hatched from the egg of night, I would not at present decide whether the fallacy was found in their premises or conclusions, never having dated my existence before the flood. When the startled alchemist discovered, as he supposed, an universal solvent, or the philosopher's stone, and the more daring Archimedes invented a lever wherewithal to pry up the universe, I cannot say that in either the principle obtained in nature or in art, or that it worked well, having never tried it. But, when by a falling apple, an immutable law was discovered, we gave it the crown of science, which is incontrovertible and capable of demonstration; hence that was wisdom and truth. When from the evidence of the senses, my reason takes cognizance of truth, although it may appear in quite a miraculous view, I must acknowledge that as science which is truth uninvestigated. Hence the following demonstration:—

Three weeks since I quitted my nurse and sick room *en route* for Portland. The belief of my recovery had died out of the hearts of those

---

[1] Letter by Mrs. M. M. Patterson (now Mrs. Mary Baker G. Eddy) in the Portland *Courier,* November 7, 1862.

who were most anxious for it. With this mental and physical depression I first visited P. P. Quimby; and in less than one week from that time I ascended by a stairway of one hundred and eighty-two steps to the dome of the City Hall, and am improving *ad infinitum*. To the most subtle reasoning, such a proof, coupled too, as it is with numberless similar ones, demonstrates his power to heal. Now for a brief analysis of this power.

Is it spiritualism? Listen to the words of wisdom. "Believe in God, believe also in me; or believe me for the very work's sake." Now, then, his works are but the result of superior wisdom, which can demonstrate a science not understood; hence it were a doubtful proceeding not to believe him for the work's sake. Well, then, he denies that his power to heal the sick is borrowed from the spirits of this or another world; and let us take the Scriptures for proof. "A kingdom divided against itself cannot stand." How, then, can he receive the friendly aid of the disenthralled spirit, while he rejects the faith of the solemn mystic who crosses the threshold of the dark unknown to conjure up from the vasty deep the awestruck spirit of some invisible squaw?

Again, is it by animal magnetism that he heals the sick? Let us examine. I have employed electro-magnetism and animal magnetism, and for a brief interval have felt relief, from the equilibrium which I fancied was restored to an exhausted system or by a diffusion of concentrated action. But in no instance did I get rid of a return of all my ailments, because I had not been helped out of the error in which opinions involved us. My operator believed in disease, independent of the mind; hence I could not be wiser than my master. But now I can see dimly at first, and only as trees walking, the great principle which underlies Dr. Quimby's faith and works; and just in proportion to my right perception of truth is my recovery. This truth which he opposes to the error of giving intelligence to matter and placing pain where it never placed itself, if received understandingly, changes the currents of the system to their normal action; and the mechanism of the body goes on undisturbed. That this is a science capable of demonstration, becomes clear to the minds of those patients who reason upon the process of their cure. The truth which he establishes in the patient cures him (although he may be wholly unconscious thereof); and the body, which is full of light, is no longer in disease. At present I am too much in error to elucidate the truth, and can touch only the keynote for the master hand to wake the harmony. May it be in essays, instead of notes! say I. After all, this is a very spiritual doctrine; but the eternal years of God are with it, and it must stand firm as the rock of ages. And to many a poor sufferer may it be found, as by me, "the shadow of a great rock in a weary land."

Her extravagance brought general ridicule upon Quimby and herself. " P. P. Quimby compared to Jesus Christ? " exclaimed the Portland *Advertiser*, in commenting on her letter, " What next? " Mrs. Patterson again took up the cudgels. She wrote in the Portland *Courier:*

Noticing a paragraph in the *Advertiser,* commenting upon some sentences of mine clipped from the *Courier,* relative to the science of P. P. Quimby, concluding, " What next? " we would reply in due deference to the courtesy with which they define their position. P. P. Quimby stands upon the plane of wisdom with his truth. Christ healed the sick, but not by jugglery or with drugs. As the former speaks as never man before spake, and heals as never man healed since Christ, is he not identified with truth? And is not this the Christ which is in him? We know that in wisdom is life, " and the life was the light of man." P. P. Quimby rolls away the stone from the sepulchre of error, and health is the resurrection. But we also know that " light shineth in darkness and the darkness comprehendeth it not."

Mrs. Patterson expressed her admiration of Quimby in verse also:

SONNET

Suggested by Reading the Remarkable Cure of
Captain J. W. Deering

To Dr. P. P. Quimby

'Mid light of science sits the sage profound,
Awing with classics and his starry lore,
Climbing to Venus, chasing Saturn round,
Turning his mystic pages o'er and o'er,
Till, from empyrean space, his wearied sight
Turns to the oasis on which to gaze,
More bright than glitters on the brow of night
The self-taught man walking in wisdom's ways.
Then paused the captive gaze with peace entwined,
And sight was satisfied with thee to dwell;
But not in classics could the book-worm find
That law of excellence whence came the spell
Potent o'er all,—the captive to unbind,
To heal the sick and faint, the halt and blind.

For the *Courier.*   MARY M. PATTERSON.

Mrs. Patterson returned in good health, as she thought, to Sanbornton Bridge. Quimby became the great possession of her life. She talked incessantly of him to all her friends, and sought to persuade the sick to visit him. In 1863 she wrote many times to Quimby. Her letters, now in the possession of George A. Quimby, describe, in the most reverential terms, her indebtedness.

The following extracts illustrate the tone of these communications:

SANBORNTON BRIDGE, January 12, 1863.
. . . I am to all who see me a living wonder, and a living monument of your power. . . . I eat, drink, and am merry, have no laws to fetter my spirit. Am as much an escaped prisoner, as my dear husband was. . . . My explanation of your *curative principle* surprises people, especially those whose minds are all matter. . . . I mean not again to look mournfully into the past, but wisely to improve the present.

In a letter dated Sanbornton Bridge, January 31, 1863, she asks for " absent treatment." " Please come to me and remove this pain." In this letter she says that her sister, Mrs. Tilton, and her son, Albert Tilton, are going to visit Mr. Quimby. She says that Albert smokes and drinks to excess, and begs Quimby to treat him for these habits, " even when Albert is not there." She explains that she herself has treated Albert to help him overcome the habit of smoking and, while doing so, felt " a constant desire to smoke! " She asks Quimby to treat her for this desire. In other letters Mrs. Patterson repeatedly asks for absent treatments, and occasionally incloses a dollar to pay for them.

In a letter from Saco, Me., September 14, 1863, Mrs. Patterson says that Quimby's " Angel Visits " (absent treatments) are helping her. " I would like to have you in your omnipresence visit me at eight o'clock this evening." On this occasion she specifies that she wishes to be treated for " small beliefs," namely, " stomach trouble, backache, and constipation."

In the early part of 1864, Mrs. Patterson again spent two or three months in Portland. She found congenial companions in one Mrs. Sarah Crosby, who was likewise a patient of Quimby's, and Miss Anna Mary Jarvis, who had brought her consumptive sister to Quimby for treatment. Mrs. Crosby and Mrs. Patterson became warm friends. They occupied adjoining rooms in the same boarding-house and spent much time together. Mrs. Patterson told Mrs. Crosby that she intended to assist Quimby in his work. The latter, says Mrs. Crosby, frequently expressed his pleasure at Mrs. Patterson's enthusiasm. " He told me many times," she adds, " that I was not so quick to perceive the Truth as Mrs. Patterson." Quimby now gave Mrs. Patterson much of his time. He was practising then mainly in the morning, and allowed Mrs. Patterson to spend nearly every afternoon at his office. " She would work with Dr. Quimby all afternoon," says Mrs. Crosby, " and then she would come home and sit up late at night writing down what she had learned during the day."

This second visit to Quimby seems to have been even more stimulating to Mrs. Patterson than the first. She gave all her time and strength to the study of this esoteric theory. It was during this visit that she first manifested a desire to become herself an active force in the teaching and practising of this " Science." The desire became actually a purpose, perhaps an ambition—the only definite one she had ever known. She was groping for a vocation. She must even then have seen before

MARY BAKER G. EDDY

From a tintype given to Mrs. Sarah G. Crosby in 1864. Mrs. Eddy was then
Mrs. Patterson

her new possibilities; an opportunity for personal growth and
personal achievement very different from the petty occupations
of her old life.   In one of her letters to Quimby, written some
months after she left Portland, there is this new note of aspiration and resolve:

Who is wise but you? . . . Doctor, I have a strong feeling of late
that I ought to be perfect after the command of science. . . . I can
love only a good, honourable, and brave career; no other can suit me.

Upon leaving Portland, after this second visit, Mrs. Patterson went to Warren, Me., to visit Miss Jarvis. Here she
seems to have tried Quimby's treatment upon Miss Jarvis,
putting into practice what she had learned from Quimby himself during the last three months. " At the mere mention of
my going," writes Mrs. Patterson, " Miss Jarvis has a relapse
and is in despair."

She confidently believes that she has benefited the sick woman.
Once, after receiving an " absent treatment " from Quimby,
she successfully transmitted its blessings to Miss Jarvis. She
became so " cheerful and uplifted " that Miss Jarvis " was gay
and not at all sad." She also writes that she has been asked
to take outside cases at Warren, but that she feels herself not
yet ready, being still in her " pupilage."

In a letter from Warren, March 31, 1864, she says:

I wish you would come to my aid and help me to sleep. Dear Doctor
what could I do without you?

In a letter dated Warren, April 5, 1864:

I met the former editor of the *Banner of Light,* and he heard for once
the truth about you. He thought you a defunct Spiritualist, before I
quitted him at Brunswick, he had endorsed your *science* and acknowledged
himself as greatly interested in it.

In another letter from Warren, under date of April 24, 1864, she says:

Jesus taught as man does *not*, who then is wise but you? Posted at the public marts of this city is this notice, Mrs. M. M. Patterson will lecture at the Town Hall on P. P. Quimby's Spiritual Science healing disease, as opposed to Deism or Rochester Rapping Spiritualism.

In a letter dated Warren, May, 1864, she writes that she has been ill, but,

I am up and about to-day, i.e., by the help of the Lord (Quimby).

Again,

Dear doctor, what could I do without you? . . . I will not bow to wealth for I cannot honour it as I do wisdom. . . . May the peace of wisdom which passeth all understanding be and abide with you.—Ever the same in gratitude.

In one letter she describes the sudden appearance of Quimby's wraith in her room. She spoke to it, she adds, " and then you turned and walked away." " That," she says, " I call dodging the issue." She repeatedly calls his treatment his " Science "; her illnesses, her " beliefs " or " errors "; and her recoveries, her " restorations."

In May, 1864, Mrs. Patterson left Miss Jarvis and went to visit another friend, her fellow-patient, Mrs. Sarah G. Crosby, at Albion, Me. Mrs. Crosby,[2] who is now living at Waterville, Me., gives an interesting account of this visit, which lasted several months. Mrs. Patterson, she says, although in a state of almost absolute destitution, retained the air of a

---

[2] Mrs. Crosby is well and creditably known in Maine. When she was a woman of forty and the mother of five children, financial reverses came to her family. She learned stenography at night without a teacher and became a court stenographer at a time when it was most unusual for a woman to hold such a position. For fifteen years she was stenographer in the highest courts of Maine, during which time she paid off her husband's debts, and reared and educated her children.

grand lady which had so characterised her in her youth. Although visiting at a farmhouse where every one had a part in the household duties, Mrs. Patterson was always the guest of honour, nor did it occur to any one to suggest her sharing the daily routine. Mrs. Crosby's servants waited upon the guest, and even her room was cared for by others. Mrs. Patterson talked incessantly of Quimby, and often urged Mrs. Crosby to leave her home and go out into the world with her to teach Quimby's " Science." Mrs. Crosby admits that she was completely under Mrs. Patterson's spell, and says that even after years of estrangement and complete disillusionment, she still feels that Mrs. Patterson was the most stimulating and invigorating influence she has ever known. Like all of Mrs. Eddy's old intimates, she speaks of their days of companionship with a certain shade of regret—as if life in the society of this woman was more intense and keen than it ever was afterward.

Mrs. Crosby says that, during this visit, both she and Mrs. Patterson became somewhat interested in spiritualism through communications from Mrs. Patterson's dead brother. Mrs. Crosby is authority for the following account: [3]

Mr. Crosby's farm was rather isolated, and the two women found relief from the tedium of country life in spirit communications from Mrs. Patterson's dead brother, Albert Baker. Mrs. Patterson had been much attached to this brother, and described his talents and personality at great length to Mrs. Crosby, making such an attractive picture that he became a very real person to the young woman. Albert, Mrs. Patterson

---

[3] This account is a condensed version of Mrs. Crosby's affidavit, which takes up the history of her entire acquaintance with Mrs. Eddy, beginning when she was a patient at Quimby's in 1864. This document is now in the writer's possession.

told her, was Mrs. Crosby's guardian spirit; he had long been trying to communicate with her, but had never been able to do so until his sister came to visit her, as Mary was his " only earthly medium." Mrs. Crosby says that she implicitly believed in Albert's care and guardianship over her, that she derived constant strength and comfort from it, and that this spirit friendship was one of the most real she has ever known.

Albert's first communication to Mrs. Crosby occurred as follows: [4]

One day Mrs. Patterson and Mrs. Crosby sat together at opposite sides of the same table. Suddenly Mrs. Patterson leaned backward, shivered, closed her eyes, and began to talk in a sepulchral, mannish voice. The voice said that " he " was Albert Baker, Mrs. Patterson's brother. " He " had been trying, the voice continued, to get control of Mrs. Patterson for many days. " He " wished to warn Mrs. Crosby against putting such entire confidence in Mrs. Patterson. " He informed me," Mrs. Crosby continues, " through her own lips, that while his sister loved me as much as she was capable of loving any one, life had been a severe experiment with her, and she might use my sacred confidence to further any ambitious purposes of her own."

Mrs. Crosby was naturally amazed at this injunction. That

---

[4] Mrs. Crosby does not assert or even imply that Mrs. Eddy was ever, in any regular or professional sense, a " medium." Mrs. Eddy herself states that she has been able to perform the signs and wonders of spiritualism, though explaining them by another cause. In the second edition of *Science and Health*, 1878, page 166, she says : " We are aware that the Spiritualists claim whomsoever they would catch and regard even Christ as an elder brother. But we never were a Spiritualist; and never were, and never could be, and never admitted we were a medium. We have explained to the class calling themselves Spiritualists how their signs and wonders were wrought, and have illustrated by doing them ; but at the same time have said, This is not the work of spirits and I am not a medium ; and they have passed from our presence and said, behold the proof that she is a medium !

Facsimile of the second sheet of the first "spirit" letter from Albert Baker, Mrs. Eddy's brother, to Mrs. Sarah Crosby

Albert should select his own sister as the medium through which to warn Mrs. Crosby against her, seemed remarkable. Again, if Mrs. Patterson consciously shammed, Mrs. Crosby could not understand why she should deliver a message so uncomplimentary to herself—unless, indeed, to make the message seem more genuine. Several times, in the course of this visit, Mrs. Patterson went into trances. In one of these, Albert Baker's spirit told Mrs. Crosby that if, from time to time, she would look under the cushion of a particular chair, she would find important written communications from him. Mrs. Crosby, following the injunction, discovered now and then a letter. One of these is interesting chiefly as containing Albert Baker's spiritistic endorsement of P. P. Quimby. The text is as follows:

Sarah dear Be ye calm in reliance on self, amid all the changes of natural yearnings, of too keen a sense of earth joys, of too great a struggle between the material and spiritual. Be calm or you will rend your mortal and your experience which is needed for your spiritual progress lost, till taken up without the proper sphere and your spirit trials more severe.

This is why all things are working for good to those who suffer and they must look not upon the things which are seen but upon those which do not appear. P. Quimby of Portland has the spiritual truth of diseases. You must imbibe it to be healed. Go to him again and lean on no material or spiritual medium. In that path of truth I first found you. Dear one, I am at present no aid to you although you think I am, but your spirit will not at present bear this quickening or twill leave the body; hence I leave you till you ripen into a condition to meet me. You will miss me at first, but afterwards grow more tranquil because of it, which is important that you may live for yourself and children. Love and care for poor sister a great suffering lies before her.

After leaving Albion, Mrs. Patterson continued to receive messages from Albert. On one occasion Mrs. Patterson sent Mrs. Crosby the following communication from her brother:

Child of earth! heir to immortality! love hath made intercession with wisdom for you—your request is answered.

Let not the letter leave your hand—nor destroy it.

Love each other, your spirits are affined. My dear Sarah is innocent, and will rejoice for every tear.

The gates of paradise are opening at the tread of time; glory and the crown shall shall be the diadem of your earthly pilgrimage if you patiently persevere in virtue, justice, and love. You twain are my care. I speak through no other earthly medium but you.

Mr. Quimby died January 16, 1866. As in the case of many mental healers, his own experience apparently belied his doctrines. He had for years suffered from an abdominal tumour. He had never had it treated medically, but asserted that he had always been able, mentally, to prevent it from getting the upper hand. The last few years of his life he worked incessantly. His practice increased enormously, and at last broke him down. In the summer of 1865 he was compelled to stop work. He closed his Portland office and went home to Belfast to devote the rest of his life to revising his manuscripts and preparing them for publication. His physical condition, however, prevented this; he became feebler every day. He now acknowledged his inability to cure himself. As long as he had his usual mental strength, he said, he could stop the disease; but, as he felt this slipping from him, his " error " rapidly made inroads. Finally, Quimby's wife, with his acquiescence, summoned a homœopathic physician. Quimby consented to this, he said, not because he had the slightest idea that the doctor could help him, but merely to comfort his family. His wife had never accepted the " theory "; his children, for the most part, had no enthusiasm for it. They all, however, loved the old man dearly and could not patiently witness his suffering without seeking all means to allay it. Quimby followed implicitly all the doctor's instructions. His son, George A. Quimby, says: [5]

An hour before he breathed his last, he said to the writer: " I am more than ever convinced of the truth of my theory. I am perfectly willing for the change myself, but I know you will all feel badly; but *I* know that I shall be right here with you, just the same as I have always been. I do not dread the change any more than if I were going on a trip to Philadelphia."

His death occurred January 16, 1866, at his residence in Belfast, at the age of sixty-four years, and was the result of too close application to his profession and of overwork. A more fitting epitaph could not be accorded him than in these words:

" Greater love hath no man than this, that a man lay down his life for his friends." For, if ever a man did lay down his life for others, that man was Phineas Parkhurst Quimby.

Many mourned Quimby's death. No one felt greater grief or expressed it more emphatically and sincerely than Mary M. Patterson. She wrote at once to Julius Dresser, asking him to take up the master's work. Her letter follows:

Mr. Dresser: Lynn, February 14, 1866.
   Sir: I enclose some lines of mine in memory of our much-loved friend, which perhaps *you* will not think overwrought in meaning: others *must* of course.

   I am constantly wishing that *you* would step forward into the place he has vacated. I believe you would do a vast amount of good, and are more capable of occupying his place than any other I know of.

   Two weeks ago I fell on the sidewalk, and struck my back on the ice, and was taken up for dead, came to consciousness amid a storm of vapours from cologne, chloroform, ether, camphor, etc., but to find myself the helpless cripple I was before I saw Dr. Quimby.

   The physician attending said I had taken the last step I ever should, but in two days I got out of my bed *alone* and *will* walk; but yet I confess I am frightened, and out of that nervous heat my friends are forming, spite of me, the terrible spinal affection from which I have suffered so long and hopelessly. . . . Now can't *you* help me? I

_____
[5] *New England Magazine*, March, 1888.

believe you can. I write this with this feeling: I think that I could help another in my condition if they had not placed their intelligence in matter. This I have not done, and yet I am slowly failing. Won't you write me if you will undertake for me if I can get to you?

Respectfully,   MARY M. PATTERSON.

The verses referred to had already been published in a Lynn newspaper.

Lines on the Death of Dr. P. P. Quimby,[6] Who Healed with the Truth that Christ Taught in Contradistinction to All Isms.

> Did sackcloth clothe the sun and day grow night,
>   All matter mourn the hour with dewy eyes,
> When Truth, receding from our mortal sight,
>   Had paid to error her last sacrifice?
>
> Can we forget the power that gave us life?
>   Shall we forget the wisdom of its way?
> Then ask me not amid this mortal strife—
>   This keenest pang of animated clay—
>
> To mourn him less; to mourn him more were just
>   If to his memory 'twere a tribute given
> For every solemn, sacred, earnest trust
>   Delivered to us ere he rose to heaven.
>
> Heaven but the happiness of that calm soul,
>   Growing in stature to the throne of God;
> Rest should reward him who hath made us whole,
>   Seeking, though tremblers, where his footsteps trod.

MARY M. PATTERSON.

Lynn, January 22, 1866.

---

[6] In a copy of these verses sent to Mrs. Sarah G. Crosby the title is worded somewhat differently and several slight variations occur in the text.

CHAPTER V

NINE years after the death of Phineas P. Quimby, Mrs. Eddy
published a book entitled *Science and Health*, in which she
developed a system of curing disease by the mind.   In this
work she mentions Quimby only incidentally, and acknowledges
no indebtedness to him for the idea upon which her system is
based.   Upon this foundation Mrs. Eddy has since established
the Christian Science Church, the sect which regards her as
the real discoverer and only accredited teacher of metaphysical
healing.   Quimby himself, though he founded no religious organisation, to-day has thousands of followers; the several schools
of Mental Scientists are convinced that he was the discoverer
and founder of mental healing in this country.   Mrs. Eddy's
partisans maintain that she received her inspiration from God,
while Quimby's adherents maintain that she obtained her ideas
very largely from Quimby.   Interrupting, for the present, the
narrative of Mrs. Eddy's life, this chapter will attempt to
present the arguments of both sides in this controversy.

Quimby's followers do not assert that Quimby wrote *Science
and Health*, or that he is the responsible author of all the
ideas now formulated in the Christian Science creed.   In brief,

their position is this: that Mrs. Eddy obtained the radical principle of her Science,—the cure of disease by the power of Divine mind,—from Quimby; that she left Portland with manuscripts which formed the basis of her book, *Science and Health;* that she publicly figured for several years after Quimby's death as the teacher and practitioner of his system; that she had, herself, before 1875, repeatedly acknowledged her obligations to him; and that since the publication of the first edition of *Science and Health,* in her determined efforts to disprove this obligation, she has not hesitated to bring discredit upon her former teacher.   They do not maintain that Quimby is, in any sense, the founder of the present Christian Science organisation; they do declare, however, that had Mrs. Eddy never visited Quimby, never listened to his ideas or studied his writings, such an organisation would probably not now exist.   On the other hand, Christian Scientists repudiate any suggestion that Mrs. Eddy, or their ecclesiastical establishment, is in the slightest degree indebted to the Portland healer.

Christian Scientists believe that Mrs. Eddy received the truths of Christian Science as a direct revelation from God.   She came to fulfil and to complete the mission of Jesus Christ.   Jesus, that is, possessed only partial wisdom.   " Our Master healed the sick," she writes in *Science and Health,* ". . . and taught the generalities of its divine Principle to his students; but he left no definite rule for demonstrating his Principle of healing and preventing disease.   This remained to be discovered through Christian Science." [1]   " Jesus' wisdom ofttimes was shown by His forbearing to speak," she writes, " as well as by His speak-

---

[1] *Science and Health* (1898), p. 41.

ing, the whole truth. . . . Had wisdom characterised all His [2] sayings, He would not have prophesied His own death and thereby hastened it or caused it." [3] In other words, Jesus, by foretelling His crucifixion, created that thought, and the thought ultimately hastened His death. In a letter written about 1877, Mrs. Eddy again suggests that her mission completes that of the New Testament:

LYNN, March 11th.

MY DEAR STUDENT:

I did not write the day your letter came, a belief was clouding the sunshine of Truth and it is not fair weather yet. But Harry, be of good cheer "behind the clouds the sun is still shining." *I know the crucifixion of the one who presents Truth in its higher aspect will be this time through a bigger error, through mortal mind instead of its lower strata or matter, showing that the idea given of God this time is higher, clearer, and more permanent than before.*[4] My dear companion and fellow-labourer in the Lord [5] is grappling stronger than did Peter with the enemy, he would cut off their hands and "ears"; you dear student, are doubtless praying for me—and so the Modern Law giver is upheld for a time. I shall go to work for the book as soon as I can think clearly for agony, or outside of the belief.

May the All Love hold and help you ever,

Your Teacher

M B G E.

In *Retrospection and Introspection,* Mrs. Eddy writes:

No person can take the individual place of the Virgin Mary. No person can compass or fulfil the individual mission of Jesus of Nazareth. No person can take the place of the author of Science and Health, the dis-

---

[2] Both this and other quotations in this article have been modified in later editions of Mrs. Eddy's books. The phrase above now stands: " This wisdom, which characterised his sayings did not prophesy his death and thereby hasten or permit it." The author thinks it hardly necessary, in what follows, to indicate the various readings of the same quotation, but will content herself with naming the particular editions in which the phrases, as quoted, appear. When no edition is mentioned, the latest edition is to be understood.
[3] *Miscellaneous Writings* (1897), pp. 83 and 84.
[4] The italics are not Mrs. Eddy's.
[5] This is apparently a reference to Asa G. Eddy, her husband.

coverer and founder of Christian Science. Each individual must fill his own niche in time and eternity.

The second appearing of Jesus is unquestionably, the spiritual advent of the advancing idea of God as in Christian Science.[6]

Mrs. Eddy believes that Christian Science is foretold in the Book of Revelation. In *Science and Health* she writes:

John the Baptist prophesied the coming of the Immaculate Jesus and declared that this spiritual idea was the Messiah who would baptise with the Holy Ghost—Divine Science. The son of the Blessed represents the fatherhood of God; and the Revelator completes this figure with the Woman, or type of God's motherhood.[7]

Again

Saint John writes, in the tenth chapter of his Book of Revelation: "And I saw another mighty angel come down from Heaven, clothed with a cloud; and a rainbow was upon his head, and his face was as it were the sun, and his feet as pillars of fire. And he had in his hand a little book open; and he set his right foot upon the sea, and his left foot upon the earth." Is this angel, or message from God, Divine Science that comes in a cloud? To mortals obscure, abstract, and dark; but a bright promise crowns its brow. When understood, it is Truth's prism and praise; when you look it fairly in the face, you can heal by its means, and it hath for you a light above the sun, for God "is the light thereof." . . . This angel had in his hand a "little book," open for all to read and understand. Did this same book contain the revelation of Divine Science, whose "right foot" or dominant power was upon the sea,—upon elementary, latent error, the source of all error's visible forms? . . . Then will a voice from harmony cry: "Go and take the little book. Take it and eat it up, and it shall make thy belly bitter; but it shall be in thy mouth sweet as honey." Mortal, obey the heavenly evangel. Take up Divine Science. Study it, ponder it. It will be indeed sweet at its first taste, when it heals you; but murmur not over Truth, if you find its digestion bitter. . . . In the opening of the Sixth Seal, typical of six thousand years since Adam, there is one distinctive feature which has *special reference to the present age.*[8]

---

[6] *Retrospection and Introspection*, pp. 95 and 96.
[7] *Science and Health* (1888), p. 513.
[8] The italics in this paragraph are not Mrs. Eddy's.

Rev. xii. 1. "And there appeared a great wonder in Heaven,—a woman clothed with the sun, and the moon under her feet, and upon her head a crown of twelve stars." . . . Rev. xii. 5. "And she brought forth a man-child, who was to rule all nations with a rod of iron; and her child was caught up unto God, and to his Throne." Led on by the grossest element of mortal mind, Herod decreed the death of every male child, in order that the man Jesus (*the masculine representative of the spiritual idea*) might never hold sway, and so deprive Herod of his crown. The impersonation of the spiritual idea had a brief history in the earthly life of our Master; but "of his kingdom there shall be no end," for *Christ, God's idea, will eventually rule all nations and peoples—imperatively, absolutely, finally—with Divine Science. This immaculate idea, represented first by man and last by woman,* will baptise with fire; and the fiery baptism will burn up the chaff of error with the fervent heat of Truth and Love, melting and purifying even the gold of human character.[9]

The following extracts from Mrs. Eddy's writings indicate the magnitude of her claims, and her conception of her own exalted mission:

She says in *Science and Health:*

In the year 1866, I discovered the Science of Metaphysical Healing, and named it Christian Science. God had been graciously fitting me, during many years, for the reception of a final revelation of the absolute Principle of Scientific Mind-healing. . . . No human pen or tongue taught me the Science contained in this book . . . and neither tongue nor pen can ever overthrow it.[10]

Science and Health, Mrs. Eddy says, continues the teachings of St. Paul.

On our subject, St. Paul first reasons upon the basis of what is seen, the effects of Truth on the material senses; thence, up to the Unseen, the testimony of spiritual sense; and right there he leaves the subject.

Just there, in the intermediate line of thought, is where the present writer found it, when she discovered Christian Science. And she has *not* left it, but continues the explanation of the power of Spirit up to its infinite meaning, its Allness.[11]

---

[9] *Science and Health* (1898), pp. 550, 551, 552, and 557.
[10] *Science and Health* (1898), pp. 1 and 4.
[11] *Miscellaneous Writings* (1897), p. 188.

Mrs. Eddy's followers believe that her discovery, in a manner, has repeated the day of Pentecost and the coming of the Holy Ghost to man. She says:

This understanding is what is meant by the descent of the Holy Ghost,— that influx of divine Science which so illuminated the Pentecostal Day, and is now repeating its ancient history. . . .

In the words of St. John: " He shall give you another Comforter, that he may abide with you *forever."* This Comforter I understand to be Divine Science.[12]

In *Miscellaneous Writings,* Mrs. Eddy further says of her Science and her ministry:

Above the fogs of sense and storms of passion, Christian Science and its Art will rise triumphant; ignorance, envy, and hatred—earth's harmless thunder—pluck not their heaven-born wings. Angels, with overtures, hold charge over both, and announce their principle and idea. . . .

No works similar to mine on Christian Science existed, prior to my discovery of this Science. Before the publication of my first work on this subject, a few manuscripts of mine were in circulation. The discovery and founding of Christian Science has cost more than thirty years of unremitting toil and unrest; but, comparing those with the joy of knowing that the sinner and the sick are helped upward, that time and eternity bear witness to this gift of God to the race, I am the debtor.

In 1895, I ordained the BIBLE, and SCIENCE AND HEALTH WITH KEY TO THE SCRIPTURES, the Christian Science Text-book, as the Pastor, on this planet, of all the churches of the Christian Science Denomination. This ordinance took effect the same year, and met with the universal approval and support of Christian Scientists. Whenever and wherever a church of Christian Science is established, its Pastor is the Bible and My Book.

In 1896, it goes without saying, preëminent over ignorance or envy, that Christian Science *is founded by its discoverer,* and built upon the Rock of Christ. The elements of earth beat in vain against the immortal parapets of this Science. Erect and eternal, it will go on with the ages, go down the dim posterns of time unharmed, and on every battlefield rise higher in the estimation of thinkers, and in the hearts of Christians.[18]

To Christian Scientists, therefore, Mrs. Eddy's discovery or revelation was a great turning-point in the history of the

---

[12] *Science and Health* (1906), pp. 43 and 55.
[13] *Miscellaneous Writings* (1897), pp. 374, 382, and 383.

human race, and the manner in which it came about is of the highest importance.

It is difficult to ascertain definitely just when Mrs. Eddy arrived at the conclusion that mortal mind, not matter, causes sin, sickness, and death, as her own recollection of her initial revelation seems to be somewhat blurred. " As long ago as 1844," she writes in the *Christian Science Journal*, in June, 1887, " I was convinced that mortal mind produced all disease, and that the various medical systems were, in no proper sense, scientific. In 1862, when I first visited Mr. Quimby, I was proclaiming—to druggists, Spiritualists, and mesmerists—that science must govern all healing."

To her discovery of the principle of mental healing, she has assigned no less than three different dates:

In a letter to the Boston *Post*, March 7, 1883, she says:

We made our first experiments in mental healing about 1853, when we were convinced that mind had a science, which, if understood, would heal all disease.

Again, in the first edition of *Science and Health* (1875), she says:

We made our first discovery that science mentally applied would heal the sick, in 1864, and since then have tested it on ourselves and hundreds of others and never found it fail to prove the statement herein made of it.

In *Retrospection and Introspection*, she says:

It was in Massachusetts, in February, 1866, . . . that I discovered the Science of Divine Metaphysical Healing, which I afterwards named Christian Science.[14]

In later editions of *Science and Health*, and in numerous other places, Mrs. Eddy definitely fixes 1866 as the year of her

---

[14] *Retrospection and Introspection,* p. 38.

discovery. This is now the generally accepted date. Her enemies have naturally made much of the seeming inconsistency of these statements. To disprove her claim that she had a knowledge of mind healing as far back as 1844 or 1853, they quote Mrs. Eddy's own words in the *Christian Science Journal* of June, 1887. She there says that before her visit to Quimby in 1862, " I knew nothing of the Science of Mind-healing. . . . Mind Science was unknown to me."

It is scarcely necessary to remark that each of these dates might be intrinsically correct, as each might mark an important advance in Mrs. Eddy's mastery of her science. It would be extremely difficult for any discoverer to date exactly the inception of an idea which eventually absorbed him completely. Doubtless these seeming inaccuracies on Mrs. Eddy's part would have been passed over as due to mere inexactness of expression, had not each date been given to meet some specific charge as to her indebtedness to Quimby—and given, as it would seem, mainly for the purpose of extricating herself from the difficulty of the moment.

As shown above, in the first edition of *Science and Health* (1875), she said that it was in 1864 that she first discovered that " science mentally applied would heal the sick."

Eight years after Mrs. Eddy had announced 1864 as the correct and authentic date of her discovery, Julius A. Dresser,[15]

---

[15] Julius A. Dresser was born in Portland, Me., February 12, 1838. He was in college in Waterville, Me., when his health failed. He had a strongly emotional religious nature and intended to become a minister in the Calvinistic Baptist Church. When he went to Mr. Quimby in the summer of 1860, he apparently had only a shcrt time to live. Quimby told him his " religion was killing him." Quimby treated him successfully for typhoid pneumonia, according to Mr. Dresser's son, Horatio W. Dresser of Cambridge, and " gave him the understanding which enabled my father to live thirty-three years after his restoration to health."

Mr. Dresser became an enthusiastic convert to the Quimby faith and for in a letter to the Boston *Post* (February 24, 1883), advanced Quimby's claim.   It was in a reply to this letter, written March 7, 1883, published in the same paper, that Mrs. Eddy first asserted: " We made our first experiments in mental healing about 1853."

Four years later (February 6, 1887), Mr. Dresser delivered an address upon " The True History of Mental Science," at the Church of Divine Unity, in Boston, in which he declared that Quimby was the originator of the present science of mental healing, and that Mrs. Eddy did not understand disease as a state of mind until she was his patient and pupil.   This address caused such comment and discussion, that four months later (June, 1887) Mrs. Eddy answered it through the *Christian Science Journal* by asserting: " As long ago as 1844, I was convinced that mortal mind produced all disease. . . . In 1862 . . . I was proclaiming . . . that science must govern all healing."

---

some years devoted himself to explaining Quimby's principle of mental healing to new patients. In this way he met Miss Annetta G. Seabury, whom he married in September, 1863, and Mrs. Eddy, then Mrs. Patterson.

After his marriage Mr. Dresser took up newspaper work in Portland and in 1866 moved to Webster, Mass., where he edited and published the Webster *Times.*

The death of Quimby was a great shock to Mr. and Mrs. Dresser. It was generally expected by Quimby's followers that Mr. Dresser would take up the work as Quimby's successor. Mrs. Dresser hesitated to attempt it publicly, knowing her own and her husband's sensitiveness, and after consideration they decided not to undertake it at that time. "This," says Mr. Horatio W. Dresser, " was a fundamentally decisive action, and much stress should be placed upon it. For Mrs. Eddy naturally looked to father as the probable successor, and when she learned from father that he had no thought of taking up the public work, *the field became free for her.* I am convinced that she had no desire previous to that time to make any claims for herself. Her letters give evidence of this."

Mr. Dresser's health again weakened from overwork, and after living in the West for a time he returned to Massachusetts and began his public work as mental teacher and healer. In Boston Mr. Dresser found that Mrs. Eddy's pupils and rejected pupils were practising with the sick, and he believed that their work was inferior to Quimby's. This gave him confidence to begin. In 1882 Mr. and Mrs. Dresser began to practise in Boston, and in 1883 they were holding class lectures, teaching from the Quimby manuscripts and practising the Quimby method.

From this the facts with regard to Mrs. Eddy and Mr. Quimby spread, **and** this was the beginning of the Quimby controversy.

The unprejudiced historian finds discrepancies, not only in the dates of Mrs. Eddy's discovery, but in her accounts of the particular episodes which occasioned it.   In the several editions of *Science and Health*, for example, there are two elaborate versions.   In the early editions Mrs. Eddy associates her discovery with experiments which she made to cure herself of dyspepsia; in later editions, as the result of a miraculous recovery from a spinal injury received in a fall on the ice in Lynn, in 1866.   Both these episodes are related in all editions of the book.   In the early versions, however, the recovery from dyspepsia receives the greater emphasis; while in recent editions the fall on the ice assumes the chief importance, with the other story forced more and more into the background.

In the first edition of *Science and Health* (1875), Mrs. Eddy gives the following account of how she was led to see the truth:

When quite a child, we adopted the Graham system for dyspepsia, ate only bread and vegetables, and drank water, following this diet for years; we became more dyspeptic, however, and of course thought we must diet more rigidly; so we partook of but one meal in twenty-four hours, and this consisted of a thin slice of bread, about three inches square, without water; our physician not allowing us with this simple meal, to wet our parched lips for many hours thereafter; whenever we drank, it produced violent retchings. Thus we passed most of our early years, as many can attest, in hunger, pain, weakness and starvation. At length we learned that while fasting increased the desire for food, it spared none of the sufferings occasioned by partaking of it, and what to do next, having already exhausted the medicine men, was a question. After years of suffering, when we made up our mind to die, our doctors kindly assuring us this was our only alternative, our eyes were suddenly opened, and we learned suffering is self-imposed, a belief, and not truth. That God never made men sick; and all our fasting for penance or health is not acceptable to Wisdom because it is not the science in which Soul governs sense. Thus Truth, opening our eyes, relieved our stomach, also, and enabled us to eat without suffering, giving God thanks; but we never afterwards enjoyed food as we expected to, if ever we were a freed slave, to eat without a master; for the new-born understanding that food could not hurt us, brought with it another point, *viz.,* that it did not help us as we had anticipated it would before our changed views on this subject; food had less power over us for evil or for good than when we consulted matter before spirit and believed in pains or pleasures of personal sense. As a natural result we took less thought about " what we should eat or what drink," and fasting or feasting, consulted less our stomachs and our food, arguing against their claims continually, and in this manner despoiled them of their power over us to give pleasure or pain, and recovered strength and flesh rapidly, enjoying health and harmony that we never before had done.

The belief that fasting or feasting enables man to grow better, morally or physically, is one of the fruits of the " tree of knowledge " against which Wisdom warned man, and of which we had partaken in sad experience; believing for many years we lived only by the strictest adherence to dietetics and physiology. During this time we also learned a dyspeptic is very far from the image and likeness of God, from having " dominion over the fish of the sea, the fowls of the air, or beasts of the field "; therefore that God never made one; while the Graham system, hygiene, physiology, materia medica, etc., did, and contrary to his commands. Then it was that we promised God to spend our coming years for the sick and suffering; to unmask this error of belief that matter rules man. Our cure for dyspepsia was, to learn the science of being, and " eat what was set before us, asking no question for conscience' sake; yea to consult matter less and God more."

In the latest editions, Mrs. Eddy relates this incident, but does not connect herself with it. " I knew a woman," she says, " who, when quite a child, adopted the Graham system to cure dyspepsia," giving the incident merely as an illustration of Christian Science healing.

At present, Christian Scientists date the dawn of the new era from February 1, 1866, on the evening of which day Mrs. Eddy fell on the ice. She says in *Retrospection and Introspection:*

It was in Massachusetts, February, 1866, and after the death of the magnetic doctor, Mr. P. P. Quimby, whom Spiritualists would associate therewith, but who was in no-wise connected with this event, that I discovered the Science of Divine Metaphysical Healing, which I afterwards named Christian Science. The discovery came to pass in this way. During twenty years prior to my discovery I had been trying to trace all physical effects to a mental cause; and in the latter part of 1866 I gained the Scientific certainty that all causation was Mind, and every effect a mental phenomenon.

My immediate recovery from the effects of an injury caused by an accident, an injury that neither medicine nor surgery could reach, was the falling apple that led me to the discovery how to be well myself, and how to make others so.

Even to the Homeopathic physician who attended me, and rejoiced in my recovery, I could not then explain the *modus* of my relief. I could only assure him that the Divine Spirit had wrought the miracle—a miracle which later I found to be in perfect Scientific accord with divine law.[16]

In a sketch of Mrs. Eddy, published by the Christian Science Publishing Society, still a later version is given:

In company with her husband, she was returning from an errand of mercy, when she fell upon the icy curbstone, and was carried helpless to her home. The skilled physicians declared that there was absolutely no hope for her, and pronounced the verdict that she had but three days to live. Finding no hope and no help on earth, she lifted her heart to God. On the third day, calling for her Bible, she asked the family to leave the room. Her Bible opened to the healing of the palsied man, Matt. ix, 2. The truth which set him free, she saw. The power which gave him strength, she felt. The life divine, which healed the sick of the palsy, restored her, and she rose from the bed of pain, healed and free.

Several documents can be brought in refutation of this claim. Mrs. Eddy's own letter to Julius A. Dresser, after the death of Quimby, apparently disproves the miraculous account given above. This letter, already quoted in full in the preceding chapter, contains the first recorded reference to this accident:

Two weeks ago I fell on the sidewalk (writes Mrs. Eddy), and struck my back on the ice, and was taken up for dead, came to consciousness amid a storm of vapours from cologne, chloroform, ether, camphor, etc., but to find myself the helpless cripple I was before I saw Dr. Quimby.

---

[16] *Retrospection and Introspection,* p. 38.

The physician attending said I had taken the last step I ever should, but in two days I got out of my bed *alone* and *will* walk; but yet I confess I am frightened, and out of that nervous heat my friends are forming, spite of me, the terrible spinal affection from which I have suffered so long and hopelessly. . . . Now can't *you* help me? I believe you can. I write this with this feeling: I think that I could help another in my condition if they had not placed their intelligence in matter. This I have not done, and yet I am slowly failing. Won't you write me if you will undertake for me if I can get to you?

In this letter, although it was written two weeks after the mishap in question, Mrs. Eddy makes no reference to a miraculous recovery. In fact, she apparently fears a return of her old spinal trouble and asks Mr. Dresser to protect her against it by the Quimby method. She adds that, although she has not placed her " intelligence in matter," she is " slowly failing."

In the first edition of *Science and Health*, Mrs. Eddy refers to this recovery, but merely as an interesting demonstration of Scientific healing. She also describes it in a letter written in 1871 to Mr. W. W. Wright. Wright, a well-known citizen of Lynn, and a prospective student, addressed several questions to Mrs. Eddy concerning Christian Science. " What do you claim for it," he says, " in cases of sprains, broken limbs, cuts, bruises, etc., when a surgeon's services are generally required? " To which Mrs. Eddy, then Mrs. Glover, replied:

I have demonstrated upon myself in an injury occasioned by a fall, that it did for me what surgeons could not do. Dr. Cushing of this city pronounced my injury incurable and that I could not survive three days because of it, when on the third day I rose from my bed and to the utter confusion of all I commenced my usual avocations and notwithstanding displacements, etc., I regained the natural position and functions of the body. How far my students can demonstrate in such extreme cases depends on the progress they have made in this Science.

Here again Mrs. Eddy cites the experience merely as a remarkable instance of the power of Christian Science; and does not connect it in any way with her revelation.

The Dr. Cushing to whom Mrs. Eddy refers in this letter is still living at Springfield, Mass. He has the clearest recollection of Mrs. Eddy and the accident in question. He is an ex-president of the Massachusetts Homœopathic Society. From his records he has made the following affidavit:

COMMONWEALTH OF MASSACHUSETTS
COUNTY OF HAMPDEN, SS.:

Alvin M. Cushing, being duly sworn, deposes and says: I am seventy-seven years of age, and reside in the City of Springfield in the Commonwealth of Massachusetts. I am a medical doctor of the homeopathic school and have practised medicine for fifty years last past. On July 13 in the year 1865 I commenced the practice of my profession in the City of Lynn, in said Commonwealth, and, while there, kept a careful and accurate record, in detail, of my various cases, my attendance upon and my treatment of them. One of my cases of which I made and have such a record is that of Mrs. Mary M. Patterson, then the wife of one Daniel Patterson, a dentist, and now Mrs. Mary G. Eddy, of Concord, New Hampshire.

On February 1, 1866, I was called to the residence of Samuel M. Bubier, who was a shoe manufacturer and later was mayor of Lynn, to attend said Mrs. Patterson, who had fallen upon the icy sidewalk in front of Mr. Bubier's factory and had injured her head by the fall. I found her very nervous, partially unconscious, semi-hysterical, complaining by word and action of severe pain in the back of her head and neck. This was early in the evening, and I gave her medicine every fifteen minutes until she was more quiet, then left her with Mrs. Bubier for a little time, ordering the medicine to be given every half hour until my return. I made a second visit later and left Mrs. Patterson at midnight, with directions to give the medicine every half hour or hour as seemed necessary, when awake, but not disturb her if asleep.

In the morning Mrs. Bubier told me my orders had been carried out and said Mrs. Patterson had slept some. I found her quite rational but complaining of severe pain, almost spasmodic on moving. She declared that she was going to her home in Swampscott whether we consented or not. On account of the severe pain and nervousness, I gave her one-eighth of a grain of morphine, not as a curative remedy, but as an expedient to lessen the pain on removing. As soon as I could, I procured a long sleigh with robes and blankets, and two men from a nearby stable. On my return, to my surprise found her sound asleep. We placed her in the sleigh and carried her to her home in Swampscott, without a moan. At her home the two men undertook to carry her upstairs, and she was so sound asleep and limp she "doubled up like a jack-knife," so I placed myself on the stairs on my hands and feet and they laid her on my back, and in that way we carried her upstairs and placed her in bed. She slept till nearly two o'clock in the afternoon; so long I began to fear there had been some mistake in the dose.

Said Mrs. Patterson proved to be a very interesting patient, and one of the most sensitive to the effects of medicine that I ever saw, which accounted for the effects of the small dose of morphine. Probably one-sixteenth of a grain would have put her sound asleep. Each day that I visited her, I dissolved a small portion of a highly attenuated remedy in one-half a glass of water and ordered a teaspoonful given every two hours, usually giving one dose while there. She told me she could feel each dose to the tips of her fingers and toes, and gave me much credit for my ability to select a remedy.

I visited her twice on February first, twice on the second, once on the third, and once on the fifth, and on the thirteenth day of the same month my bill was paid. During my visits to her she spoke to me of a Dr. Quimby of Portland, Maine, who had treated her for some severe illness with remarkable success. She did not tell what his method was, but I inferred it was not the usual method of either school of medicine.

There was, to my knowledge, no other physician in attendance upon Mrs. Patterson during this illness from the day of the accident, February 1, 1866, to my final visit on February 13th, and when I left her on the 13th day of February, she seemed to have recovered from the disturbance caused by the accident and to be, practically, in her normal condition. I did not at any time declare, or believe, that there was no hope for Mrs. Patterson's recovery, or that she was in a critical condition, and did not at any time say, or believe, that she had but three or any other limited number of days to live. Mrs. Patterson did not suggest, or say, or pretend, or in any way whatever intimate, that on the third, or any other day, of her said illness, she had miraculously recovered or been healed, or that, discovering or perceiving the truth of the power employed by Christ to heal the sick, she had, by it, been restored to health. As I have stated, on the third and subsequent days of her said illness, resulting from her said fall on the ice, I attended Mrs. Patterson and gave her medicine; and on the 10th day of the following August, I was again called to see her, this time at the home of a Mrs. Clark, on Sumner Street, in said City of Lynn. I found Mrs. Patterson suffering from a bad cough and prescribed for her. I made three more professional calls upon Mrs. Patterson and treated her for this cough in the said month of August, and with that, ended my professional relations with her.

I think I never met Mrs. Patterson after August 31, 1866, but saw her often during the next few years and heard that she claimed to have discovered a new method of curing disease.

Each of the said visits upon Mrs. Patterson, together with my treatment, the symptoms and the progress of the case, were recorded in my own hand in my record book at the time, and the said book, with the said entries made in February and August, 1866, is now in my possession.

I have, of course, no personal feeling in this matter. In response to many requests for a statement, I make this affidavit because I am assured it is wanted to perpetuate the testimony that can now be obtained, and be used only for a good purpose. I regard it as a duty which I owe to posterity to make public this particular episode in the life of Mary Baker G. Eddy.

ALVIN M. CUSHING.

On this second day of January, in the year one thousand, nine hundred and seven, at the City of Springfield, Massachusetts, personally appeared before me, Alvin M. Cushing, M.D., to me personally known, and made oath that he had read over the foregoing statement, and knows the contents thereof, and that the same are true; and he, thereupon, in my presence, did sign his name at the end of said statements, and at the foot of each of the three preceding pages thereof.

RAYMOND A. BIDWELL, *Notary Public.*

It will be noted that although Mrs. Eddy's revelation and miraculous recovery occurred on February third, Dr. Cushing visited her professionally three times after she had been restored to health by divine power. Dr. Cushing says that he visited her on the third day—when, writes Mrs. Eddy, she had her miraculous recovery; and also two days later. In August, seven months after her discovery of Christian Science, he was called in to treat her for a cough, and made four professional visits during that month.

Quimby's adherents believe that Mrs. Eddy's own contradictory statements invalidate her claims that God miraculously

revealed to her the principle of Christian Science.   They assert
that, on the other hand, they can clearly prove that she obtained the basic ideas of her system from Phineas P. Quimby.
They can prove their contention, they add, from the sworn
testimony of many reputable witnesses.   They do not rely,
however, chiefly upon personal testimony.   They put forth as
the chief witness against Mrs. Eddy, Mrs. Eddy herself.   They
seek to disprove practically all her later statements regarding
Quimby by quoting from her own admitted writings and from
letters.

They assert that Mrs. Eddy obtained from Quimby, not
only her ideas, but the very name of her new religion.   Mrs.
Eddy herself says that in 1866 she named her discovery Christian Science.   Quimby, however, called his theory Christian
Science at least as early as 1863.   In a manuscript written
in that year, entitled " Aristocracy and Democracy," he used
these identical words.   In the main, however, Quimby called
his theory the " Science of Health and Happiness," the " Science
of Christ," and many times simply " Science."

CHAPTER VI

THE controversy is chiefly upon two points: whether Quimby healed mentally, through the divine power of mind, or physically, through mesmerism or animal magnetism; and whether he himself developed his own theory and wrote his own manuscripts or obtained his ideas from Mrs. Eddy. Mrs. Eddy, when accused of having appropriated Quimby's theories, has always declared that her system had not the slightest similarity to his. Christian Scientists heal by the direct power of God, precisely as did Jesus Himself. They regard mesmerism, or hypnotism, as the supreme error. " Animal magnetism," once wrote the Rev. James Henry Wiggin, Mrs. Eddy's literary adviser, " is *her* devil. No church can long get on without a devil, you know." Therefore, if Mrs. Eddy proves that Quimby practised this art, and healed by it, to her followers she has more than proved her case. In *Retrospection and Introspection*, she says that Quimby was a " magnetic doctor," and implies that he was a spiritualist. " It was in Massachusetts, February, 1866," she says, " and after the death of the magnetic doctor, Mr. P. P. Quimby, whom Spiritualists would associate therewith, but who was in no-wise connected with this event, that I discovered the Science of Divine Metaphysical Healing, which I afterwards named Christian Science." This idea she has elaborated many times. In *Miscellaneous Writings* she tells the story of her visit to Quimby in these words:

About the year 1862, while the author of this work was at Dr. Vail's Hydropathic Institute in New Hampshire, this occurred: A patient considered incurable left that institution, and in a few weeks returned apparently well, having been healed, as he informed the patients, by one Mr. P. P. Quimby, of Portland, Maine.

After much consultation among ourselves, and a struggle with pride, the author, in company with several other patients, left the Water Cure, *en route* for the aforesaid doctor in Portland. He proved to be a magnetic practitioner. His treatment seemed at first to relieve her but signally failed in healing her case.

Having practised Homeopathy, it never occurred to the author to learn his practice, but she did ask him how manipulation could benefit the sick. He answered kindly and squarely, in substance, " Because it conveys *electricity* to them." That was the sum of what he taught her of his medical profession.[1]

In the *Christian Science Journal* for June, 1887, Mrs. Eddy repeats the same idea:

I never heard him intimate that he healed disease mentally; and many others will testify that, up to his last sickness, he treated us magnetically, manipulating our heads, and making passes in the air while he stood in front of us. During his treatments I felt like one having hold of an electric battery and standing on an insulated stool. His healing was never considered or called anything but Mesmerism.

In numerous other articles, Mrs. Eddy has declared that Quimby healed by animal magnetism; that he never said he healed mentally, never recognised the superiority of mind to matter, or any divine principle in his work. These statements, however, hardly agree with that made in the letter to W. W. Wright, written in 1871 and quoted in this chapter, in which

---

[1] *Miscellaneous Writings* (1897), p. 378.

she refers to Quimby as " an old gentleman who had made it a research for twenty-five years, starting from the standpoint of magnetism, thence going forward and leaving that behind."

In the letter published on November 7, 1862, in the Portland *Courier*, Mrs. Eddy herself defended Quimby from the very charge which she now brings against him—that he healed by animal magnetism.   On this point, she wrote:

Again, is it by animal magnetism that he heals the sick? Let us examine. I have employed electro-magnetism and animal magnetism, and for a brief interval have felt relief, from the equilibrium which I fancied was restored to an exhausted system or by a diffusion of concentrated action. But in no instance did I get rid of a return of all my ailments, because I had not been helped out of the error in which opinions involved us. My operator believed in disease, independent of the mind; hence I could not be wiser than my master. But now I can see dimly at first, and only as trees walking, the great principle which underlies Dr. Quimby's faith and works; and just in proportion to my right perception of truth is my recovery. This truth which he opposes to the error of giving intelligence to matter and placing pain where it never placed itself, if received understandingly, changes the currents of the system to their normal action; and the mechanism of the body goes on undisturbed. That this is a science capable of demonstration, becomes clear to the minds of those patients who reason upon the process of their cure. The truth which he establishes in the patient cures him (although he may be wholly unconscious thereof); and the body, which is full of light, is no longer in disease. . . . After all, this is a very spiritual doctrine; but the eternal years of God are with it, and it must stand firm as the rock of ages. And to many a poor sufferer it may be found, as by me, "the shadow of a great rock in a weary land."

Hardly anything could be more specific than this.

In 1862, Mrs. Eddy, while she was still Quimby's patient, declared that he healed, not by animal magnetism, but by the " truth which he opposes to the error of giving intelligence to matter and placing pain where it never placed itself."   Again, " the truth which he establishes in the patient cures him . . .

and the body, which is full of light, is no longer in disease."

In 1871, while teaching and practising Quimby's method for a livelihood, she declared that he started " from the standpoint of magnetism, thence going forward and leaving that behind." [2]

In 1887, when at the head of a great organisation of her own, she says: " he treated us magnetically. . . . His healing was never considered or called anything but Mesmerism."

Now Mrs. Eddy says that Quimby's method was purely " physical "; then, in 1862, she wrote that, " after all, this is a very spiritual doctrine," and describes it as " the great principle which underlies Dr. Quimby's faith and works." In another communication to the Portland *Courier*, written November, 1862, Mrs. Eddy specifically declared that Quimby healed after Christ's method. She said:

P. P. Quimby stands upon the plane of wisdom with his truth. Christ healed the sick, but not by jugglery or with drugs. As the former speaks as never man before spake, and heals as never man healed since Christ, is he not identified with truth? And is not this the Christ which is in him? We know that in wisdom is life, "and the life was the light of man." P. P. Quimby rolls away the stone from the sepulchre of error, and health is the resurrection. But we also know that " light shineth in darkness and the darkness comprehendeth it not."

Mrs. Eddy repeated the same thought in the verses which she published, over her own name, in a Lynn newspaper, on February 22, 1866. She entitled them, " Lines on the Death of Dr. P. P. Quimby, Who Healed with the Truth that Christ Taught in Contradistinction to All Isms." The letters written by Mrs. Eddy to Quimby in the years 1862, '63, '64, and '65, extracts from which were printed, express the same conviction.

---

[2] See extract from letter to Mr. W. W. Wright, p. 101 of this chapter.

On September 14, 1863, in asking for an " absent treatment,"
Mrs. Eddy wrote: " I would like to have you in your omnipresence visit me at eight o'clock this evening." In a letter
dated Warren, May, 1864, she writes that she has been ill,
but adds, " I am up and about today, i.e., by the help of the
Lord (Quimby)." In the quotation from *Retrospection and
Introspection* above, Mrs. Eddy associates Quimby with spiritualists. Yet, forty years ago, she delivered a public lecture
to prove that he was not a spiritualist. She records the event
in a letter to Quimby, dated Warren, April 24, 1864:

Jesus taught as man does *not,* who then is wise but you? Posted at
the public marts of this city is this notice, Mrs. M. M. Patterson will
lecture at the Town Hall on P. P. Quimby's Spiritual Science healing
disease, as opposed to Deism or Rochester Rapping Spiritualism.

Quimby's manuscripts, his defenders assert, clearly show that
when Mrs. Eddy knew him he had dropped mesmerism for his
new system. In 1859—three years before he ever saw Mrs.
Eddy—he clearly distinguished between physical and spiritual
healing—between the permanent healing of disease through
God, Wisdom, or the Christ method, and its temporary and
ineffectual healing through ignorance, symbolically called
Beelzebub.

The question is asked me by some, is the curing of disease a science?
I answer yes. You may ask who is the founder of that science? I
answer Jesus Christ. Then comes the question, what proof have you that
it is a science? Because Christ healed the sick, that of itself is no proof
that he knew what he was doing. If it was done, it must have been done
by some law or science, for there can be no such thing as accident with
God, and if Christ was God, he did know what he was doing. When he was
accused of curing disease through Beelzebub or ignorance, he said, If I
cast out devils or disease through Beelzebub or ignorance, my kingdom or
science cannot stand, but if I cast out devils or disease through a science

or law, then my kingdom or law will stand, for it is not of this world. When others cast out disease they cured by ignorance, or Beelzebub, and there was no science in the cure, although an effect was produced, but not knowing the cause, the world was none the wiser for their cures. At another time when told by his disciples, that persons were casting out devils in his name, and they forbid them, he said, they that are with us are not against us, but they that are not with us, or are ignorant of the laws of curing, scattereth abroad, for the world is none the wiser. There you see, he makes a difference between his mode of curing and theirs. If Christ's cures were done by the power of God, and Christ was God, he must have known what that power or science was, and if he did, he knew the difference between his science, and their ignorance. His science was His Kingdom, therefore it was not of this world, and theirs being *of* this world, he called it the Kingdom of Darkness. To enter into Christ's Kingdom, or science, was to enter into the laws of knowledge, of curing the evils of this world of darkness. As disease is an evil, it is of this world and in this kingdom of darkness. To separate one world from another, is to separate life, the resurrection of one is the destruction of the other.[3]

Mrs. Eddy, to prove that Quimby was merely a mesmerist, emphasises the fact that he frequently rubbed his patients' heads. According to the present Christian Science belief, that is the cardinal sin. Physical contact with the patient implies that the treatment is of this world; in order that healing be Divine, Christ-like, its only instrument must be mind. On this one point the controversy has been long and bitter. It figures as conspicuously in this dispute as did the word *filioque* in the contentions of the early Christian Church. Mrs. Eddy, in the *Christian Science Journal* of June, 1887, says:

If, as Mr. Dresser says, Mr. Quimby's theory (if he had one) and practice were like mine, purely mental, what need had he of such physical means as wetting his hands in water and rubbing the head? Yet these appliances he continued until he ceased practice; and in his last sickness the poor man employed a homeopathic physician. The Science of Mind-healing would be lost by such means and it is a moral impossibility to understand or to demonstrate this science through such extraneous aids. Mr. Quimby,

---

[3] From a manuscript written in 1859.

never to my knowledge, thought that matter was mind; and he never intimated to me that he healed mentally, or by the aid of mind. Did he believe matter and mind to be one, and then rub matter in order to convince the mind of truth? Which did he manipulate with his hands, matter or mind? Was Mr. Quimby's entire method of treating the sick intended to hoodwink his patients?

Quimby's followers freely admit that, on some occasions, he dipped his hands in water and rubbed the patient's head. They deny, however, that this was an essential part of the cure. Mr. Julius A. Dresser explains the circumstances thus:

Some may desire to ask, if in his practice, he ever in any way used manipulation. I reply that, in treating a patient, after he had finished his explanations, and the silent work, *which completed the treatment,* he usually rubbed the head two or three times, in a brisk manner, for the purpose of letting the patient see that something was done. This was a measure of securing the confidence of the patient at a *time when he was starting a new practice,* and stood alone in it. I knew him to make many and quick cures at a distance sometimes with persons he never saw at all. He never considered the touch of the hand as at all necessary; but let it be governed by circumstances, as was done eighteen hundred years ago.[4]

In Mrs. Eddy's early days, she treated in precisely the same way. As will be described in the next chapter, she lived in several Massachusetts towns, teaching and practising the Quimby cure. She always instructed her students, after treating their patients mentally, to rub their heads. In addition, Mrs. Eddy would dip her hands in water and lay them over the stomach of the patient, repeating, as she did this, the words: " Peace, be still." Several of Mrs. Eddy's students of that time are still practising, and they still, in accordance with her instructions of nearly forty years ago, manipulate their patients. It was not until 1872 that she learned that the

---

[4] *The True History of Mental Science,* p. 25.

practice was pernicious. She tells the story as follows, in a pamphlet, *The Science of Man,* published in 1876:

When we commenced this science, we permitted students to manipulate the head, ignorant that it could do harm, or hinder the power of mind acting in an opposite direction, viz., while the hands were at work and the mind directing material action. We regret to say it was the sins of a young student that called our attention to this question for the first time, and placed it in a new moral and physical aspect. By thorough examination and tests, we learned manipulation hinders instead of helps mental healing; it also establishes a mesmeric connection between patient and practitioner that gives the latter opportunity and power to govern the thoughts and actions of his patients in any direction he chooses, and with error instead of truth. This can injure the patients and must always prevent a scientific result. . . . Since our discovery of this malpractice in 1872, we have never permitted a student with our consent to manipulate in the least, and this process unlearned is utterly worthless to benefit the sick.[5]

This is an admission on Mrs. Eddy's part that, for six years after her discovery of the " absolute principle of metaphysical healing," she herself taught the method which she now asserts disproves that Quimby ever healed by the power of mind. Quimby's adherents maintain that the fact that during these six years she followed his instructions implicitly and rubbed her patients' heads, is merely another proof that she obtained her original conception of mental healing from him. In *Miscellaneous Writings* Mrs. Eddy explains this head-rubbing on the same ground as did Quimby,—that is, that the average weak and doubting mind needed an outward sign:

It was after Mr. Quimby's death, that I discovered, in 1866, the momentous facts relating to Mind and its superiority over matter, and named my discovery Christian Science. Yet, there remained the difficulty of adjusting in the scale of Science a metaphysical *practice,* and settling the question, What shall be the outward sign of such a practice: if a

[5] P. 12.

Divine Principle alone heals, what is the human modus for demonstrating this? . . . My students at first practised in slightly different forms. Although *I* could heal mentally, without a sign save the immediate recovery of the sick, my students' patients, and people generally, called for a sign— a material evidence wherewith to satisfy the sick that something was being done for them; and I said, " Suffer it to be so now," for thus saith our Master. Experience, however, taught me the impossibility of demonstrating the Science of Metaphysical Healing by any outward form of practice.[6]

Other pupils of Quimby, among them Mr. Julius A. Dresser, resented his being presented to the world by Mrs. Eddy as a mesmerist and magnetic healer. They asserted again and again that he healed by mental science purely, and that Mrs. Eddy had misrepresented him and his methods. Mr. Dresser made a statement to that effect in the Boston *Post*, February 24, 1883. Mrs. Eddy replied to this letter (Boston *Post*, March 7, 1883), admitting that Quimby " may have had a theory in advance of his method," but making the claim that it was she who first asked him to " write his thoughts out," and that she would sometimes so transform his manuscripts that they were virtually her own compositions. She says:

We never were a student of Dr. Quimby's. . . . Dr. Quimby never had students, to our knowledge. He was an Humanitarian, but a very unlearned man. He never published a work in his life; was not a lecturer or teacher. He was somewhat of a remarkable healer, and at the time we knew him he was known as a mesmerist. We were one of his patients. He manipulated his patients, but possibly back of his practice he may have had a theory in advance of his method. . . . We knew him about twenty years ago, and aimed to help him. We saw he was looking in our direction, and asked him to write his thoughts out. He did so, and then we would take that copy to correct, and sometimes so transform it that he would say it was our composition, which it virtually was; but we always gave him back the copy and sometimes wrote his name on the back of it.

---

* *Miscellaneous Writings* (1897), pp. 379 and 380.

In a revised edition of Julius A. Dresser's pamphlet, *The True History of Mental Science*, Mr. Dresser's son, Horatio W. Dresser, says:

It has frequently been claimed that Mrs. Eddy was Quimby's secretary, and that she helped him to formulate his ideas. It has also been stated that these manuscripts were Mrs. Eddy's writings, left by her in Portland; that the articles printed in this pamphlet were Mrs. Eddy's words, as nearly as she can recollect them (*Christian Science Sentinel*, February 16, 1899). *There is absolutely no truth* in any of these statements or suppositions. Mrs. Eddy never saw a page of the *original* manuscripts; and Volume I, loaned her by my father in 1862, was his *copy from a copy*. Mrs. Eddy may have made a copy of this volume for her own use, but the majority even of the copied articles Mrs. Eddy never saw. I have read and copied all of these articles, and can certify that they contain a very original and complete statement of the data and theory of mental healing. There are *over eight hundred closely written pages,* covering one hundred and twenty subjects, written previous to March, 1862, more than six months before Mrs. Eddy went to Dr. Quimby.

In the 1884 edition of *Science and Health*, Mrs. Eddy, writing of Quimby, says:

The old gentleman to whom we have referred had some very advanced views on healing, but he was not avowedly religious neither scholarly. We interchanged thoughts on the subject of healing the sick. I restored some patients of his that he failed to heal, and left in his possession some manuscripts of mine containing corrections of his desultory pennings which I am informed, at his decease, passed into the hands of a patient of his, now residing in Scotland. He died in 1865 and left no published works. The only manuscript that we ever held of his, longer than to correct it, was one of perhaps a dozen pages, most of which we had composed.

This manuscript of "perhaps a dozen pages," is clearly the one called by Quimby, *Questions and Answers.* The original copy, now in the possession of the writer, in the handwriting of Quimby's wife, is dated February, 1862, eight months before

Quimby had ever seen Mrs. Eddy. From this manuscript Mrs. Eddy taught for several years after Quimby's death, and she sold copies of it to her early students for $300 each.[7] Its history will be given in detail and its contents analysed in the next chapter.

In refutation of Mrs. Eddy's general assertion that she herself taught Quimby what he knew about mental science, and that she corrected and so largely contributed to the Quimby manuscripts, Quimby's defenders again quote Mrs. Eddy herself. They once more draw upon her early letter to the Portland *Courier*. This, they say, does not read like a letter written by master to pupil. If Mrs. Eddy were the teacher and Quimby the student, would she, they ask, speak of him in this wise? " Now, then, his works are but the result of superior wisdom, which can demonstrate a science not understood. . . . But now I can see dimly at first, and only as trees walking, the great principle which underlies Dr. Quimby's faith and works; and just in proportion to my right perception of truth is my recovery." If Mrs. Eddy, they add, were at that time writing Quimby's manuscripts, would she, in this same letter, have expressed herself thus :—" At present I am too much in error to elucidate the truth, and can touch only the keynote for the master hand to wake the harmony. . . . To many a poor sufferer may it be found, as by me, ' the shadow of a great rock in a weary land.' "

Mrs. Eddy's poem on Quimby's death, already quoted, is apparently the grateful tribute of pupil to teacher. Its concluding lines ill sustain Mrs. Eddy's present position:

---

[7] For the $300 Mrs. Eddy's students also obtained twelve lessons in the Quimby cure.

"Rest should reward him who hath made us whole,
Seeking, though tremblers, where his footsteps trod."

Her letters to Quimby, 1862-'65, also fail to substantiate this impression that Quimby was under Mrs. Eddy's instruction. "I have the utmost faith in your philosophy," she wrote in 1862. Other phrases, scattered through the letters, read: [8]

"Dear doctor, what could I do without you? . . . I am to all who see me a living wonder, and a living monument of your power. . . . My explanation of your *curative principle* surprises people. . . . Who is wise but you? " She wrote from Warren, Me., in the spring of 1865, that she had been asked to treat sick people after the Quimby method. She refuses to do so, she adds, because she considers that she is still in her "pupilage."

In connection with Mrs. Eddy's claim that she herself largely wrote the Quimby manuscripts, the following extract from an affidavit of Mrs. Sarah G. Crosby of Waterville, Me., an intimate friend of Mrs. Eddy when she was under Quimby's treatment, is also of interest:

I know little of the history of said Mrs. Patterson between 1866 and 1877, when she called me professionally [9] to Lynn, in February, 1877, a few weeks after her marriage to Asa G. Eddy, to report a course of lessons to a class of nine pupils. She told me she wished a copy of these lessons for Mr. Eddy to study, that he, too, might teach classes. These lectures were in all material respects the same as I had myself been taught by said Dr. Quimby and that Mrs. Patterson and I had so often discussed, and which she had tried so hard to make me understand and adopt when we were together in Portland and later in Albion;—the same teaching about Truth and Error and matter and disease, the same method of curing disease by Truth casting out Error, the same claim that it was the method

---

[8] For further extracts from Mrs. Eddy's letters to Quimby, see Chapter IV.
[9] Mrs. Crosby was an expert court stenographer.

adopted by Jesus. I do not hesitate to say that Mrs. Eddy's teachings in 1877, and Dr. Quimby's teachings in 1864 were substantially the same; in fact, as I heard them both, *I know they were.*

In June, 1883, an attorney representing said Mrs. Patterson came to see me at Waterville, my present home, and interviewed me regarding her work with Dr. Quimby in Portland in 1864. I refused to answer his questions and he left, but returned the next day bearing an affectionate letter from said Mrs. Patterson. The following is a copy thereof:—

" MY DEAR SISTER,

SARAH,—

I wanted to see you myself but it was impossible for me to leave my home and so have sent the bearer of this note to see you for me.

Two nights ago I had a sweet dream of *Albert* [10] and the dear face was so familiar, Oh how I loved him! and in the morning a thought popped into my head to ask Sarah to help me in this very trying hour.

These are the circumstances. A student [11] of my husband's took the class-book of mine that he studied, put his name to most of it, and published it as his own after he was through with the class.

Then was the time I ought to have sued him, but Oh, I do so dislike a quarrel that I hoped to get over it without a law-suit.

So I noticed in my next edition of ' Science and Health ' his infringement with a sharp reprimand thinking that would stop him, but this winter he issued another copy of my work as the author, and then I sued him. The next thing he did was to publish the falsehood that I stole my works from the late Dr. Quimby. When everything I ever had published has been written or edited by me as spontaneously as I teach or lecture.

---

[10] It will be remembered that the "spirit" friendship of Mrs. Patterson's dead brother, Albert Baker, for Mrs. Crosby, formed a close bond in the friendship of the two women, and that he communicated with Mrs. Crosby through his sister.—See Chapter IV.

[11] In the early '80's, Edward J. Arens published a pamphlet entitled *Old Theology in its Application to the Healing of the Sick; the Redemption of Man from the Bondage of Sin and Death, and His Restoration to an Inheritance of Everlasting Life.* In this Arens borrowed liberally, in word and idea, from *Science and Health.* In 1883 Mrs. Eddy sued Arens for infringement of copyright. Arens said, in defence, that he had not borrowed from Mrs. Eddy, but from the late P. P. Quimby, of Portland, Me. He added that Mrs. Eddy had herself appropriated Quimby's ideas,—in other words, that both had drawn their philosophy from the same source. The court decided in Mrs. Eddy's favour, and issued a perpetual injunction restraining Arens from circulating his books. On the strength of this decision Mrs. Eddy and her followers have declared that the United States courts have decided the issue of the Quimby controversy in her favour. There is nothing in this decision contrary to the claims of Quimby's friends. The court, they agree, simply decided that Mrs. Eddy held a valid copyright upon *Science and Health* and that Arens had violated that copyright. They have never denied either of these facts. They freely admit that Mrs. Eddy wrote *Science and Health* as it stands, and that she has a property interest in it. They are not discussing legal technicalities, but only the moral issue involved,—which, they add, did not and properly could not, be considered by the court.

Now dear one, I want you to tell this man, the bearer of this note, that you know that Dr. Quimby and I were friends and that I used to take his scribblings and fix them over for him and give him my thoughts and language which as I understood it, were far in advance of his.

Will you do this and give an affidavit to this effect and greatly oblige your Affectionate Sister Mary."

I read the foregoing appeal for help from said Mrs. Patterson, then Eddy, and as it was clearly a request that I should make oath to what was not true, I informed the attorney that I should not make the affidavit asked by his client, as it would not be a true statement. He then threatened to summon me to the trial, but I think I made him understand that I would not be a desirable witness on his side of the case. He thereupon departed, and I was not summoned to testify. And since that interview, I have only a public knowledge of said Mrs. Patterson-Eddy.

In her private correspondence, Mrs. Eddy has said, in so many words, that she taught the Quimby system. Reference has already been made to the correspondence in March, 1871, between Mrs. Eddy—then Mrs. Glover—and Mr. W. W. Wright of Lynn. Mr. Wright specifically asked this question:

6th: Has this theory ever been advertised or practised before you introduced it, or by any other individual?

To this Mrs. Eddy replied:

6th: Never advertised, and practised by only one individual who healed me, Dr. Quimby of Portland, Me, an old gentleman who had made it a research for twenty-five years, starting from the stand-point of magnetism thence going forward and leaving that behind. *I* discovered the art in a *moment's time,* and he acknowledged it to me; he died shortly after and since then, eight years, I have been founding and demonstrating the science. . . . please preserve this, and if you become my student call me to account for the truth of what I have written

Respectfully

M M B Glover

Mrs. Eddy has never attempted to reconcile the statements which she made before the publication of *Science and Health* with the very different ones which she has made since.

The explanation by which she seeks to account for her early expressions of devotion and gratitude to Quimby is not one which tends to lessen the perplexities of the historian. She simply asserts that she wrote these tributes to Quimby while under mesmeric influence and is not properly responsible for them at all.

In the Boston *Post*, in a letter dated March 7, 1883, after Julius A. Dresser had made public some of the letters already quoted, she wrote as follows:

Did I write those articles purporting to be mine? I might have written them twenty or thirty years ago, for I was under the mesmeric treatment of Dr. Quimby from 1862 until his death in 1865. He was illiterate and I knew nothing then of the Science of Mind-healing, and I was as ignorant of mesmerism as Eve before she was taught by the serpent. Mind Science was unknown to me; and my head was so turned by animal magnetism and will-power, under his treatment, that I might have written something as hopelessly incorrect as the articles now published in the Dresser pamphlet. I was not healed until after the death of Mr. Quimby; and then healing came as the result of my discovery in 1866, of the Science of Mind-healing, since named Christian Science.

In 1887, when Julius A. Dresser published his *True History of Mental Science*, the Quimby-Eddy controversy reached its climax. Mrs. Eddy, says Horatio W. Dresser, requested her literary adviser, Rev. James Henry Wiggin, to answer the pamphlet. Mr. Wiggin asked Mrs. Eddy if she had written the letters in the Portland newspapers, the letter to Dresser, the poem on Quimby's death, and other effusions. Mrs. Eddy admitted that she had. " Then," replied Mr. Wiggin, " there is nothing to say," and declined the task. In a personal letter Mr. Wiggin says:

What Mrs. Eddy has, as documents clearly prove, she got from P. P. Quimby, of Portland, Me., whom she eulogised after death as the great leader and her special teacher. . . . She has tried to answer this charge of the adoption of Quimby's ideas, and called me in to counsel her about it; but her only answer (in print!) was that if she said such things twenty years ago, she must have been under the influence of Animal Magnetism.

Mrs. Eddy, however, issued the following challenge:

To whom it may concern:

Mr. George A. Quimby son of the late Phineas P. Quimby, over his own signature and before witnesses, stated in 1883, that he had in his possession at that time all the manuscript that had been written by his father. And I hereby declare that to expose the falsehood of parties publicly intimating that I have appropriated matter belonging to the aforesaid Quimby, I will pay the cost of printing and publishing the first edition of those manuscripts with the author's name:

Provided, that I am allowed first to examine said manuscripts, and do find that they were his own compositions, and not mine, that were left with him many years ago, or that they have not since his death, in 1865, been stolen from my published works. Also that I am given the right to bring out this one edition under the copyright of the owner of said manuscripts, and all the money accruing from the sales of said book shall be paid to said owner. Some of his purported writings, quoted by Mr. D—, were my own words as near as I can recollect them.

There is a great demand for my work, "Science and Health, with Key to Scriptures," hence Mr. D—'s excuse for the delay to publish Quimby's manuscripts namely, that this period is not sufficiently enlightened to be benefited by them (?) is lost, for if I have copied from Quimby, and my book is accepted, it has created a demand for his.

MARY BAKER G. EDDY.

This proposition was ignored by Mr. Quimby, owing to his own knowledge of Mrs. Eddy and of his father's manuscripts. Quimby's adherents declare that the provisions made in her offer indicate what her claims would have been if the manuscripts had been given into her hands—as she had already announced that Dr. Quimby's writings were her own—and that the proposition was made with the object of securing possession of the manuscripts.

In a letter to Mr. A. J. Swartz, a mental healer of Chicago who interested himself in the case, dated February 22, 1838, George A. Quimby explained his position:

> Your letter with enclosure at hand. I judge that you offer to defend the memory of my father, the late P. P. Quimby. . . . Please permit me to say that I have no doubt of your kind intention to come to the rescue of my father, but I do not feel that there is the slightest necessity for it. . . . If I were in prison, in solitary confinement for life, I should be too busy to get into any kind of a discussion with Mrs. Eddy.
>
> I have my father's manuscripts in my possession, but will not allow them to be copied nor to go out of my hands. Answering your further inquiries, I have no written article of Mrs. Eddy's in my possession, have never had, nor did my father ever have, nor did she ever leave any with either of us. Neither of us have ever " stolen " any of her writings nor anything else. In fact, we both have been able to make a living without stealing. . . .
>
> Yours truly,
>
> GEORGE A. QUIMBY.

From the history of this controversy, it is evident that, for Mrs. Eddy, there have existed two Phineas P. Quimbys: one the Quimby who was her physician and teacher, who roused her from the fretful discontent of middle-age, and who gave her purpose and aspiration; the other the Quimby who, after the publication of *Science and Health,* became, in a sense, her rival,—whom she saw as an antagonist threatening to invalidate her claims. If she has been a loser through this controversy, it is not because of what she borrowed from Quimby, but because of her later unwillingness to admit her obligation to him. Had she observed the etiquette of the regular sciences, where personal ambition is subsidiary to a desire for truth, and where discoverers and investigators are scrupulous to acknowledge the sources from which they have obtained help, it would have strengthened rather than weakened her position.

CHAPTER VII

DR. AND MRS. PATTERSON IN LYNN—THEIR SEPARATION—MRS.
PATTERSON AS A PROFESSIONAL VISITOR—SHE TEACHES
HIRAM CRAFTS THE QUIMBY " SCIENCE "—MRS. PATTERSON
IN AMESBURY

ALTHOUGH after Mrs. Eddy's second visit to Quimby in the
early part of 1864 she always desired to teach his doctrines
and could think and talk of little else, it was not until 1870
that she was able to establish herself as a teacher of metaphysical
healing.   The six years intervening are important chiefly as
the period of Mrs. Eddy's novitiate.   During that time she
drifted from one to another of half a dozen little towns about
Boston; but amid all vicissitudes one thing remained fixed and
constant,—her conviction that she was the person destined to
teach and popularise Quimbyism.

Mrs. Patterson's long visit at the home of Mrs. Sarah Crosby,
at Albion, Me., has already been referred to in the fourth
chapter of the present volume.   She went to Mrs. Crosby's
house in May, 1864, remaining there most of the summer and
leaving in the early autumn.   She then rejoined her husband,
Dr. Patterson, at Lynn, Mass., where the doctor had begun
to practise and had taken an office at 76 Union Street.   In the
Lynn *Weekly Reporter*, of June 11, 1864, the following advertisement appears for the first time:

DENTAL NOTICE

DR. D. PATTERSON

Would respectfully announce to the public that he has returned to
Lynn, and opened an office in B. F. & G. N. Spinney's new building, on
Union St., between the Central Depot & Sagamore Hotel, where he will
be happy to greet the friends and patrons secured last year while in the
offices of Drs. Davis and How, and now he hopes to secure the patronage
of "all the rest of mankind" by the exhibition of that skill which close
study and many years of first-class and widely-extended practice enable
him to bring to the aid of the suffering. He is aware that he has to
compete with able practitioners, but yet offers his services fearlessly,
knowing that competition is the real stimulus to success, and trusting to
his ability to please all who need Teeth filled, extracted or new sets.
He was the first to introduce LAUGHING GAS in Lynn for Dental
purposes and has had excellent success with it. Terms lower than anywhere else for the same quality of work.

Dr. Patterson and his wife first boarded at 42 Silsbee Street,
where they remained for some months, afterward moving to the
house of O. A. Durall, in Buffum Street.

The doctor's dental practice in Lynn was fairly good, and
people liked him for a bluff, jovial fellow, none too clever, but
honest and kind of heart. Both he and his wife were at this
time prominent members of the Linwood Lodge of Good Templars, at Lynn, and old members of the lodge remember the
active part which Mrs. Patterson took in their meetings. She
was often called upon to read, or to speak on matters under
discussion, and was always ready to do so. Her remarks never
failed to command attention, and the Good Templars of Lynn
considered her " smart but queer." Members of the lodge who
are still living say that she discussed Quimbyism whenever she
found opportunity to do so, and, although they were considerably amused by her extravagant metaphors and could make
nothing of her " philosophy," they had no doubt that it was

very profound and recondite. It was when she was returning from one of these Good Templar meetings, February 1, 1866, that Mrs. Patterson had the fall from the effects of which she says she was miraculously healed. She, with a party of fellow Templars, was passing the corner of Oxford and Market Streets, when she slipped upon the icy sidewalk and fell. She was carried into the house of Samuel Bubier, where Dr. Cushing attended her, and the next day, at her urgent request, she was moved to the house on the Swampscott Road, where she and her husband were then boarding. It was on the following day, according to Mrs. Eddy's account, that she received her revelation, and in this house Christian Science was born. In the following spring the Pattersons took a room in the house of P. R. Russell, at the corner of Pearl and High Streets, Lynn. Here, after about two months, Dr. Patterson finally left his wife, and they never lived together after this time. In referring to her husband's desertion of her, Mrs. Eddy says:

In 1862[1] my name was Patterson; my husband, Dr. Patterson, a distinguished dentist. After our marriage I was confined to my bed with a severe illness, and seldom left bed or room for seven years, when I was taken to Dr. Quimby, and partially restored. I returned home, hoping once more to make that home happy, but only returned to a new agony,— to find my husband had eloped with a married woman from one of the wealthy families of that city, leaving no trace save his last letter to us, wherein he wrote " I hope some time to be worthy of so good a wife." [2]

[1] Letter to the Boston *Post*, March 7, 1883.
[2] From Mrs. Eddy's statement it is impossible to tell whether by " that city " she means Sanbornton Bridge, where she returned after her first visit to Quimby, or Lynn, where she joined her husband after her second visit. Neither in Lynn nor Sanbornton Bridge do the people who knew the Pattersons recall any elopement on Dr. Patterson's part. P. R. Russell, in whose house the Pattersons were living when the Doctor deserted his wife, says in his affidavit:
" While they were living at my house, Dr. Patterson went away and did not return. I do not know the cause of his going. I never heard that he eloped with any woman, and I never heard Mrs. Patterson say that he had eloped with any woman. Mrs. Patterson never said anything whatever to me on the subject of her husband's departure. I never heard anything against Dr. Patterson's character either then or since."

After leaving his wife, Dr. Patterson went to Littleton, N. H., where he practised for some years. Afterward he led a roving life, wandering from town to town, until he at last went back to the home of his boyhood, at Saco, Me., where he secluded himself and lived the life of a hermit until his death in 1896.

Bitter experience awaited Mrs. Patterson after her husband's desertion. Whatever may have been the cause for his leaving, Mrs. Patterson did not, at that time, claim the sympathy of her friends on account of it, and to her landlord and his wife she maintained silence on the subject, merely saying in answer to inquiries, that he had gone away. According to Mrs. Patterson's relatives, her husband went about the separation deliberately, announcing his intention and his reason [3] to her family, and making what provision he was able for her support.[4]

In the fall of 1865 Mark Baker, Mrs. Patterson's father, died, and at about the same time her sister, Mrs. Tilton, closed her door forever against Mrs. Patterson.[5] Her only child, George Glover, at that time a young man, she had sent away in his childhood. Mrs. Patterson was, therefore, for the first time in her life, practically alone in the world and largely dependent upon herself for support. Untrained in any kind of paid work, she fell back upon the favour of her friends or chance acquaintances, living precariously upon their bounty, and obliged to go from house to house, as one family after

[3] To her family Dr. Patterson said that he was unable to endure life with Mrs. Patterson any longer.
[4] For several years after their separation Dr. Patterson gave his wife an annuity of $200, which was paid in small instalments.
[5] When Mrs. Tilton, who had taken care of Mrs. Patterson from childhood and supported her in her widowhood, finally turned against her sister, she was as hard as she had been generous before. " I loved Mary best of all my sisters and brothers," she said to her friends, " but it is all gone now." The bitterness of her feeling lasted to the day of her death. She instructed her family not to allow Mary to see her after death nor to attend her funeral, and her wishes were carried out.

another wearied of her. For a while she stayed on at the Russells', but as she was unable to pay even the $1.50 a week rental which they charged her, she was served with eviction papers and dispossessed of her room within a month after Dr. Patterson's departure. Mr. Russell, her landlord, says that the matter of the rent was merely a pretext. He wished Mrs. Patterson to go because his wife, who had greatly admired her when she first came into the house, soon declared that she could not endure Mrs. Patterson's remaining there. His father, Rev. P. R. Russell, also strongly objected to Mrs. Patterson's presence.

The month of August, or a part of it, Mrs. Patterson spent with Mrs. Clark, in Summer Street, Lynn, and it was there that Dr. Cushing treated her for a severe cough. She next stayed with Mrs. Armenius Newhall, but soon afterward left the house, at Mrs. Newhall's request.

Mrs. James Wheeler of Swampscott, in her own town known as " Mother " Wheeler from her gentle qualities and her eagerness to help and comfort every one, then offered Mrs. Patterson a shelter.

At the Wheelers', as elsewhere, Mrs. Patterson talked continually of Quimby and declared that it was the ambition of her life to publish his notes on mental healing. Mrs. Julia Russell Walcott, a sister of Mrs. Patterson's former landlord, and an intimate friend of Mrs. Wheeler, says in her affidavit:

Mrs. Patterson was the means of creating discord in the Wheeler family. She was unkind in her language to and treatment of Mrs. James Wheeler, at the same time exacting extra personal service and attention to her daily wants.

One morning I sat in the parlour at the Wheeler house when Mrs.

Patterson came down to breakfast. The family breakfast was over, but Mrs. Wheeler, according to her usual custom, had prepared a late breakfast for Mrs. Patterson. Mrs. Wheeler, Mrs. Patterson, and myself were alone in the house. I had come in late the previous evening and Mrs. Patterson did not know of my presence in the house. She entered the breakfast room from the hall, and began at once, and without any apparent cause, to talk to Mrs. Wheeler in a most abusive manner, using violent and insulting language.

I immediately went into the breakfast room and commanded her to stop, which she did at once. I indignantly rebuked Mrs. Patterson and informed her that I should tell Mrs. Wheeler's family of her conduct.

Mrs. Wheeler did not respond to Mrs. Patterson. To me she said, "Thank God, Julia, that you were here, this time. I have often borne this."

Mrs. Patterson was, soon after this, requested to leave the Wheeler house, and did so. Mrs. Wheeler received nothing in payment for Mrs. Patterson's board. When Mrs. Wheeler asked Mrs. Patterson for a settlement, Mrs. Patterson replied to the effect that she had "treated" a wounded finger for Mr. Wheeler and that this service was equivalent to what she had received from Mr. and Mrs. Wheeler, in board, lodging, etc.

Upon leaving the Wheelers, Mrs. Patterson took refuge with the Ellis family. Mrs. Mary Ellis lived at Elm Cottage, Swampscott, with her unmarried son, Fred Ellis, master of a boys' school in Boston. Both she and her son were cultivated persons, and they felt a certain sympathy with Mrs. Patterson's literary labours. Wherever she went, Mrs. Patterson was preceded by the legend that she was writing a book. During the time which she spent with Mrs. Ellis, she remained in her room the greater part of each day, working upon the manuscript which eight years later was to be published under the title, *Science and Health*. In the evening she often joined Mr. Ellis and his mother downstairs, and read them what she had written during the day, telling them of Dr. Quimby and his theories of mind and matter, and explaining how she meant to develop them.

While in Lynn Mrs. Patterson continued to take an interest in Spiritualism. The older Spiritualists of Lynn remember her taking part as a medium in a circle which met at the home of Mrs. George Clark in Summer Street. Mrs. Richard Hazeltine says: [6]

My husband, Richard Hazeltine, and I went to the circle at Mrs. Clark's and saw Mrs. Glover [7] pass into the trance state, and heard her communicate by word of mouth messages received from the spirit world, or what she said and we believed were messages from the spirit world. I cannot forget certain peculiar features of these sittings of Mrs. Glover's. Mrs. Glover told us, as we were gathered there, that, because of her superior spiritual quality, and because of the purity of her life, she could only be controlled in the spirit world by one of the Apostles and by Jesus Christ. When she went into the trance state and gave her communications to members of the circle, these communications were said by Mrs. Glover to come, through her as a medium, from the spirit of one of the Apostles or of Jesus Christ.

Mrs. Mary Gould, a Spiritualist medium in Lynn, remembers that at one time Abraham Lincoln was one of Mrs. Glover's controls.

In the winter of 1866-67 Mrs. Patterson met Hiram Crafts at a boarding-house in Lynn. Crafts was a shoe-worker of East Stoughton, who had come to Lynn to work in a shoe factory there for the winter. Mrs. Patterson tried to interest every one she met in Quimby's theories and saw in the serious shoemaker a prospective pupil. What she told Crafts of this new system of doctoring appealed to him strongly; he was a Spiritualist and was deeply interested in psychic phenomena. After he returned home, he sent for Mrs. Patterson to come to East

[6] From the affidavit of Mrs. Richard Hazeltine of Lynn.
[7] Although Mrs. Patterson did not divorce Dr. Patterson until 1873, she resumed her former name of Glover soon after he went away.

Stoughton and teach him.   She joined the Crafts, accordingly, in the early part of 1867, and lived for some months in their home at East Stoughton—now Avon—instructing Mr. Crafts in the Quimby method of healing.   Early in the spring Crafts

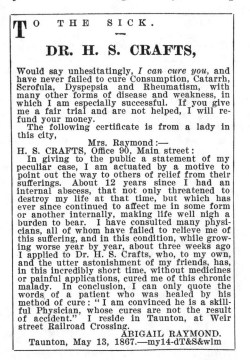

An advertisement of Hiram S. Crafts, which appeared in a Taunton newspaper, May 13, 1867. Mr. Crafts had moved from East Stoughton to Taunton, taking his wife and Mrs. Eddy with him.

went to Taunton, taking his wife and Mrs. Patterson with him, and opened an office.   He was the first of Mrs. Eddy's students to go into practice.   His advertisement in a Taunton paper is reprinted herewith.   Mrs. Patterson did not practise herself, but remained with the family to teach and advise Crafts.   Concerning Mrs. Patterson and her relation to the Crafts,[8] Ira Holmes, brother of Mrs. Crafts, makes the following affidavit:

Ira Holmes, being duly sworn, deposes and says:

I am 76 years of age. I reside in Stoughton, Massachusetts. I first met Mrs. Mary Patterson, now known as Mary Baker G. Eddy, of Concord, New Hampshire, in the year 1867. She was then living at the home of Mr. and Mrs. Hiram S. Crafts in East Stoughton, which is now called Avon. Mrs. Hiram S. Crafts is my sister, and Hiram S. Crafts is a brother of my wife, Mrs. Ira Holmes. The two families were, therefore, intimately connected, and I was acquainted with what occurred in the Crafts home.

Hiram Crafts and his wife, Mary Crafts, told me that they first met Mary Patterson in a boarding house in Lynn, Mass., where Hiram and Mary Crafts lived temporarily while Hiram Crafts was working in a Lynn shoe manufactory. Mr. and Mrs. Crafts were Spiritualists, and they have told me that Mrs. Patterson represented to them that she had learned a " science " that was a step in advance of Spiritualism. She wished to teach this science to Hiram Crafts, and after Mr. and Mrs. Crafts had returned from Lynn to their home in East Stoughton, Massachusetts, Mrs. Patterson came to their home for the purpose of teaching this new science to Hiram Crafts. I have heard her say many times, while she was living at Crafts' that she learned this science from Doctor Quimby. I have heard her say these words: " I learned this science from Dr. Quimby, and I can impart it to but one person." She always said this in a slow, impressive manner, pronouncing the word " person " as if it were spelled " pairson."

From my sister, Mary Crafts, and her husband, Hiram S. Crafts, I learned that Hiram Crafts had entered into an agreement with Mrs. Patterson to pay her a certain sum of money for instructing him in Quimby's science.

After Hiram Crafts had learned it, he took some patients for treatment, in East Stoughton, but in a short time he, with Mrs. Crafts and Mrs. Patterson, moved to Taunton, Mass., for the purpose of practising the healing system which Mrs. Patterson had taught him. I never knew of Mrs. Patterson treating, or attempting to treat, any sick person. I understood, from her and from Mr. and Mrs. Crafts, that she could not practise this science, but could teach it, and could teach it to only one person.

While Mrs. Patterson lived in the home of Mr. and Mrs. Crafts, she caused trouble in the household, and urged Mr. Crafts to get a bill of divorce from his wife, Mary Crafts. The reason Mrs. Patterson gave for

---

[8] Hiram Crafts died last year. His widow is now living with a brother in Brockton, Mass.

urging Mr. Crafts to divorce his wife was, that Mrs. Crafts stood in the way of the success of Mr. Crafts and Mrs. Patterson in the healing business. Mrs. Crafts, my sister, was gentle, kind, and patient, and in no way merited Mrs. Patterson's dislike of her. Mrs. Crafts waited upon Mrs. Patterson, did the housework and marketing, and in every way sought to advance the interests of her husband, Hiram S. Crafts. When Mrs. Crafts discovered that Mrs. Patterson was attempting to influence Mr. Crafts to apply for a divorce, she, my sister, Mary Crafts, prepared to pack up her possessions and to leave her husband's house. The result of this was that Mr. Crafts would not consent to lose his wife, and as Mrs. Crafts would not remain unless Mrs. Patterson went away, Mrs. Patterson was obliged to leave the home of Mr. and Mrs. Crafts. This was while they were residing in Taunton, Mass. After Mrs. Patterson's departure, Mr. and Mrs. Crafts returned to East Stoughton to live, and Hiram S. Crafts no longer practised the healing system taught by Mrs. Patterson.

I make this statement of my own free will, solely in the interest of justice.

IRA HOLMES.

COMMONWEALTH OF MASSACHUSETTS
NORFOLK, ss:

STOUGHTON, February 7, 1907.

Then personally appeared the above named Ira Holmes and acknowledged the foregoing instrument by him subscribed, to be his free act and deed, before me.

GEO. O. WENTWORTH, *Notary Public.*

Many years afterward, when the Crafts were living in Hebron, N. H., and Mrs. Eddy had retired to Concord, N. H., she sent for Mr. Crafts and paid his expenses to Pleasant View to deliver into her hands his copy of the manuscript which she had used in teaching him,—probably a copy of the Quimby manuscript,—which he did.

After leaving the Crafts, Mrs. Patterson seems to have gone to Amesbury to the home of Captain and Mrs. Nathaniel Webster. Concerning Mrs. Webster and Mrs. Patterson's stay at her house, Mrs. Mary Ellis Bartlett, a granddaughter of Mrs. Webster, makes the following affidavit:

Photograph by H. F. Currier

MARY BAKER G. EDDY

From a photograph taken in Amesbury, Mass., in   From a tintype. Mrs. Eddy helping an Amesbury
1870   photographer to get a successful picture of a baby

Mary Ellis Bartlett, being duly sworn, deposes and says:

I am 55 years of age, and I am a citizen of Boston, Massachusetts. I am the daughter of William R. Ellis and Mary Jane Ellis, and the granddaughter of Captain Nathaniel Webster and Mary Webster, who for many years resided in Amesbury, Massachusetts. In the years between 1865 and 1870 my grandparents, Captain and Mrs. Webster, were living in Amesbury, Mass., at what is now No. 5 Merrimac Street. Captain Webster was a retired sea captain, and at that time was superintendent of cotton mills in Manchester, New Hampshire, of which E. A. Straw, his son-in-law, who was later Governor of New Hampshire, was agent for many years. My Grandmother Webster was a well-known Spiritualist. Grandfather Webster was away from home, attending to his business in Manchester, much of the time, returning home to Amesbury about once in two weeks, to remain over Sunday. My grandmother was, therefore, much alone, and because of this, and for the further reason that she was deeply interested in Spiritualism in all its forms, she had at her house constant visitors and charity patients who were Spiritualists. Invalids, cripples, and other unfortunate persons were made welcome, and my grandmother took care of them when they were ill and lodged and boarded them free of charge. She had, or believed she had, spiritual communications in regard to their various ailments, which she followed in prescribing for them and in her treatment of them. My grandmother was what was called a " drawing medium " and a " healing medium." She drew strange pictures under the influence of the spirits. Many of these pictures are now in existence, and some of them are in my possession, having been given to me by my grandmother.

Grandmother Webster had a room in her house which was used for spiritual séances, and for all grandmother's spiritistic work. This room was on the ground floor, situated in the rear of the front parlour. It was decorated in blue, according to the direction of grandmother's spirit control,—blue being a colour favoured by the spirits. The room was furnished with the usual chairs, tables, couch, etc., but this furniture was called by my grandmother and her Spiritualist friends, " spiritual furniture," because it was used only for spiritual purposes. There was a couch which grandmother called her " spiritual couch." She thought she could sleep upon it when she could not sleep elsewhere. Upon it she took her daytime naps, and sometimes during a restless night she was able to sleep if she lay upon this couch. There was a table in the room which was used for the laying on of hands by the Spiritualists at the séances held in the room, and there was an old chair which had belonged to Captain Webster's mother, in which grandmother always sat for her spirit communications. Above this room, which was known as the " spiritual room," was a bedroom.

One night in the autumn of 1867, as nearly as I can fix the date, a woman, a stranger, came to my grandmother's door, and told her that she had been led by the spirits to come to her house, for the reason that it was " a nice, harmonious home." My grandmother, who was sympathetic and hospitable, and, above all, a devoted Spiritualist, who would never turn another Spiritualist away, upon hearing this, exclaimed, " Glory to God! Come right in!" The woman thus admitted told my grandmother that she was Mrs. Mary Glover, a Spiritualist, and that she had been drawn as above described to my grandmother's house. Mrs. Glover did not explain further why she came and did not say from what place she had come. My grandmother gave her the use of the bedroom over the spiritual room, and also the use of the spiritual room. Here grandmother and Mrs. Glover continued to hold spiritualistic séances, in which Mrs. Glover took an active part, passing into the trance state and giving what grandmother believed to be communications from the spirits.

Mrs. Glover became permanently settled at Grandmother Webster's house. She was treated as a guest, was waited upon, and was cared for in every respect. My Grandfather Webster, coming home and finding Mrs. Glover established in the house, was displeased because she was there. He told my grandmother that he did not want Mrs. Glover to remain. . . . But Mrs. Glover continued to live in the house, and after a few months, during which my grandmother's admiration for Mrs. Glover had begun to grow less, Mrs. Glover informed my grandmother that she had learned a new science which she thought was something beyond Spiritualism. She said she had learned it from Dr. Quimby of Portland, Maine, and that she had brought copies of some of his manuscripts with her. She talked about it and read the manuscripts to my grandmother, who did not, however, believe that the " science " was an improvement or a step beyond Spiritualism. From that time forward Mrs. Glover talked of Quimby's science. She was writing what she told grandmother was a revision of the Bible. She always sat in the spiritual chair at the spiritual table in grandmother's spiritual room to do her writing, and sometimes after she had written for hours, she would gather up all the pages she had filled with writing and tear them up, because she could not make them read as she wished.

My father, William R. Ellis, was in 1867 living in New York, with his three children—myself, my sister, and my brother. My mother had died three or four years before. Our family had always spent the summer school vacation at my grandparents' home in Amesbury, Mass., and when it was time for us to leave New York, my father always went to Amesbury in advance of the rest of us, in order to clear my grandmother's house of broken-down Spiritualists and sick persons, so that we might have enough room in the house and because he thought the atmosphere of so much sickness and Spiritualism was unwholesome for young children.

My father, upon first seeing Mrs. Glover in the house, had told my grandmother that she, Mrs. Glover, should not be permitted to remain. . . . . My grandmother, upon being urged by my father and grandfather to dismiss Mrs. Glover, at last told her that she was no longer welcome and asked her to go away. Mrs. Glover ignored my grandmother's request and continued to live in the house . . . .

Failing to succeed in getting Mrs. Glover to leave the house, my grandmother sent for my father. He arrived in the early evening of the following Saturday. When grandmother had told him of the trouble and how Mrs. Glover refused to go away, she asked my father to see if he could not make Mrs. Glover leave the house. My father commanded Mrs. Glover to leave, and when she steadfastly refused to go, he had her trunk dragged from her room and set it outside the door, insisted upon her also going out the door, and when she was outside he closed the door and locked it. I have frequently heard my father describe this event in detail, and I have heard him say that he had never expected, in his whole life, to be obliged to put a woman into the street. It was dark at the time, and a heavy rain was falling. My grandparents and my father considered it absolutely necessary to take this step, harsh and disagreeable as it seemed to them.

The above statement is made partly from my own personal knowledge, and partly from hearing it many, many times from my father, my grandmother, and my Grandfather Webster, who have related it to me and others of the family until it has come to be a well-known part of our family history. I make this statement of my own free will, solely in the interests of justice.

MARY ELLIS BARTLETT

STATE OF MASSACHUSETTS,
SUFFOLK, SS:

Personally appeared the above named Mary Ellis Bartlett, and made oath that the foregoing statements covering eleven sheets, each of which is subscribed by her, are true to the best of her knowledge and belief, this sixth day of February, 1907.

HERBERT P. SHELDON, *Notary Public.*

When Mrs. Glover was thus left without a lodging-place for the night, Mrs. Richardson, another of Mrs. Webster's Spiritualist guests, who was in the house at the time, was

moved to compassion and took Mrs. Glover down the street
to the house of Miss Sarah Bagley, a dressmaker, who was a
fellow Spiritualist.

DR. ROUNDY AND WIFE,

CLAIRVOYANT, Magnetic and Electric Physicians, have recently furnished a house on
Quincy avenue, in QUINCY, MASS., where they are
still Healing the Sick with good success. Board
and treatment reasonable.   Address, QUINCY,
MASS.   6w*—June 6.

ANY PERSON desiring to learn how to heal the
sick can receive of the undersigned instruction
that will enable them to commence healing on a
principle of science with a success far beyond
any of the present modes. No medicine, electricity, physiology or hygiene required for un-
paralleled success in the most difficult cases. No
pay is required unless this skill is obtained. Address, MRS. MARY B. GLOVER, Amesbury, Mass.,
Box 61.   tf†—June 20.

MRS. MARY LEWIS, by sending their autograph,
or lock of hair, will give psychometrical de-
lineations of character, answer questions, &c.
Terms $1.00 and red stamp. Address, MARY
LEWIS, Morrison, Whiteside Co., Ill.
                              June 20.—20w*.

The above advertisement, in which Mrs. Eddy offers to teach a new
kind of healing based on a " principle of science," appeared July 4, 1868,
in the *Banner of Light,* the official organ of New England Spiritualists.
Mrs. Eddy was then living at the home of the Websters in Amesbury,
and the number of Captain Webster's post-office box was 61.

Miss Bagley took the friendless woman into her home, and
here, in addition to the small sum which she paid for her
board, Mrs. Glover taught Miss Bagley the Quimby method
of treating disease. Miss Bagley developed such powers as a
healer that she soon abandoned her needle and began to practise
" professionally." Mrs. Glover was generally known in Amesbury as a pupil of Dr. Quimby, and it was rumoured in the
village that before Mrs. Glover was through with her " science "
she was going to walk on the waters of the Merrimac. Two
Amesbury girls were so interested in this report that, one

afternoon when Mrs. Glover attended some merrymaking on the river bank, they went down and lingered on the bridge, hoping that she might be tempted to try her powers on that festal occasion.

To-day the Christian Scientists of Lynn draw a pathetic picture of the persecuted woman, driven from door to door, carrying her great truth in her bosom, and finding no man ready to receive it. And it is not to be wondered at that those who regard Mrs. Eddy as the recipient of God's most complete revelation, find here material for legend, and liken her wanderings to those of the persecuted apostles.

There is no indication that these harsh experiences ever, in the least, subdued Mrs. Glover's proud spirit. Wherever she went, she took her place as the guest of honour, and she consistently assumed that she conferred favour by accepting hospitality. She did not hesitate to chide and reprimand members of the families she visited, to criticise and interfere with the administration of household affairs. She seems never to have known discouragement or to have felt apprehension for the future, but was content with dominating the house in which she happened to be and with striving to win a following among the friends of the family. While she certainly cherished a vague, half-formulated plan to go out into the world some day and teach the Quimby doctrine, her imperative need was to control the immediate situation; to be the commanding figure in the lodge, the sewing-circle, the family gathering. The one thing she could not endure was to be thought like other people. She must be something besides plain Mrs. Glover,—invalid, poetess, healer, propagandist, guest; she must be exceptional at any cost.   Even while she was dependent upon precarious hospitality, Mrs. Glover managed to invest her person and her doings with a certain form and ceremony which was not without its effect.   She spent much time in her room; was not always accessible; had her meals prepared at special hours; made calls and received visitors with a certain stress of graciousness and condescension.   She had the faculty of giving her every action and word the tone of importance.   She was now a woman of forty-seven; her wardrobe was shabby and scant; she still rouged her cheeks; the brown hue of her hair was crudely artificial; her watch and chain and several gold trinkets were, with the Quimby manuscripts, her only treasures.   Certainly, neither village gossips nor rustic humourists had spared her. But the stage did not exist that was so mean and poor, nor the audience so brutal and unsympathetic, that Mrs. Glover could not, unabashed, play out her part.

CHAPTER VIII

WHEN Mrs. Glover left Amesbury, she went to Stoughton, to the home of Mrs. Sally Wentworth, whom she had met when she was with Hiram Crafts. Mrs. Wentworth had a consumptive daughter whom she took to Hiram Crafts for treatment, and in his house she met Mrs. Glover and became much interested in her system of healing. Her curiosity about the Quimby mind cure was not surprising, as she was a practical nurse and had much to do with illness. She was frequently called upon to care for the sick in the neighbourhood, and was locally famous for the comfort she could give them by rubbing their limbs and bodies. She was a Spiritualist and believed in the healing power of Spiritualism. " Old Ase Holbrook," a Spiritualist and clairvoyant " doctor," often asked Mrs. Wentworth to assist him in the care of his patients. In Mrs. Glover's system of healing she hoped to find something which she could put into beneficial practice in her work. Mrs. Glover went into Mrs. Wentworth's house to teach her the Quimby system for a consideration of three hundred dollars, which sum was to cover her board and lodging for a considerable period of time.

The Wentworth household then consisted of the parents and

two children, Charles and Lucy, the daughter being about fourteen years of age. The married son, Horace T. Wentworth, often dropped in to see his mother, and Mrs. Wentworth's niece—a spirited girl, now Mrs. Catherine Isabel Clapp, was in and out of the house continually. Mrs. Glover lived with the Wentworths for about two years, leaving them only to make occasional visits in the neighbourhood or at Amesbury. At first all the family took great pleasure in her visit. Although Mrs. Glover seldom held her friends long, and although her friendships often terminated violently, when she exerted herself to charm, she seldom failed. Mrs. Wentworth used reproachfully to declare to her less impressionable niece, " If ever there was a saint upon this earth, it is that woman." Both the children were fond of Mrs. Glover, but Lucy abandoned herself to adoration. The child followed her about, waited upon her, and was eager to anticipate her every wish, even at the cost of displeasing her parents. She resented the slightest criticism of their guest, and was deeply hurt by the jests which were passed in the village at Mrs. Glover's expense.

Mrs. Glover's highly coloured speech, her odd clothes, and grand ways, her interest in strange and mysterious subjects, her high mission to spread the truths of her dead master, made her an interesting figure in a humdrum New England village, and her very eccentricities and affectations varied the monotony of a quiet household. Her being " different " did, after all, result in material benefits to Mrs. Glover. All these people with whom she once stayed, love to talk of her, and most of them are glad to have known her,—even those who now say that the experience was a costly one. She was like a patch of colour in those gray communities. She was never dull, her old hosts say, and never commonplace. She never laid aside her regal air; never entered a room or left it like other people. There was something about her that continually excited and stimulated, and she gave people the feeling that a great deal was happening.

Except for occasional angry outbursts, it was this engaging aspect of Mrs. Glover that, for many months, the Wentworths saw. She was tiresome only when she talked of Dr. Quimby, and then only because she discoursed upon him and his philosophy so often. Mrs. Clapp describes how, after long dissertations on mind and matter, Mrs. Glover would fold her hands in her lap, tilt her head on one side, and gently nodding, would, in mincing tones, enunciate this sentence:

" I *learned* this from Dr. *Quimby,* and he made me *promise* to teach it to at least *two* persons before I *die.*"

She confided this fact to every one, always in the same phrase, with the same emphasis, and with the same sweetness, until it became a fashion for the village girls to mimic her.

The estrangement which resulted in Mrs. Glover's leaving the house began in a difficulty between her and Mr. Wentworth. Mr. Wentworth was indignant because Mrs. Glover had attempted to persuade his wife to leave him and to go away with her and practise the Quimby treatment. After this, Mrs. Glover's former kindly feeling toward the family seemed to disappear altogether. Mrs. Clapp remembers going to the house one day and being disturbed by the sound of violent pounding on the floor upstairs. Her aunt, with some embarrassment, explained that Mr. Wentworth was sick in bed, and that Mrs. Glover had shut herself in her room and was deliberately pounding on the floor above his head to annoy him. Other things of a similar nature occurred, and Mrs. Wentworth was finally compelled to ask Mrs. Glover to leave the house as soon as she could find another place to stay.   Horace T. Wentworth, in his affidavit, says:

" Mrs. Wentworth consulted a member of the family as to the best way to bring about Mrs. Glover's departure.   By this time my mother was almost in a state of terror regarding Mrs. Glover.   She was so afraid of her that she hardly dared to go to sleep at night.   She had a lock put on the door of her room so that Mrs. Glover could not get access to her, and ordered her to leave the house."

Mrs. Glover chose for her departure a day when all the members of the Wentworth family were away from home. She took the train for Amesbury, without a word of good-bye to any one.   When the Wentworths returned that night, they went to Mrs. Glover's room and knocked, but could get no reply.   Horace, the son, suggested forcing the lock, but his mother would not permit it, saying that such a liberty might offend Mrs. Glover, who had probably gone to spend the night with one of the neighbours.   The next day they inquired among their friends, but could get no news of their missing guest. Several days went by, and Mrs. Wentworth, becoming alarmed lest some mischance might have befallen Mrs. Glover, told her son to force the door and see if any clue to her whereabouts could be found in her room.

Horace T. Wentworth, in his affidavit, thus describes his entering the room:

A few days after Mrs. Glover left, I and my mother went into the room which she had occupied. We were the first persons to enter the room after Mrs. Glover's departure. We found every breadth of matting slashed up through the middle, apparently with some sharp instrument. We also found the feather-bed all cut to pieces. We opened the door of a closet. On the floor was a pile of newspapers almost entirely consumed. On top of these papers was a shovelful of dead coals. These had evidently been left upon the paper by the last occupant. The only reasons that they had not set the house on fire evidently were because the closet door had been shut, and the air of the closet so dead, and because the newspapers were piled flat and did not readily ignite—were folded so tight, in other words, that they would not blaze.

Mrs. Clapp, in her affidavit, substantiates this statement.

The Wentworths never saw or directly heard from Mrs. Glover again.

While Mrs. Glover was in Stoughton, she apparently had no ambition beyond expounding Quimby's philosophy and declaring herself his disciple. She made no claim to having originated anything she taught.

Although Mrs. Eddy now believes that she discovered the secret of health through divine revelation in 1866, she was often ill while in the Wentworth house, 1868-1870, and on several occasions was confined to her bed for considerable periods of time. During her illnesses Mrs. Wentworth nursed and cared for her, rubbing her and treating her after the Quimby method.

During her stay in Stoughton she made no claim to having received a divine revelation, or to having discovered any system of her own. She seldom associated her teachings with religion as such, and preached Quimbyism merely as an advanced system of treating disease. In instructing Mrs. Wentworth she used a manuscript, which, she always

said, had been written by " Dr. Quimby of Portland, Me." She
held this document as her most precious possession. " One day
when I was at the Wentworths'," recently said Mrs. Clapp,
" Mrs. Wentworth was busy copying this manuscript. I went
to the buttery to get what I wanted, but couldn't find it, and
called Mrs. Wentworth. She got up to get it for me, but
before doing so, she put the manuscript in the desk and locked
it. I expressed surprise that she should take such pains when
she was only stepping across the room for a moment, and she
said: ' Mrs. Glover made me promise never to leave this manuscript, even for a moment, without locking the desk.' "

Mr. Horace T. Wentworth of Stoughton now has his mother's
manuscript. He has made affidavit [1] that this is the document

----

[1] COMMONWEALTH OF MASSACHUSETTS,

COUNTY OF NORFOLK, SS.

Horace T. Wentworth, being duly sworn, deposes and says:
I am sixty-four years of age, and reside in the Town of Stoughton, in the
Commonwealth of Massachusetts, and have resided there for upwards of
sixty-two years past. I am the son of Alanson C. and Sally Wentworth, and
my mother resided in said town of Stoughton from her birth to the time of
her death, in 1883.
I became acquainted with Mrs. Mary Baker G. Eddy, now of Concord, N. H.,
and known as the Discoverer and Founder of Christian Science, in the year
1868, when she was the wife of one Daniel Patterson, with whom she was
not living, and was known by the name of a former husband, one George W.
Glover, and called herself Mrs. Mary M. Glover.
In 1867, Mrs. Glover came to Stoughton, and took up her residence at the
house of one Hiram Crafts in said Town of Stoughton, and in 1868, after
leaving said Crafts, she went upon the invitation of my mother, to the residence of said Mrs. Sally Wentworth, of said Stoughton, and there continuously
resided until the spring of the year 1870. Very often during the years 1868,
1869, and 1870, I saw and talked with said Mrs. Glover at my mother's said
residence. Mrs. Wentworth invited said Mrs. Glover to visit her for the
express purpose of being taught, by said Mrs. Glover, a system of mental
healing, which said Mrs. Glover said she had been taught by one Dr. Phineas
P. Quimby, of Portland, Me. Said Mrs. Glover often spoke to me of said
system of mental healing and always ascribed its origin and discovery to said
Quimby. Said Mrs. Glover was outspoken in her acknowledgment that she learned
her mental healing system from said Quimby, and never, to my knowledge,
while at my mother's house, made the slightest claim or pretensions to having
discovered or originated it herself.
Said Mrs. Glover, upon coming to my mother's house, lent my mother her
manuscript copy of what she, Mrs. Glover, said were writings of said Quimby,
and permitted my mother to make a full manuscript copy thereof, and said
manuscript copy of the writings of said Quimby, in my mother's handwriting,
and with corrections and interlineations in the handwriting of Mrs. Glover, is
now, and has been since my mother's death, in my possession.
On the outside, said copy is entitled " Extracts from Doctor P. P. Quimby's
Writings," and at the head of the first page, on the inside, said copy is

copied by his mother from Mrs. Glover's, and that he has himself heard Mrs. Glover attribute the original to Dr. Quimby. His brother, Charles O. Wentworth; his sister, Mrs. Arthur L. Holmes (then Miss Lucy Wentworth), and his cousin, Mrs. Catherine Isabel Clapp, have made affidavits to the same effect. This includes all members of the Wentworth household now living.

The Wentworth manuscript itself powerfully supports these affidavits. Of chief interest are the title-page and the first

further entitled "The Science of Man, or the Principle which Controls all Phenomena." There is a preface of two pages with Mrs. Mary M. Glover's name signed at the end. The extracts are in the form of fifteen questions and answers and are labelled, "Questions by patients, Answers by Dr. Quimby."

Annexed hereto, marked "Exhibit A," is a full and complete copy of my mother's said copy of Mrs. Glover's said copy of Dr. Quimby's writings. . . .

Annexed hereto and marked "Exhibit B" is a photograph of the first page of Mrs. Wentworth's manuscript plainly showing the additions made in a handwriting not my mother's. All of the said first page shown in Exhibit B is my mother's handwriting except the words "Wisdom Love &" added to the beginning of the fifteenth line, the word "of" and the symbol "&" added to the sixteenth line and the words "is in it" added to the seventeenth line, none of which additions is in my mother's handwriting.

Annexed hereto and marked "Exhibit C" is a photograph of the second page of said manuscript plainly showing further additions in a handwriting not my mother's. All of the said second page shown in Exhibit C is in my mother's handwriting except the words "wisdom love &" added to the second line, the word "believe" added to the eleventh line, none of which additions is in my mother's handwriting.

I am perfectly familiar with my mother's handwriting; but am not familiar enough with said Mrs. Glover's handwriting to state positively from my acquaintance with it, that the said added words are written by her. This manuscript, however, came directly into my hands from my mother's desk at the time of her death; the added words are not in the handwriting of any member of my family; they are, as will be seen, in the nature of corrections to my mother's writing of said Mrs. Glover's signed preface to Dr. Quimby's teachings, and, having compared them with unquestionable writing of said Mrs. Glover's, found with my mother's papers, and seen them to be strikingly similar, I am confidently of the opinion that they are the writing of the only person interested in the correction of said Mrs. Glover's preface to said Dr. Quimby's writings, to wit, said Mrs. Mary M. Glover—Mrs. Mary Baker G. Eddy—herself.

I have been often urged to make these facts known in the public interest, and have for years felt it my duty to tell the truth and the whole truth. . . .

HORACE T. WENTWORTH.

On this 9th day of February, 1907, at the Town of Stoughton, in the Commonwealth of Massachusetts, personally appeared before me, Horace T. Wentworth, to me personally known, and made oath before me that he had read over the foregoing statement and knows the contents thereof, and that the same are true; and he, thereupon, in my presence, did sign his name at the end of said statement, and at the foot of the cover.

EDGAR F. LEONARD, *Justice of the Peace.*

And before me a Notary Public appeared Horace T. Wentworth and made oath to above statement.   HENRY W. BRITTON, *Notary Public.*

Stoughton, Mass.
    Feb. 9th, 1907.

two pages, which are here reproduced in facsimile. The title-page reads, " Extracts from Doctor P. P. Quimby's Writings." On the first page of the manuscript appears the title, " The Science of Man or the principle which controls all phenomena." Then follows a preface, signed " Mary M. Glover." Following this is a marginal note, " P. P. Q.'s Mss.," and at this point begins the Quimby paper. Others who have copies of this same document declare that Mrs. Glover taught from them and sold them as copies of Quimby's manuscript.

By examining the pages reproduced in facsimile, the reader will observe that some one has edited them,—that certain words are written in, not in the handwriting of Mrs. Wentworth. Beginning the fourth paragraph of the first page, are the words, " Wisdom Love & "; two lines below this, are the words, " is in it "; on the second page, second line, again, " wisdom love & "; and on the eleventh line of the same page, " believe." Mrs. Clapp, who was familiar with Mrs. Glover's handwriting at the time, having copied many pages of her manuscript, takes oath that she believes these interlineations to be Mrs. Glover's. Mr. William G. Nixon of Boston, who, as the publisher for several years of Mrs. Eddy's books, handled thousands of pages of her manuscript, also takes oath that in his opinion these words are in her handwriting. George A. Quimby of Belfast, Me., has lent to the writer one of his father's manuscripts, entitled, " Questions and Answers." This is in the handwriting of Mr. Quimby's mother, the wife of Phineas P. Quimby, and is dated, in Mrs. Quimby's handwriting, February, 1862,—nine months before Mrs. Eddy's first visit to Portland. For twenty closely written pages, Quimby's manuscript, " Questions and

Title page and part of the first page of the manuscript from which Mrs. Glover taught Mrs. Wentworth the system of mental healing which she ascribed to P. P. Quimby

Answers," is word for word the same as Mrs. Glover's manuscript, " The Science of Man." [2]

The relation of Quimby's " Questions and Answers " to the Christian Science doctrine will be discussed in a later chapter. The following quotations, taken at random, illustrate the fact that the Quimby manuscript abounds in ideas and phrases familiar to every Christian Scientist.

If I understand how disease originates in the mind and fully believe it, why cannot I cure myself?

Disease being made by our beliefs or by our parents' beliefs or by public opinion, there is no one formula of argument to be adopted, but every one must be hit in their particular case. Therefore it requires great shrewdness or wisdom to get the better of the error.

I know of no better counsel than Jesus gave to His Disciples when He sent them forth to cast out devils, and heal the sick, and thus in practice to preach the Truth " Be ye wise as serpents and harmless as doves." Never get into a passion, but in patience possess ye your soul, and at length you weary out the discord and produce harmony by your Truth destroying error. Then it is you get the case. Now, if you are not afraid to face the error and argue it down, then you can heal the sick.

The patient's disease is in his belief.

Error is sickness. Truth is health.

In this science the names are given thus: God is Wisdom. This Wisdom is not an individuality but a principle, embraces every idea form, of which the idea, man, is the highest—hence the image of God, or the Principle.

Understanding is God.

All sciences are part of God.

Truth is God.

There is no other Truth but God.

God is Wisdom. God is Principle.

Wisdom, Love, and Truth are the Principle.

Error is matter.

Matter has no intelligence.

To give intelligence to matter is an error which is sickness.

Matter has no intelligence of its own, and to believe intelligence is in matter is the error which produces pain and inharmony of all sorts; to

---

[2] The manuscript *Science of Man,* from which Mrs. Glover taught, is not the same work as her printed pamphlet of that title.

hold ourselves we are a principle outside of matter, we would not be influenced by the opinions of man, but held to the workings only of a principle, Truth, in which there are no inharmonies of sickness, pain or sin.

For matter is an error, there being no substance, which is Truth, in a thing which changes and is only that which belief makes it.

Christ was the Wisdom that knew Truth dwelt not in opinion, and that matter was but opinion that could be formed into any shape which the belief gave to it, and that the life which moved it came not from it, but was outside of it.

In teaching Mrs. Wentworth, Mrs. Glover supplemented the Quimby manuscripts with oral instruction. She taught Mrs. Wentworth to rub her patient's head, precisely as did Quimby, and to say, as she did so: "It is not necessary for me to rub your head, but I do it to concentrate my thoughts." In addition she taught Mrs. Wentworth to lay her hands over the patient's stomach.

Mrs. Eddy left a few scraps of writing at the Wentworths', all connected with her teachings. Of especial interest are the instructions which she wrote out to direct Mrs. Wentworth in treating the sick. These Mr. Horace T. Wentworth has in her own handwriting. The first two pages of this manuscript read as follows: (The spelling, punctuation, etc., follow the original MS.)

An argument for the sick having what is termed fever chills and heat with sleepless nights, and called spinal inflammation.

The patient has been doctoring the sick one patient is an opium eater, with catarrh, great fear of the air, etc. Another had inflammation of the joints or rheumatism, and liver complaint another scrofula and rheumatism, and another dyspepsia, all of them having the most intense fear.

First the fever is to be argued down. What is heat and chills we answer nothing but an effect produced upon the body by images of disease before the spiritual senses wherefore you must say of heat and chill you are not hot you are not cold you are only the effect of fright there is no such thing as heat and cold if there were you would not grow hot when angry or abashed or frightened and the temperature around not changed in the least.

Inflammation is not inflammation or redness and soreness of any part this is your belief only and this belief is the red dragon the King of beasts which means this belief of inflammation is the leading lie out of which you get your fright that causes chills and heat. Now look it down cause your patient to look at this truth with you call upon their spiritual senses to look with your view which sees no such image and thus waken them out of their dream that is causing them so much suffering, etc.

In her autobiographical sketches, Mrs. Eddy does not mention the years she spent in Stoughton, Taunton, and Amesbury. In *Restrospection and Introspection,* page 39, she says, after recounting the manner of her miraculous recovery and revelation in 1866:

I then withdrew from society about three years,—to ponder my mission, to search the Scriptures, to find the Science of Mind, that should take the things of God and show them to the creature, and reveal the great curative Principle,—Deity.

The record of these wandering, vagarious years from 1864 to 1870 is far from being satisfactory biography; the number of houses in which she lived, her quarrels and eccentricities, by no means tell us the one thing which is of real importance: what, all this time, was going on in Mrs. Glover's own consciousness. Wherever she went, she taught, now a shoemaker, now a dressmaker, now a boy in the box factory; and wherever she went, she wrote. Her first book was not published until 1875, but for eight years before she was always writing; working upon articles and treatises which were eventually incorporated in this first edition of *Science and Health.* As early as 1866, when she was in Lynn, she said that she was writing a Bible, and was almost through Genesis. Several years later, at the Wentworths', she pointed affectionately to a pile of note-paper tied up with a string, which lay on her desk, and told Mrs. Clapp that it was her Bible, and that she had completed the Book of Genesis. Mrs. Clapp at that time copied for Mrs. Glover a bulky manuscript, which she believes was one of the early drafts of *Science and Health.* She recalls many passages, and remembers her amusement in copying the following passage, which now occurs on page 413 of *Science and Health:*

The daily ablutions of an infant are no more natural or necessary than would be the process of taking a fish out of water every day and covering it with dirt in order to make it thrive more vigorously thereafter in its native element.

After Mrs. Clapp had finished copying the manuscript, Mrs. Glover took it to Boston to find a publisher. Six hundred dollars, cash, in advance, was the only condition on which a publisher would undertake to get out the book, and Mrs. Glover returned to Stoughton and vainly besought Mrs. Wentworth to mortgage the farm to raise money.

Mrs. Glover's persistence was all the more remarkable in that the trade of authorship presented peculiar difficulties for her. Although from her youth she had never lost an opportunity to write for the local papers, and although when she first went to Dr. Quimby she introduced herself to him as an " authoress," her contributions in the old files of the Lynn papers show that she had had no training in the elementary essentials of composition. The quoted extracts from her written instructions to Mrs. Wentworth are indicative of her difficulties with punctuation, which was always a laborious second thought with her. From her letters and early manuscripts it is evident that lucid, clean-cut expression was almost impossible to Mrs.

Glover.   Some of her first dissertations upon Quimbyism were so confused as to be almost unintelligible.   She had, indeed, to fashion her own tools in those years when she was carpentering away at her manuscript and struggling to get her mass of notes into some coherent form.   Her mind was as untrained as her pen.   Logical thought was not within her compass, and even her sporadic ideas were vague and befogged.   Yet, strangely enough, her task was to present an abstract theory, and to present it largely in writing.

Everything depended upon her getting a hearing.   In the first place, her doctrine was her only congenial means of making a living.   In the second, it was the one thing about which she knew more than the people around her, and it gave her that distinction which was necessary to her.   Above all, she had a natural aptitude for the subject and absorbed it until it literally became a part of her.   Mercenary motives were always strong with Mrs. Glover, but no mercenary motive seems adequately to explain her devotion to this idea.   After Quimby's death in '66, his other pupils were silent; but Mrs. Glover, wandering about with no capital but her enthusiasm, was preaching still. Her fellow-students in Portland were people of wider experience than she, and had more than one interest; but only one idea had ever come very close to Mrs. Glover, and neither things present nor things to come could separate her from it. But Mrs. Glover had not the temperament of the dreamer and devotee.   There was one thing in her stronger even than her monomania, and that was her masterfulness.   Others of his pupils lost themselves in Quimby's philosophy, but Mrs. Glover lost Quimby in herself.

CHAPTER IX

WHEN Mrs. Glover left Stoughton early in the year 1870, she went directly to the home of her friend, Miss Sarah Bagley, in Amesbury, Mass.

During her former stay in Amesbury, more than two years before, she had undertaken the instruction of a boy in whom she saw exceptional possibilities. When she first met Richard Kennedy, he was a boy of eighteen, ruddy, sandy-haired, with an unfailing flow of good spirits and a lively wit which did not belie his Irish ancestry. From his childhood he had made his own way, and he was then living at Captain Webster's and working in a box factory. Mrs. Glover recognised in him, as she did in every one she met, excellent capital for a future practitioner. He studied zealously with her while she remained at the Websters', and when she was compelled to leave the house, Kennedy, with Quixotic loyalty becoming his years, left with her. After she went to Stoughton, Mrs. Glover wrote to him often, and whenever he could spare the time, he went over from Amesbury to take a lesson. After her break with the Wentworths, Mrs. Glover at once sought him out. He was then her most promising pupil, and her only hope of getting

134

the Quimby science upon any practical basis.   Her experiment
with Hiram Crafts had failed and she had not succeeded in
her efforts to induce Mrs. Crosby in Albion, or Mrs. Wentworth
in Stoughton, to give up their homes and go into the business
of teaching and practising the Quimby system with her.   What
Mrs. Glover most wanted was a partner, and she now saw one
in Richard Kennedy.   He was nearly twenty-one and sufficiently well-grounded in the principles of mind-cure to begin
practising.   Mrs. Glover had not, up to this time, achieved
any success as a healer herself, and she had come to see that
her power lay almost exclusively in teaching the theory.   Without a practical demonstration of its benefits, however, the
theory of her Science excited little interest, and it was in con-
junction with a practising student that she could teach most
effectively.   She entered into an agreement with young Kennedy
to the effect that they were to open an office in Lynn, Mass.,
and were to remain together three years.

In June, 1870, Mrs. Glover and Richard Kennedy went to
Lynn.   They stayed temporarily at the home of Mrs. Clarkson
Oliver, whom Kennedy had known in Amesbury, while he looked
about for suitable offices.   He heard that Miss Susie Magoun,
who conducted a private school for young children, had just
leased a building on the corner of Shepard and South Common
Streets and was desirous of subletting the second floor.   Miss
Magoun, now Mrs. John M. Dame of Lynn, remembers how
one June evening, when she was looking over the building to
decide upon the arrangement of her schoolrooms, a very boyish-
looking young man appeared and nervously asked whether she
intended to let a part of the house.   He said he was looking

for offices for a physician. Miss Magoun, misled by his youthful appearance, at once supposed that he wanted the rooms
for his father, which caused the boy some embarrassment. He
told her that the five rooms upstairs would not be too many
for him, as he should bring with him " an elderly woman who
was writing a book," and they would each need offices and
sleeping-rooms. Miss Magoun liked the boy's candour and told
him he might move in. He drew a sigh of relief, telling her
that so many people had refused him that he had almost lost
heart. Even when Miss Magoun's friends prophesied that she
would lose her rent, she did not repent of her bargain; and
she never afterward had occasion to do so. Miss Magoun's
first meeting with Mrs. Glover occurred some days later, when
her new tenants came to take possession of their rooms. As
she was hurrying through the hall to her classroom, young
Kennedy stopped her and introduced his partner. Mrs. Glover
bowed and at once began to explain to her astonished landlady
the Quimby theory of the universe and the non-existence of
matter.

Kennedy's sign, which was put on a tree in the yard, read
simply: " Dr. Kennedy." The rooms upstairs were very plainly
furnished, for Mrs. Glover had no money and her student very
little. They bought only such articles of furniture as were
absolutely necessary, covered the floor with paper oil-cloth, and
put up cheap shades at the windows. Much to Miss Magoun's
surprise, patients began to come in before the first week was
over, and at the end of the month Kennedy was able to pay
his rent promptly. By the first of September the young man's
practice was flourishing. Miss Magoun's school was in excel-

lent standing, and the fact that his office was in the same building recommended the young practitioner, while she herself was
glad to say a good word for him whenever she could.   It
became a common thing for the friends of discouraged invalids
to say: " Go to Dr. Kennedy.   He can't hurt you, even if he
doesn't help you."   His offices were sometimes so crowded that
he would have to ask his patients to await their turn below
in Miss Magoun's parlour.   The children in the school were fond
of him, and he often found time to run downstairs about dismissal hour and help Miss Magoun and her assistant get the
younger pupils into their wraps and overshoes.   He knew them
all by name, and sometimes joined in their games.

Mrs. Glover herself, during these first months, remained much
in the background, a solitary and somewhat sombre figure, applying herself to her work with ever-increasing seriousness.
For the first time she was free from pecuniary embarrassments,
and she concentrated her energies upon her teaching, and
writing with a determination which she had never before shown.
She seldom went out of the house, was usually silent at Miss
Magoun's dinner-table, and the school children, when they met
her in the hall, hurried curiously past the grave, abstracted
woman, who never spoke to them or noticed them.   Far from
relaxing in an atmosphere of comparative prosperity, she was
impatient of the easy-going friendliness of the people about her.
She was contemptuous of the active part which Kennedy took
in the social life around him, and resented his having much to
do with Miss Magoun's young friends.   She continually urged
him to put aside every other interest and concentrate himself
wholly upon Science.   She was annoyed at the women patients

who came often for treatment, and when she saw them sitting in the front office awaiting their turn, she sometimes referred to them as " the stool-pigeons." She began in these days to sense the possibilities of the principle she taught, and to see further than a step ahead. She often told Kennedy that she would one day establish a great religion which would reverence her as its founder and source. " Richard," she would declare, looking at him intently, " you will live to hear the church-bells ring out my birthday." And on July 16, 1904, they did— her own bells, in her own church at Concord.

The feeling of at last having her foot in the stirrup seemed to crystallise and direct Mrs. Glover's ambition as adversity had never done. She had something the world had waited for, she told Kennedy, and she meant to make the world pay for it. She often declared that she had been born an unwelcome child, and that from the first every man's hand had been against her. Although she was in her fiftieth year, Mrs. Glover had not reached the maturity of her powers. During these early years in Lynn she becomes in every way a more commanding and formidable person. Since she no longer had to live by her wits, certain affectations and ingratiating mannerisms became less pronounced. The little distinction for which she had fought so tenaciously, and which she had been put at such shifts to maintain, was now respectfully admitted by all her students—and by some even reverently. She began to dress better. Her thin face filled out, her figure lost its gauntness and took on an added dignity. People who were afraid of her complained that her " hawk-eye " looked clear through them, and persons who admired her compared her eye to an eagle's.

Once relieved of the necessity of compelling attention from hither and yon, she conserved her powers and exerted herself only when she could hope for a commensurate result. In following her through the six years prior to 1870, one is struck with her seeming helplessness against herself and against circumstances, and with the preponderant element of blind chance in her life. Before she had been in Lynn a year, she had come to work with some sort of plan, and her life was more orderly and effective than it had ever been before. Her power was one of personality, and people were her material;—her church, which so persistently denies personality, is built upon it. Her abilities were administrative rather than executive, and without a cabinet she exemplified the old fable of the impotence of the head without the body.

Mrs. Glover at first called the thing she taught merely " science," but when she had her professional cards printed they read:

> MRS. MARY M. GLOVER,
> TEACHER OF
> MORAL SCIENCE.

Her first students in Lynn were persons whom Richard Kennedy had cured or friends of his patients. The case of two young men in her first class will serve to illustrate. Mrs. Charles S. Stanley, who was suffering from tuberculosis in an advanced stage, was greatly benefited by Kennedy. She entreated her husband and her half-brother to take instruction under Mrs. Glover, and they did so. Her husband at first felt that he had an aptitude for the subject and eventually became a practising student. As to the half-brother, George Tuttle, Mrs. Glover felt that there she had cast her seed upon stony ground; and certainly he must have been an incongruous figure in the little circle which met in her rooms to " unlearn matter." A stalwart, strapping lad, he had just returned from a cruise to Calcutta on the sailing vessel *John Clark,* which carried ice from Boston Harbour to the Indies. The young seaman, when asked what he thought he would get out of Mrs. Glover's class, replied that he didn't think about it at all, he joined because his sister asked him to. He even tried, in a bashful way, to practise a little, but he says that when he actually cured a girl of dropsy, he was so surprised and frightened that he washed his hands of Moral Science.

Mrs. Glover's course consisted of twelve lectures and extended over a period of three weeks. Her students were required to make a copy of the Quimby manuscript which Mrs. Glover called " The Science of Man," and although each was allowed to keep his copy, he was usually put under a formal three-thousand-dollar bond not to show it. As soon as the student had taken the final lesson, Mrs. Glover addressed him or her as " Doctor," and considered that a degree had been conferred. Often she wrote her students a congratulatory letter upon their graduation, addressing them by their newly acquired titles.

The members of her first class in Lynn each paid one hundred dollars for the lessons. Each also agreed to give Mrs. Glover a percentage on the income from his practice. Tuttle and Stanley executed an agreement with her which was substantially in the following words:

" Lynn, Aug. 15, 1870. We, the undersigned, do hereby

agree in consideration of instruction and manuscripts received from Mrs. Mary Baker Glover, to pay one hundred dollars in advance and ten per cent. annually on the income that we receive from practising or teaching the science. We also agree to pay her one thousand dollars in case we do not practise or teach the above-mentioned science that she has taught us. (Signed) G. H. Tuttle, Charles S. Stanley."

Trouble arose between George Tuttle and Charles Stanley and their teacher, and Mrs. Glover dismissed Stanley from the class. Although he afterward practised mental healing with some success, it was not with Mrs. Glover's sanction, and he finally became a homœopathic physician. In 1879 Mrs. Glover brought a suit in equity in the Essex County Court against Tuttle and Stanley for unpaid tuition. Judge George F. Choate,[1] the referee in the case, at his death left among his papers his book of minutes on this case of " Mary B. Eddy vs. G. H. Tuttle et al."—written out in long hand, which throws light on Mrs. Glover's methods of teaching and on her relation to her pupils. Judge Choate's notes on Stanley's testimony are in part as follows:

I went to Mrs. Eddy for the purpose of taking lessons—She pretended to teach me—She never taught me anything—I never told anybody I practised her method.

I was acquainted with Dr. Kennedy in Lynn. He practised physical manipulation. He first led me to commence practice, etc.—My wife was doctored by Dr. Kennedy—My wife told me Mrs. Eddy wanted to see me. I went, and Mrs. Eddy said she was about starting a class for others like me—She said she had manuscripts, not books, etc. She said she taught setting bones and obstetrics—she said she could teach me in six weeks to be as good a physician as any in the city. She wanted $100. I said I was too poor and could not pay—I left. My wife and I went

---

[1] George F. Choate of Salem was for many years probate judge in Essex County, Mass.

again in the evening, and she urged me—finally I paid her $25 advance. Then I saw Tuttle with a manuscript. He said to get one to copy. I got paper. I asked her to postpone my lessons till, etc.—She said you don't require to eat in order to live. I said yes. She said she had got so far that she could live without eating. She called me and Tuttle to a room, showed me a paper. When she asked us to sign, I objected— She said when we had learned this and the other one (manuscript) which she would have for us, she would go with us and find a place, etc., and on these conditions, i. e., that she would teach us obstetrics, setting bones, and would go with us and find place, etc., I signed the agreement.[2]

She said she always went with students to see them well located, that she required this agreement—that she furnished other manuscripts, that this one was only a commencement.

She turned me out of the class at the end of three weeks. She told me I couldn't practise her method anyway because I was a Baptist—We were to have a six weeks' course, and it was at end of two weeks she told me to leave.

Finding that I could have a good effect upon my wife when she was sick and would have severe coughing spells, I thought likely I could have a good effect upon others. I saw what was in those manuscripts and asked her when the others she spoke of were coming. I asked her what to do if called to a person with a broken limb—She said if so, tell them there isn't any broken limb, that it is all belief, etc.

The testimony of George H. Tuttle, in the same suit, is recorded in Judge Choate's minutes as follows:

In 1870 I knew Mrs. Eddy—was a student of hers. My sister was being attended by Dr. Kennedy, and through my sister I was induced to go up to Mrs. Eddy's with Dr. Stanley and my sister. We signed an agreement—This is the agreement—She showed us how all diseases could be cured and that there was no sort of disease that she could not cure—Said that she would make us more successful than any physician.

The instructions were simply that we were to understand the teachings of the manuscript and that fully understanding it we should be able to heal all disease—We took lessons for a week and a half to two weeks, in the evenings only,—but every day, I think—There used to be an abundance of talk between her and Stanley—Considerable misunderstanding—about payments—and about his religion. She said that he couldn't be a success in this line so long as he adhered to the Baptist faith.

---

[2] The text of this agreement is given above.

She said she could walk on the water—Could live without eating—He disputed with her—Offered to stand it without eating as long as she, and she backed down—She was to enable us to heal *all* diseases—bone-setting—obstetrics—and to treat everything successfully,—and she was to go with us and see that we had success.

She used to hold up consumption and tell us that there was no such thing as lungs—no liver—and they were all imagination—She became dissatisfied sometimes with him (Stanley) and sometimes with me—Finally she recalled the manuscripts, claiming that she wanted to make some alterations. I haven't got mine back, but she gave me another one finally. This is the one. Our instructions ceased—She had taken our manuscripts, and we were literally turned out—I learned from Stanley that he had been dismissed.

We went to see her and demanded our manuscripts—Did not get them— She complained of him, said she was dissatisfied—that he had fallen from grace and was going back on it—was attracted to the Baptist belief, etc., and he could not go on—Dr. Stanley and I went up together for the manuscripts. I don't remember the talk, but there were faultfindings.

She was dissatisfied with him—because he didn't pay—and with his dulness and inability to comprehend it (her Science)—In the first place she had held out to us that the knowledge of her principle and the possession of this power would surely attract patients to us, so that we couldn't fail to get patients—She said she had seen the dead raised—I didn't know if dead could be raised—I in part believed that those apparently dead had been raised.

I got treatment by Dr. Kennedy—In as much as she sent us out to Dr. Kennedy for a (practical) example, I suppose,—She taught rubbing, putting hand in water and upon the stomach, etc.

She claimed that Stanley must surrender everything, surrender the Baptist as every other creed—At the time we went for our manuscripts we were both turned out—Stanley gave her a piece of his mind—told her she was a fraud, etc.

I never regularly practised, because I never understood it.

Stanley said to her she was a fraud in getting the manuscripts back and generally—He was very mistrustful throughout. I don't think he had studied even the three weeks out.

She said she would give us other manuscripts in reference to bone setting—I don't remember what she said about obstetrics; she said generally that he would have only to walk into the room and be filled with the understanding, and all pain would disappear—I don't know but that something further was to be done in cases of bone setting.

When Mrs. Eddy took the stand, she said:

I told the defendant it was a very good method and better than I had found before of healing sick. I taught him the method. I told him it was through the action of mind upon the body—Don't recollect that I said it would cure *all* diseases. I didn't limit or unlimit it. I don't know that I meant for him to understand that it will heal everything—I presume I intended him to understand that it was a better method than any other. I don't think I ever told any student that it would heal every disease. I cannot give you an explanation—you have not studied it. The principle is mind operating on the body.

The mind is cause of disease—Through mind scarlet fever and diphtheria are cured—I have found that through the action of mind I could cure, as I have done, apoplexy, paralysis, etc.,—Heart disease, enlargement of heart, consumption are cured by mind—I have cured cases of consumption found hopeless by action of mind, blindness, deafness, etc.

The Prisoner of Chillon found that gray hairs are produced through the mind—I haven't tried my system on old age yet.

I didn't promise to teach him bone setting or obstetrics. Nor that I would furnish other manuscripts, nor that I would go with him to find his place, etc. Might have said I would make him a good physician— I taught him the application of hands and water—He told me he hadn't the means to pay me and that if I would take him by installments, he would study—I didn't dismiss him, but he said " I understand enough now to do more than any of your students," that he knew enough now to go right into practice.

I never taught mesmerism. I did teach the laying on of hands—not with power—I did teach manipulation in 'sixty-seven, 'sixty-eight and 'sixty-nine and in 'seventy—I ceased—I can't tell the date—Can't tell if 'seventy, 'seventy-one.

I did teach Mr. Stanley manipulation—that was not my principle, it was my method—My method was metaphysical—I taught it—I don't know for what—it was because I saw a hand helped me—I thought it was a good method—I can't say whether it is a science, I can't say whether a part or the whole of it is a science—if it is practised right it is a science—that part which is effective and heals the sick is a science—I don't know as I can explain it. *I do not claim it as a discovery* (manipulation), *I had known of it always. Can't tell if I knew of this will power before I knew Dr. Quimby*—It is not always necessary to know what is the belief.

I should generally require them (my students) to keep the ten commandments—Should require them to be moral.

I can argue to myself that striking my hand upon the table will not produce pain—I don't think I could produce the effect that this knife would not produce a wound, but that I could argue myself out of the pain. I have not claimed to have gone as far as that. I have said that belongs to future time. I can alleviate—I cannot prevent a broken bone. I would send for a surgeon and set the bone—and after that I would alleviate the pain and inflammation. Can't do more in my present development—*I have seen the dead in understanding raised* [3]—The infant is the son of the parent and the parents' mind governs its mind—Through the parents' mind I cure the infant.

Before 1872 I taught manipulation and the use of water.

That was not all I taught—I never said that was the science, but I said it was a method, and until I saw a student doing great evil, etc. [4]

Richard Kennedy in his testimony said:

I went to Lynn to practise with Mrs. Eddy. Our partnership was only in the practice, not in her teaching.

I practised healing the sick by physical manipulation—The mode was operating upon the head giving vigorous rubbing—This was a part of her system that I had learned—The special thing she was to teach me was the science of healing by soul power—I have never been able to come to knowledge of that principle—She gave me a great deal of instruction of the so-called principle, but I have not been able to understand it—She claimed that it would cure advanced stages of consumption and the worse cases of violent disease, that these were but trifles under her Science.

I was there at the time Stanley was there—I made the greatest effort to practise upon her principle, and I have never had any proof that I had attained to it or had any success from it.

I had nothing to do with the instructions—She told me that she had expelled Mr. Stanley from the class—of his incompetency to understand her science—that it was impossible to convince him of the folly of his times—*that his faith in a personal God and prayer was such that she could not overcome it—She used the word Baptist in connection with him because he was a Baptist—but it was the same with all other creeds.*

So long as they believed in a personal God and the response to prayer, they could not progress in the scientific religion—I performed the manipulation of Mr. Stanley as follows:

Mrs. Eddy requested me to rub Mr. Stanley's head and to lay special stress upon the idea that there was no personal God, while I was rubbing him.

I never entirely gave up my belief in a personal God, though my belief was pretty well shaken up.

---

[3] See letter to W. W. Wright on page 149.
[4] Reference to Richard Kennedy.

In rendering a decision in favour of Tuttle and Stanley, Judge Choate said:

Upon a careful examination I do not find any instructions given by her nor any explanations of her "science" or "method of healing" which appear intelligible to ordinary comprehension, or which could in any way be of value in fitting the Defendant as a competent and successful practitioner of any intelligible art or method of healing the sick, and I am of opinion that the consideration for the agreement has wholly failed, and I so find.

Within a few weeks after her first class was organised, Mrs. Glover raised her tuition fee to three hundred dollars, which price was never afterward changed. Concerning her reasons for fixing upon this sum, Mrs. Eddy says:

When God impelled me to set a price on my instruction in Christian Science Mind-healing, I could think of no financial equivalent for an impartation of a knowledge of that divine power which heals; but I was led to name three hundred dollars as the price for each pupil in one course of lessons at my college,—a startling sum for tuition lasting barely three weeks. This amount greatly troubled me. I shrank from asking it, but was finally led, by a strange providence, to accept this fee.

God has since shown me, in multitudinous ways, the wisdom of this decision; and I beg disinterested people to ask my loyal students if they consider three hundred dollars any real equivalent for my instruction during twelve half-days, or even in half as many lessons.[5]

In 1888 Mrs. Eddy reduced the course of twelve lessons to seven, but the tuition fee still remained three hundred dollars. In the *Christian Science Journal* for December, 1888, she published the following notice:

Having reached a place in teaching where my students in Christian Science are taught more during seven lessons in the primary class than they were formerly in twelve, and taught all that is profitable at one time, hereafter the primary class will include seven lessons only. As this number of lessons is of more value than twice this number in times past, no change is made in the price of tuition, three hundred dollars. Mary Baker G. Eddy.

[5] *Retrospection and Introspection*, p. 71.

Most of Mrs. Glover's early students were artisans; many of them shoe-workers.   Lynn was then a city of about thirty thousand inhabitants, and shoemaking was, as it now is, the large and characteristic industry.   Many of the farmers about the country had little shoeshops in their backyards, and during the winter season took out piecework from the factories.   The majority of the village and country boys had had something to do with shoemaking before they went into business or chose a profession, and when Whittier went from the farm to attend the academy at Haverhill, he was able to pay his way by making slippers.   Among Mrs. Glover's first students were S. P. Bancroft, a shoe-worker; George W. Barry, foreman in a shoeshop; Dorcas Rawson, a shoe-worker, and her sister Mrs. Miranda R. Rice; Charles S. Stanley, a shoe-worker; Miss Frances Spinney, who had a shop in which she employed a score of girls to sew on women's shoes; Mrs. Otis Vickary; George H. Allen, who was employed in his father's box factory, and Wallace W. Wright, then accountant in a bank.

Liberal religious ideas flourished in New England thirty-five years ago, and although one woman left the class because " Mrs. Glover was taking Christ away from her," most of the students were ready to accept the idea of an impersonal God and to deny the existence of matter.   Even Dorcas Rawson, who was an ardent Methodist and had " professed holiness," unhesitatingly accepted the statement that God was Principle.

From the very beginning of her teaching Mrs. Glover had with her students those differences which later made her career so stormy.   After the defection of Stanley and Tuttle, Mrs. Vickary, dissatisfied with her instruction, sued for and recovered the one hundred and fifty dollars which she had paid in advance for tuition.[6]   Wallace Wright, one of the most intelligent of her early students, publicly attacked in the Lynn press the " Moral Science," as it was then called, which he had studied under Mrs. Glover.

Wallace W. Wright was the son of a Universalist clergyman of Lynn, and a brother of Carroll D. Wright, who afterward became United States Commissioner of Labour.   He was regarded as one of the most promising young business men in Lynn, when he was drowned in the wreck of the *City of Columbus*, off Gayhead Light, January 18, 1884.   When he first studied under Mrs. Glover, he was very enthusiastic over her Science and, much to his own surprise, made several successful demonstrations.

Before he entered her class, he had made careful inquiries about the nature of what she taught.   Both he and his father were interested in her claims and wished to pin Mrs. Glover down to exact statements concerning her Science.   He wrote her a letter, asking her nine questions, and requesting an answer to each in writing.

(*Here follow the most significant of Mr. Wright's questions, together with Mrs. Glover's answers*):[7]

QUESTION 1—Upon what principle is your science founded?
ANSWER 1—On God, the principle of man.

---

[6] The suit, Mrs. Otis Vickary *versus* Mary M. B. Patterson, was entered in the Lynn Police Court on August 3, 1872.   (Mrs. Glover had not yet obtained legal right to use her former name.)   The Lynn Five Cent Savings-Bank was summoned as Trustee.   Both the Savings-Bank and the Defendant were defaulted, apparently for failure to appear and answer, and judgment was rendered for the Plaintiff, and execution issued for the amount of $150 and $5.73 for costs, on August 9th.

[7] Mr. Wright's sixth question and Mrs. Glover's answer, in which she admits that Dr. Quimby practised her Science and had made it a subject of research for twenty-five years, was quoted on page 101.

QUESTION 2—Is a knowledge of anatomy necessary to the success of the student or practitioner?

ANSWER 2—It is a hindrance instead of help, anatomy belongs to knowledge, the Science I teach, to God, one is the tree whereof wisdom forbade man to partake, the other is the " tree of life."

QUESTION 3—Will it meet the demands of extreme, acute cases?

ANSWER 3—Yes, beyond all other known methods of healing; it is in acute and extreme cases that this science is seen most clearly in its demonstrations over matter.

QUESTION 4—Is a knowledge of disease necessary to effect cures?

ANSWER 4—This " knowledge " is what science comes to destroy.

.   .   .   .

QUESTION 7—Does it admit of universal application?

ANSWER 7—*Yes,* even to raising or restoring those called dead. I have witnessed this myself, therefore I testify of what I have seen.[8]

In June, 1871, Mr. Wright went to Knoxville, Tenn., and there entered into practice. Of this experience he afterward wrote:

The 9th of last June found me in Knoxville, Tennessee, as assistant to a former student. We met with good success in a majority of our cases, but some of them utterly refused to yield to the treatment. Soon after settling in Knoxville I began to question the propriety of calling this treatment " Moral Science" instead of mesmerism. Away from the influence of argument which the teacher of this so-called science knows how to bring to bear upon students with such force as to outweigh any attempts they may make at the time to oppose it, I commenced to think more independently, and to argue with myself as to the truth of the positions we were called upon to take. The result of this course was to convince me that I had studied the science of mesmerism.[9]

Wright accordingly wrote to Mrs. Glover from Knoxville, asking her to refund the three hundred dollars which he had paid for his tuition and also to compensate him for the two hundred dollars which his venture had cost him. On his return to Lynn

---

[8] In Mrs. Eddy's testimony in her suit against Stanley and Tuttle, printed in this article. she states that she has seen the *dead in understanding* awaken through her Science.—See page 145.

[9] Lynn *Transcript,* January 13, 1872.

he called upon Mrs. Glover and repeated this request. On January 13, 1872, Mr. Wright published a signed letter in the Lynn *Transcript*, stating that he believed Moral Science and Mesmerism to be one and the same thing, and warning other students against being misled. Mrs. Glover replied to this letter in the same paper, January 20th, stating that Mr. Wright had made an unreasonable demand to which she had refused to accede, and that he was now attacking her Science from motives of revenge:

'Tis but a few weeks since he called on me and threatened that if I did not refund his tuition fee and pay him $200 *extra* he would prevent my ever having another class in this city. Said he, "my simple purpose now is revenge, and I will have it"—and this, too, immediately after saying to individuals in this city that the last lesson the class received of which he was a member, was alone worth all he had paid for tuition. . . . Very soon after this, however, I received a letter from him requesting me to pay him over and above all I had received from him, or in case I should not, he would ruin the Science. I smiled at the threat and told a lady at my side, "If you see him, tell him first to take a bucket and dip the Atlantic dry, and then try his powers on this next scheme." . . .

My few remaining years will be devoted to the cause I have espoused, viz:—to teach and to demonstrate the Moral and Physical Science that can heal the sick. Well knowing as I do that God hath bidden me, I shall steadfastly adhere to my purpose to benefit my suffering fellow-beings, even though it be amid the most malignant misrepresentation and persecution.

MARY M. B. GLOVER

This controversy continued several weeks, occupying columns of the *Transcript*, and on February 10th, Mr. Wright issued the following challenge:

And now in conclusion I publicly challenge Mrs. Mary Baker Glover to demonstrate her science by any of the following methods, promising, if she is successful, to retract *all* I have said, and humble myself by asking forgiveness publicly for the course I have taken. Her refusal to do this, by silence or otherwise, shall be considered a failure of her cause:

1st: To restore the dead to life again as she claims she can.

2nd: To walk upon the water without the aid of artificial means as she claims she can.

3rd: To live 24 hours without air, or 24 days without nourishment of any kind without its having any effect upon her.

4th: To restore sight when the optic nerve has been destroyed.

5th: To set and heal a broken bone without the aid of artificial means.

I am, respectfully,

W. W. WRIGHT

At this point Mrs. Glover retired from the controversy, but five of her students, George W. Barry, Amos Ingalls, George H. Allen, Dorcas Rawson, and Miranda Rice wrote a protest to the Lynn *Transcript*, February 17th, ignoring Mr. Wright's challenge, but defending their teacher and her Science, and declaring that his charges against both were untrue. Mr. Wright had the last word and ended the controversy, February 24th, by exultantly declaring that Mrs. Glover and her Science were practically dead and buried; which certainly suggests that the gift of prophecy was denied him.

Mrs. Glover's pen at this period was not employed exclusively in controversy. In the Lynn *Transcript*, November 4, 1871, appear the following verses:

LINES ON RECEIVING SOME GRAPES

By Mary Baker Glover

Beautiful grapes would I were thee,
  Clustering round a parent stem,
The blessing of my God to be,
  In woodland, bower or glen;

Where friend or foe had never sought
  The angels " born of apes,"
And breathed the disappointed thought,
  Behold ! They're sour grapes.

And such, methinks, e'en Nature shows
    The fate of Beauty's power—
Admired in parlour, grotto, groves,
    But faded, O how sour!

Worth,—unlike beauty—fadeless, pure,
    A blessing and most blest,
Beyond the shadows will endure,
    And give the lone heart rest.

For the *Transcript*.

Though Mrs. Glover's classes grew larger, and Richard Kennedy's practice steadily increased, frequent disagreements occurred between him and his teacher.   He found that the Quimby method was, like every other method of treating disease, limited in its scope, and urged Mrs. Glover to modify her sweeping statements concerning its possibilities—which greatly angered her.   His common-sense rebelled when Mrs. Glover told her students that she could hold her finger in the flame of a candle without feeling pain, and her grim ambition rather repelled him.   Although he was almost filial in his dutifulness, her tyranny in trivial matters tried even his genial temper.   About a year after they opened their office, Miss Magoun married John M. Dame of Lynn, and gave up her school, leaving the Moral Scientists to sublet from another tenant.

On Thanksgiving night of that year (1871) Mrs. Glover and Kennedy went to Mrs. Dame's new home to play cards. At the card-table Kennedy and Mrs. Glover played against each other, Kennedy and his partner playing, apparently, the better game.   Mrs. Glover, who could not endure to be beaten in anything, lost her temper and declared that Richard had cheated.   The young man was chagrined at being thus

RICHARD KENNEDY

From a photograph taken in Lynn, Mass., in 1871

taken to task before his friends.   The frequent scenes caused by Mrs. Glover's jealous and exacting disposition had worn out his patience.   When he and Mrs. Glover reached home that night, he tore his contract with her in two and threw it into the fire, telling her that he would no longer consider himself bound by it.   Mrs. Glover threatened and entreated, but to no purpose, and even when she fell to the floor in a swoon Kennedy was not to be moved.

From that night Kennedy prepared to leave Mrs. Glover. Their separation took place in the spring of 1872.   When they settled their accounts, Mrs. Glover was left with about six thousand dollars in money.   While they remained together, Kennedy had paid their living expenses and had given Mrs. Glover half of whatever money was left from his practice, while Mrs. Glover's income from teaching was entirely her own.

After this separation Kennedy took another office in Lynn, and Mrs. Glover remained for some months in their old rooms. She afterward boarded with the Chadwells on Shepard Street, later stayed at the home of Dorcas Rawson, and still later lived for some time in a boarding-house at Number 9 Broad Street, opposite the house which she eventually purchased.

The Essex County registry of deeds shows that on March 31, 1875, Francis E. Besse, in consideration of $5,650, deeded to " Mary M. B. Glover, a widow woman of Lynn," the property at Number 8 Broad Street, which became the first official headquarters of Christian Science.[10]   This house, a small two-and-a-half story building, is still standing.   When Mrs. Glover moved in, shortly after her purchase, she occupied only the second

---

[10] When Mrs. Glover bought this property, she assumed the mortgage on it of $2,800.

floor, renting the first floor of the house to a succession of tenants. She used as her study a little low-ceiled room on the third floor, lighted by one window and a skylight. Here she completed the manuscript of *Science and Health,* read the proofs of the first edition, and prepared the second and third editions. The Christian Science reading-room of Lynn is now in this building. At the time of the June communions [11] at the Mother Church in Boston, thousands of people go out to visit the little skylight room which they regard as the cradle of their faith. The room has, of course, been changed since Mrs. Eddy worked there. The woodwork has been painted white, and the walls and ceiling are now pale blue and cream colour, dotted with gold stars. None of the original furniture remains; but the chair and table are said to be very like those which Mrs. Eddy used, and on the shelf is a clock like that which used to count the hours while Mrs. Eddy measured time out of existence. On the low wall there hangs—not without a stirring effect of contrast—a very light and airy water-colour of the gray tower of the original Mother Church in Boston. Over the door is frescoed the First Commandment:

" Thou shalt have no other Gods before me."

---

[11] These yearly communions at the Mother Church in Boston have this year (1908) been discontinued by order of Mrs. Eddy.

CHAPTER X

WHATEVER disagreement Mrs. Glover had with individual
students, their number constantly increased, and for every de-
serter there were several new adherents. Her following grew
not only in numbers but in zeal; her influence over her students
and their veneration of her were subjects of comment and astonishment in Lynn. Of some of them it could be truly said that
they lived only for and through Mrs. Glover. They continued
to attend in some manner to their old occupations, but they
became like strangers to their own families, and their personalities seemed to have undergone an eclipse. Like their teacher,
they could talk of only one thing and had but one vital interest.
One disciple let two of his three children die under metaphysical
treatment without a murmur. Another married the woman
whom Mrs. Glover designated. Two students furnished the
money to bring out her first book, though Mrs. Glover at that
time owned the house in which she lived, and her classes were
fairly remunerative.

The closer students, who constituted Mrs. Glover's cabinet
and bodyguard, executed her commissions, transacted her business, and were always at her call. To-day some of these who

have long been accounted as enemies by Mrs. Eddy, and whom she has anathematised in print and discredited on the witness-stand, still declare that what they got from her was beyond equivalent in gold or silver.   They speak of a certain spiritual or emotional exaltation which she was able to impart in her classroom; a feeling so strong that it was like the birth of a new understanding and seemed to open to them a new heaven and a new earth.   Some of Mrs. Glover's students experienced this in a very slight degree, and some not at all, but such as were imaginative and emotional, and especially those who had something of the mystic in their natures, came out of her class-room to find that for them the world had changed.   They lived by a new set of values; the colour seemed to fade out of the physical world about them; men and women became shadow-like, and their own humanity grew pale.   The reality of pain and pleasure, sin and grief, love and death, once denied, the only positive thing in their lives was their belief—and that was almost wholly negation.   One of the students who was closest to Mrs. Glover at that time says that to him the world outside her little circle seemed like a madhouse, where each inmate was given over to his delusion of love or gain or ambition, and the problem which confronted him was how to awaken them from the absurdity of their pursuits.   It is but fair to say that occasionally a student was more of a royalist than the king, and that Mrs. Glover herself had a very sound sense of material values and often reminded an extravagant follower to render unto Cæsar what was his due.

Among the enthusiasts of Mrs. Glover's following was Daniel Harrison Spofford, who became a very successful practitioner of mental healing, and at one time had offices in Boston, Haverhill, and Newburyport, dividing his time among the three places. Spofford was one of the most interesting of Mrs. Glover's students and an important factor in the early development of Christian Science.[1] He was born at Temple, N. H., and when he was a boy of ten came to eastern Massachusetts with his brother and widowed mother. He was put out to work for farmers about the country, and, although he was a frail boy, he did a man's work. He was working as a watchmaker's apprentice when, in his twentieth year, he entered the army. He enlisted in '61 and served in the Army of the Potomac, in Hooker's brigade, until he was mustered out in '64, taking part in some twenty engagements, among them Gettysburg and the second battle of Bull Run. On his return from the army he went to work in a shoe factory in Lynn. He first met Mrs. Glover in 1871, when she was with Richard Kennedy, and he had access, through another student, to the manuscripts from which she taught. During the next three years, which he spent in the South and West, he carried these manuscripts with him and studied them. He was thoughtful and reflective by nature, and even when he was a chore boy on the farm he read the Bible diligently and went about his work in the barn and in the field, pondering deeply upon the paradoxes of the old theology. He had worked out a kind of transcendentalism of his own, and he found something in the Quimby manuscripts which satisfied a need of his nature. When he came back to Lynn, in the spring of 1875, he began to experiment among his friends in the healing power of this

---

[1] Mr. Spofford now lives opposite the old Whittier homestead, on the road between Haverhill and Amesbury.

system, and made several cures which were much talked about. Mrs. Glover soon heard of this and sent Spofford a letter, in which she said: " Mr. Spofford I tender you a cordial invitation to join my next class and receive my instruction in healing the sick without medicine, without money and without price."

Spofford, who was then about thirty-three years of age, accordingly entered Mrs. Glover's class in April, 1875, and in a few weeks her teaching had become to him the most important thing in the world. Mr. Spofford still says that no price could be put upon what Mrs. Glover gave her students, and that the mere manuscripts which he had formerly studied were, compared to her expounding of them, as the printed page of a musical score compared to its interpretation by a master. His teacher recognised in him a mind singularly adapted to her subject, and a nature sincere and free from self-seeking. She turned many of her students over to him for instruction in Scriptural interpretation, addressed him as " Harry," and showed her appreciation of his loyalty by presenting to him, in a silver case, the gold pen with which *Science and Health* was written.

In May, a month after he entered her class, Mr. Spofford opened an office in Lynn and put out his sign, " Dr. Spofford, Scientific Physician." His success was as rapid as Richard Kennedy's had been, although it would be difficult to find two men more unlike than these, who were perhaps the most intelligent and able of all Mrs. Glover's practising students. Kennedy was cheerful, impulsive, practical, and blessed with a warm enjoyment of the world as it is. He made a host of friends, whom he managed to see very often, and always found a thousand agreeable duties which he discharged punctiliously. Spofford was an idealist, somewhat tinged with the gentle melancholy of the dreamer—a type with which the literature of New England has made us all familiar. His frame was delicate, his hands and features finely cut, and his eyes were intense and very blue in colour. His voice was low, and his manner gentle and somewhat aloof.

Foremost in loyalty among Mrs. Glover's women students was Mrs. Miranda Rice, who remained in constant attendance upon her, acting as mediator between her and recalcitrant students, and attending her in those violent seizures of hysteria which continued to torture her. Mrs. Rice says that during these attacks the poor woman would often lie unconscious for hours together; at other times she would seem almost insane, would denounce all her friends, declare that they were all persecuting and wronging her, and that she would run away, never to come back.

In spite of the hardships of her service, Mrs. Rice remained Mrs. Glover's friend for about twelve years—Mrs. Glover rarely kept her friends so long. Mrs. Rice always felt under obligation to her teacher, for she had paid no tuition when she entered her class, and one of Mrs. Glover's most noted demonstrations—for years recounted in succeeding editions of *Science and Health*—occurred when she attended Mrs. Rice in childbed. Mrs. Rice still affirms that the birth was absolutely painless.

George W. Barry, a student who avowed that Mrs. Glover had cured him of consumption, was long active in her service and he always addressed her as " Mother." Once when Bronson Alcott, that undiscouraged patron of metaphysical cults, went

to Lynn upon an invitation from Mrs. Glover and addressed
her class, he turned to Barry and, struck by his youthful
appearance, asked, " How old are you, young man? " Barry
replied, " I am five years old, sir," explaining that it was five
years ago that he first began to study under Mrs. Glover. Two
years after he had thus defined existence, Barry sued Mrs.
Glover, then Mrs. Eddy, for money due him for services to her
extending over a period of five years; some of the instances
set forth in his bill of particulars give an interesting glimpse
of life at Number 8 Broad Street. Among the services rendered, as stated in this bill, was: " Copying the manuscript of
the book entitled *Science and Health*, and aiding in arrangement of capital letters and some of the grammatical construc-
tions." (The Referee in the case found that Barry had copied
out in long hand twenty-five hundred pages, and allowed him
more than the usual copyist rate, " on account of the difficulty
which a portion of the pages presented to the copyist by reason
of erasures and interlineations.") Other services mentioned in
Barry's bill were: " Copying manuscript for classes and helping to arrange the construction of some of the sentences ";
" copying Mrs. Glover's replies to W. W. Wright's newspaper
articles "; " searching for a publisher "; " moving her goods
from the tenement on South Common Street, Lynn, i.e., dispos-
ing of some at the auction room, storing others in my uncle's
barn, and storing trunks and goods at my father's house,
clearing up rooms, paying rent for the same "; " attending
to her financial business, i.e., withdrawing monies from Boston
savings banks, going to Boston to get United States coupon
bonds, taking in my care two mortgages," etc.

Further services mentioned in Barry's bill were: "Aiding in buying and caring for the place at Number 8 Broad Street; aiding in selection of carpets and furniture, helping to move, putting down carpets, etc., and working in the garden." In his bill of expenditures he said that he had paid out money on Mrs. Glover's account for rent, car-fare, postage, stationery, printing, express charges, and boots. In her reply Mrs. Glover stated that she had repaid him for all these expenditures, and that the boots were a present from the plaintiff. On the witness-stand she further stated that she taught him "how to make an interrogation point and what capitals to attach to the names of the Deity." She affirmed that she had cured him of disease. "I gave him mind as one would treat a patient with material medicine," she told the judge. Mrs. Glover later reproachfully published some verses which she said Barry wrote her before his defection:

> O, mother mine, God grant I ne'er forget,
> Whatever be my grief or what my joy,
> The unmeasured, unextinguishable debt
> I owe to thee, but find my sweet employ
> Ever through thy remaining days to be
> To thee as faithful as thou wast to me.[2]

Surrounded as she was by these admiring students, who hung upon her words and looked to her for the ultimate wisdom, Mrs. Glover gradually became less acutely conscious of Quimby's relation to the healing system she taught. She herself was being magnified and exalted daily by her loyal disciples, in whose extravagant devotion she saw repeated the attitude of

---

[2] *Science and Health* (1881), Vol. II., p. 15.

many of Quimby's patients—herself among them—to their healer. Instead of pointing always backward and reiterating, " I *learned* this from Dr. *Quimby*," etc., she began to acquiesce in the belief of her students, who regarded her as the source of what she taught. Her infatuated students, indeed, desired to see no further than their teacher, and doubtless would not have looked beyond her had she pointed. Consequently she said less and less about Quimby as time went on, and by 1875, when her first book, *Science and Health*, was issued, she had crowded him altogether out of his " science." [3]

In the history of the Quimby manuscript, from which she taught during the five years, 1870-1875, one can trace the steps by which Mrs. Glover, starting as the humble and grateful patient of Quimby, arrived at the position of rival, and pre-tender to his place. We have seen that while she was in Stoughton, Mrs. Glover wrote a preface, signed " Mary M. Glover," to her copy of Quimby's manuscript, " Questions and Answers," and that she made slight changes in, and additions to, the text. In examining the copies of this manuscript which were given out to her students in Lynn, 1870-1872, we find that this signed preface has been incorporated in the text, so that the manuscript reads like the composition of one person, and that instead of being issued with a title-page, reading " Extracts from P. P. Quimby's Writings," as was the Stough-ton manuscript, the copies given out in Lynn were unsigned. This manuscript Mrs. Glover called " The Science of Man, or the Principle which Controls Matter." In 1870 she took out a copyright upon a book entitled: *The Science of Man by which*

---

[3] There is only a casual mention of Quimby in the first edition of *Science and Health*.

*the Sick are Healed Embracing Questions and Answers in Moral
Science Arranged for the Learner by Mrs. Mary Baker Glover.*
This seems to have been only a precautionary measure, however,
as she took no steps to publish the pamphlet until 1876.   When
it appeared, it contained allusions to events which happened
after 1872, and it must have been largely rewritten after the
date of the copyright.

In Stoughton " The Science of Man " was the only manuscript from which Mrs. Glover taught.   By the time she arrived
in Lynn, however, she had worked out another treatise, which
she sometimes entitled " Scientific Treatise on Mortality, As
Taught by Mrs. M. B. Glover," and sometimes gave no title
at all.   Mr. Horatio Dresser and Mr. George A. Quimby, the
two persons best acquainted with Phineas P. Quimby's writings,
say that this second manuscript is only partially his, and
seems to be made up of extracts from his writings, woven together and interspersed with much that must have been Mrs.
Glover's own.   In her early teaching in Lynn she gave out
this new manuscript, first requiring her pupils to learn it by
heart, and following it up with " The Science of Man," which
still formed the basis of her lectures.   She occasionally reinforced her instruction by giving to a promising pupil still a
third manuscript, also a combination of Quimby and herself,
which she called " Soul's Inquiries of Man."   At first, however,
Mrs. Glover gave Quimby credit for the authorship of the three
manuscripts, even for the two which seem to have been partly
her own composition.

The next important change in her manuscript occurred in the
spring of 1872, when Richard Kennedy left her.   Mrs. Glover

was then without a practising student—a serious disadvantage to her—and she was so angered that she conceived for Kennedy a violent hatred, from which, without the slightest provocation on his part, she suffered intensely for many years, and from which it may be justly said she still suffers. Kennedy simply changed his office, refused to discuss Mrs. Glover at all, and went on practising. His success so annoyed Mrs. Glover that she wished to repudiate him and his methods, and to do this it was necessary to repudiate what she herself had taught him. She therefore announced that she had discovered that the method of treatment which she had taught Kennedy (i.e., wetting and rubbing the patient's head) was harmful and pernicious. Mr. Wright's articles in the Lynn *Transcript* had apparently suggested mesmerism to her, and she now declared that Kennedy was a mesmerist and his treatment mesmerism.[3][1-2] In the first edition of *Science and Health*, page 193, she says:

Sooner suffer a doctor infected with smallpox to be about you than come under the treatment of one that manipulates his patients' heads, and is a traitor to science.

And on page 371:

There is but one possible way of doing wrong with a mental method of healing, and this is mesmerism, whereby the minds of the sick may be controlled with error instead of Truth. . . . For years we had tested the benefits of Truth on the body, and knew no opposite chance for doing evil through a mental method of healing until we saw it traduced by an erring student, and made the medium of error. Introducing falsehoods into the minds of the patients prevented their recovery, and the sins of the doctor was visited on the patients, many of whom died because of this. . . .

Soon after her break with Kennedy she had all her students strike out from their manuscript, "Scientific Treatise on Mortal-

---

[1-2] The story of the beginning and growth of Mrs. Eddy's belief in mesmerism is told in full in Chapter XII.

ity," the passages regarding the manipulation of the patient's head. These passages are within parentheses in the following:

That is, do not be discouraged but hold calmly and persistently on to science that tells you you are right and they are in error, (and wetting your hand in water, rise and rub their head, this rubbing has no virtue only as we believe and others believe we get nearer to them by contact, and now you would rub out a belief and this belief is located in the brain, therefore as an M.D. lays a poultice where the pain is, so you lay your hands where the belief is to rub it forever out) do not address your thoughts for a moment to their body as you mentally argue down their beliefs (and rub their heads) but take yourself, the Soul, to destroy the error of life, sensation and substance in matter to your own belief, as much as in you lies, etc.

" Manipulation," as she called it, became a thing of horror to Mrs. Glover; it was the taint which distinguished the false science from the true.   Now, manipulation had been Quimby's method of treating his patients, and as Mrs. Glover was a person of singularly literal mind, breaking away from that method gave her a sense not only of independence but of conquest.   She considered that she had improved upon the original Quimby method and left it behind her.   She still taught her students to put their fingers upon the patient's head, but the rubbing and the bowl of water were now symbols of the dark abuses of " mental malpractice."   Having abjured them, Mrs. Glover felt that this Science was hers as it had never been before. She felt that she had now a system which was practically her own, and told Dr. Spofford she considered that Quimby had been a detriment to her growth in Science.   The more one studies the illogical and literal quality of Mrs. Glover's mind as evinced in her life and writings, the better one understands how she could readily persuade herself that this was true.

The progress of this assimilation is easily followed:

First—The writing of a signed preface to and the amending of the original Quimby manuscript.

Second—The incorporating of this preface in the text.

Third—The composition of a second manuscript, partly her own, from which she was able to teach successfully.

Fourth—The discontinuation of " manipulation " in treatment.

Fifth—The belief, fostered by her students, that her interpretation of the Quimby manuscript was far beyond the manuscript itself in scope and understanding.

Sixth—The writing of the book, *Science and Health*, begun in the later '60's and finished in 1875, in which Mrs. Glover undoubtedly added much extraneous matter to Quimbyism, and developed self-confidence by presenting ideas of her own.

Although the Christian Science Church was not chartered until 1879, the first attempt at an organisation was made in 1875.   Her students desired Mrs. Glover to conduct services of public worship in Lynn, and to this end formed an association, electing officers, and calling themselves the " Christian Scientists."   In a memorandum book, kept by Daniel H. Spofford in the spring of that year, appears the following entry:

May 26—At a meeting of students, 8 Broad street, there was a committee of three appointed, consisting of Dorcas B. Rawson, George W. Barry and D. H. Spofford, to ascertain what a suitable hall could be rented for, and the amount which could be raised weekly toward sustaining Mrs. Glover as teacher and instructor for one year. Committee to report night of June 1.

This committee entered heartily into its labours and drew up the following pledge, which was signed by eight students:

Whereas, in times not long past, the Science of Healing new to the age, and far in advance of all other modes was introduced into the city of Lynn by its discoverer, a certain lady, Mary Baker Glover,

And, whereas, many friends spread the good tidings throughout the place, and bore aloft the standard of life and truth which had declared freedom to many manacled with the bonds of disease or error,

And, whereas, by the wilful and wicked disobedience of an individual,[4] who has no name in Love Wisdom or Truth, the light was obscured by clouds of misinterpretation and mists of mystery, so that God's work was hidden from the world and derided in the streets,

Now therefore, we, students and advocates of this moral science called the Science of Life, . . . have arranged with the said Mary Baker Glover, to preach to us or direct our meetings on the Sabbath of each week, and hereby covenant with one another, and by these presents do publish and proclaim, that we have agreed and do each and all agree to pay weekly, for one year, beginning with the sixth day of June, A.D., 1875, to a treasurer chosen by at least seven students the amount set opposite our names, provided nevertheless the moneys paid by us shall be expended for no other purpose or purposes than the maintenance of said Mary Baker Glover as teacher or instructor, than the renting of a suitable hall and other necessary incidental expenses, and our signatures shall be a full and sufficient guarantee of our faithful performance of this contract.

Mr. Spofford's memorandum book continues the story of this association:

June 1—On receiving the report of the committee it was decided to rent Templars' Hall, Market street, and the first regular meeting to be June 6. Also a business meeting appointed June 8.

June 6—There were probably sixty in attendance at the meeting this evening.

June 8—At the meeting this evening, George H. Allen was chosen president, George W. Barry, secretary, and Daniel H. Spofford, treasurer, the society to be known as the " Christian Scientists." [5]

For five successive Sundays Mrs. Glover discoursed to her pupils in the Templars' Hall, receiving five dollars for each address. The remaining five dollars of the amount subscribed

---

[4] Presumably Richard Kennedy.
[5] This, so far as can be learned, was the first time that Mrs. Glover's students were called " Christian Scientists."

went toward paying incidental expenses. After the first two meetings a number of Spiritualists were attracted to the services. In the discussions following Mrs. Glover's talks they asked questions which annoyed her, and she finally refused to continue her lectures and abolished public services.

Toward the end of the same year the book, *Science and Health,* made its first appearance in print.[6] Mrs. Glover was convinced that it was through this volume that she was to make her way, and that the most important task before her was to advertise it and push its sale. She accordingly entrusted this work to her leading practitioner and chief adviser, Daniel Spofford, persuading him to hand over his thriving practice to one of her new students, Asa Gilbert Eddy.

Mrs. Glover first met Mr. Eddy through Mr. Spofford, to whom Eddy had come as a patient. Although destined to become the husband of Mrs. Glover and his name to be indissolubly associated with Christian Science and made famous throughout two continents, this new student was personally unpretentious and had no suspicion of his future greatness. He was of humble origin, coming from the village of South Londonderry in the Green Mountains, where his father, Asa Eddy, was, according to his neighbours and friends, a hard-working, plodding farmer. His mother, Betsey Smith Eddy, was a more original character, and the children inherited many of her peculiarities. Farm life was not congenial to Mrs. Eddy or her children. Their tastes and inclinations were not for the established and the orderly, and they consequently had little or nothing to do with the routine work of either farm or house.

---

[6] A detailed account of the publication of this important book is given in the next chapter.

ASA GILBERT EDDY

Mrs. Eddy's third husband.   He died in 1882

Mrs. Eddy was not a very marked example of New England housewifely thrift, and she was pretty generally criticised for her " slack " housekeeping and her inattention to her children. The children, indeed, grew up as they would, satisfying their hunger from the " mush-pot " in which they boiled the corn-meal porridge which formed their main diet, and regulating their habits and conduct, each to suit himself.   They met with no interference from their mother, who was much away from home.   Every morning after the children had been sent over to the district school, which was only a few steps from the house, it was Mrs. Eddy's invariable custom to hitch up her horse and set forth on a trip through the country or to the neighbouring towns.   This drive usually lasted all day, and it was the one thing that was performed with promptness and regularity in the Eddy ménage.   To protect herself from rough weather on her expeditions, Mrs. Eddy devised an ingenious costume.   From the front of her large poke bonnet she hung a shawl, in which was inserted a 9 x 10 pane of window glass, so placed that when she donned the costume the glass was opposite her face.   This handy contrivance kept out the wind or rain or snow, without obscuring her vision ; and thus equipped, Mrs. Eddy daily defied the vagaries of Vermont weather.   The children of the village called her " the woman with the looking-glass."

Neighbourly comment and rebuke were lost on mother and children alike.   They themselves enjoyed the unhampered life they led.   It was only those who had a sense of order and regularity who suffered from the Eddy method, and they were all outside the Eddy family, unless indeed, it were Asa Eddy, the father, who may sometimes have grown tired of returning from his day's work in the fields to a deserted house, to make a fire and prepare his own food.

As the boys grew older they were very ingenious about the house. They learned to wash and iron their own clothes as well as to make them, and while none of them would work on the farm with their father they all knew how to run the loom, which their mother kept in the kitchen, and upon which she sometimes wove. They took naturally to the trades, and when they started out for themselves one chose that of a carpenter, another became a cobbler, a third a stone-cutter, a fourth a clock-maker, and Asa Gilbert, the future husband of the founder of the Christian Science Church, was a weaver. As a boy Gilbert had been much with his mother, often accompanying her on her drives and winding the " quills " for her loom on the rare occasions when she felt like spinning or weaving. At school, where he was nicknamed " Githy," [7] he was backward in everything except penmanship, in which he excelled and in which he took great satisfaction. He had considerable personal pride of a kind which showed itself in his odd choice of clothes, his mincing gait, and the elaborate arrangement of his hair, which he trained to curl under in a roll at the back and combed up into a high " roach " in front. Like his brothers he was fond of hunting and spent much of his time shooting at birds or at a target. Sometimes he hired out to a farmer, but only for a few days or weeks at a time, for he had no taste for farming.

The family had no church connections or religious prefer-

---

[7] This nickname was won because Gilbert had a lisp and could not pronounce the words, " geese eggs."

ences, but Mrs. Eddy had pinned her faith to a famous clairvoyant called " Sleeping Lucy," who lived up the valley at Cavendish. " Sleeping Lucy," [8] whose real name was Mrs. Lucy Cook, possessed what she called " a gift of nature," by means of which she passed into a sleep or trance and was able, when in this sleeping state, to diagnose cases of sickness and to prescribe remedies for them. Mrs. Eddy's faith in " Sleeping Lucy " was profound, and whenever any of her family were ill she bundled them up and took them to Cavendish to see the clairvoyant. When Spiritualism was introduced, it appealed at once to Mrs. Eddy, and she and her son Gilbert became ardent believers, attending the Spiritualist meetings and séances for miles around.

When Gilbert left home, about 1860, he went to Springfield, Vt., to run a " spinning jack " in a woollen mill, and later when the woollen mill burned, he found employment in a baby-carriage factory in the same village. Altogether he was in Springfield until late in the 'sixties, and after spending some time again in Londonderry, he drifted to East Boston and became agent for a sewing machine. In spite of the shiftlessness of his bringing up, Gilbert developed a strain of thrift and economy. While in Springfield he had worked regularly and hoarded his savings. He lived by himself in meagre quarters and did his own housework, including his washing, and he made his own trousers. His sister-in-law, Mrs. Washington Eddy of New Haven, Conn., says, that when he visited his brother, he always helped her with the housework, especially with the ironing. She says that " he could do up a shirt as well as any

[8] " Sleeping Lucy " later went to Montpelier and to Boston, where, under another name, she became well known and prosperous.

woman." By means of his good management Gilbert was able to purchase from his parents the deed of their farm, which at his own death went by will to his wife, Mary Baker G. Eddy, who sold it for $1,500 to Stephen Houghton, a neighbour of the Eddys in Londonderry.

It was while Gilbert was acting as sewing machine agent in East Boston that he heard of Daniel H. Spofford as a healer and went to him as a patient. Spofford talked with him about the method he practised and when Eddy became interested, Spofford advised him to study the system and become a practitioner himself. Eddy eagerly accepted the advice and Spofford introduced him to Mrs. Glover, who at once enrolled him as a member of her next class.

People who knew Eddy well in Lynn describe him as a quiet, dull little man, docile and yielding up to a certain point, but capable of a dogged sort of obstinacy. He was short of stature, slow in his movements, and always taciturn. When he first came to Lynn people remarked upon his old-fashioned dress and singular manner of wearing his hair. He usually wore a knitted Cardigan jacket and a long surtout gathered very full at the waist and a light cinnamon in colour.

From their first acquaintance he and his teacher manifested a cordial regard for each other. He alone of all her students was permitted to call her by her first name, Mary, and she addressed him as Gilbert, often speaking of him to other pupils, and extolling his willingness and obedience. After Mr. Spofford's patients had been transferred to Eddy, some of Mrs. Glover's students began to feel that her interest in the new practitioner was out of all proportion to his usefulness in the

Science. Mrs. Glover became aware of this jealousy and was greatly distressed by it. She felt that her students were leaning on her too heavily, and that by demanding her attention and even by thinking about her so constantly, they drained her powers and unfitted her for her work. She spoke much in these days of a temperamental quality which compelled her to take on the ills and perplexities of her friends and to suffer from them as if they were her own. She continually besought her students not to " call upon her " in thought when they were sick or in trouble. For some months before her marriage to Gilbert Eddy she seems to have felt completely at the mercy of her students' minds, and that she must find some way to put a barrier between their thoughts and her own. An almost incoherent letter, written to Daniel Spofford two days before her marriage, indicates great mental distress, and she evidently felt that her favouritism toward Eddy had been the subject of criticism.

" Now, Dr. Spofford," she writes, " won't you exercise *reason* and let me live or will you *kill* me?   Your mind is just what has brought on my relapse and I shall never *recover* if you do not govern yourself and TURN YOUR THOUGHTS wholly away from me.   Do for God's sake and the work I have before me let me get out of this suffering I never was worse than last night and you say you wish to do me good and I do not doubt it.   Then won't you *quit thinking* of me.   I shall write no more to a male student and never more trust one to live with.   It is a hidden foe that is at work read Science and Health page 193, 1st paragraph.

" No STUDENT nor mortal has tried to have you leave me

that I know of. Dr. Eddy has tried to have you stay you are in a *mistake*, it is *God* and not man that has separated us and for the reason I *begin* to learn. Do not think of returning to me again I shall never again trust a *man* They know not what manner of temptations assail God produces the separation and I submit to it so must you. There is no cloud between us but the way you set me up for a Dagon is wrong and now I implore you to return forever from this error of *personality* and go alone *to God* as I have taught you.

"It is mesmerism that I feel and is killing me it is *mortal* mind that only can make me suffer. Now stop thinking of me or you will cut me off *soon* from the face of the earth."

Gilbert Eddy called on his teacher that same evening, and must have reassured the distracted woman as to the trustworthiness of his sex, for on the next day he was the proud bearer to Spofford of the following note, even the date line of which breathes peace:

SABBATH EVE, Dec. 31, '76.

DEAR STUDENT:

For reasons best known to myself I have changed my views in respect to marrying and ask you to hand this note to the Unitarian clergyman and please wait for his answer.

Your teacher,

M. B. G.

Hand or deliver the reply to Dr. Eddy.

When Mr. Spofford read the note he remarked:

"You've been very quiet about all this, Gilbert."

"Indeed, Dr. Spofford," protested the happy groom, "I didn't know a thing about it myself until last night."

He then produced the marriage license from his pocket,

and Mr. Spofford noticed that the ages of both the bride and groom were put down as forty years. Knowing that Mrs. Glover was in her fifty-sixth year, he remarked upon the inaccuracy, but Mr. Eddy explained that the statement of age was a mere formality and that a few years more or less was of no consequence.

On New Year's Day, 1877, the Rev. Samuel B. Stewart performed the marriage ceremony at Mrs. Glover's home on Broad Street. The wedding was unattended by festivities, but several weeks later Mrs. Eddy's friends and students assembled one evening to offer the usual bridal gifts and congratulations. An interesting picture of this friendly gathering is found in an account published in the Lynn *Recorder*, February 10, 1877.

CHRISTIAN SCIENTISTS' FESTIVAL

MR. EDITOR—A very pleasant occasion of congratulations and bridal gifts passed off at the residence of the bride and bridegroom, Dr. and Mrs. Eddy, at No. 8 Broad St., on the evening of the 31st ult. The arrival of a large number of unexpected guests at length brought about the discovery that it was a sort of semi-surprise party, and thus it proved, and a very agreeable surprise at that. It afterwards appeared that the visitors had silently assembled in the lower parlour, and laden the table with bridal gifts, when the door was suddenly thrown open and some of the family invited in to find the room well packed with friendly faces; all of which was the quiet work of that mistress of all good management, Mrs. Bixby. One of the most elaborate gifts in silver was a cake basket. A bouquet of crystallised geranium leaves of rare varieties encased in glass was charming, but the presents were too fine to permit a selection. Mr. S. P. Bancroft gave the opening address—a very kind and graceful speech, which was replied to by Mrs. Glover-Eddy with evident satisfaction, when alluding to the unbroken friendship for their teacher, the fidelity to Truth and the noble purposes cherished by a number of her students and the amount of good compared with others of which they were capable. The happy evening was closed with reading the Bible, remarks on the Scriptures, etc. Wedding cake and lemonade were served, and those from out of town took the cars for home.

SPECTATOR.

CHAPTER XI

THE book upon which Mrs. Glover had been at work for so long, was first published in 1875. For eight years she had been writing and rewriting, with unabated patience, and wherever she went she had enlisted the interest of her friends and had set them to copying her manuscripts and getting them ready for a possible printer. While she was staying with the Wentworths in Stoughton she carried her copy to Boston to look for a publisher, and when the printer to whom she showed it asked to be paid in advance, Mrs. Glover tried to persuade Mrs. Wentworth to lend her the money. Had Mrs. Glover then been successful in her search for a publisher, Christian Science in its present form would never have existed; for at that time she had not dreamed of calling the system anything but Quimby's " science."

By 1875, however, Mrs. Glover had persuaded herself that she owed very little to the old Maine philosopher,[1] and when her book appeared she said no more of Quimby or of her promise to teach his science " to at least *two* persons before I *die*."

Neither Mrs. Glover nor the printer took any financial risk

[1] The story of Mrs. Glover's absorption of Quimby is told in Chapter X.

in the publication of the book, when it was at last brought out; but two of Mrs. Glover's students, Miss Elizabeth Newhall and George Barry, were prevailed upon to advance $1,500. Owing, however, to the many changes in the proofs which Mrs. Glover made after the plates were cast, the edition cost $2,200, which Miss Newhall and Mr. Barry paid. Mrs. Glover, in spite of her reluctance to risk money on it, believed intensely in her book, and from the first she declared that it would sell. Even when the first edition of 1,000 copies fell flat on the market and Daniel Spofford was obliged to peddle them about personally, Mrs. Glover did not lose confidence in the future of her book, but immediately set about revising the volume for a second edition.

Mrs. Glover and Mr. Spofford advertised the book by means of handbills and through the newspapers, printing testimonials of the wonderful cures made by the application of the science, and urging all to buy the book which would tell them all about it. Copies were sent to the leading New England newspapers for review, accompanied by a request to the editors to print nothing about the book if a favourable notice could not be given. This request was respected by some of the papers, but others criticised the book severely or referred to it flippantly. Copies were also sent to the University of Heidelberg, to Thomas Carlyle, and to several noted theologians and literary men. But the book made no stir, and outside of the little band of devoted Christian Scientists, its advent was unobserved. Whatever imperishable doctrine the book may have contained it was not suggested by the outward form of the volume, which was an ill-made, cheap-looking affair. It contained 456 pages and sold for $2.50 at first, but later, when the sales fell off, it went willingly for $1.

Mrs. Glover called her book *Science and Health*,[2] an adaptation of Quimby's name for his healing system, " The Science of Health." It contained eight chapters entitled in their order: " Natural Science," " Imposition and Demonstration," " Spirit and Matter," " Creation," " Prayer and Atonement," " Marriage," " Physiology," and " Healing the Sick." In these chapters Mrs. Glover attempted to set forth the theory of her " Science " of healing and the theological and metaphysical systems upon which it was based. It was a serious undertaking, but Mrs. Glover, with no preparation but her study of the Quimby manuscripts, and no resources but an illimitable confidence in the success of her undertaking, felt equal to the task; and judged by Mrs. Glover's standard, her venture was a success.

Even after her eight years struggle with her copy, the book, as printed in 1875, is hardly more than a tangle of words and theories, faulty in grammar and construction, and singularly vague and contradictory in its statements. Although the book is divided into chapters, each having a title of its own, there is no corresponding classification of the subject, and it is only by piecing together the declarations found in the various chapters that one may make out something of the theories which Mrs. Glover had been trying for so long to express.

The basic ideas of the book and much of the terminology were, of course, borrowed from the Quimby papers which Mrs. Glover had carried reverently about with her since 1864, and

---

[2] The *Key to the Scriptures,* which now forms a part of the title, was not yet written.

from which she had taught his doctrines.   But in the elabora-
tion and amplification of the Quimby theory, Mrs. Glover
introduced some totally new propositions and added many an
ingenious ornament.

On its metaphysical side Mrs. Glover's science went a step
beyond the conclusions of the idealistic philosophers—that we
can have no absolute knowledge of matter, but only a sense
impression of its existence; she asserted that there *is* no matter
and that we *have* no senses.   The five senses being non-existent,
Mrs. Glover pointed out that " all evidence obtained therefrom "
is non-existent also.   " All material life is a self-evident falsehood."   But while denying the existence of matter, Mrs. Glover
gave it a sort of compulsory recognition by calling it " mortality."   And as such it assumes formidable proportions.   It
is error, evil, a belief, an illusion, discord, a false claim, darkness, devil, sin, sickness, and death; and all these are non-
existent.   Her denials include all the physical world and mankind, and all that mankind has accomplished by means of his
reason and intelligence.   " Doctrines, opinions, and beliefs, the
so-called laws of nature, remedies for soul and body, *materia
medica,* etc., are error," Mrs. Glover declared; but she tempered
the blow by adding: " This may seem severe, but is said with
honest convictions of its Truth, with reverence for God and
love for man."

In Mrs. Glover's system all that exists is an immortal
Principle which is defined as Spirit, God, Intelligence, Mind,
Soul, Truth, Life, etc., and is the basis of all things real.
This universal Principle is altogether good.   In it there is no
evil, darkness, pain, sickness, or other forms of what Mrs.

Glover called "error." Man is a Spiritual being only, and the world he inhabits is a Spiritual world. The idea that he is a physical body as well as an immortal soul, is an illusion introduced into the world by Adam and strengthened by all the succeeding generations. In this philosophy it is impossible for man to be both spiritual and material. "We are Spirit, Soul, and not body, and all is good that is Spirit." "The parent of all discord is this strange hypothesis, that Soul is in body, and Life in matter." But by one of the contradictions which abound on every page, Mrs. Glover, in accounting for what seems to be the existence of the body, said that even when man shall have attained the realisation that he is Spirit only, his *body* will still be here but that it will have no sensation: "How are we to escape from flesh, or mortality, except through the change called death? By understanding we never were flesh, that we are Spirit and not matter. When the belief that we inhabit a body is destroyed we shall live, but our body will have no sensation."

To live by this " science " man must clear his mind of all his previous beliefs, and must understand that all he has believed himself to be, is a falsehood, and that his conduct and the conduct of the whole human race from the beginning have been erroneous. He must ignore his physical body and the material things about him, and he must no longer depend upon the laws of nature or of man, but be governed by spiritual law only. "There is no material law that creates or governs man, or that man should obey; obedience to spiritual law is all that God requires, and this law abrogates matter," wrote Mrs. Glover.

What seems to be the physical world, Mrs. Glover said, is a vision created by " mortal mind," that error or belief in matter which is forever at war with Immortal Mind, and which Mrs. Glover's philosophy denied yet constantly recognised. " Material man," she wrote, " and a world of matter, reverse the science of being and are utterly false; nothing is right about them; their starting point is error, illusion."

The physical forces of nature are likewise illusory. They exist, according to Mrs. Glover, not in fact, but because mortal mind at some time imagined matter and imagined it to contain certain properties. " Vertebrates, articulates, mollusks, and radiates are simply what mind makes them. They are technicalised mortality that will disappear when the radiates of Spirit illumine sense and destroy forever the belief of Life and Intelligence in matter." " Repulsion, attraction, cohesion, and power supposed to belong to matter, are constituents of mind." " The so-called destructive forces of matter, and the ferocity of man and beast are animal beliefs."

All this is a part of what Mrs. Glover called the " dream of life in matter." In time, when the world shall have accepted Christian Science, Mrs. Glover believed, all this will be changed: " All this must give place to the spiritualised understanding. . . . Material substance, geological calculations, etc., will be swallowed up in the infinite Spirit that comprehends and evolves all idea, structure, form, colouring, etc., that we now suppose are produced by matter."

In Christian Science, as Mrs. Glover stated it, all human knowledge which, she held, has done so much harm in the world, will be wiped out, and as man proceeds in the Christian Science

faith, he will gain a complete understanding of the true science
of life.   This understanding will come through spiritual insight
which " opens to view the capabilities of being, untrammelled
by personal sense, explains the so-called miracles, and brings
out the infinite possibilities of Soul, controlling matter, discern-
ing mind, and restoring man's inalienable birthright of dominion."

When man shall have reached this summit of understanding
he will be infallible, unable to make mistakes, for " Mistakes
are impossible to understanding, and understanding is all the
mind there is."

In giving a religious foundation to her science, Mrs. Glover
allowed herself a free hand, for here she was not restrained
by the limits of Quimbyism.   Quimby had not aimed to give
his system a religious tone, but he dealt with the same problems
that religion has tried to solve, and he believed that the severe
doctrines of the churches overlooked the real solution of man's
destiny, and did incalculable damage in the world by spreading
fear and the belief that man was naturally born to sin.   His
own theory, it will be remembered, was that man had had these
beliefs of sin and fear and disease so borne in upon him and
impressed upon him that he was spiritually weakened and
made impotent by an overruling conviction of his own unworthiness.   Quimby's gospel was the gospel of healthy-mindedness.
He assumed that the vivifying principle which pervaded the
universe was absolutely good and that goodness was man's
natural inheritance.   Quimby also taught that the mission of
Jesus Christ was to restore to man his birthright of goodness
and happiness and health; to point the way, as he put it, to

Harmony; and Harmony, in Quimby's philosophy, was Heaven. He also presented the theory of the dual nature of Christ. Jesus, he said, was the human man; Christ, the man of God.[3]

In making out her theological system, Mrs. Glover took in these modest ideas of Quimby, borrowed something from the Shaker sect (see Appendix C) and the " revelations " of Andrew Jackson Davis (see Appendix B), and introduced new and quite original ideas of her own. She made argument futile at the outset by claiming for her religion the advantage of direct inspiration and revelation. " The Bible," she wrote, " has been our only text-book. . . . The Scriptures have both a literal and spiritual import, but the latter was the especial interpretation we received, and that taught us the science of Life outside of personal sense." " We can not doubt the inspiration that opened to us the spiritual sense of the Bible." [4]

Mrs. Glover described the process by which she arrived at the true meaning of the Bible: " The only method of reaching the Science of the Scripture, hence, the Truth of the Bible, is to rise to its spiritual interpretation, then compare its sayings, and gain its general tenor, which enables us to reach the ascending scale of being through demonstration; as did prophet and apostle." By pursuing this method she came, inevitably, to some curious conclusions concerning the beginning of the world and the origin of man. Parts of the Bible she accepted literally, other parts were declared to be allegorical, and some of its statements she rejected altogether as mistakes of the

---

[3] An exposition of Quimby's doctrine is contained in Chapter III of this volume.
[4] In later editions of *Science and Health* the idea of revelation is greatly enlarged upon and emphasised.

early translators and copyists. " From the original quotations," wrote Mrs. Glover, " it appears the Scriptures were not understood by those who re-read and re-wrote them. The true rendering was their spiritual sense." And again: " The thirty thousand different readings given the Old, and the three thousand the New Testament, account for the discrepancies that sometimes appear in the Scriptures."

In the chapter called " Creation," Mrs. Glover stated that the Trinity as commonly accepted is an error. " There is but one God. . . . That three persons are united in one body suggests a heathen deity more than Jehovah. . . . Life, Truth, and Love are the triune Principle of man and the universe; they are the great Jehovah, and these three are one, and our Father which art in heaven." In later editions Christian Science is said to be the Holy Comforter.

The creation of the universe and man had its origin in this triune Principle. The creation was the Idea of Principle; and man and the universe began to exist, not at the moment they received visible form, but before that—at the very moment, in fact, that the Idea of them occurred to Principle. " Intelligence " [that is, Principle], said Mrs. Glover, " made all that was made, and every plant before it was in the ground; every mineral, vegetable, and animal were ideas of the eternal thought." Their form was only a " shadowing forth " of what Principle or Intelligence had already mentally created; for all that was made and all that grew was not developed by natural law, but was literally ordered into being by the First Principle or Creative Wisdom: " The seed yields not an herb because of a propagating principle in itself; for there is none, inasmuch

as Intelligence made all that was made; the idea was only to
shadow forth what Intelligence had made."

" Water," in Mrs. Glover's interpretation, was made to corre-
spond to Love, out of which Wisdom produced the " dry land "
which is, said Mrs. Glover, " the condensed idea of the universe."
The statement in the Bible that God divided the light from the
darkness is said to mean that " Truth and error were distinct
in the beginning and never mingled."   This statement was made
without explanation of how " error " came to be co-existing
with Truth in the beginning, or by whom it was created.   Mrs.
Glover apparently had forgotten for the moment that " error "
is a belief only and that this illusion originated with Adam.

The firmament which God placed in the midst of the waters
to divide them, was, according to *Science and Health,* the
understanding that divided the waters into those " above " and
those " below," into the spiritual and material, that we learn
are separated forever. . . . Understanding interpreted God
and was the dividing line between Truth and error; to separate
the waters which were under the firmament from those above
it; to hold Life and Intelligence that made all things distinct
from what it made, and superior to them, controlling and pre-
serving them, not through laws of matter, but the law of
spirit."

Mrs. Glover did not mention even here why the " spiritual "
should be separated from the " material " by the firmament
of understanding, if, as she taught, there is and never has
been any material life.   But, " Unfathomable Mind," as Mrs.
Glover said, " had expressed itself."

" It was in obedience to Intelligence and not matter," that

the earth brought forth grass, and trees yielded fruit.   Nature was like the setting of a stage, where scenes could be shifted at will.   Intelligence brought forth landscapes [4] [1-2] " even as a picture is produced by the artist."   " The grass and the trees grew," not from the ground, but " from out the infinite thought that expressed them."   In the creation of the solar system Mrs. Glover saw a complete endorsement of her theory that vegetation lived by Intelligence only: " The Scripture gives no record of solar light until after time had been divided into day and night, and vegetation was formed, showing you light was the symbol of the Life-giving Creator, and not a source of life to the vegetable kingdom. . . . Matter never represented God; geology cannot explain the earth, nor one of its formations."

The animal creation, according to Mrs. Glover's idea, was originally mild and harmless.   " Beast and reptile," she said, " were neither carnivorous nor poisonous."   Wisdom held dominion over reptiles in those first days, and the savage traits of wild animals to-day are the result of erroneous human thinking.   Mortal mind has impressed these qualities into the animal kingdom.   It was because they understood this that Moses " made a staff as a serpent," and Daniel feared not the hungry lions.   " When immortality is better understood," Mrs. Glover said, " there will follow an exercise of capacity unknown to mortals."

In the story of the creation of man as recorded in Genesis,

[4] [1-2] Mrs. Glover also taught that the natural law which produces flowers and fruit can be changed at will, even now, if one has a grasp of her science. In a personal letter written in 1896 she stated that she had caused an apple tree to blossom in January, and had frequently performed " some such trifles in the floral line," while living in Lynn.

Mrs. Glover found much that would not fit into her plan of the universe, but she explained this: " In Genesis, the spiritual record of the universe and man is lost sight of, it was so materialised by uninspired writers." And, " the scripture not being understood by its translators was misinterpreted." " The translators of that record wrote it in the error of being . . . hence their misinterpretations. . . . They spake from error, of error . . . which accounts for the contradictions in that glorious old record of Creation." " A wrong version of the Scriptures has hidden their Truth." According to Mrs. Glover's version, man was formed as follows:

When, as recorded in the first chapter of Genesis, God said: " Let *us* make man in *our* image, after *our* likeness, and let *them* have dominion . . . over all the earth," He meant by the word " us " to indicate His triune Principle of Life, Truth, and Love. The word, " them," referred to man in the plural. It " signifies plurality, for man was the generic name of mankind." Therefore, we have the conclusion that God, in his triune capacity of Life, Truth, and Love, made, not one man, but all mankind: " In contradistinction to the belief that God made one man, and man made the rest of his kind, science reveals the fact that he made all."

" So God created man in His own image, male and female created He them," means, in the *Science and Health* version, that mankind thus created, merely " reflected the Principle of male and female, and was the likeness of ' Us,' the compound Principle that made man." It is to be understood that God, himself, not being a person, can have no " gender," " inasmuch as He is Principle embracing the masculine, feminine, and neuter." Indeed, if one of these genders predominates over another in the triune Principle, it is the feminine, for "We have not," said Mrs. Glover, "as much authority in science, for calling God masculine as feminine, the latter being the last, therefore the highest idea given of him." Also: "Woman was a higher idea of God than man, insomuch as she was the final one in the scale of being; but because our beliefs reverse every position of Truth, we name supreme being masculine instead of feminine." [5]

This creation of man, as recorded in the first chapter of Genesis, and explained by *Science and Health*, was, according to Mrs. Glover, the only real creation of man. This man is not given a name in the Bible. He was mankind, the immortal Idea of the First Principle, and he inhabited the inanimate universe, and was given dominion over it. "All blessings and power," said *Science and Health*, "came with the creations of Spirit and as such they were to multiply and replenish the earth on this basis of being, and subdue it, making matter subservient to spirit, and all would be harmonious and immortal." That is, that as intended in the beginning, this spiritual universe was to continue its existence, and Idea or man was to "multiply and replenish the earth" solely by the will of the Spirit. The products of the earth were to come forth when and how original man dictated. "In this science of being the herb bore seed and the tree fruit, not because of root, seed or blossom, but because their Principle sustained these ideas."

There were no laws of nature, or of man, for none was

---

[5] In more recent years Christian Scientists have declared their belief that Mrs. Eddy is the "feminine principle of Deity," and much has been written by her followers in defence of this position.

needed. All was Mind or Infinite Spirit. Man, the male and female Idea of God, was to bring forth his kind, through the law of Spirit only.[6] "That matter propagates itself through seed and germination is error, a belief only."

When God had thus made mankind, according to Mrs. Glover's version, he rested, and he had nothing to do with making anything that came later. Of the Bible statement: "Thus the heavens and earth were finished and all the hosts of them," Mrs. Glover said: "Here the scripture repeats again the science of creation, namely, that all was complete and finished, *therefore that nothing has since been made.*" Having finished creation, God rested on the seventh day, and this again supplied to Mrs. Glover proof that whatever was created thereafter was not of God, but a myth only. Creation was finished, and the Great Principle was at rest.

But somehow, and because of the carelessness, no doubt, of the early translators, a second creation was started, after the seventh day. But the story of this supplementary creation, related in the second chapter of Genesis, is purely mythical and imaginary, Mrs. Glover declared. It is due entirely to misinterpretation, and is wholly untrustworthy. How this belief in a further creation started is not explained, even in *Science and Health*, but it seemed to originate with the discovery that "God had not caused it to rain upon the earth, and there was

---

[6] This theory is the basis of the Christian Science belief that children born of the flesh are not born according to the "science of being." Christian Science discourages the birth of children in the usual way, but permits it as "expedient" for the present. In the future when, as they believe, the world shall be more spiritual, children will appear as products of Spirit only, and they will come by whatever means they are desired. "Should universal mind or belief adopt the appearing of a star as its formula of creation, the advent of mortal man would commence as a star." "Belief may adopt any condition whatever, and that will become its imperative mode of cause and effect." "Knowledge will . . . diminish and lose estimate in the sight of man; and Spirit instead of matter be made the basis of generation."

not a man to till the ground." Mrs. Glover had already pointed out that rain and light were not necessary to the growth of vegetation, and there was not a man to till the ground because, to quote Mrs. Glover, " there was no necessity of it," for " the earth brought forth spontaneously, and man lived not because of matter." " Man was the Idea of Spirit, and this Idea tilled not the ground for bread."

" But," we are told in that fatal second chapter of Genesis, " there went up a mist from the earth and watered the whole face of the ground." That was error, " the figurative mist of earth," and " that which started from a matter basis," in Mrs. Glover's interpretation. " And," to quote Genesis again, " the Lord God formed man of the dust of the ground, and breathed into his nostrils the breath of life, and man became a living soul." Here, then, was the beginning of a " belief of life in matter," and this belief has accompanied us throughout the ages. " The first record," says *Science and Health*, " was science ; the second was metaphorical and myth-ical," and " the supposed utterances of matter."

Mrs. Glover thought it was unfortunate that whoever wrote the first reports of the creation had not, by making judicious comments, indicated which was the true and which the make-believe record: " Had the record divided the first statement of creation from the fabulous second, by saying ' after Truth's creation we will name the opposite belief of error, regarding the origin of the universe and man,' it would have separated the tares from wheat, and we should have reached sooner the spiritual significance of the Bible." But there was no clue, and the error went on.

This man of error, who was formed after creation was finished, was named Adam. The significance of his name is not explained in the first edition of *Science and Health*, but in later editions, Mrs. Eddy, ignoring the Hebraic origin of the word, gives it this literal interpretation: " Divide the name Adam into two syllables, and it reads, *A dam*, or obstruction." Adam was to obstruct our growth in spirituality. Adam, the belief of life in matter, was the first " mortal man," and with him came sickness, sin, and death, and all the troop of error.

Adam, being a " product of belief," and Eve a product of Adam, " both were beliefs of Life in matter." At once they set about their " mortal " mischief. They ate of the tree of knowledge, which was " the symbol of error," in which originated " theology, *materia medica*, mesmerism, and every other 'ology and 'ism under the sun." The fruit of the tree which Eve gave to Adam was, Mrs. Glover suggested, " a medical work, perhaps."

The driving of Adam out of Eden is " a clear and distinct separation of Adam, error, from harmony and Truth, wherein Soul and Sense, person and Principle, Spirit and matter, are forever separate." The history of Adam and his descendants, then, is one of mortality and error, an evil dream that has no reality, and this is Mrs. Glover's contention. " There is no mortal man, or reality to error," she declared. We are not as we have thought, the descendants of Adam; but we are the offspring of that first nameless man who dwelt with God before Adam was. We have been so influenced, however, by the Adam belief that we have lost sight of our true inheritance.

The immediate outlook for the sons of error is not encouraging, for we are told that " error will continue for seven thousand years, from the time of Adam, its origin.   At the expiration of this period Truth will be generally comprehended, and science roll back the darkness that now hides the eternal sunshine and lift the curtain on Paradise, where earth produces at the command of Intelligence, and Soul, instead of sense, govern man."

Mrs. Glover believed thoroughly that, in the meantime, it was her mission to restore to man his original state of spirituality.   Throughout the centuries since Adam, there has been but one other who brought the message of " science " to mankind.   " Jesus of Nazareth," Mrs. Glover wrote, " was the most scientific man of whom we have any record."   " The Principle He demonstrated was beyond question, science," and she refers to Him as " The great Teacher of Christian Science," and the " Pioneer of the science of Life."

Mrs. Glover's explanation of the dual nature of Christ was like Quimby's.   Christ she defined as God, or " the Principle and Soul of the man Jesus; constituting Christ-Jesus, that is, Principle and Idea."   But Mrs. Glover went farther than Quimby and presented a new explanation of the origin and birth of Christ.   She said: " Why Jesus of Nazareth stood higher in the scale of being, and rose proportionately beyond other men in demonstrating God, we impute to His spiritual origin.   He was the offspring of Soul, and not sense; yea, the son of God.   The science of being was revealed to the virgin mother, who in part proved the great Truth that God is the only origin of man.   The conception of Jesus illustrated this Truth and finished the example of creation."   The birth of Christ without a physical father was, in Mrs. Glover's idea, an advance toward the science of being, which dispenses not only with the physical father, but the physical mother as well, and declares that man is born of Spirit only. In support of her argument, Mrs. Glover referred to the fact that some of the lower forms of animal life propagate their kind by self-division, and she said: " the butterfly, bee, etc., propagating their species without the male element . . . corroborates science, proving plainly that the origin of the universe and man depends not on material conditions." Self-division and parthenogenesis are, apparently, held to be less material methods of reproduction, and less in accordance with natural law, than methods in which the " male element " is employed.

The idea that " God is the only author of man " came first, Mrs. Glover said, to the mother of Christ, and she demonstrated it, producing the child Jesus. " The illumination of spiritual sense had put to silence personal sense with Mary, thus mastering material law, and establishing through demonstration that God is the father of man," she wrote. Also: " The belief that life originates with the sexes is strongest in the most material natures; whereas the understanding of the spiritual origin of man cometh only to the pure in heart. . . . Jesus was the offspring of Mary's self-conscious God-being in creative Wisdom."

But the virgin mother, we are told, " proved the great Truth that God is the only origin of man," only " in part." If she had proved it completely she would have had to dispense with herself as mother; and in that case Jesus would have been a perfect demonstration of Mrs. Glover's " science of being." Being born, however, of an actual and visible mother, Jesus was not altogether free from the universal illusion of personal sense. He was the Idea of Principle, it is true, " but born of woman, that is, having in part a personal origin, he blended the idea of Life, that is, God, with the belief of Life in matter, and became the connecting link between science and personal sense; thus to mediate between God and man."

Although Mrs. Glover wrote many a page to prove that Spirit and matter cannot unite and must forever be separate, and was almost violently emphatic in her statement of this principle, she seemed unconscious of the fact that, in making God the spiritual father of Jesus, and Mary His personal mother, and their producing together, the child in whom was " blended " the idea of God with the belief of Life in matter, she was contradicting at all points the very thing she was so laboriously trying to prove. But Mrs. Glover was never afraid of contradicting herself, and her explanation accounted, in some manner, for the origin and nature of Christ, and such as it was, it was made to serve her purpose.

It was, she said, the Son of God, or Christ, who " walked the wave and stilled the tempest," healed the sick, restored the blind, and declared that " I and the Father are one "; and it was Mary's son, or Jesus, who endured temptation, suffered in Gethsemane, and died upon the cross. " Christ, understanding that Soul and body are Intelligence and its Idea, destroyed the belief that matter is something to be feared and that sickness and death are superior to harmony and Life. His kingdom was not of this world, He understood Himself Soul and not body, therefore He triumphed over the flesh, over sin and death. He came to teach and fulfil this Truth, that established

the Kingdom of Heaven, or reign of harmony on earth." But
the man Jesus was not unconscious of "matter conditions."
Although, Mrs. Glover thought, He "experienced few of the
so-called pleasures of personal sense; perhaps He knew its
pains." This illustrated, also, that "Truth, in contact with
error, produced chemicalisation." Chemicalisation, in Mrs.
Glover's vocabulary, meant that when Truth and error, which
cannot mingle, first come together, the contact of these two
opposing forces, like the two parts of a Seidlitz powder, sets
up a violent agitation and eruption. This is chemicalisation,
and during its process Truth may sometimes seem to be affected
by error, but when it subsides it is found that error is van-
quished, and Truth has prevailed. "Hence," said Mrs. Glover,
"our Master's sufferings came through contact with sinners;
but Christ, the Soul of man, never suffered." She taught that
"Had the Master utterly conquered the belief of Life in matter,
He would not have felt their infirmities, but," she continued,
"He had not yet risen to this His final demonstration."

The death on the cross is interpreted as a "demonstration"
of "science." "He permitted them the opportunity to destroy
His body mortal, that He might furnish the proof of His
immortal body in corroboration of what He taught, that the
Life of man was God, and that body and Soul are inseparable.
. . . Neither spear nor cross could harm Him; let them think
to kill the body, and, after this, He would convince those He
had taught this science, He was not dead, and possessed the
same body as before. Why His disciples saw Him after the
burial, when others saw Him not, was because they better understood His explanations of the phenomenon." Christ had "tri-

umphed over sense, and sat down at the right hand of the Father, having solved being on its Principle."

The atonement received a new interpretation. Atonement means " at-one-ment " with God, Mrs. Glover said. " Jesus of Nazareth explained and demonstrated his oneness with the Father, for which we owe Him endless love and homage." But that is all. There was no sacrifice on Calvary. Christ's mission was to show us how to forsake the belief of life in matter, " but not to do it for us, or to relieve us of a single responsibility in the case." " ' Work out your own salvation,' is the demand of Life and Love," said Mrs. Glover, " and to this end God worketh with you."

Prayer, as commonly practised, had no place in Mrs. Glover's religion, in which God is Principle and not Person. " To address Deity as a Person," she said, " impedes spiritual progress and hides Truth." " Prayer is sometimes employed, like a Catholic confession, to cancel sin, and this impedes Christianity. Sin is not forgiven; we cannot escape its penalty. . . . Suffering for sin is all that destroys it." " When we pray aright, we shall . . . shut the door of the lips, and in the silent sanctuary of earnest longings, deny sin and sense, and take up the cross, while we go forth with honest hearts, labouring to reach Wisdom, Love, and Truth."

Mrs. Glover gave a spiritual interpretation of the Lord's prayer, converting it from a supplication to an affirmation of the properties of the Deity as she conceived them:

Harmonious and eternal Principle of man,
Nameless and Adorable Intelligence,
Spiritualise man;
Control the discords of matter with the harmony of Spirit.

Give us the understanding of God,
And Truth will destroy sickness, sin, and death, as it destroys the belief
of intelligent matter,
And lead man into Soul, and deliver him from personal sense,
For God is Truth, Life, and Love forever.[7]

When *Science and Health* was first published, Mrs. Glover
believed that church organisations, church buildings, and
" creeds, rites, and doctrines," were obstructions to spiritual
growth. " We have no need of creeds and church organisations." " The mistake the disciples of Jesus made to found
religious organisations and church rites, if indeed they did
this, was one the Master did not make." " No time was lost
by our Master in organisations, rites, and ceremonies, or in
proselyting for certain forms of belief." " We have no record
that forms of church worship were instituted by our great
spiritual teacher, Jesus of Nazareth, . . . a magnificent edifice
was not the sign of Christ's church." " Church rites and ceremonies have nothing to do with Christianity . . . they draw
us toward material things . . . away from spiritual Truth."
" Worshipping in temples made with hands . . . is not the true
worship." " The soft palm upturned to a lordly salary, and
architectural power—making dome and spire tremulous with

---

[7] This prayer has been re-interpreted in the successive editions of *Science
and Health*, and in the last edition (1909) it reads as follows, the lines alter-
nating with the Lord's Prayer as given in the New Testament:
Our Father which art in heaven,
Our Father-Mother God, all Harmonious,
Hallowed be thy name,
Adorable One,
Thy Kingdom come,
Thy Kingdom is come; Thou art ever present.
Thy will be done on earth as it is in Heaven.
Enable us to know,—as in Heaven, so on earth,—God is omnipotent, supreme.
Give us this day our daily bread;
Give us grace for today; feed the famished affections;
And forgive us our debts as we forgive our debtors;
And Love is reflected in love;
And lead us not into temptation, but deliver us from evil;
And God leadeth us not into temptation, but delivereth us from sin, disease,
and death.
For Thine is the Kingdom, and the power, and the glory, forever.
For God is infinite, all power, all Life, Truth, Love, over all and All.

beauty, that turns the poor and stranger from the gate, shuts the door on Christianity." " The man of sorrows was not in danger from salaries or popularity." [8]

Mrs. Glover's theory of the origin of disease was based upon Quimby's science of health. Her fundamental proposition was, like Quimby's, that mind is the only causation, and that disease, as well as all other disharmonies of man, is due to man's stead-fast belief that his body contains certain properties over which his mind has no control. But, enlarging upon the Quimby theory, Mrs. Glover declared that the body itself is a mere supposition which mankind has imagined for itself and has come to believe in implicitly. Starting from her standpoint that man is an immortal, spiritual being, having a form, it is true, as he at present believes, but that form being a " sensa-tionless body," an inanimate figure, which may live, breathe, and move, not in accordance with any laws of its own, but in response only to the will of its owner, who is Spirit, Mrs. Glover argued that this spiritual body of man cannot see, hear, feel, smell, or taste, except as Spirit desires. He can not think, or reason, or perform any of the physical or mental functions commonly attributed to man, only as Spirit wills. Spirit, in her idea, is the man. The body is the mere instru-ment of Spirit.

This Spirit, which governs the body and owns it, is not an individual spirit. There are not just so many bodies and an equal number of spirits to govern them. Spirit, as described,

[8] Since 1875 Mrs. Eddy's ideas of church buildings and church organisations have been considerably broadened. Her organised churches are now more than six hundred in number, and her congregations worship in costly temples, and have a very complete ecclesiastical system ; and the founder of the church and the head of the entire church system is Mrs. Eddy herself.

is singular, general, and pervasive; and mankind, as well as trees, animals, and all phenomena, is simply the furniture of the universe, made for the use and convenience of universal Spirit. These sensationless bodies of Spirit were not very clearly defined, but in some places in her book Mrs. Glover said that they are " immortal " and " indestructible."

It follows that this sensationless body cannot, by any possibility, know, of and by itself, either sickness or health. It can have no sensation whatever, and in Mrs. Glover's system, this spiritual man, whose body is sensationless, is the only man that exists. Man, as we know him, a combination of brain, nerves, muscle, etc., is that false, hereditary image of physical life which we inherited from Adam. Along with our belief in this physical body, we have inherited a deeply-rooted conviction that this mythical body is capable of certain sensations, such as sight, hearing, etc., and is susceptible to the influences of the mythical physical conditions about it. This belief has given rise to other beliefs, and the result is that man has invented a very intricate and complicated system of physical life, giving names and attributes to various parts of his body, and clothing it and feeding it, in the belief that it requires clothes and food for comfort and nourishment. And, most remarkable of all, he has come to believe that his body can be sick, and can suffer from a derangement of its parts. Labouring under this delusion, man has imagined that, by administering certain remedies to his body, this mythical body will be pleased, and will often consent to get well. If not, if man believes very firmly that his body is very sick, and that it cannot get well, then the remedies do not please his body and it will not consent to get well.   Then man becomes convinced that his body ceases, of its own volition, to live, and that it is then dead and has no longer power to see, smell, hear, think, or suffer.   He believes also that his spirit, which he imagined had been imprisoned within his body, is, by the death of his body, set free, and that it then goes off to a world inhabited by other spirits of other dead bodies, and there continues to dwell.

This, according to *Science and Health,* is the status of " material mankind " to-day.   The mission of Jesus Christ was to lead man back to the way of Truth and to restore to him his rightful spiritual character and the power over his body and over all created things.   But the work of Christ was incomplete.   Although He gave His message, and made His demonstration, He could not finish His task because of " the materiality of the age " in which He lived.   He practised and taught Christian Science, and Mrs. Glover went so far as to call Him its " pioneer "; but He left no written statement of its theory, no text-book, and no formulæ by which His disciples could permanently confound disease.   That was left to Mrs. Glover, who, after centuries of ignorance, and when the world had lost sight of the real mission of its Saviour, appeared to " this age " to teach and demonstrate and write all Truth in its fulness.

In applying her principle to the present material conditions, Mrs. Glover was emphatic and radical; and it must be admitted that her discussions showed a wonderfully scant knowledge of matters that are merely temporary and mortal.   This, however, in the light of her science, would have been considered a proof of her fitness for the task of demolishing mortality, for Mrs.

Glover came, not to save, but to destroy all man-made knowledge and human institutions. In her world of Spirit, knowledge was an outcast, and the less she knew about what she called the " 'ologies and 'isms " the clearer and more searching was her spiritual vision.

If man would get out of his material state and into the realm of Spirit and Intelligence, he must first, she told him, unlearn all that he had learned. All knowledge is harmful, particularly a knowledge of physiology, for it creates false beliefs, and, like obedience to " the so-called laws of health," it multiplies diseases and increases the death rate. *Materia medica*, physiology, hygiene, and drugs were the deadliest enemies to Mrs. Glover's science. The hardly-won knowledge of the physical scientists was, she declared, the densest and most harmful ignorance. Again and again she repeated, " there is no physical science," and taught her readers that all the laws of nature were to be defied and set at naught. In accordance with his spiritual nature and origin, man should never admit the belief that he has a physical body, or that he dwells in a world of matter which can affect his body. All things are at his command, and the beliefs of cold, heat, pain, or discomfort, should be dismissed at once; and they will disappear. " Why," Mrs. Glover demanded, " should man bow down to flesh-brush, flannel, bath, diet, exercise, air, etc.? " The belief that man requires food, clothing, and sleep, she said, is strengthened by the doctors, and it is the doctors, too, who are principally to blame for the existence and continuance of disease. Disease is a habit, and the habit grows more prevalent as education and enlightenment spread, in proof of which she pointed out that there is less sickness among the uncivilised races and among animals than among the highly cultivated classes. "The less mind there is manifested in matter, the better. When the unthinking lobster loses his claw, it grows again." If man would believe that matter has no sensation "then the human limb would be replaced as readily as the lobster's claw." "Epizootic is an educated finery that a natural horse has not." "The snowbird sings and soars amid the blasts; he has no catarrh from wet feet."

"Obesity," Mrs. Glover wrote, "is an adipose belief of yourself as a substance." "All the diseases on earth," said *Science and Health*, "never interfered for a moment with man's Life. Man is the same after, as before a bone is broken, or a head chopped off." But for the present, Mrs. Glover advised, if such accidents seem to occur one might as well seem to call a surgeon. "For a broken bone, or dislocated joint," she wrote naïvely, "'tis better to call a surgeon, until mankind are farther advanced in the treatment of mental science. To attend to the mechanical part, a surgeon is needed to-day . . . but the time approaches when mind alone will adjust joints and broken bones, if," she added, "such things were possible then."

Food is not necessary to nourish and sustain the body. "We have no evidence," said Mrs. Glover, "of food sustaining Life, except false evidence." "We learn in science food neither helps nor harms man." Yet Mrs. Glover took care to warn her readers not to be too radical on this point. "To stop utterly eating and drinking," she said, "until your belief changes in regard to these things, were error," and she admonished them to " get rid of your beliefs as fast as possible."

In treating a patient, who is under the delusion of sickness, there is a stated method.   It must first be thoroughly understood that his disease has its origin in the mind.   His body may seem to suffer because it is at the mercy of his mind, and as long as his mind retains " a mental image " of toothache, cancer, tuberculosis, fever, dyspepsia, or any form of bodily discomfort, his body will respond and will seem to develop the particular belief of sickness that is in his mind.   The object, then, is to abolish the mental picture of disease.   The Christian Science healer " in case of decaying lungs, destroys in the mind of his patient this belief, and the Truth of being and immortality of man assert themselves . . . and the lungs become sound and regain their original proportions."   The belief in the mind of the patient is not always easily destroyed, but the healer must be patient.   " When healing the sick," said Mrs. Glover, " make your mental plea, or better, take your spiritual position that heals, silently at first, until you begin to win the case, and Truth is getting the better of error."   That is, while the patient is lying before you, convulsed with pain, you must retreat within yourself and fight out the disease in a mental argument with error, contending that there is no pain and that the patient is deluded.   This course, faithfully pursued, according to *Science and Health*, will result in an overwhelming conviction that the patient is not held in the throes of error, and the disease will begin to subside.   " Then your patient is fit to listen," said Mrs. Glover, " and you can say to him, ' Thou art whole,' without his scorn."   She advised the healer to " explain to him audibly, sometimes, the power mind has over body. and give him a foundation . . . to lean upon, that he may brace himself against old opinions." " The battle lies wholly between minds, and not bodies, to break down the beliefs of personal sense, or pain in matter, and stop its supposed utterances, so that the voice of Soul, the immortality of man, is heard."

As a preventative of disease, Christian Science is equally effective. " You can prevent or cure scrofula, hereditary disease, etc., in just the ratio you expel from mind a belief in the transmission of disease, and destroy its mental images ; this will forestall the disease before it takes tangible shape in mind, that forms its corresponding image on the body." " When the first symptoms of disease appear, knowing they gain their ground in mind before they can in body, dismiss the first mental admission that you are sick; dispute sense with science, and if you can annul the false process of law, alias your belief in the case, you will not be cast into prison or confinement." " Speak to disease as one having authority over it." " Not to admit disease, is to conquer it."

One of the signs that the healer's efforts are successful, and that Truth is working against error in the patient is " chemicalisation," which has been previously referred to in this chapter. In healing, chemicalisation first shows itself in a violent aggravation of all the patient's symptoms of disease, but neither the patient nor the healer should be alarmed at this. It is a beneficial process, and during it the error or poisonous thought in the patient's system will be thrown off, and when it is over the patient will be well.

The patient can be treated just as effectively without the

bodily presence of his healer, for the healer's mind can work upon the mind of his patient equally well, be he absent or present. Absent treatment is, therefore, regularly practised in Christian Science.

Despite Mrs. Glover's protest against all " knowledge," she seemed to admit that her healers should know something of physiology and *materia medica,* sufficient, at least, to recognise symptoms and to understand the names of both symptoms and diseases. " When healing mentally," she wrote, " call each symptom by name, and contradict its claims, as you would a falsehood uttered to your injury," for " if you call not the disease by name when you address it mentally, the body will no more respond by recovery than a person will reply whose name is not spoken ; and you can not heal the sick by argument, unless you get the name of the disease."   That is, if a patient happened to be labouring under the belief that he was afflicted with yellow fever, and the lay healer, whose knowledge of medical science is, by the terms of his religion, as limited as he can possibly make it, did not recognise the disease, and was ignorant of its name, then the healer could not heal, and Truth would stand powerless while the patient died of this rare and unfamiliar belief.

In the contemplation of death, Mrs. Glover did not weaken in theory.   Death is the great and final test of Christian Science.   It is, she said, " the last enemy to be overcome," and " much is to be understood before we gain this great point in science."   Healers must " never consent to the death of man, but rise to the supremacy of spirit."   But whether or not they consent to it, Mrs. Glover recognised that death, although false, is, for the present, an incontrovertible fact. " Contemplating a corpse," she wrote, " we behold the going out of a belief." One might conclude, from Mrs. Glover's reasoning, that a " corpse " might be exactly that " immortal " and " sensationless " body which belongs to Spirit. The belief of Life in matter has " gone out." It is as " sensationless " as it is possible to be. Yet the all-powerful and all-pervading Principle, of which she said so many things, never quickens a " corpse " nor works its wonders through the dead.

But in spite of her statement that death is " the going out of a belief," Mrs. Glover said in another passage: " If the change called death dispossessed man of the belief of pleasure and pain in the body, universal happiness were secure at the moment of dissolution; but this is not so; every sin and every error we possess at the moment of death remains after it the same as before, and our only redemption is in God, the Principle of man, that destroys the belief of intelligent bodies."

The system seems altogether hopeless if one attempts to follow Mrs. Glover's reasoning. If a mortal man's belief in material life continues even after his mortal and material life is dissolved, it being all the time understood that " belief," " material life," and " mortal man " are one and the same, then what chance has man to become separated from his belief in himself? Mrs. Glover had a suspicion that all this was confusing and tried to help it out. " From the sudden surprise," she wrote, " of finding all that is mortal unreal, . . . the question arises, who or what is it that believes? "

" God is the only Intelligence, and can not believe because He understands. . . . Intelligence is Soul and not sense, Spirit and not matter, and God is the only Intelligence, and there is but one God, hence there are no believers!" That is the answer. "So far as this statement is understood, it will be admitted," said Mrs. Glover; and who shall say that she is not right?

Among the many incidental ideas which Mrs. Glover added to Quimbyism is her qualified disapproval of marriage. Quimby had a large family and saw nothing unspiritual in marriage; and although Mrs. Glover had twice been married, and became a wife for the third time a year later, she believed that marriage had not a very firm spiritual basis. In defining the real purpose of marriage she said nothing about children. "To happify existence by constant intercourse with those adapted to elevate it, is the true purpose of marriage." "The scientific *morale* of marriage is spiritual unity. . . . Proportionately as human generation ceases, the unbroken links of eternal harmonious being will be spiritually discerned." [9]

In addition to the development of her "science," Mrs. Glover described a later discovery in regard to it. Some of her "false students," she said, were substituting mesmerism for "science" when healing the sick. The chapters called "Imposition and Demonstration," and "Healing the Sick," are largely taken up with an account of how this false doctrine, which is a perversion of Christian Science, originated, and a warning of its evil effects. This practice of mesmerism was the forerunner of what she later called "Malicious Animal Magnetism." The

[9] In a chapter called "Wedlock," in *Miscellaneous Writings* (1897), Mrs. Eddy, after an evasive discussion of the subject, squarely puts the question: "Is marriage nearer right than celibacy? Human knowledge inculcates that it is, while Science indicates that it is *not*." Also: "Human nature has bestowed on a wife the right to become a mother; but if the wife esteems not this privilege, by mutual consent, exalted and increased affections, she may win a higher."

story of its origin and development will be told in the next chapter.

The book, *Science and Health,* has, since 1875, been through nearly five hundred editions.   It has been revised and edited many times since the original version appeared, and there have been important additions to the doctrine from time to time; but the first edition contained, in the main, the body of the Christian Science faith as it is to-day.   The first three editions of *Science and Health* were marred by bitter personal references to those whom Mrs. Glover considered her enemies.   These denunciations were summed up in a chapter called " Demonology," which was published in the third edition (see chapter xii). Mrs. Glover was persuaded by Rev. James H. Wiggin, her literary adviser, to omit this chapter from later editions, on the ground that it was libellous.   The " Key to the Scriptures " was added to the book in 1884.   It consisted originally of a " Glossary," in which certain words in the Bible were given new meanings through Mrs. Glover's spiritual interpretation. For example, " death " is said to mean " an illusion "; " Mother," should read " God "; evening is " mistiness of mortal thought "; " bridegroom " is " spiritual understanding," etc.   This glossary was for the use of her students in reading the Bible.   The most conspicuous addition to the doctrine is contained in the chapter called " Apocalypse," which was first printed in 1886.   In this chapter Mrs. Eddy adopts a belief similar to the belief the Shakers entertain of their founder, Ann Lee, namely, that she is the woman referred to in the Apocalypse, and represents the " feminine principle of Deity." [10]

[10] For other similarities to be found between the religious beliefs of the Shakers and Christian Science, see Appendix C.

From the study of Quimby's theory, as given in chapter iii, and the foregoing statement of Mrs. Glover's more elaborate system, as contained in *Science and Health*, it will be seen that Quimby's " science of man," as he tried to teach and practise it, was simply a new way of applying an old truth; and that Mrs. Glover, in the process of making Quimby's idea her own, merely added to it certain abnormalities, which, if universally believed and practised, would make of Christian Science the revolt of a species against its own physical structure; against its relation to its natural physical environment; against the needs of its own physical organism, and against the perpetuation of its kind. But in spite of the radical doctrines laid down in *Science and Health*, neither Mrs. Glover nor her followers attempted to practise them in their daily lives; nor do they do so now. In relation to their physical existence and surroundings, Mrs. Eddy and all Christian Scientists live exactly as other people do; and while they write and teach that physical conditions should be ignored, and the seeming life of the material world denied, they daily recognise their own mortality, and have a very lively sense of worldly thrift and prosperity. Mrs. Eddy's philosophy makes a double appeal to human nature, offering food both to our inherent craving for the mystical and to our desire to do well in a worldly way, and teaching that these extremes are not incompatible in " science." Indeed, as one of the inducements offered to purchasers of the first edition of *Science and Health*, Mrs. Glover advertised it as a book that " affords opportunity to acquire a profession by which you can accumulate a fortune," and in the book itself she said that " Men of business have said this science was of great advantage from a secular point of view." And in later and more prosperous days Mrs. Eddy has written in satisfied retrospect: " In the early history of Christian Science among my thousands of students few were wealthy. Now, Christian Scientists are not indigent; and their comfortable fortunes are acquired by healing mankind morally, physically, and spiritually." Whatever may be the Christian Science theories regarding the nothingness of other forms of matter, the various forms of currency continue to appear very real to the spiritualised vision of its followers. Mrs. Eddy insists that her healers shall be well paid. The matter of payment has, she thinks, an effect upon the patient who pays. She says: " Christian Science demonstrates that the patient who pays what he is able to pay is more apt to recover than he who withholds a slight equivalent for health." Worldly prosperity, indeed, plays an important part in the Christian Science religion to-day. It is, singularly enough, considered a sign of spirituality in a Christian Scientist. Poverty is believed to be an error, like sin, sickness, and death; [11] and Christian Scientists aim to make what they call their " financial demonstration " early in their experience. A poor Christian Scientist is as much of an anomaly as a sick Christian Scientist.

[11] We were demonstrating over a lack of means, which we had learned was just as much a claim of error to be overcome with Truth as ever sickness or sin was.—Contributor to the *Christian Science Journal*, September, 1898.

The lack of means is a lupine ghost sired by the same spectre as the lack of health, and both must be met and put to flight by the same mighty means of our spiritual warfare.—Contributor to the *Christian Science Journal*, October, 1904.

CHAPTER XII

MRS. EDDY'S BELIEF THAT SHE SUFFERED FOR THE SINS OF OTHERS
—LETTERS TO STUDENTS—THE ORIGIN AND DEVELOPMENT
OF MALICIOUS ANIMAL MAGNETISM—A REVIVAL OF WITCH-
CRAFT

Indeed, one of the most primitive and fundamental shapes which the relation of cause and effect takes in the savage mind, is the assumed connection between disease or death and some malevolent personal agency. . . . The minds of civilised people have become familiar with the conception of natural law, and that conception has simply stifled the old superstition as clover chokes out weeds. . . . The disposition to believe was one of the oldest inheritances of the human mind, while the capacity for estimating evidence in cases of physical causation is one of its very latest and most laborious acquisitions.—JOHN FISKE.

AT the beginning of 1877, her seventh year as a teacher in Lynn, Mrs. Eddy and her Science were little known outside of Essex County, though the first edition of *Science and Health* had been published more than a year before, and the author was busy preparing a second edition. Her loyal students, however, believed that she was on the way to obtain wider recognition. Miss Dorcas Rawson, Mrs. Miranda Rice, and Daniel Spofford laboured unceasingly for her interests. Mr. Eddy, immediately upon his marriage, withdrew from practice, dropping the patients he had taken over from Mr. Spofford, and devoted himself entirely to his wife's service. Three days after her marriage Mrs. Eddy wrote to one of her students concerning Mr. Eddy: " I feel sure that I can teach my husband up to a higher usefulness, to purity, and the higher development of all his *latent noble* qualities of head and heart."

In spite of the frequent jars and occasional lawsuits between Mrs. Eddy and her students, new candidates for instruction were constantly attracted by the Science taught at Number 8 Broad Street, where the large sign, " Mary B. Glover's Christian Scientists' Home " still aroused the curiosity of the stranger.

The Christian Science faith has, from the beginning, owed its growth to its radical principle that sickness of soul and body are delusions which can be dispelled at will, and that the natural state of the human creature is characterised by health, happiness, and goodness. The message which Mrs. Eddy brought to Lynn was substantially that God is not only all-good, all-powerful, and all-present, but that there is nothing but God in all the Universe; that evil is a non-existent thing, a sinister legend which has been handed down from generation to generation until it has become a fixed belief. Mrs. Eddy's mission was to uproot this implanted belief and to emancipate the race from the terrors which had imprisoned it for so many thousands of years. " Ye shall know the Truth," she said, " and the Truth shall make you free."

Yet Mrs. Eddy herself was not always well, was not always happy. She used at first to account for this seeming inconsistency by explaining that she bore in her own person the ills from which she released others. When sick or distraught, Mrs. Eddy frequently reminded her students that Jesus Christ was bruised for our transgressions and bore upon His shoulders the sin and weakness of the world He came to save. She apparently did not realise that Christ, by the very act of His atonement, admitted the reality of sin, while she, having denied its existence, had forfeited any logical right to suffer because of it.   The missionary who frees the savage from the fear of demons and witchcraft, and the nurse who assures the child that there is no evil thing lurking for him in the dark, do not suffer from the enlightenment they bring, and they do not assume the fear which the child casts off.   Mrs. Eddy, on the contrary, for many years believed that she herself suffered from the torturing belief she had taken away from others.   The reader will remember that in 1863 Mrs. Eddy wrote to Dr. Quimby that while treating her nephew, Albert Tilton, to rid him of the habit of smoking, she herself felt a desire to smoke. By 1877 Mrs. Eddy not only believed that she suffered from the physical ills from which her students were released, but declared that her students followed her in thought and selfishly took from her to feed their own weakness.   The work upon the second edition of her book could not go on because they nourished themselves upon her and sapped her powers.

By the 1st of April, three months after her marriage to Mr. Eddy, she was almost in despair, and on April 7th she wrote one of her students: " I sometimes think I can not hold on till the next edition is out.   Will you not help me so far as is in your power, in this way?   Take Miss Norman, she is an interesting girl and help her *through*.   She will work for the cause but she will swamp me if you do not take hold.   I am at present such a tired swimmer, unless you do this I have more than I can carry at present.   Direct your thoughts and everybody's else that you can away from me, don't talk of me."

A week later she fulfilled an old threat, and, attended by her husband, went away for some weeks, leaving no address; " driven," as she said, " into the wilderness." She felt that if her students did not know her whereabouts, their minds could not so persistently prey upon hers. The following letter to Daniel Spofford is postmarked Boston, April 14th, but seems to have been written upon the eve of Mrs. Eddy's flight from Lynn.

DEAR STUDENT—This hour of my departure I pick up from the carpet a piece of paper write you a line to say I *am* at length driven into the wilderness. *Everything* needs me in science, my doors are thronged, the book lies waiting, but those who *call on me mentally* in suffering are in belief killing me! *Stopping my work* that none but me can do in their supreme selfishness; how unlike the example I have left them! Tell this to Miss Brown, Mr. McLauthlen, Mrs. Atkinson, and Miss Norman [1] but do not let them know they *can call* on me thus if they are doing this ignorantly and if they do it consciously tell *McLauthlen* and *them all* it would be no greater crime for them to come directly and thrust a dagger into my heart they are just as surely in belief killing me and committing murder.

The sin lies at their door and for them to meet its penalty *sometime. You can teach* them better, see you do this.

O! Harry,[2] the book must stop. I can do no more now if ever. They lay on me suffering inconceivable.   MARY.

If the students will continue to think of me and call on me, I shall at *last* defend myself and this will be to cut them off from me utterly in a spiritual sense by a bridge they cannot pass over and the effect of this on them they will then learn.

I will let you hear from me as soon as I can bear this on account of my health; and will return to prosecute my work on the Book as soon as I can safely. I am going far away and shall remain until you will do your part and give me some better prospect.

Ever *truly,*

MARY.

---

[1] Four of Mrs. Eddy's students. Miss Brown was an invalid of Ipswich. Miss Norman was also of Ipswich, and a friend of Miss Brown. Mrs. Atkinson was the wife of Mayor Atkinson of Newburyport. Mr. George T. McLauthlen was a manufacturer of machinery in Boston.

[2] Mr. Spofford's Christian name is Daniel Harrison. Mrs. Eddy always called him " Harry."

Mrs. Eddy believed that her students not only depended upon her for their own moral and physical support, but that, when treating their patients, their minds naturally turned to her, in whom dwelt the healing principle, and unconsciously coupled her in thought with the ill of the patient, which was thus transferred to her.

Even after she had escaped into solitude, the book progressed but slowly, and she complained that whenever she had succeeded in concentrating herself upon her work, the beliefs (illnesses) of other people would seize her " as sensibly as a hand." From Boston, shortly after her departure, she wrote to a trusted student one of those incoherent letters which indicate the excitement under which Mrs. Eddy sometimes laboured.

April, 1877, Sunday.

DEAR STUDENT: I am in Boston to-day feeling very very little better for the five weeks that are gone. I cannot finish the Key [3] yet I will be getting myself and all of a sudden I am seized as sensibly by some others belief as the hand could lay hold of me my sufferings have made me utterly weaned from this plane and if my husband was only willing to give me up I would gladly yield up the ghost of this terrible earth plane and join those nearer my Life. . . . Cure Miss Brown [4] or I shall never finish my book. Truly yrs.   M.

A letter to Mr. Spofford, written a week after she left Lynn, and postmarked Fair Haven, Conn., shows that despite her sufferings she was eagerly planning for the second edition of her book and that, notwithstanding the cold reception of the first edition, her faith in its ultimate success was unshaken.

April 19, 1877.

MY DEAR STUDENT, . . . I will consider the arrangement for embellishing the book. I had fixed on the picture of Jesus and a sick man— the hand of the former outstretched to him as in rebuke of the disease;

---

[3] *Key to the Scriptures.*
[4] The student from Ipswich referred to in the preceding letter.

or *waves* and an *ark*. The last will cost less I conclude and do as well. No rainbow can be made to look right except in colours and that cannot be conveniently arranged in gilt. Now for the printing—would 480 pages include the Key to Scriptures and the entire work as it now is? The book entitled Science and Health is to embrace the chapter on Physiology all the same as if this chapter was not compiled in a separate volume; perhaps you so understand it. If the cost is what you stated, I advise you to accept the terms for I am confident in the sale of two editions more there can be a net income over and above it all. If I get my health again I can make a large demand for the book for I shall lecture and this will sell one edition of a thousand copies (if I can stand it). I am better, some. One circumstance I will name. The night before I left, and before I wrote you those fragments, Miss Brown went into convulsions from a chemical, was not expected to live, but came out of it saying she felt perfectly well and as well as before the injury supposed to have been received. I thought at that time if she was not "born again" the Mother would die in her labours. O, how little my students *can* know what it all costs me. Now, I thank you for relieving me a little in the other case, please see her twice a week; in healing you are *benefitting yourself,* in teaching you are benefitting others. I would not advise you to change business at present the rolling stone gathers no moss; persevere in *one line* and you can do much more than to continually scatter your fire. Try to get students into the field as practitioners and thus healing will sell the book and introduce the science more than aught but *my* lecturing can do. Send the name of any you can get to study for the purpose of practising and in six months or thereabouts we will have them in the field helping you. If you have ears to hear you will understand. Send all letters to Boston. T. O. Gilbert will forward them to me at present.

Now for the writings you named. I will make an agreement with you to publish the book the three years from the time you took it and have twenty-five per cent royalty paid me; at the end of this period we will make other arrangements or agreements or continue those we have made just as the Spirit shall direct me. I feel this is the best thing for the present to decide upon. During these years we shall have a treasurer such as we shall agree upon and the funds deposited in his or her hands and drawn for specified purposes, at the end of these three years if we dissolve partnership the surplus amount shall be equally divided between us; and this is the best I can do. All the years I have expended on that book, the labour I am still performing, and all I have done for students and the cause gratuitously, entitle me to *some income* now that I am unable to work. But as it is I have none and instead am sued for $2,700 [5]

---

[5] Reference to George W. Barry's suit for payment for services rendered. See Chapter X.

for what? for just this, I have allowed my students to think I have no rights, and they can not wrong me!

May God open their eyes at length.

If you conclude not to carry the work forward on the terms named, it will have to go out of edition as I can do no more for it, and I believe this hour is to try my students who think they have the cause at heart and see if it be so. My husband is giving all his time and means to help me up from the depths in which these students plunge me and this is all he can do at present. Please write soon.

As ever,
MARY.

Send me the two books that are corrected and just as soon as you can, and I with Gilbert will read them.[6]

Please tell me if you are going to have the chapter on Physiology in a book by itself that I may get the preface ready as soon as I am able.

I do nothing else when I have a day I can work. Will send you the final corrections *soon*.

Think of me when you feel *strong* and well only, and think only of me as well

Ever yrs. in
Truth
MARY.

It is an interesting fact that, however incoherent Mrs. Eddy became in other matters, she was never so in business. Through hysteria and frantic distress of mind, her shrewd business sense remained alert and keen. When, upon receipt of this letter, Mr. Spofford wrote her that he did not see how he could pay all the cost of printing, advertising, and putting the second edition upon the market, and still pay Mrs. Eddy her twenty-five cent. royalty upon each copy sold, she replied to him that her work upon the book would more than offset his invested capital:

" The conditions I have named to you," she wrote, " I think are *just*. I *give three years and more* to offset the capital

---

[6] Mr. Spofford had agreed to mark the typographical and other errors in two copies of the first edition of *Science and Health*.

you put into printing. . . . Now dear student you can work as your teacher has done before you, unselfishly, as you wish to and gain the reward of such labour; meantime you can be fitting yourself for a higher plane of action and its reward."

The above letters, with their refrain of dread, seem anomalous from one who had discovered the secret of health and happiness. Although she absolutely denied the influence of heredity, Mrs. Eddy told her students that she had a congenital susceptibility to assume the mental and physical ills of others. She felt that such a state was incompatible with a full realisation of the principles of Christian Science, and in the first edition of *Science and Health* she says of Christ:

He bore their sins in his own person; that is, he felt the suffering their error brought, and through this consciousness destroyed error. Had the Master utterly conquered the belief of Life in matter, he would not have felt their infirmities; he had not yet risen to this his final demonstration.[7]

Mrs. Eddy believed that she herself in time overcame this weakness, and says in the edition of 1881:

In years past we suffered greatly for the sick when healing them, but even that is all over now, and we cannot suffer for them. But when we did suffer in belief, our joy was so great in removing others sufferings that we bore ours cheerfully and willingly. This self-sacrificing love has never left us, but grows stronger every year of our earth life.[8]

Malicious mesmerism, an important addition to Mrs. Eddy's Science, was developed gradually, almost by chance. Even the most haphazard philosopher is likely at some time to have to account for the element of evil, but Mrs. Eddy came to do so purely through the exigencies of circumstances, and was quite unconscious that she was repeating history. She added to her

---

[7] *Science and Health* (1875), p. 130.
[8] *Science and Health* (1881), chapter vi. p. 38.

philosophy from time to time, to meet this or that emergency, very much as a householder adds an ell or a wing to accommodate a growing family. Christian Science as it stands today is a kind of autobiography in cryptogram; its form was determined by a temperament, and it retains all the convolutions of the curiously duplex personality about which it grew.

When Richard Kennedy left Mrs. Eddy in 1872, she was confronted by a trying situation. It was inconceivable to her that, having broken away, he should not try to harm her, and she felt that his very popularity put her in the wrong. The means with which Mrs. Eddy met emergencies were often, indeed almost always, in themselves ill-adapted to her ends; but she had a truly feminine adroitness in making the wrong tool serve. When she thought it necessary to discredit Mr. Kennedy and to demonstrate that his success was illegitimate, she caught up the first weapon at hand, which happened to be mesmerism. Mesmerism loomed large in Mrs. Eddy's vision just then, for only a few months before Wallace W. Wright had published a number of articles in the Lynn *Transcript*, asserting that the Science taught by Mrs. Eddy was identical with mesmerism. She had been obliged to confess that there was an outward similarity. Here was the solution, ready made. When Kennedy left her, he left true Metaphysics behind. How, then, could he still succeed? By mesmerism, that dangerous counterfeit which so resembled the true coin. Mrs. Eddy thus explained her discovery:

Some newspaper articles falsifying the science, calling it mesmerism, etc., but especially intended, as the writer informed us, to injure its author, precipitated our examination of mesmerism in contradistinction to our metaphysical science of healing based on the science of Life. Filled with revenge and evil passions, the mal-practitioner can only depend on manipulation, and rubs the heads of patients years together, fairly incorporating their minds through this process, which claims less respect the more we understand it, and learn its cause. Through the control this gives the practitioner over patients, he readily reaches the mind of the community to injure another or promote himself, but none can track his foul course.[9]

Without a doubt Mrs. Eddy had speculated somewhat upon the possibility of a malignant use of mind power before Kennedy's separation from her, but she never got very far with abstractions until she had a human peg to hang them on.   Her indignation against Kennedy gave her reflections upon the subject of malignant mind power a vigorous impetus, and she fell to work to develop the converse of her original proposition with almost as much fervour and industry as she had bestowed upon the proposition itself.   She thus explained her discovery of Kennedy's " malpractice " :

Some years ago, the history of one of our [10] young students, as known to us and many others, diverged into a dark channel of its own, whereby the unwise young man reversed our metaphysical method of healing, and subverted his mental power apparently for the purposes of tyranny peculiar to the individual. A stolid moral sense, great want of spiritual sentiment, restless ambition, and envy, embedded in the soil of this student's nature, metaphysics brought to the surface, and he refused to give them up, choosing darkness rather than light. His motives moved in one groove, the desire to subjugate; a despotic will choked his humanity. Carefully veiling his character, through unsurpassed secretiveness, he wore the mask of innocence and youth. But he was young only in years; a marvelous plotter, dark and designing, he was constantly surprising us, and we half shut our eyes to avoid the pain of discovery, while we struggled with the gigantic evil of his character, but failed to destroy it. . . . The second year of his practice, when we discovered he was malpractising, and told him so, he avowed his intention to do whatever he chose with his mental power, spurning a Christian life, and exulting in the absence of moral

---

[9] *Science and Health* (1875), p. 375.
[10] Throughout this chapter on Demonology Mrs. Eddy uses the editorial " we " in referring to herself. Mr. Eddy is designated as " our husband."

restraint. The sick clung to him when he was doing them no good, and he made friends and followers with surprising rapidity, but retained them only so long as his mesmeric influence was kept up and his true character unseen. The habit of his misapplication of mental power grew on him until it became a secret passion of his to produce a state of mind destructive to health, happiness, or morals. . . . His mental malpractice has made him a moral leper that would be shunned as the most prolific cause of sickness and sin did the sick understand the cause of their relapses and protracted treatment, the husband the loss of his wife, and the mother the death of her child, etc.[11]

Mrs. Eddy had always been able to wring highly-coloured experiences from the most unpromising material, and she never accomplished a more astonishing feat than when she managed to see a melodramatic villain in Richard Kennedy. Her hatred of Kennedy was one of the strongest emotions she had ever felt, really a tragic passion in its way, and since the cheerful, energetic boy who had inspired it was in no way an adequate object, she fell to and made a Kennedy of her own. She fashioned this hypothetical Kennedy bit by bit, believing in him more and more as she put him together. She gave him one grisly attribute after another, and the more terrible she made her image, the more she believed in it and hated and feared it; and the more she hated and feared it, the more furiously she wrought upon it, until finally her creation, a definite shape of fear and hatred, stood by her day and night to harry and torment her.

Without Malicious Mesmerism as his cardinal attribute, the new and terrible Kennedy could never have been made. It was like the tragic mask which presented to an Athenian audience an aspect of horror such as no merely human face could wear. By a touch really worthy of an artist Mrs. Eddy made the

[11] *Science and Health* (1881), chapter vi, p. 2.

boy's youth, agreeable manner, and even his fresh colour con-
ducive to a sinister effect.   Given such a blithe and genial
figure, and suppose in him a power over the health and emotions of other people, and a morbid passion for using it to the
most atrocious ends, and you have indeed the young Nero,
which title Mrs. Eddy so often applied to Kennedy.

Mrs. Eddy feared this imaginary Kennedy as only things
born of the imagination can be feared, and dilated upon his
corrupt nature and terrible power until her new students, when
they met the actual, unconscious Kennedy upon the street, shud-
dered and hurried away.   During the sleepless nights which
sometimes followed an outburst of her hatred, Mrs. Eddy would
pace the floor, exclaiming to her sympathetic students: "Oh,
why does not some one kill him?   Why does he not die?"

She afterward wrote of him:

> Among our very first students was the mesmerist aforesaid, who has
> followed the cause of metaphysical healing as a hound follows his prey,
> to hunt down every promising student if he cannot place them in his track
> and on his pursuit.   Never but one of our students was a voluntary mal-
> practitioner; he has made many others. . . . This malpractitioner tried
> his best to break down our health before we learned the cause of our
> sufferings.   It was difficult for us to credit the facts of his malice or to
> admit they lie within the pale of mortal thought.[12]

To Richard Kennedy and his mesmeric power Mrs. Eddy
began to attribute, not only her illnesses, but all her vexations
and misfortunes; any lack of success in her ventures, any
difficulties with her students.

In the famous chapter on Demonology she enumerates a long
list of friends whose warm regard for her was destroyed by
Kennedy's mesmeric power.   "Our lives," she writes, "have

---

[12] *Science and Health* (1881), chapter vi, p. 34.

since floated apart down the river of years." She charges this " mental assassin " with even darker crimes.

The husband of a lady who was the patient of this malpractitioner poured out his grief to us and said: " Dr. K— has destroyed the happiness of my home, ruined my wife, etc."; and after that, he finished with a double crime by destroying the health of that wronged husband so that he died. We say that he did these things because we have as much evidence of it as ever we had of the existence of any sin. The symptoms and circumstances of the cases, and the diagnosis of their diseases, proved the unmistakable fact. His career of crime surpasses anything that minds in general can accept at this period. We advised him to marry a young lady whose affection he had won, but he refused; subsequently she was wedded to a nice young man, and then he alienated her affections from her husband.[13]

The real Richard Kennedy must not be confounded with the smiling Elagabalus of Mrs. Eddy's imagination. While she was perfecting her creation, the flesh-and-blood Kennedy was establishing an enviable record for uprightness, kindliness, and purity of character. In 1876 he became prosperous enough to move his office to Boston. There he was, as he had been in Lynn, an active agent for good. He had made many friends and had built up a good practice, when, in 1881, in the third edition of *Science and Health*, Mrs. Eddy broke forth into that tirade of invective which she called " Demonology "—the flower of nine years of torturing hatred. Kennedy's old friends in Lynn were stirred to mirth rather than indignation when a passage like the following was applied to a man whose amiability was locally proverbial:

The Nero of to-day, regaling himself through a mental method with the tortures of individuals, is repeating history, and will fall upon his own sword, and it shall pierce him through. Let him remember this when, in the dark recesses of thought, he is robbing, committing adultery, and

[13] *Science and Health* (1881), chapter vi, p. 6.

killing; when he is attempting to turn friend away from friend, ruthlessly stabbing the quivering heart; when he is clipping the thread of life, and giving to the grave youth and its rainbow hues; when he is turning back the reviving sufferer to her bed of pain, clouding her first morning after years of night; and the Nemesis of that hour shall point to the tyrant's fate, who falls at length upon the sword of justice.[14]

In the beginning, then, Malicious Mesmerism was advanced merely as a personal attribute of Richard Kennedy, and was a means by which Mrs. Eddy sought to justify her hatred. In the first edition of *Science and Health*, though she usually links it with some reference to Kennedy, Mrs. Eddy occasionally refers to mesmerism as an abstract thing, apart from any personality.

In coming years the person or mind that hates his neighbour, will have no need to traverse his fields, to destroy his flocks and herds, and spoil his vines; or to enter his house to demoralise his household; for the evil mind will do this through mesmerism; and not in *propria personæ* be seen committing the deed. Unless this terrible hour be met and restrained by *Science,* mesmerism, that scourge of man, will leave nothing sacred when mind begins to act under direction of conscious power.

The sign of the mesmerist, however, the plague spot which he could not conceal, was " Manipulation "—the method which she had taught Kennedy and afterward repudiated. " Sooner suffer a doctor infected with smallpox to be about you," she cries, " than come under the treatment of one who manipulates his patients' heads." And again, " the malpractitioner can depend only on manipulation." From 1872 to 1877 Mrs. Eddy counted many victims of Kennedy's mesmeric power, but charged no other student with consciously and maliciously practising mesmerism. In 1877, however, an open rupture occurred between Mrs. Eddy and Daniel Spofford. Now, Mr. Spofford

---

[14] *Science and Health* (1881), chapter vi, p. 38.

was, like Kennedy, a man with a personal following, and his secession would mean that of his party. Though she never hated Spofford as bitterly as she hated Kennedy, he was the second of her seceding students who was deemed important enough to merit the charge of mesmerism—a charge which conferred a certain distinction, as only those who had stood in high places ever incurred it.

But in her book, published only two years before, Mrs. Eddy had clearly and repeatedly stated that the mesmerist could " depend only on manipulation," and could always be detected thereby. Now Mr. Spofford did not manipulate—he had been so soundly taught that he would sooner have put his hands into the fire. Accordingly, Mrs. Eddy got out a postscript to *Science and Health.* The second edition, which Mr. Spofford had laboured upon and helped to prepare, was hastily revised and converted into a running attack upon him, hurried to press, labeled Volume II., and sent panting after *Science and Health,* which was not labeled Volume I., and which had already been in the world three years. This odd little brown book, with the ark and troubled waves on the cover, is made up of a few chapters snatched from the 1875 edition, interlarded with vigorous rhetoric such as the following apostrophe to Spofford:

Behold! thou criminal mental marauder, that would blot out the sunshine of earth, that would sever friends, destroy virtue, put out Truth, and murder in secret the innocent befouling thy track with the trophies of thy guilt,—I say, Behold the " cloud, no bigger than a man's hand," already rising in the horizon of Truth, to pour down upon thy guilty head the hailstones of doom.

The purpose of this breathless little courier—a book of 167

pages—in looks very unlike the sombre 480-page volume which had preceded it—was to announce that mesmerism could be practised without manipulation—indeed, that the practice was more pernicious without a sign than with it. Mrs. Eddy thus explained her new light upon the subject:

> Mesmerism is practised through manipulation—and without it. And we have learned, by new observation, the fool who saith "There is no God" attempts more evil without a sign than with it. Since "Science and Health" first went to press, we have observed the crimes of another mesmeric outlaw, in a variety of ways, who does not as a common thing manipulate, in cases where he sullenly attempted to avenge himself of certain individuals, etc. But we had not before witnessed the mal-practitioner's fable without manipulation, and supposed it was not done without it; but have learned it is the addenda to what we have described in a previous edition, but without manipulating the head.[15]

Malicious Mesmerism, or Malicious Animal Magnetism, first conceived as a personal attribute of Richard Kennedy, was six years later stretched to accommodate Daniel Spofford. By 1881, when the third edition of *Science and Health* appeared, a personal animosity had fairly developed into a doctrine, and Mrs. Eddy was well on the way toward admitting a general principle of evil—a thing she certainly never meant to admit. She had decided that mesmerism was not merely a trick employed in practice, but a malignant attitude of mind, and that a person evilly disposed, by merely wishing his neighbour harm, could bring it to him—unless the object of his malice were wise in Metaphysics and could treat against this evil mind-power. Unless a man were thus protected by Christian Science, his enemy might, through Mesmerism or Mortal Mind, bring upon him any kind of misfortune; might ruin his business, cause a

---

[15] *Science and Health* (1878), p. 136.

rash to break out upon his face, vex his body with grievous humours, cause his children to hate him and his wife to become unfaithful.

Having instanced a few cases of the evil workings of the hidden agency in our midst, our readers may feel an interest to learn somewhat of the indications of this mental malpractice of demonology. It has no outward signs, such as ordinarily indicate mesmerism, and its effects are far more subtle because of this. Its tendency is to sour the disposition, to occasion great fear of disease, dread, and discouragement, to cause a relapse of former diseases, to produce new ones, to create dislikes or indifference to friends, to produce sufferings in the head, in fine, every evil that demonology includes and that metaphysics destroys. If it be students of ours whom he attacks, the malpractitioner and aforesaid mesmerist tries to produce in their minds a hatred towards us, even as the assassin puts out the light before committing his deed. He knows this error would injure the student, impede his progress, and produce the results of error on health and morals, and he does it as much for that effect on him as to injure us.[16]

The question is often asked, " How did Mrs. Eddy justify this evil power with her scheme of metaphysics? If God is all and all is God, where does Malicious Mesmerism come in?" The answer is evident; when the original Science of Man, as she had learned it from Quimby, and as she at first taught it, no longer met the needs of her own nature, Mrs. Eddy simply went ahead and added to her religion out of the exuberance of her feelings, leaving justification to the commentators— and she has rapped them soundly whenever they have attempted it.

No philosophy which endeavours to reduce the universe to one element, and to find the world a unit, can admit the existence of evil unless it admits it as a legitimate and necessary part of the whole. But the very keystone of Mrs. Eddy's Science

[16] *Science and Health* (1881), chapter vi, p. 35.

is that evil is not only unnecessary but unreal. Admitting evil as a legitimate part of the whole would be to deny that the whole was good and was God. Admitting evil in opposition to good would be to deny that good and God were the whole. Whenever a train of reasoning seemed to be leading to the wrong place, Mrs. Eddy could always drop a stitch and begin a new pattern on the other side. Since neither the allness of God nor the Godhood of all could explain the injuries and persecutions which she felt were inflicted upon her, she fell back upon Mortal Mind.

"As used in Christian Science," she says, " animal magnetism is the specific term for Error, or Mortal Mind."

Mortal Mind is Mrs. Eddy's explanation of the seeming existence of evil in the world.[17]   Whatever seems to be harmful,— sin, sickness, earthquakes, convulsions of the elements,—are due to the influence of Mortal Mind. Now, Mortal Mind, she says, has no real existence except as a harmful tradition; she affirms that its very name is a fallacy, and she admits it merely for the sake of argument. Hence, though there is no such thing as evil, there is an accumulated belief in evil, a tradition which overshadows us, as Mrs. Eddy says, " like the deadly Upas tree." The belief in evil, then, is the only evil that exists. This belief is Mortal Mind, and Mortal Mind is Mesmerism.

---

[17] Mortal mind includes all evil, disease, and death; also, all beliefs relative to the so-called material laws, and all material objects, and the law of sin and death.

The Scripture says, " The carnal mind (in other words mortal mind) is enmity against God; for it is not subject to the law of God, neither indeed can be." Mortal mind is an illusion; as much in our waking moments as in the dreams of sleep. The belief that Intelligence, Truth, and Love, are in matter and separate from God, is an error; for there is no intelligent evil, and no power besides God, Good. God would not be omnipotent if there were in reality another mind creating or governing man or the universe. *Miscellaneous Writings,* p. 36, Sixty-sixth Edition (1883-1896).

Mrs. Eddy says:

The origin of evil is the problem of ages. It confronts each generation anew. It confronts Christian Science. The question is often asked, if God created only the good, whence comes the evil?

To this question Christian Science replies: Evil never did exist as an entity. It is but a belief that there is an opposite Intelligence to God. This belief is a species of idolatry, and is not more true or real than that an image graven on wood or stone is God.[18]

But concerning the origin of the *belief* in evil, Mrs. Eddy is silent; and certainly with the belief we are immediately concerned, since that and that alone "brought death into the world, and all our woe." The cause of this knot or tangle in the human consciousness, however, remains unexplained down to the very last page of the very last edition of *Science and Health*.

The Rev. James Henry Wiggin, for some years Mrs. Eddy's literary adviser, said that "Mesmerism was her Devil," and it does seem that she has routed Satan from pillar to post only to be confronted by him at last. By designating evil as Mortal Mind, and declaring that it was non-existent, Mrs. Eddy evidently believed herself well rid of it; and she was bewildered to find that she was still afraid of it, and that it could do her harm. Unwittingly she was demonstrating Kant's proposition that " a dream which we all dream together, and which we all must dream, is not a dream, but a reality."

Mrs. Eddy's method of protecting herself against Malicious Mesmerism—the " adverse treatment " which later became such a prolific source of scandal in the Christian Science Church— was first practised by her students about 1875. By now mesmerism had become an indispensable household convenience.

---

[18] *Miscellaneous Writings* (1896) p. 346.

After she moved into her Broad Street house, Mrs. Eddy had
a long succession of tenants and housekeepers, all of whom
she at first found satisfactory, but against whom she soon had
a grievance. She accused nearly all of them of stealing; of
taking her coal, her blankets, her feather pillows, her silver
spoons, and especially of taking her knives and forks, which
kept magically disappearing like the food to which the clown
sits down in the pantomime. It seemed as if the only way
in which she could keep these knives and forks at all was actually
to hold them in her hands. All this trouble she bitterly accredited to Kennedy. People came into her house well disposed
toward her, she said; he set his mind to work upon their minds,
and in a few days she could see the result. They avoided her,
looked at her doubtfully, and her spoons and pillows began
playing hide and seek again.

Mrs. Eddy talked of Kennedy continually, and often in
her lectures she wandered away from her subject, forgot that
her students were there to be instructed in the power of universal
love, and would devote half the lesson hour to bitter invective
against Kennedy and his treachery. This, of course, made an
unfavourable impression upon new students, and Mrs. Eddy's
advisers, Mr. Spofford, Mrs. Rice, and Miss Rawson, besought
her to control her feeling and not to darken the doctrine of
Divine love by the upbraidings of hatred. When thus advised
she would tell her students how she had withdrawn herself from
the world and laboured night and day through weary years,
" standing alone with God," that she might give this great
truth to men; and how Kennedy had perverted it and put it
to evil uses. Not only did he rob her of her students and set

the minds of men against her, she declared, but he pursued her mind " as a hound pursues its prey," causing her torment, sleeplessness, and unrest. She explained that even his cures were made at her expense; that when standing beside his patients and " rubbing their heads years together," he took up Mrs. Eddy in thought, united her mentally with the sick, and cured them by throwing the burden of their disease upon her. Thus weighed down by the ills of his patients, she could go no further. Unless some means were found of protecting her against Kennedy, she must sink under his persecution and her mission be unfulfilled. In this extremity she implored her students to save her by treating against Kennedy and his power.

Those of Mrs. Eddy's students who did not know Mr. Kennedy believed that their teacher was suffering acutely at his hands. She so wrought upon their sympathies that they actually consented to meet at her house and take part in this treatment, which they believed would injure the young man. One of the faithful students present in the circle would say to the others:

Now all of you unite yourselves in thought on Kennedy; that he cannot heal the sick, that he must leave off calling on Mrs. Glover mentally, that he shall be driven out of practice and leave the town, etc.

Mrs. Eddy was never present at these sessions, and her students soon discontinued them. One of the number, who used to meet with the others to treat against Kennedy, explains that he was unwilling to go on with it because he discovered that the more he wished evil to Kennedy, the more he felt the presence of evil within himself. He writes that " while thoughts born of love or its attributes are unlimited in their power to help both their author and their object, thoughts born of malice influence only those who originate them."

Although no open rupture occurred between Mrs. Eddy and Daniel Spofford until the summer of 1877, by the spring of 1877 Mrs. Eddy's feeling for him had begun to cool. It will be remembered that she had turned a number of her students over to Mr. Spofford for instruction in the Interpretation of the Scriptures. As a teacher, Mr. Spofford proved so popular that Mrs. Eddy repented the authority she had given him. His success in practice also made her restive,—doubtless one of the causes which led her to insist upon his turning his practice over to Asa Gilbert Eddy and devoting his time to pushing the sale of her book. It would be scarcely fair to draw the conclusion that Mrs. Eddy resented the success of her students in itself, but she certainly looked upon it with apprehension if the student showed any inclination to adopt methods of his own or to think for himself. Mrs. Eddy required of her students absolute and unquestioning conformity to her wishes; any other attitude of mind she regarded as dangerous. She often told Mr. Spofford that there was no such thing as devotion to the principle of revealed truth which did not include devotion to the revelator. " I am Wisdom, and this revelation is mine," she would declare when a student questioned her decision.

In July, 1877, Mr. Spofford closed out the stock of *Science and Health*, which he had received from George H. Barry and Elizabeth M. Newhall, the students who had furnished the money to publish the book. Mr. Spofford paid over the money which he had received for the books, something over six hundred dollars, to these two students, and although Mrs. Eddy had agreed to ask for no royalty upon the first edition, she was exceedingly indignant that the money had not been paid to her. She declared that Mr. Barry and Miss Newhall had advanced the money to further the cause, and that whatever was realised from the sale of the first edition should have gone toward getting out a second. Mr. Spofford told her that if Mr. Barry and Miss Newhall wished to put the money into a second edition, there was nothing to prevent their doing so, but that he had received from them a number of books which were their property, and he was in duty bound to turn over to them any money received for the same. Mr. Barry and Miss Newhall lost over fifteen hundred dollars on the edition, and Mr. Spofford paid out five hundred dollars of his own money for advertising and personal expenses, besides giving his time for several months. Mrs. Eddy made no effort to reimburse them.

The estrangement thus brought about between Mrs. Eddy and Mr. Spofford continued until, in January, 1878, Mr. Spofford was expelled from the Christian Scientists' Association and received the following notice:

Dr. D. H. Spofford of Newburyport has been expelled from the Association of Christian Scientists for immorality and as unworthy to be a member.

Lynn, Jan. 19th, 1878.

Secretary of the Christian Scientists' Association, Mrs. H. N. Kingsbury.

A notice also appeared in the Newburyport *Herald*, stating that Daniel H. Spofford had been expelled for alleged immorality from the Christian Scientists' Association of Lynn. Mr. Spofford brought no action against the Association, as he thought the charge would be considered absurd and could do him no harm.

" Immorality " was a favourite charge of Mrs. Eddy's; she insisted it meant that a student had been guilty of disloyalty to Christian Science. The very special and wholly unauthorised meanings which Mrs. Eddy had given to many common words in writing *Science and Health* doubtless confirmed her in the habit of empirical diction. An amusing instance of this occurred years afterward, when Mrs. Eddy quarrelled with a woman prominent in the Mother Church in Boston, and declared that she was an adulteress. When the frantic woman appealed to her to know what in Heaven's name she meant, Mrs. Eddy replied gravely, " You have adulterated the Truth; what are you, then, but an adulteress? "

The test of loyalty in a disciple was obedience. " Whosoever is not for me is against me," Mrs. Eddy declared in an angry interview with Mr. Spofford. If a student were " against " her, there could be but one cause for his hardening of heart—Richard Kennedy and Malicious Mesmerism. Mr. Spofford was amazed, therefore, in the spring of 1878, to find that a bill had been filed before the Supreme Judicial Court at Salem, charging him with practising witchcraft upon one of Mrs. Eddy's former students, Lucretia L. S. Brown of Ipswich.

Lucretia Brown was a spinster about fifty years of age, who lived with her mother and sister in one of the oldest houses in Ipswich, facing upon School-house Green. When she was a child, Miss Brown had a fall which injured her spine, and she was an invalid for the greater part of her life. Although not absolutely bedridden, she had often to keep to her bed for weeks together, and seldom walked further than the church. She conducted a crocheting agency, taking orders for city dealers, and giving out piece-work to women in the village who wished to earn a little pin-money. Miss Lucretia was noted for her system and her neatness. On certain days of the week she gave out this crochet work at exactly two o'clock in the afternoon, and whoever arrived a few minutes early had to await the stroke of the clock, as Miss Brown was not visible until then. The women who came for work gathered in the sitting-room, and one by one they were admitted to Miss Lucretia's sleeping chamber, where she received them in a bed incredibly white and smooth. They used to wonder how Miss Lucretia could lie under a coverlid absolutely wrinkleless, and how she could handle her worsted and give all her directions without rumpling the smoothness of the turned-back sheet, or marring the geometrical outline of her pillow. As the candidate retired from Miss Brown's presence, her bundle of yarn was sharply eyed by the other women who waited in the sitting-room, as there was a rumour that Miss Lucretia gave more work to her favourites than to others, and that they rolled their worsted up tightly to conceal the evidence of her partiality.

In the matter of good housewifery, the three Brown ladies were triumphant and invincible. They carried their daintiness even into their diet, regarding anything heavier than the most ethereal food as somewhat too virile and indelicate for their spinster household. The assertion was once made that Essex was the cleanest county in Massachusetts, and Ipswich was the cleanest town in Essex, and the Browns were the cleanest people in Ipswich. Even when Miss Lucretia was suffering from her worst attacks and was supposed to be helpless in bed, she was occasionally discovered late at night, slipping about the house and " tidying up " under cover of darkness.

Before Miss Lucretia knew Mrs. Eddy and Miss Rawson, she was a Congregationalist, but after she was healed by Christian Science she withdrew from her old church. Her cure was much talked about. After she was treated by Miss Rawson, she was able to be up and about the house all day and to walk a distance of two or three miles, whereas before she had made much ado to call upon a neighbour at the other end of the Green. After her healing she made some effort to practise upon other people, but Ipswich folk were slow to quit their family doctors in favour of the new method.

Miss Brown, however, remained a devout Scientist until her death in 1883, and up to that time occasionally took a case. The story goes that she got the cold she died of by airing the house too thoroughly after having treated one of her patients. Fifty years of frantic cleanliness were not to be overcome in an instant; and although Miss Lucretia well knew that disease was but a frame of mind, that contagion was a myth, and that dirt itself was only a " belief," the moment a patient was out of the house, up went the windows, and the draperies went out on the clothes-line.

In her last illness she called in her old family physician, but refused to let him prescribe for her, explaining that she merely wished him to diagnose her case so that her Christian Science healer would know what to treat her for. Her death was as orderly as her life. When she felt that her " belief " (pneumonia) was gaining on her, she called in her mother and sister, talked over her business, and put her affairs in order, telling them where they would find all her things. When she had given all her directions, she asked them if there were any-thing about which they wished to question her. When they replied in the negative, she said, " Good-bye, Mother. Good-bye, Sister," and smoothing once again that never-wrinkled, turned-back sheet, she folded her hands and almost instantly died.

In 1878, when Miss Brown believed that Mr. Spofford had bewitched her, she was a patient of Miss Dorcas Rawson. Miss Rawson and her sister, Mrs. Rice, it will be remembered, were among Mrs. Eddy's first students in Lynn. They were daugh-ters of a large family in Maine, and when they were very young girls came to Lynn to make their way in the shoe shops. Miranda soon married Mr. Rice and left the factory. After the two sisters had studied with Mrs. Eddy, Dorcas also left the factory and became a practising healer. She was as ardent in her new faith as she had been before in Methodism. While a Methodist she had been one of a number who " professed holiness," that is, who felt that in their daily walk they were so near to God that His presence protected them from even the temptation to sin. Miss Rawson was a thoroughly good and unselfish woman, and so earnest and forceful that perhaps in a later day she would have been called " strong-minded." However devoted in service, such a firm and independent nature would almost inevitably clash with Mrs. Eddy's at times, and Miss Rawson had more than one painful difference with her teacher. But it was hard for Miss Rawson to give up a friend, harder than to bear with Mrs. Eddy's unreasonableness. After these disagreements she always came back, telling her friends that she could not endure to be separated from Mrs. Eddy in spirit, and that, when she was, she felt her health failing and discouragement threatening to overwhelm her.

When, under her treatment, Miss Brown suffered a relapse, Miss Rawson, in her perplexity, went to Mrs. Eddy. Mrs. Eddy had the solution at her tongue's end. Daniel Spofford, in his general opposition to truth, was exercising upon Miss Brown his mesmeric arts. Miss Rawson was at first loath to believe this. Mr. Spofford was an old and trusted friend; even had he been subsidised by Richard Kennedy, why should Mortal Mind, as exercised by Mr. Spofford, prevail over Divine Mind as employed by Miss Rawson? But Mrs. Eddy convinced her, with her will or against it, and also convinced poor Miss Brown.

Mr. Spofford's acquaintance with Miss Brown had been slight. When she was studying with Mrs. Eddy, she, with other students, had entered his class in the Interpretation of the Scriptures. When Miss Brown's health began to fail, he had not seen her for some months and was ignorant alike of her illness and the supposed cause of it. After Miss Lucretia had begun to regard him as the author of her ills, Mr. Spofford was in Ipswich one day and bethought him of calling upon his old student. Accordingly he went down to the Green and knocked at her cottage. Miss Brown herself came to the door and immediately fell into great agitation. Ordinarily a pale woman, her cheeks and forehead flushed so hotly that Mr. Spofford innocently thought that she must be making preserves and had just come from the stove. She stood for a moment, very ill at ease, and, without asking him to come in, begged him to excuse her and ran back into the house.   When she reappeared, she seemed even more distracted than before, and Mr. Spofford now felt sure that he had intruded upon some critical moment in preserve-making, and told her that he would call again when he next happened to be in Ipswich.   He went away, leaving Miss Brown to wonder whether he had merely come to see how his victim did, or whether he had come to do her further harm.

By this time Mrs. Eddy had Mr. Spofford upon her mind almost as constantly as she had Richard Kennedy.   In April, a month before the charge of witchcraft was made against him, Mrs. Eddy filed a bill in equity against Mr. Spofford to recover tuition and a royalty on his practice.   This suit was still pending when the witchcraft case came up, and was dismissed June 3d because of defects in the writ and insufficient service.   The Newburyport *Herald* of May 16th, in commenting editorially upon the witchcraft case, said: "Mrs. Eddy tried, some time since, to induce us to publish an attack upon Spofford, which we declined to do, and we understand that similar requests were made to other papers in the county."

In preparing to prosecute the witchcraft case, Mrs. Eddy first selected twelve students from the Christian Scientists' Association—she has always been partial to the apostolic number—and called on these students to meet her at her house and treat Mr. Spofford adversely, as other students had formerly treated Richard Kennedy.   She required each of these twelve students, one after another, to take Mr. Spofford up mentally for two hours, declaring in thought that he had no power to heal, must give up his practice, etc.   Mr. Henry F. Dunnels of Ipswich was one of the chosen twelve.   He says in his affidavit: " When the Spofford lawsuit came along, she took twelve of us from the Association and made us take two hours apiece, one after the other.   She made a statement that this man Spofford was adverse to her and that he used his mesmeric or hypnotic power over her students and her students' patients, and hindered the students from performing healing on their patients, and we were held together to keep our minds over this Spofford to prevent him from exercising this mesmeric power over her students and patients.   This twenty-four hours' work was done in her house."

Having thus prepared her case through the agency of Divine Mind, Mrs. Eddy next set about making the most of human devices.   She went to her lawyer in Lynn and had him draw up a bill of complaint in Miss Brown's name, setting forth the injuries which Miss Brown had received from Mr. Spofford's mesmeric malice, and petitioning the court to restrain him from exercising his power and using his arts upon her.   The text of the bill is in part:

Humbly complaining, the Plaintiff, Lucretia L. S. Brown of Ipswich in said County of Essex, showeth unto your Honours, that Daniel H. Spofford, of Newburyport, in said County of Essex, the defendant in the above entitled action, is a mesmerist and practises the art of mesmerism and by his said art and the power of his mind influences and controls the minds and bodies of other persons and uses his said power and art for the purpose of injuring the persons and property and social relations of others and does by said means so injure them.

And the plaintiff further showeth that the said Daniel H. Spofford has at divers times and places since the year eighteen hundred and seventy-five, wrongfully and maliciously and with intent to injure the plaintiff, caused the plaintiff by means of his said power and art great suffering of body and mind and severe spinal pains and neuralgia and a temporary suspension of mind, and still continues to cause the plaintiff the same. And the plaintiff has reason to fear and does fear that he will continue in the future to cause the same. And the plaintiff says that said injuries are great and of an irreparable nature and that she is wholly unable to escape from the control and influence he so exercises upon her and from the aforesaid effects of said control and influence.

As Mrs. Eddy's attorney flatly refused to argue the case in court, she arranged that one of her students, Edward J. Arens, should do so. At the opening of the Supreme Judicial Court in Salem May 14, 1878, Mrs. Eddy and Mr. Arens appeared under power of attorney for Miss Brown, attended by some twenty witnesses, " a cloud of witnesses," as the Boston *Globe* put it in an account of the hearing. When they were assembled at the railway station in Lynn to take the train for Salem, one of the witnesses went to Mrs. Eddy and protested that he knew nothing whatever about the case and would not know what to say were he called upon to testify. " You will be told what to say," replied Mrs. Eddy reassuringly.

Having arrived at the Salem Court House, Mrs. Eddy and her loyal band awaited in the jury-room the entrance of the chief justice. As soon as Judge Horace Gray had taken his seat, Mr. Arens arose and presented his petition for a hearing on the bill of complaint. He then made an exposition of the case to the Judge, who ordered that an order of notice be served upon Mr. Spofford, and appointed Friday, May 17th, for a hearing of the case. Mr. Arens at once took the train for Newburyport to search for Mr. Spofford, as Mrs. Eddy feared that he might escape into another State.

Meanwhile the Massachusetts press was making the most of

the novel legal proceedings at Salem. A reporter from the Boston *Globe* called at Miss Brown's house in Ipswich, but was told that she was away from home. Of this call the *Globe* published the following account:

In an interview with a sister of Miss Brown, the latter being out of town, the lady informed the *Globe* reporter that she and her family believed that there was no limit to the awful power of mesmerism, but she still had some faith in the power of the law, and thought that Dr. Spofford might be awed into abstaining from injuring her sister further. That he does so she believes there is no possibility of a doubt. In answer to a query put by the reporter, she admitted that should Dr. Spofford prove so disposed, even though he be incarcerated behind the stone walls at Charlestown, he could still use his mesmeric power against her sister.

On Friday morning the crowd which had assembled at the Salem Court House was disappointed. Mr. Spofford himself did not appear, but his attorney, Mr. Noyes, appeared for him and filed a demurrer, which Judge Gray sustained, declaring with a smile that it was not within the power of the Court to control Mr. Spofford's mind. The case was appealed, and the appeal waived the following November.

So, after a lapse of nearly two centuries, another charge of witchcraft was made before the court in Salem village. But it was an anachronism merely, and elicited such ridicule that it was hard to realise that, because of charges quite as fanciful, one hundred and twenty-six persons were once lodged in Salem jail, nineteen persons were hanged, and an entire community was plunged into anguish and terror.

During the long years that the grass had been growing and withering above the graves of Martha Corey and Rebecca Nurse and their wretched companions, one of the most important of all possible changes had taken place in the world—a change in the mode of thinking. The work of Descartes, Locke, and Sir Isaac Newton had become a common inheritance; the relation of physical effect with physical cause had become established even in ignorant and unthinking minds, and a schoolboy of 1878 would have rejected as absurd the evidence upon which Judge Hawthorne condemned a woman like Mary Easty to death.

Mrs. Eddy's attempt to revive the witch horror was only a courtroom burlesque upon the grimmest tragedy in New England history. It is interesting only in that it demonstrates how surely the same effects follow the same causes. When Mrs. Eddy had succeeded in overcoming in her students' minds the tradition of sound reasoning of which they and their century were the fortunate heirs, when she had convinced them that there were no physical causes for physical ills, she had unwittingly plunged them back into the torturing superstitions which it had taken the world so long to overcome. The capacity for estimating evidence in cases of physical causation, which John Fiske calls " one of the world's latest and most laborious acquisitions," once denied, the Christian Scientists had parted with that rational attitude of mind which is the basis of the health and sanity of modern life; which has abolished religious persecution as well as controlled contagious disease, and has made a revival of the witchcraft terror as impossible as a recurrence of the Black Death. This rational habit of mind once broken down, two good women like Lucretia Brown and Dorcas Rawson could suspect a good man of the malice of a fiend. Among this little group of people who had been friends and fellow-seekers after God, there broke out, in a milder form, that same scourge of fear and distrust which demoralised Salem from 1692 to 1694. In the attempt to bring the glad tidings of emancipation from the operation of physical law, which is sometimes cruel, Mrs. Eddy had come back to the cruelest of all debasing superstitions—that of attributing disease and misfortune to a malevolent human agency.

CHAPTER XIII

FROM 1877 to 1879 Mrs. Eddy was in the law-courts so
frequently that the Boston newspapers began to feature her
litigations and to refer to them and to her with disrespectful
jocularity.

In March, 1877, George W. Barry,[1] one of her students,
brought his suit against Mrs. Eddy for twenty-seven hundred
dollars for services rendered her in copying the manuscript of
Science and Health, attending to her business, storing her goods,
putting down her carpets, working in her garden, and paying
out money for her on various accounts. This suit dragged
on until October, 1879, when it was decided in Barry's favour,
the referee awarding him three hundred and ninety-five
dollars and forty cents, with interest from the date of his
writ.

In February of 1878, Mrs. Eddy brought suit against
Richard Kennedy in the Municipal Court of Suffolk County
to recover seven hundred and fifty dollars upon a promissory
note which bore the date February, 1870, several months previ-

---

[1] A full account of this action was given in Chapter X.

ous to the date upon which Mrs. Eddy and Kennedy went to Lynn to practise, and which read as follows:

> February, 1870.
>
> In consideration of two years' instruction in healing the sick, I hereby agree to pay Mary M. B. Glover, one thousand dollars in quarterly instalments of fifty dollars commencing from this date.
>
> (Signed) RICHARD KENNEDY.

Mr. Kennedy admitted having signed the note, but testified that when Mrs. Eddy asked him to do so she said that she would never collect it, and that she wanted the paper simply to show to prospective students to convince them of the monetary value of her instruction. He further testified that though, when he signed the note, he had been studying with Mrs. Glover-Eddy for two years, he believed at the time that she was withholding from him the final and most illuminating secrets of her Science, and that he had reason to believe that, if he complied with her request in regard to the note, she would disclose them to him.

In his answer he stated that Mrs. Eddy had " obtained the promissory note declared on by pretending that she had important secrets relating to healing the sick which she had not theretofore imparted to defendant, and which she promised to impart after the making and delivery to her of said note, and she then had no such secrets and never afterward undertook to impart or imparted such secrets."

The Municipal Court awarded judgment for the plaintiff of seven hundred and sixty-eight dollars and sixty-three cents, but the case was carried to the Superior Court and tried before a jury, which returned a verdict for Mr. Kennedy.

In April, 1878, came Mrs. Eddy's suit against George H. Tuttle and Charles S. Stanley, two of her earliest students, to discover the amount of their practice and to recover a royalty thereon, which was decided in favour of the defendants.[2]

In April, 1878, Mrs. Eddy brought her action against Daniel Spofford to discover the amount of his practice and to recover royalty thereon. Her original idea was to collect a royalty from all her practising students, which arrangement, could she have held them to it, would, in time, have been very remunerative. This case was dismissed for insufficient service.

In May of the same year came the witchcraft case, Brown *vs.* Spofford, of which Mrs. Eddy was the instigator, and in which she represented the plaintiff in court.

These lawsuits reached a sensational climax when, in October, 1878, Asa Gilbert Eddy and Edward J. Arens were arrested on the charge of conspiracy to murder Daniel H. Spofford.

It will be remembered that Mr. Spofford had been one of the most earnest and trusted of Mrs. Eddy's students. She had permitted him to assist in her teaching, had given him the pen with which *Science and Health* was written, and had intrusted to him the sale of her book. She seems at one time even to have considered the possibility of his being her successor.

In a letter dated October 1, 1876, she writes:

My joy at having *one* living student after these dozen years of struggle, toil and defeat, you at present cannot understand, but will know at a future time when the whole labour is left with you. . . . The students make all their mistakes *leaning on me,* or *working against me.* You are not going to do either, and certainly the result will follow that you will be faithful over a few things and be made ruler *over* many.

---

[2] This suit has already been referred to in Chapter IX. From Judge Choate's finding it would seem that his decision was based largely on the fact that when Mrs. Eddy taught Tuttle and Stanley in 1870 she still instructed her students to " manipulate " the heads of their patients, whereas she later repudiated this method and declared before Judge Choate that it was of no efficacy in healing the sick, thus discrediting the instruction she had given the defendants.

She continually consulted Mr. Spofford in the preparation of the second edition of *Science and Health* (the little book which was eventually converted into an intermittent attack upon him), and in a letter written several weeks after the above she says:

LYNN, Oct. 22, '76.

DR. SPOFFORD—

Dear Student—Your interesting letter just read. I am in a condition to feel all and more than all you said. The mercury of my mind is rising as the world's temperature of thought heats up and the little book "sweet in the mouth" but severe and glorious in its proof, is about to go forth like Noah's dove over the troubled waves of doubt, infidelity and bigotry, to find if possible a foothold on earth. . . . I have great consolation in you, in your Christian character that I read yet more and more, the zeal that should attend the saints, and the patient waiting for our Lord's coming.

Press on; You know not the smallest portion, comparatively, of your ability in science. . . . Inflammation of the spinal nerves are what I suffer most in belief.[3]

There was no middle ground with Mrs. Eddy, and it was her policy to strike before she could be struck. After her disagreement with Mr. Spofford concerning his disposition of the money he had received from the sale of her book, she denounced him as an enemy to truth, had her students begin to treat against him, expelled him from the Christian Scientists' Association, tried to induce the county papers to publish attacks upon him, and launched two lawsuits at him within a month of each other. Mrs. Eddy and her husband gave such wide circulation to the charge that Mr. Spofford had been dishonest in regard to the sale of the book, that the publishers of the book felt called upon to publish the following statement:

---

[3] This refers to Mrs. Eddy's continued ill health.

TO THE PUBLIC

Having heard certain malicious statements concerning our business transactions with Dr. D. H. Spofford of Newburyport, we, the undersigned, original publishers of " Science and Health," written by Mary Baker Glover of Lynn, in justice to him desire to correct them. He settled with us July 25th, 1877, paying several hundred dollars cash and giving notes (which were promptly taken up when due) for the further amount of his indebtedness. His account had been carefully examined by counsel and found correct and satisfactory. We desire to STOP the untruths which some person or persons have set afloat.

GEORGE W. BARRY,

Jan. 21st, 1878.   E. M. NEWHALL,

Mrs. Eddy was now convinced that Spofford was a mesmerist and openly denounced him as a malpractitioner.[4] Her students had orders to discredit him as widely as possible, and Mr. Spofford soon began to see the result of their efforts in the falling off of his practice. It was Mr. Arens' practice which Mrs. Eddy was now endeavouring to build up.

Edward J. Arens was a Prussian who had come to Lynn as a young man, where he worked as a carpenter until he was able to open a cabinet-making shop. He was a good workman, but was not particularly successful in his business, and was frequently involved in litigation. Although his educational oppor-

---

[4] She thus explained her position in the local press :

" BOTH SIDES

" Mr. EDITOR :—We desire to say through the columns of your interesting weekly, that certain threatening letters received by ourself, and an esteemed citizen of one of your adjacent towns, had better be discontinued.

" These letters are from a Mr. Noyes [Spofford's attorney] of Newburyport, under orders of D. H. Spofford, who is already prosecuted by us to answer at a higher tribunal than the prejudice, falsehood or malice, before which some people would arraign others.

" We have befriended this former student of ours when friendless, we have effected cures for him professionally, not only in the cases of Mrs. Atkinson, Miss Tandy, and Miss Ladd, but others, and we did this without any reward, but to gain some place for him in the public confidence.

" As the founder of a Metaphysical practice, we have a warm interest in the success of all our students, and have always promoted it, unless compelled in some especial instances, by a strong sense of our duty to the public, to speak of a MALPRACTICE.

" AUTHOR OF SCIENCE AND HEALTH."

tunities had been limited, he had an active mind. He read a great deal, was restless, eager, and ambitious. When he became a student of Mrs. Eddy's, he gave up his cabinet business and, naturally hot-headed and impulsive, he threw himself into metaphysical healing with great enthusiasm. He came to Mrs. Eddy's succour in a critical hour, when she desperately needed a man who could devote himself effectively to her cause. Mr. Eddy had never been a man of much initiative, and his terror of mesmerism had cowed him beyond his natural docility.

By this time Mrs. Eddy's hatred for Mr. Spofford had reached the acute stage, where it kept her walking the floor at night, declaring that Spofford's mind was pursuing and bullying hers, and that she could not shake it off. Mr. Eddy, a helpless spectator of his wife's misery, used to declare that the man ought to be punished for persecuting her, and believed that Mr. Spofford's mind was on their track night and day, seeking to break down Mrs. Eddy's health, to get their property away from them, and to overthrow the movement. Mr. Spofford, on the other hand, was scarcely less distraught. He still believed that Mrs. Eddy had brought him the great truth of his life, and that, however unworthy, she had a divine message. He felt his separation from her deeply, and was amazed and terrified by her vindictiveness. He feared that Mrs. Eddy would not stop until she had entirely destroyed his practice, and he never knew what weapon she would use against him next. Only a state of panic on both sides can explain the developments of the autumn of 1878.

One morning early in October a heavy-set, rather brutal-looking man knocked at the door of Mr. Spofford's Boston office, Number 297 Tremont Street, and said he wanted to see the Doctor. Mr. Spofford glanced at the man and, thinking he was not the sort of person who would be likely to consult a mental healer, asked him if he were sure that he had come to the right kind of a doctor. The man introduced himself as James L. Sargent, a saloon-keeper, took from his pocket a card which Mr. Spofford had left on the door of his Newburyport office, and, pointing to the name on it, said that was the doctor he had come to see. After taking a seat in the consulting-room, Sargent asked Mr. Spofford whether he knew two men named Miller and Libby. Mr. Spofford replied that he did not.

" Well, they know you," insisted Sargent, " and they want to get you put out of the way. Miller, the young man, says you are going with the old man's daughter and he wants to marry her himself." Sargent went on to explain that these two men had offered him five hundred dollars to put Mr. Spofford out of the way and had paid him seventy-five dollars in advance. He declared that, while he meant to get all the money he could out of it, he had no intention of risking his neck, and said that he had already notified State Detective Hollis C. Pinkham and had asked him to watch the case.

Mr. Spofford immediately called upon Pinkham and found that Sargent had told him the same story. Pinkham said, however, that he had paid very little attention to the story, as Sargent had a criminal record, and he had thought that the man was up to some game to square himself with the Police Department. He promised to look into the matter more carefully, and Mr. Spofford went away.

Several days later Sargent came in and said that Miller and

Libby were pressing him. He had gone to them for more money, assuring them that Mr. Spofford was already dead, but they had sent a young man to Spofford's office to investigate, and accused Sargent of playing them false.

Mr. Spofford was now thoroughly alarmed. Sargent suggested that he accompany him to his (Sargent's) brother's house at Cambridgeport and conceal himself there while he (Sargent) tried to collect the money promised him by Miller and Libby. Mr. Spofford consulted with Detective Pinkham and then disappeared. Sargent, so he later declared in court, informed Miller and Libby, whom he identified as Edward J. Arens and Asa Gilbert Eddy, that he had disposed of Mr. Spofford, whereupon he received a part of the money promised him. Mr. Spofford left Boston Tuesday, October 15th, and remained about two weeks at the house of Sargent's sister-in-law. Sargent had promised to come out and give him news of the case, but as he failed to do so, Mr. Spofford then returned to Boston, going first to his brother's store in Lawrence. In the meantime his friends had been greatly alarmed at his disappearance, had advertised him as missing, and had published a description of him in the Boston papers.

On October 29th Edward J. Arens and Asa G. Eddy were arrested and held in three thousand dollars bail for examination in the Municipal Court on November 7th.

As Mrs. Eddy afterward indignantly wrote, " the principal witnesses for the prosecution were convicts and inmates of houses of ill fame in Boston." A motley array of witnesses, certainly, confronted the judge when the Municipal Court con-

Photograph by H. S. Dunshee

DANIEL H. SPOFFORD

Photograph by Kendall

EDWARD J. ARENS

vened on the afternoon of November 7th.   Sargent was a bartender with a criminal record.   George Collier, his friend, was,
at that time, under bonds, waiting trial on several most un-
savoury charges.   Laura Sargent, the sister of James Sargent,
who kept a disorderly house at Number 7 Bowker Street,
appeared with several of her girls, all vividly got up for the
occasion and ingenuously pleased at coming into court in the
dignified rôle of witnesses for the Commonwealth.   Mr. H. W.
Chaplin appeared for the prosecution, and Russell H. Conwell
appeared for the defendants.   Mr. Chaplin briefly opened the
case for the Government, contending that he should be able
to prove directly that the defendants had conspired to take
the life of Mr. Spofford, and that Sargent had been paid
upwards of two hundred dollars toward the five hundred dollars
due him for the job.   The evidence adduced at the hearing
was in substance as follows:

James L. Sargent testified that he was a saloon-keeper in
Sudbury Street,[5] that he had become acquainted four months
before with a man who called himself " Miller," but whom
he recognised as the defendant, Arens; that Miller, or Arens,
came to his saloon to tell fortunes; that Arens had told him
he knew of a good job where three or four hundred dollars
could be made; that he, Sargent, inquired about the job, and
Arens asked him if he could be depended on; that Sargent
assured him on that point, and Arens then told him that he
wanted a man " licked," and " he wanted him licked so that
he wouldn't come to again."

---

[5] Sargent stated in court that, when he first met Mr. Arens, he was a
bartender in a saloon on Portland Street.   He had been running a place of
his own for about six weeks when the hearing occurred.

I told him [said Sargent] that I was just the man for him, and Arens said the old man [Libby] would not pay out more than was absolutely necessary to get the job done, as he had already been beaten out of seventy-five dollars. I met Arens the following Saturday at the corner of Charles and Leverett streets at five o'clock, and we walked down Charles Street into an alleyway. He said Libby was not satisfied and wanted to see me himself. . . . We selected a spot in a freight-yard where he and the old man [Libby] would meet me in half an hour. In the meantime, fearing that the affair might be a plot of some kind against myself, I borrowed a revolver of a friend and got another friend named Collier to go with me. Collier secreted himself in a freight-car with the door partially opened, so that he could overhear any conversation, and at the appointed time I met Arens and a man who was known to me as "Libby," but whom I recognise as the defendant, Eddy. . . . Eddy asked me how much money I wanted to do the job, and I told him I ought to have one hundred dollars to start with. He asked if I would take seventy-five dollars at the outset, and I said I would. He wanted to know if I would be square, and I told him yes. He then said he had but thirty-five dollars with him that night, which he would give me, and would send the remainder by Arens on the following Monday. I told him no, I must have the whole at that time. Just then a man came walking down the freight-yards, and Arens told me in a quick tone to meet him Monday morning. I did so, and Arens passed me seventy-five dollars. . . . A few days later I met Arens again, and he said he would bring me directions where to find Dr. Spofford. He gave me an advertisement, clipped from some newspaper, giving the days when I could find Dr. Spofford at his offices in Haverhill and Newburyport.

After telling in detail of his own delay in following instructions and of spending the money and putting Arens off, Sargent's testimony continued:

We went to the Hotel Tremont, and Arens gave me sixteen dollars, with which I went to the Doctor's office in Newburyport. I did not see the Doctor, but brought away one of his business cards; came back and called at Dr. Spofford's office and had a conversation with him. I afterward met Arens on the Common by appointment, and told him I had made arrangements to have the Doctor go out of town. . . . In a few days he met me on the Common again. He said I was playing it on him and that the whole thing was a put-up job, for Dr. Spofford was in his office. He had sent a boy to find out.

Sargent said he met Arens several times after that, and finally they agreed that Sargent should take Spofford into the country on the pretence that he had a sick child. He took the Doctor to his brother's in Cambridgeport and kept him there about two weeks. The fact that Spofford had disappeared was published in the papers. Sargent said he had met Arens after that, and told him that he had made away with the Doctor, and that he had done it about half-past seven in the evening. Sargent said that Arens replied that he had known this—that he had felt it, and had a way of telling such things that other people knew nothing of.

He saw him several times afterward, and finally Arens agreed to pay him some money. They met in Lynn on Monday, after the disappearance of Spofford. Mr. Eddy was also there, and Arens paid the witness twenty dollars.

Their plan, Sargent said, had been to take Spofford out on some lonely road and have him knocked in the head with a billy, afterward causing the horse to run away, first entangling the body with the harness, so it would appear that death was caused by accident.

Another witness was Jessie Macdonald, who had lived as housekeeper with Mr. and Mrs. Eddy eight months. She had never seen Spofford, but she had heard Mr. Eddy say that Spofford kept Mrs. Eddy in agony, and that he would be glad if Spofford were out of the way. She had heard Mrs. Eddy read a chapter from the Old Testament which says that all wicked people should be destroyed.

James Kelly testified to holding a conversation with Sargent, who told him of the job he had on hand.

John Smith, Sargent's bartender, testified that he saw **Arens** in Sargent's saloon four times.

Laura Sargent, James Sargent's sister, who kept a house of ill-fame in Bowker Street, testified that Sargent had a room in her house, and that Arens had come there three or four times to see him; also that Sargent had given her seventy-five dollars to keep for him, saying he was going away to his brother's in Cambridgeport.

Hollis C. Pinkham, the detective employed on the case, said that Sargent had laid the case before him, and that he had told Sargent to go ahead and find out what he could; that he had seen Sargent and Arens together in conversation on the Common; that he had followed Eddy to his home in Lynn, and had seen Sargent go toward the door of Eddy's house there; that he had asked Eddy if he had arranged to put Spofford out of the way; that Eddy had denied having been in Sargent's saloon or meeting him in a freight-yard; that Arens had maintained he had never seen or known Sargent, even when confronted with Sargent.

Detective Chase Philbrick, also employed on the case, testified to seeing Sargent at Eddy's house in Lynn; saw him try to get in, but fail to do so.   He corroborated the evidence of Pinkham.

George A. Collier, a carpenter, was an important witness. He said he worked in Sargent's saloon when he was out of a job, and told of going with Sargent to the freight-house and concealing himself in an empty car, leaving the door ajar, so that he might hear a conversation between Sargent and another man. He corroborated Sargent's testimony as to what transpired.

This closed the case for the Government. The defence offered no evidence, as this was a case where only probable cause for suspicion was to be shown, and it was then to go to a higher court. Mr. Conwell, counsel for the defendants, did not indicate what line the defence would take.

Counsel for the Government submitted no argument, but called the attention of the court to the chain of circumstances which had been brought out by the evidence, and which he believed was strong enough to justify holding the defendants.

Judge May remarked that the case was a very anomalous one, but that there was, in his opinion, sufficient evidence to show that the parties should be held to appear before the Superior Court. He therefore fixed the amount of bail at three thousand dollars each for the appearance of the defendants at the December term of the Superior Court.

The case was called in the Superior Court in December, 1878, and an indictment was found on two counts.[6]

The Superior Court record reads:

This indictment was found and returned into Court by the Grand Jurors at the last December term, when the said Arens and Eddy were severally set at the bar and having said indictment read to them, they severally said thereof that they were not guilty.

---

[6] The first read: "That Edward J. Arens and Asa G. Eddy of Boston aforesaid, on the 28th day of July in the year of our Lord, one thousand eight hundred and seventy-eight, Boston aforesaid, with Force and Arms, being persons of evil minds and dispositions did then and there unlawfully conspire, combine, and agree together feloniously, wilfully, and of their malice aforethought, to procure, hire, incite, and solicit, one James L. Sargent, for a certain sum of money, to wit, the sum of five hundred dollars, to be paid to said Sargent by them, said Arens and Eddy, feloniously, wilfully, and of his, said Sargent's malice aforethought, in some way and manner and by some means, instruments, and weapons, to said jurors unknown, one, Daniel H. Spofford, to kill and murder. Against the law, peace, and dignity of said Commonwealth."

The second count charged the prisoners with hiring Sargent "with force and arms in and upon one, Daniel H. Spofford, to beat, bruise, wound, and evil treat, against the law, peace, and dignity of said Commonwealth."

This indictment was thence continued to the present January term, and now the District Attorney, Oliver Stevens, Esquire, says he will prosecute this indictment no further, on payment of costs, which are thereupon paid. And the said Arens and Eddy are thereupon discharged. January 31, 1879.

There is no memorandum filed with the papers in the case to show the reason for the *nol. pros.*, and a letter of inquiry sent July, 1905, to the late Oliver Stevens, the District Attorney, elicited the reply that he had kept no data concerning the case, and the circumstances which caused him to enter a *nol. pros.* had gone from his mind.

On October 9th, six days before Mr. Spofford fled to Cambridgeport, he received a letter from Mrs. Eddy, dated from Number 8 Broad Street, Lynn. It read as follows:

DEAR STUDENT,

Won't you make up your mind before it is forever too late to stop sinning with your eyes wide open? I pray for you that God will influence your thoughts to better issues and make you a good and great man, and spare you the penalty that must come if you do not forsake sin.

I am ready at any time to welcome you back, and kill for you the fatted calf, that is, destroy in my own breast the great material error of rendering evil for evil or resenting the wrongs done us. I do not cherish this purpose toward any one. I am too selfish to do myself this great injury. I want you to be good and *happy in being good* for you never can be happy without it. I rebuke error only to destroy it not to harm *you,* but to do you *good.* Whenever a straying student returns to duty, stops his evil practice or sin against the Holy Ghost, I am ready to say, "neither do I condemn thee, go and sin no more." I write you at this time only from a sense of the high and holy privilege of charity, the greatest of all graces. Do not mistake my motive, I am not worldly selfish in doing this, but am only desirous to do you good. Your silent arguments to do me harm have done me the greatest possible good; the wrath of man has praised Thee. In order to meet the emergency, Truth has lifted me above my former self, enabled me to know who is using this argument and when and what is being spoken, and knowing this, what is said in secret is proclaimed on the house top and affects me no more than for you to say it to me audibly, and tell me I have so and so; and to hate my husband; that I feel others; that arguments cannot do good; that Mrs. Rice cannot; that my husband cannot, etc., etc. I have now no need of human aid. God has shut the mouth of the lions. The scare disappears when you know another is saying it and that the error is not your own.

May God save you from the effects of the very sins you are committing and which you have been and will be the victim of when the measure you are meting shall be measured to you. *Pause,* think, solemnly and selfishly of the cost to you. Love instead of hate your friends, and *enemies* even. This alone can make you happy and draw down blessings infinite.

Have I been your friend? Have I taught you faithfully the way of happiness? and rebuked sternly that which could turn you out of that way? If I have, then I was your friend and risked much to do you good. May God govern your resolves to do right from this hour and strengthen you to keep them. Adieu,

M. B. GLOVER EDDY.

In the 1881 edition of *Science and Health* Mrs. Eddy takes up this conspiracy case at length, giving a careful and detailed explanation of it.[7] In her exposition she quotes this letter as a proof of the fact that she was still trying to reclaim Mr. Spofford when the conspiracy was invented.   Mr. Spofford, on the other hand, since he had not heard from Mrs. Eddy for seventeen months, believed that Mrs. Eddy intended this letter should be found in his mail-box after his disappearance, to avert suspicion from her.

In her exposition of the case Mrs. Eddy explains it entirely as the result of demonology or mesmerism. She implies that it was a conspiracy hatched by Richard Kennedy and Mr. Spofford to injure the sale of the second edition of her book, which had been out but a few weeks when her husband was placed under arrest:

The purpose of the plotters was evidently to injure the reputation of metaphysical practice, and to embarrass us for money at a time when they hoped to cripple us in the circulation of our book. This is seen

---

[7] *Science and Health* (1881), chapter vi, pp. 20-33.

in the fact that our name was in any way introduced in the case when we were not implicated by the law and by the gospel.[8]

Mrs. Eddy attributed Mr. Kennedy's participation in the plot to the fact that her suit against him for the amount of the promissory note signed in Amesbury in 1870 was still pending. She says:

> The mental malpractitioners managed that entire plot; and if the leading demonologist can exercise the power over mind, and govern the conclusions and acts of people as he has boasted to us that he could do, he had ample motives for the exercise of his demonology from the fact that a civil suit was pending against him for the collection of a note of one thousand dollars, which suit Mr. Arens was jointly interested in.[9]

In her exposition of the case Mrs. Eddy published affidavits from Caroline Fifield and Margaret Dunshee, in which they testified that Mr. Eddy was instructing a class in Metaphysics in Boston Highlands at the hour when Sargent and Collier declared they had seen him in a freight-yard in East Cambridge. She also published the following confession which, she said, Mr. Eddy had received from Collier a few weeks after the hearing before the Grand Jury:

> TAUNTON, Dec. 16, 1878.
>
> To DRS. ASIA G. EDDY and E. J. ARNES—feeling that you have been greatly ingered by faulse charges and knowing their is no truth in my statement that you attempted to hire James L. Sargent to kil Dr. Spoford and wishing to retract as far as poserble all things I have sed to your ingury, I now say that thair is no truth whatever in the statement that I saw you meet James L. Sargent at East Cambridge or any outher place and pay or offer to pay him any money that I never hurd a conversation betwene you and Sargent as testifyed to by me whouther Spoford has anything to do with Sargent I do not know all I know is that the story I told on the stand is holy faulse and was goton up by Sargent.
>
> GEO. A. COLLIER.

---

[8] *Science and Health* (1881), chapter vi, p. 22.
[9] *Science and Health* (1881) chapter vi, p. 29.

This letter was subsequently reinforced by an affidavit said to have been made by Collier before a justice in Taunton, on December 17, 1878, in which he makes a similar declaration.

The evidence on both sides is of the most anomalous and inconsequential character and reads like the testimony heard in the nightmare of some plethoric judge. The witnesses for the prosecution were, with the exception of Jessie Macdonald and the two detectives, utterly worthless as sources of testimony.

Mrs. Eddy's charge that the plot was the malicious invention of Mr. Kennedy and Mr. Spofford can be regarded only as the delusion of an unreasonable and over-wrought woman. The only other possible solution would advance Sargent as the instigator of the plot. If a double blackmailing enterprise could be attributed to Sargent, the tangle could be easily explained. But this hypothesis is weakened by the fact that he never asked for or received any money from Mr. Spofford. And why a saloon-keeper from Sudbury Street should have gone so far from his familiar haunts and associates, and should have aspired to play a part in the quarrels of the Christian Scientists, remains a difficult question.

CHAPTER XIV

MRS. EDDY ADDRESSES BOSTON AUDIENCES—SHE IS TORTURED BY HER FEAR OF MESMERISM—ORGANISATION OF " THE CHURCH OF CHRIST, SCIENTIST "—WITHDRAWAL OF EIGHT LEADING MEMBERS—MRS. EDDY'S RETREAT FROM LYNN

As early as 1878, Mrs. Eddy began to give occasional lectures in a Baptist church on Shawmut Avenue, in Boston, and in 1879 she gave Sunday afternoon talks in the Parker Fraternity Building on Appleton Street. Her audiences were not large. Sometimes, on a fine afternoon as many as fifty persons would be present, while again the number would fall as low as twenty-five. Mrs. Eddy came up from Lynn on Sunday afternoon, attended by Mr. Eddy, and often by several of her students. She usually wore a black silk gown and a hat when she spoke, used gold-bowed spectacles, and was confident and at ease upon the rostrum. Mr. Eddy, dressed in a black frock-coat, acted as usher and passed the collection-plate. Mrs. Eddy spoke on the curative aspect of her Science almost entirely, relating many individual instances of the astonishing cures she and her students had performed. The religious element in her discussions was incidental and rather cold. She never hinted at repentance, humility, or prayer in the ordinary sense, as essential to regeneration. Moral reform came naturally as a result of adopting Christian Science. Mrs. Eddy possessed on the platform that power of moving people to a state of emotional exaltation which had already proved so effective in her classroom.

After the lecture Mrs. Eddy always came down from the platform and shook hands cordially with her audience. The company usually separated into two groups, one surrounding Mr. Eddy and the other gathering about his wife. Mr. Eddy, in a low voice, would recommend the interested inquirer to join one of Mrs. Eddy's classes and thus come into a fuller understanding of the subject. Occasionally a visitor would ask Mrs. Eddy why she used glasses instead of overcoming the defect in her eyesight by mind. This question usually annoyed her, and on one occasion she replied sharply that she " wore glasses because of the sins of the world," probably meaning that the belief in failing eyesight had become so firmly established throughout the ages that she could not at once overcome it.

Mrs. Eddy's audiences were largely made up of people who were interested in some radical theory of theology or medicine. Mr. Arthur T. Buswell, for instance, who afterward became prominent in the Christian Science movement, had been employed in the New England Hygiene Home, a water-cure sanatorium at West Concord, Vt., and had come to Boston to practise hydropathy.[1] His friend, James Ackland, who attended the lectures with him, was a professor of phrenology.

When Mrs. Eddy felt that one of the Sunday afternoon visitors had become interested in her lectures, Mr. Eddy mildly but persistently followed him up. He used often to drop in

---

[1] Mr. Buswell had first become interested in mind cure through Dr. John A. Tenney, now a physician at Number 2 Commonwealth Avenue, who, in turn, had become interested in the subject through Dr. Evans, a pupil of Quimby's.

at Mr. Buswell's office and lay before him the material and spiritual advantages of a course with Mrs. Eddy, telling him that it was impossible to realise the wonder of Mrs. Eddy's teaching from her public lectures. He always entered the office quietly, glancing back over his shoulder to see whether he were being followed, and spoke in a very low tone, looking nervously about him as he talked. He explained that the mesmerists were constantly on his trail, and that to avoid them extreme caution was necessary on his part. If he walked with Mr. Buswell on the street, he slipped along as if trying to avoid observation, and would sometimes suddenly catch Buswell's sleeve and pull him into a doorway, as if he felt mesmerism in the air, telling him it was very important that they should not be seen together, as the mesmerists were always shadowing him, ready to set to work upon the minds of prospective students and prejudice them against Mrs. Eddy.

Mr. Buswell and his friend Ackland, the phrenologist, were finally persuaded to go to Lynn and study under Mrs. Eddy. They both roomed in Mrs. Eddy's house, and Mr. Buswell's experience there was a pleasant one. Mrs. Eddy's fortunes were then at a low ebb. There was now a good deal of feeling against her in the town, and her frequent differences with her followers and the scandal caused by the witchcraft and conspiracy cases had reduced the number of her students. There were but three in Mr. Buswell's class, and one of these dropped out, leaving only Mr. Ackland and himself to complete the course. Other students who came under Mrs. Eddy's instruction at about this time were: Hanover P. Smith, a young man who worked in his aunt's boarding-house in Boston and who afterward became incurably insane; Joseph Morton, who was a maker of flavoring extracts in Boston, and who was interested in astrology; and Edward A. Orne.

Litigation had been a heavy drain upon Mrs. Eddy financially. She and Mr. Eddy let the lower floor of their house, occupying, themselves, only the upstairs rooms, and now they rented one of those. They did their own housework, and Mrs. Eddy was exceedingly cheerful and courageous about it. Mr. Buswell remembers finding her on her knees with soap and pail one afternoon, scrubbing her back stairs. When he reproved her for undertaking such heavy work, she laughed and replied that it was good for her to stir about after writing all morning, adding that she could not get good help, as the mesmerists immediately affected her servants. Mr. Buswell remembers that in her classroom she sometimes related how once when she was driving through Boston in an open carriage, a cripple had come up to the carriage, and she had put out her hand and healed him. She also told of returning home after several days' absence to find her window plants drooping and dying. She had discovered that when she was in the house the plants could live without sunlight or moisture, so, instead of watering them, she put them in the attic and treated them mentally, after which they were completely restored.[2] Sometimes, on the same morning that she related one of these extravagant anecdotes, she would tell, with apparent apprecia-

---

[2] This incident may have been one of the "floral demonstrations" referred to in a letter sent from Pleasant View, March 21, 1896, which says:

". . . While Mrs. Eddy was in a suburban town of Boston she brought out one apple blossom on an apple tree in January when the ground was covered with snow. And in Lynn demonstrated in the Floral line some such small things. But Mrs. Woodbury was never with her in a single instance of these demonstrations.

"Respectfully

"MARY BAKER EDDY."

tion, · how Bronson Alcott, after reading *Science and Health,* had said that no one but a woman or a fool could have written it.

At this time the skeleton in the house was still Malicious Mesmerism. Ever since his arrest upon the charge of conspiracy to murder, Mr. Eddy had seemed stupefied by fear, and he went about like a man labouring under a spell. He was trying to teach a little, but said that the mesmerists broke up his classes. He had a tendency to brood upon the few things in which he was interested at all, and he used to become deeply despondent, confiding to the loyal students his fear that the work would be utterly broken down and trampled out.

Mrs. Eddy was nervous about her mail, and believed that her letters were intercepted. When she wrote letters now, she had one of her students take them to some remote part of the town and drop them into one of the mail-boxes farthest away from her house. She believed that the mesmerists kept her under continual espionage, and she seldom went out of the house alone. When Mr. Eddy got home after a trip to Boston, ten miles distant, she would embrace him and thank God that he had escaped the enemy once again. Mrs. Eddy's heaviest cross was that the mesmerists were apparently triumphant. She was greatly chagrined by the fact that Richard Kennedy had been able to build up a practice in Boston, and his prosperity hurt her like a personal affront. He had stolen his success, she said. Within a year after the conspiracy trouble, Edward Arens also incurred her displeasure, and she added him to the list of mesmerists. She kept photographs of Kennedy, Spofford, and Arens in her desk, Kennedy's picture marked with a black cross, and the other two marked with red

crosses. Kennedy was still regarded as the Lucifer of mesmerism and the source of the corrupting influence. In the course
of time he had fellows, but never a rival. It was when Mrs.
Eddy would become agitated in talking of these three men
that her students first noticed that violent trembling of the
head, which was the beginning of the palsy which afterward
afflicted Mrs. Eddy. Mesmerism became the dominating conception of her life, and it is difficult to find a parallel for such
a constant and terrifying sense of evil unless one turns to
Bunyan in the days before his conversion, or to Martin Luther
in the monastery of Wittenberg, when he lived under such a
continual oppression of sin that the gates of hell seemed always
open just under the flagstones as he paced the cloisters.[3] Her
illnesses, like Luther's earache, were purely the result of a
consciously malicious agency; but, unlike Luther's, Mrs. Eddy's
depression never came from a feeling of unworthiness or a sense
of sin.

After she left Richard Kennedy, Mrs. Eddy seems for some
years to have given little thought to the project which she used
to discuss with him of founding a new church. It is quite
possible that even then by " church " she meant a new faith
rather than an organised sect. In the first edition of *Science
and Health* she expressed her opinion that church organisation
was a hindrance rather than a help to the highest spiritual
development.

We have no need of creeds and church organisation to sustain or explain
a demonstrable platform, that defines itself in healing the sick, and casting

---

[3] " In the monastery of Wittenberg, he constantly heard the Devil making a
noise in the cloisters; and became at last so accustomed to the fact, that he
related that, on one occasion, having been awakened by the sound, he perceived
that it was *only* the Devil, and accordingly went to sleep again. The black
stain in the castle of Wartburg still marks the place where he flung an ink-
bottle at the Devil."   Lecky, *Rationalism in Europe.*

out error. The uselessness of drugs, the emptiness of knowledge that puffeth up, and the imaginary laws of matter are very apparent to those who are rising to the more glorious demonstration of their God-being.

The mistake the disciples of Jesus made to found religious organisations and church rites, if indeed they did this, was one the Master did not make; but the mistake church members make to employ drugs to heal the sick, was not made by the students of Jesus. Christ's church was Truth, " I am Truth and Life," the temple for the worshippers of Truth is Spirit and not matter. . . .

No time was lost by our Master in organisations, rites, and ceremonies, or in proselyting for certain forms of belief.[4]

The very fact, however, that Christian Science was irreconcilable with the doctrines of any of the established churches must have suggested that it should have an organisation of its own. A belief which presented a new theory of the Godhead, of sin and the atonement, which declared that petitions to a personal Deity could not obtain for man truth, life, or love,[5] needed an organisation behind it if it were to be successfully propagated. Mrs. Eddy's most useful and effective students had been active in church work before they came into Christian Science. They missed their old church associations and wanted a church to work for. They believed that their new faith was a revival of the apostolic method of healing, a new growth from the original root of Christianity, and it was as a religion, rather than a philosophy, that they liked to regard it. While most of these students had first allied themselves with Christian Science chiefly because they wished to heal or to be healed, a mere scheme of therapeutics, even metaphysical therapeutics, was too deficient in sentiment to hold them together and fire them with the zeal which the cause demanded. Mrs. Eddy began to realise this and to see that the time had come to

---

[4] *Science and Health* (1875), pp. 166, 167.
[5] *Science and Health* (1875), p. 289.

emphasise the more expressly religious features of Christian Science.

The first Christian Science organisation was that formed June 8, 1875, when eight of Mrs. Eddy's students banded together, calling themselves " the Christian Scientists," and pledging themselves to raise money enough to have Mrs. Eddy address them every Sunday. On July 4, 1876, the students reorganised into " The Christian Scientists' Association," and this society still held occasional informal meetings when first a church organisation was talked of.

In 1879 Mrs. Eddy and her students took steps to form a chartered church organisation. They elected officers and directors, and chose a name, " The Church of Christ (Scientist)." On August 6th they applied to the State for a charter. The officers and directors were: Mary B. G. Eddy, president; Margaret J. Dunshee, treasurer; Edward A. Orne, Miss Dorcas B. Rawson, Arthur T. Buswell, James Ackland, Margaret J. Foley, Mrs. Mary Ruddock, Oren Carr, directors.

All proceedings were conducted with the greatest secrecy, as Mrs. Eddy felt that it was imperative that the infant church should be hidden from the knowledge of the mesmerists, Spofford and Kennedy. When it was necessary for the newly elected officers and directors to meet before a notary and to sign the agreement of incorporation, Mrs. Eddy had a long list of notaries looked up, and finally selected one in Charlestown, a man who was known to Margaret Dunshee, and for whom she could vouch that he had no affiliations with mesmerists. The students met at Mrs. Dunshee's house in Charlestown, and, one by one, by circuitous routes, they went to the notary's office, where the papers were made out and signed. This meeting of the subscribers to the articles of incorporation occurred August 15th, and the papers were filed and a charter issued August 23, 1879. The purpose of the corporation was given as " to carry on and transact the business necessary to the worship of God," and Boston was named as the place within which it was established. There were in all twenty-six charter members, but by no means all of these were active in the work. The membership roll represented, like those of most new churches in small towns, all who could be persuaded to ally themselves with the sect.

For the first sixteen months of its existence the church had no regular place of meeting, but Sunday services were held at the houses of various members in Lynn and Boston. The Lynn meetings were usually held at the house of Mrs. F. A. Damon, who was one of the most earnest workers in the new church. A copy of the secretary's minutes of the Lynn meetings shows that, in Mrs. Eddy's absence, either Mrs. Damon or Mrs. Rice usually conducted the service. These minutes are interesting in that they make one realise what a small organisation the Christian Science Church then was. Half a dozen members, gathered in Mrs. Damon's parlour on Jackson Street, constituted a congregation. The minutes show that on one Sunday five members were present; on another four; on another seven, etc. The Boston circle of Christian Scientists, which met at the house of Mrs. Clara Choate, was scarcely larger. The service itself, however, was very much like the service now used in the great church in Boston. The meeting opened with silent prayer or with Mrs. Eddy's interpretation of the Lord's

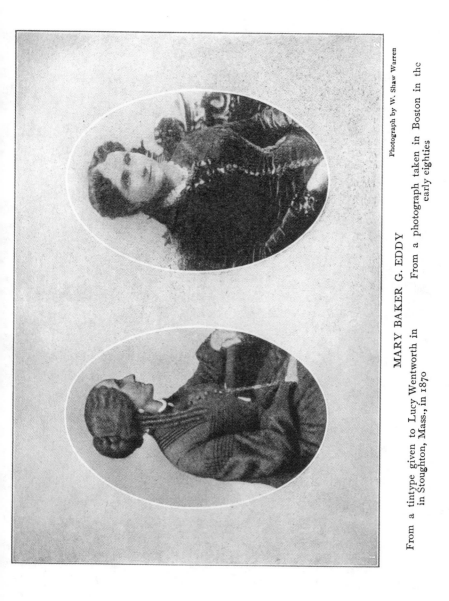

MARY BAKER G. EDDY

Photograph by W. Shaw Warren

From a tintype given to Lucy Wentworth in in Stoughton, Mass., in 1870

From a photograph taken in Boston in the early eighties

Prayer; then Mrs. Damon read from *Science and Health,* after which Mrs. Rice read from the Scriptures. The following record occurs for the meeting on September 5, 1880:

Meeting opened by Mrs. Damon in the usual way. Mrs. M. B. G. Eddy, having completed her summer vacation, was present and delivered a discourse on Mesmerism.

Whole number in attendance, twenty-two.

On the following Sunday the subject was again Mesmerism. Mrs. Eddy's resuming of her duties seems to have been marked by a vigorous return to this subject and by a marked increase in the attendance.

On December 12, 1880, the Christian Scientists began to hold their services in the Hawthorne rooms, on Park Street, Boston. Mrs. Eddy usually preached and conducted the services, though occasionally one of her students took her place, and now and again a minister of some other denomination was invited to occupy the pulpit. In spite of the fact that she was always effective on the rostrum, Mrs. Eddy seemed to dread these Sunday services. The necessity for wearing spectacles embarrassed her. When she sometimes wore glasses in her own home, she apologised for doing so, explaining that it was a habit she often rose above, but that at times the mesmerists were too strong for her. She believed that the mesmerists set to work upon her before the hour of the weekly services, and on Sunday morning her faithful students were sometimes called to her house to treat her against Kennedy, Spofford, and Arens, until she took the train for Boston. Certain ones of the students were delegated to attend her from Lynn to Boston and to occupy front seats in the Hawthorne rooms for the purpose of treating her while she spoke. On the way back to Lynn the party frequently discussed the particular kind of evil influence which had been brought to bear upon Mrs. Eddy during the service. Already Mrs. Eddy thought she could tell which was Kennedy's influence and which was Spofford's, and she could even liken their effect upon her to the operation of certain drugs. Later Arens' malevolence, too, came to have an aroma of its own, so that when Mrs. Eddy rose in the morning she could tell by the kind of depression she experienced which of the three was to be her tormentor for the day. At times she was convinced that Kennedy and Spofford were both annoying her, and not infrequently she declared that the three mesmerists had all set upon her at once.

During the last few years the attitude of the Lynn public toward Mrs. Eddy had changed from one of amused indifference to one of silent hostility. Mrs. Eddy attributed this change entirely to Kennedy and Spofford, and despairing of ever bringing her work to a successful issue in Lynn, she began planning to take Christian Science up bodily and flee with it to some place far removed from mesmerists. She decided to send Arthur Buswell to some other part of the country, there to seek out a spot for the planting of her church. Where to send him was the question. Mrs. Eddy and Mr. Buswell got out a map of the United States and studied it together. But, however topical the map, there were no red or green lines to indicate where mesmerism ran light or heavy, and they realised that the venture would be largely a leap in the dark. They finally selected Cincinnati, attracted, Mr. Buswell says, by its central location and by the number of railroads which seemed, on the map, to pass through that city.   Mr. Buswell was, accordingly, despatched, at his own expense, to make straight the path in Cincinnati, with the understanding that Mrs. Eddy would follow him in six weeks.[6]   She did not go, however, and was greatly annoyed when Mr. Buswell ran out of money and wrote to her for help.   She replied that it was very evident to her that mesmeric influences were abroad in Cincinnati as well as in Lynn, and had inspired him with disloyal sentiments.

In the meantime Mrs. Eddy's forerunners in Boston had been meeting with some success.   Mrs. Clara Choate and her husband had taken a house on Shawmut Avenue and were introducing the Christian Science treatment of disease.   Edward J. Arens came to Boston immediately after the unfortunate conspiracy tangle, and fell to work with industry and courage. He took an office at 32 Upton Street and began to do missionary work among the marketmen down about Faneuil Hall, treating a bronchial cold here and a case of rheumatism there.   He spoke occasionally in a hall in Charlestown, lecturing on Metaphysical Healing, and charging an admission fee of ten cents. Among his first patrons was James C. Howard, a bookkeeper who came to arrange for treatments for his invalid wife.   This was before Mrs. Eddy had entirely renounced Mr. Arens, and it was in his office that Mr. Howard first met Mrs. Eddy.   He became interested in Christian Science and made one of a class of two which Mrs. Eddy taught at Mrs. Choate's house.   Mrs. Eddy was then in need of practitioners, and she urgently needed an active man of affairs to succeed Mr. Arens, toward whom

---

[6] At about the same time that Mrs. Eddy sent Mr. Buswell to Cincinnati to prepare a way for her, she sent Joseph Morton to New York on the same mission, promising to follow later. He opened an office on Ninth Street, but, as he found no patients, he soon returned to Boston.

she had begun to feel deep resentment. She was also desirous of letting the lower floor of her Broad Street house, which had been tenantless for some time, in spite of the fact that she had tried very hard to rent it. In fact, Mrs. Eddy's differences with her tenants, servants, and students had created a general impression in Lynn that life at Number 8 Broad Street was difficult and complicated. Mr. Howard, when he moved there with his wife and children, certainly found it so. The Eddys were in such perpetual terror of mesmerism that they could give very little attention to anything else. They felt that the sentiment toward them in Lynn had changed, and Mrs. Eddy was so anxious and nervous that she easily gave way to petulance and anger. Mr. Howard and Mr. Eddy were indefatigable in their efforts to please her, but whatever they did, it usually proved to be the wrong thing. She had lost all patience with Mr. Eddy's slowness and had begun to exhibit annoyance at his somewhat rustic manner and appearance. Mr. Eddy had never been a particularly efficient man, and now his fear of mesmerists kept him in a semi-somnambulant condition. He sometimes became deeply discouraged in his efforts to help his wife, and once bitterly confided to Mrs. Rice that he did not believe God Almighty could please Mrs. Eddy.

Mr. Howard was an alert, adaptable young man who made himself useful in a great many ways. He took charge of the sale of the third edition of Mrs. Eddy's book, often acted as her private secretary, and played the cornet at the Sunday services in Hawthorne Hall. Mrs. Eddy at first seemed fond of him and seemed to enjoy his musical accomplishment. But she soon tired of him as she had tired of so many others, and grew so exacting that when he went out to do her errands he found it expedient to take down her instructions in writing, so that if, by the time he returned, she had changed her mind as to what she wanted done, he would have his notes to justify himself. When Mr. Howard left Mrs. Eddy's house in October, 1881, six months after he had moved into it, he had decided to leave the Church as well.

Mr. Howard was not the only Christian Scientist who came to this decision. Discouragement and discontent had been growing among Mrs. Eddy's oldest and most devout followers. For a long while they said nothing to each other, and each bore his disappointment and disillusionment as best he could. They believed firmly in the principles of Christian Science and hesitated to do anything which might injure the Church, but they felt that no good, either to her or to themselves, could come from their further association with Mrs. Eddy. Mr. Howard, when he went to explain his position to Mrs. Rice before he took the final step, found, to his amazement, that both she and her sister, Miss Rawson, felt that they had come to the end of their endurance and could follow Mrs. Eddy no further. Five others of the leading women of the Church confessed that they were discouraged and dissatisfied.   They were tired of being dragged as witnesses into lawsuits which they believed were unwise, and which they knew brought discredit upon the Church and, discouraged by the outbursts of rage which Mrs. Eddy apparently made no effort to control. and which they believed helped to bring on the violent illnesses for which they were perpetually called to treat her.   Above all, they were tired of Malicious Mesmerism.   Several of her

students really believed that this subject had become a monomania with Mrs. Eddy.   Christian Science seemed, for the time,
to have been superseded, and Demonology was the living and
important issue.   After earnest discussion and consultation,
eight of Mrs. Eddy's most prominent students agreed to
withdraw from the Church together.   They held a meeting
and drew up a memorial which each of them signed, and
of which each preserved a copy.   This resolution read as
follows:

We, the undersigned, while we acknowledge and appreciate the understanding of Truth imparted to us by our Teacher, Mrs. Mary B. G. Eddy,
led by Divine Intelligence to perceive with sorrow that departure from the
straight and narrow road (which alone leads to growth of Christ-like
virtues) made manifest by frequent ebullitions of temper, love of money,
and the appearance of hypocrisy, *cannot* longer submit to such Leadership;
therefore, without aught of hatred, revenge or petty spite in our hearts,
from a sense of duty alone, to her, the Cause, and ourselves, do most
respectfully withdraw our names from the Christian Science Association
and Church of Christ (Scientist).

S. Louise Durant,
Margaret J. Dunshee,
Dorcas B. Rawson,
Elizabeth G. Stuart,
Jane L. Straw,
Anna B. Newman,
James C. Howard,
Miranda R. Rice.

21st October, 1881.

On the night of October 21st this memorial was read aloud
by Mrs. F. A. Damon at the regular meeting of the Christian
Scientists' Association.   This meeting, which was a heated
session, was prolonged until after midnight.   The eight resignations were a complete surprise to Mrs. Eddy, and she expressed her indignation at length, declaring that the resigning

members were all the victims of mesmerism. The next day she made an effort to see in person several of the signers of the memorial, but they kept well within their doors and refused her admittance. Mr. Howard had been Mrs. Eddy's business representative; Mrs. Dunshee, Mrs. Newman, and Mrs. Stuart were all able and intelligent women, and their membership had been a source of great pride to Mrs. Eddy. Mrs. Rice and Miss Rawson had been her friends and followers for more than eleven years, and were the only ones of her early students who had been faithful until the founding of the Church. They had believed in her sincerely, and had served her, heart and soul. Because of Mrs. Rice's robust health, Mrs. Eddy liked to have her much about her. Mrs. Rice had been more successful than any other student in treating Mrs. Eddy in her illnesses, and a messenger from Broad Street often summoned her to Mrs. Eddy's side in the hours after midnight. When Mr. Eddy was arrested on the charge of conspiracy and thrown into jail, it was Mrs. Rice who persuaded her husband to furnish bail. On the morning after her resignation from the Church, Mrs. Rice saw Mrs. Eddy a moment from her window, but from that day to this she has never seen her again.

Instead of accepting the eight resignations, Mrs. Eddy notified the resigning members that they were liable to expulsion, and summoned them to meet the Church on October 29th. They did not appear, but at this meeting Mrs. F. A. Damon, at whose house the church services were formerly held, and Miss A. A. Draper, secretary of the Church, also resigned. In their letters of resignation they stated that they " could no longer entertain the subject of Mesmerism which had lately

been made uppermost in the meetings and in Mrs. Eddy's talks."
Edward A. Orne had quietly left the Church some time before,
and Mr. Buswell was in Cincinnati. There were scarcely a
dozen students left to whom Mrs. Eddy could turn in an hour
of need. During the next few months she worked incessantly
to rally her shattered ranks, and on February 3, 1882, the
few remaining members of the Christian Scientists' Association
published in the Lynn *Union* resolutions [7] censuring the act of
the seceding members, stamping their charges as untrue, and
indorsing Mrs. Eddy to the extent of affirming her " the chosen
messenger of God to the nations," and declaring that " unless
we hear Her voice we do not hear His voice."

Ardent as these resolutions were, they were the swan-song
of the movement in Lynn, and to this day the Christian Science
Church there has never prospered. Its members declare that

[7] The following is a copy of these resolutions:
" At a meeting of the Christian Scientist association the following resolutions were unanimously adopted:
" *Resolved*, That we the members of the Christian Scientist association, do
herein express to our beloved teacher, and acknowledged leader, Mary B.
Glover Eddy, our sincere and heartfelt thanks and gratitude for her earnest
labours in behalf of this association, by her watchfulness of its interest, and
persistent efforts to maintain the highest rule of Christian love among its
members.
" *Resolved*, That while she has had little or no help, except from God, in the
introduction to this age of materiality of her book, *Science and Health,* and
the carrying forward of the Christian principles it teaches and explains, she
has been unremitting in her faithfulness to her God-appointed work, and we
do understand her to be the chosen messenger of God to bear his truth to the
nations, and unless we hear ' Her Voice,' we do not hear ' His Voice.'
" *Resolved*, That while many and continued attempts are made by the mal-
practise, as referred to in the book, *Science and Health,* to hinder and stop
the advance of Christian science, it has with her leadership attained a success
that calls out the truest gratitude of her students, and when understood, by
all humanity.
" *Resolved*, That the charges made to her in a letter, signed by J. C. Howard,
M. R. Rice, D. B. Rawson, and five others, of hypocrisy, ebullitions of temper,
and love of money, are utterly false, and the cowardice of the signers in refusing to meet her and sustain or explain said charges, be treated with the
righteous indignation it justly deserves. That while we deplore such wicked-
ness and abuse of her who has befriended them in their need, and when wrong,
met them with honest, open rebuke, we look with admiration and reverence
upon her Christ-like example of meekness and charity, and will, in future,
more faithfully follow and obey her divine instructions, knowing that in so
doing we offer the highest testimonial of our appreciation of her Christian
leadership.
" *Resolved*, That a copy of these resolutions be presented to our teacher and
leader, Mary B. Glover Eddy, and a copy be placed on the records of this
Christian Scientist association."

there is an error in belief there regarding Mrs. Eddy which they find hard to overcome.

Mrs. Eddy at last despaired of conquering the prejudice that had arisen in Lynn against her and her religion. While she attributed this to the influence of the mesmerists, her seceding students attributed it to the unpleasant notoriety given her by her lawsuits and her quarrels with her followers. Whether these lawsuits were really discreditable to Mrs. Eddy or not, they were generally considered to be so in Lynn. People did not stop to discover whether they arose on reasonable grounds. The general public caught only the obvious paradox that here were a group of people teaching a new religion and professing to overcome sin and bodily disease through their superior realisation of Divine love, and that they were constantly quarrelling and bickering among themselves, accusing each other of fraud, dishonesty, witchcraft, bad temper, greed of money, hypocrisy, and finally of a conspiracy to murder. Unquestionably Mrs. Eddy, as the accepted messenger of God, was more severely criticised for her part in these altercations than if she had appeared before the courts merely as a citizen of Lynn, and this criticism had much to do with the cloud of suspicion and distrust which hung over the Church when, in the early part of the winter of 1882, Mrs. Eddy left Lynn forever behind her and went to Boston.

Mrs. Eddy's departure from Lynn was distinctly in the nature of a retreat. A neutral field had become pronouncedly hostile; her oldest friends and most ardent workers had left her. *Science and Health* had been through three editions, but less than four thousand copies of the book had been sold.

Her following was now, for the most part, made up of indifferent material—discontented women, and young men who had not
succeeded in finding their place in the world, or who had drifted
away from other professions.   The Christian Science Church
was a struggling organisation with considerably less than fifty
members; its history had been one of dissension, and its good
standing was all to make—and Mrs. Eddy was then sixty-one
years old.

CHAPTER XV

THE organisation of the Christian Science Church in August, 1879, seems to have suggested the organisation of another institution, which, in the history of the Christian Science movement, is second in importance only to the Church itself. The Massachusetts Metaphysical College was chartered January 31, 1881, and between that date and 1889, when it closed, about four thousand persons studied Christian Science in this institution, and to-day many practising healers have the degree of C.S.B., C.S.D., or D.S.D. from Mrs. Eddy's college.

The college was organised something more than a year before Mrs. Eddy removed permanently to Boston, and was, in the beginning, one of the experiments by which she strove to rehabilitate herself in Lynn. Its charter was issued under an act passed in 1874,[1] an act so loose in its requirements, resulting in the chartering of so many dubious institutions and the granting of so many misleading diplomas, that, in 1883,

---

[1] Acts and Resolves passed by the General Court of Massachusetts, 1874, Chapter 375, Section 2: "Such association may be entered into for any educational, charitable, benevolent, or religious purpose ; for the prosecution of any antiquarian, historical, literary, scientific, medical, artistic, monumental, or musical purposes," etc., etc. This Chapter 375 was later merged into Chapter 115 of the Public Statutes.

medical institutions chartered under this act were prohibited from conferring degrees.   The purpose of the Massachusetts Metaphysical College, as stated in the articles of agreement, was: " To teach pathology, ontology, therapeutics, moral science, metaphysics, and their application to the treatment of diseases." The signers to the articles of agreement were: Mary B. G. Eddy, president; James C. Howard, treasurer; Charles J. Eastman, M.D., Edgar F. Woodbury, James Wiley, William F. Walker, and Samuel P. Bancroft, directors; all students of Mrs. Eddy's except Charles J. Eastman, who had been a pupil in the little " dame's school " which Mrs. Eddy taught at Tilton for a few months during her first widowhood, and who at this time had a doubtful medical practice in Boston.

The name " Massachusetts Metaphysical College " is somewhat misleading. During the nine years of its existence this institution never had a building of its own, or any other seat than Mrs. Eddy's parlour, and, with very incidental exceptions, Mrs. Eddy herself, during all this time, constituted the entire faculty.[2]   In short, the Massachusetts Metaphysical College, subsequently of such wide fame among Christian Scientists, was simply Mrs. Eddy, and its seat was wherever she happened to be.   To call it an institution was a very literal application of the boast of the old Williams alumni that Mark Hopkins on one end of a saw-log and a student on the other would make a college.

The organisation of the college in 1881 in no way changed Mrs. Eddy's manner of instruction. Her new letter-heads,

---

[2] Mrs. Eddy states that her husband taught two terms in her college, that her adopted son, E. J. Foster Eddy, taught one term, and that Erastus N. Bates taught one class.

indeed, told the public that the Massachusetts Metaphysical College was located at Number 8 Broad Street, Lynn, but the name was the only thing which was new. Classes of from two to five students continued to meet on the second floor of Mrs. Eddy's house, as before, and she gave but one course of study: twelve lessons in mental healing, very similar to those she had given to Miss Rawson, Mrs. Rice, and their fellow-students eleven years before—except that " manipulation " was now discountenanced, and denunciation of mesmerism was a prominent feature of the lectures. The tuition fee was still three hundred dollars, the price which Mrs. Eddy says she fixed under Divine guidance; although, in many instances where the student was unable to pay that amount, she took one hundred dollars instead.

When Mrs. and Mr. Eddy moved to Boston in the early spring of 1882, they soon took a house at 569 Columbus Avenue, Mrs. Eddy's first permanent home in Boston, and on the door placed a large silver plate bearing the inscription, " Massachusetts Metaphysical College." At about this time Mr. Eddy's health began to decline, and both he and his wife believed that he was suffering from the adverse mental treatments of Edward J. Arens.

After the charge of conspiracy to murder, brought in 1878, a coldness developed between Mr. Arens and the Eddys. He came to Boston, and began to exercise some originality in his practice and teaching, which was, of course, very obnoxious to Mrs. Eddy. In 1881 Mr. Arens published a pamphlet entitled *Theology, or the Understanding of God as Applied to Healing the Sick*. In this pamphlet Mr. Arens quoted extensively from *Science and Health*, using the text of Mrs.

Eddy's work where it answered his purpose, but substituting his own ideas for many of her statements which he believed were extreme or untenable.   In his preface he announced that he made no claim to the authorship of the doctrine which he advanced, stating that it had been practised by Jesus and the apostles, by the secret association of priests known as the Gottesfreunde in the fourteenth century, and in the nineteenth century by P. P. Quimby of Belfast, Me.   He added that he had made use of " some thoughts contained in a work by Eddy." The third edition of *Science and Health* appeared a few months later, containing a preface signed by Asa G. Eddy, which scathingly denounced Arens as a plagiarist, and paid the following tribute to Mrs. Eddy:

" Mrs. Eddy's works are the outgrowths of her life.   I never knew so unselfish an individual, or one so tireless in what she considers her duty.   It would require ages and God's mercy to make the ignorant hypocrite who published that pamphlet originate its contents.   His pratings are coloured by his character, they cannot impart the hue of ethics, but leave his own impress on what he takes.   He knows less of metaphysics than any decently honest man."

From this time on, the Eddys credited Mr. Arens with the same malicious intervention in their affairs with which they had already charged Mr. Kennedy and Mr. Spofford.   As has been mentioned before, Mrs. Eddy believed that the mesmeric influence of each of these three men affected her differently, and that each operated upon her in a manner analogous to the effect of certain harmful drugs.   The influence of Mr. Arens, she insisted, affected her like arsenic.   Hence, when Mr. Eddy's

health began to fail, she diagnosed his case as the result of
Mr. Arens' mesmeric influence, or, as she expressed it, " arsenical
poison, mentally administered." To say that Mr. Eddy believed in malicious mesmerism more sincerely than did his wife
would perhaps be incorrect; but his was the more passive nature,
and he had less power of reaction and recuperation. He was
convinced that he was being slowly poisoned, and daily treated
himself against Mr. Arens and his alliterative chemical equivalent.

When Mr. Eddy continued to grow steadily worse, Mrs. Eddy
became alarmed, and sent for a regular physician. She called
Dr. Rufus K. Noyes, then of Lynn, a graduate of the Dartmouth Medical School, and who has now for many years been
a physician in Boston. Dr. Noyes found Mr. Eddy's case very
simple, and told Mrs. Eddy that her husband was suffering
from a common and very well-defined disease of the heart, and
that he might die at any moment. He came to see Mr. Eddy
twice after this, gave him advice as to diet, hygiene, and rest,
and suggested the usual tonics for the heart and general
system.

Mr. Eddy's death occurred on the morning of Saturday,
June 3d, some hours before daybreak, and almost immediately
Mrs. Eddy telegraphed Dr. Noyes to come up from Lynn and
perform an autopsy.[3] The autopsy was private, and was
conducted at the widow's request. Dr. Noyes found that death
had resulted from an organic disease of the heart, the aortic

---

[3] Only the year before, Mrs. Eddy had expressed herself strongly against
post-mortem examinations: " A metaphysician never gives medicine, recommends
or trusts in hygiene, or believes in the ocular or the *post-mortem* examination
of patients." *Science and Health* (1881), Vol. I., p. 269.
" Many a hopeless case of disease is induced by a single post-mortem examination." *Science and Health* (1881), Vol. I., p. 163.

valve being destroyed and the surrounding tissues infiltrated with calcareous matter.

It is necessary to remember that, fantastic as the theory of poisoning by mental suggestion may sound, Mrs. Eddy thoroughly believed in it, and she considered her husband's death absolute proof of the power of malicious mesmerism to destroy life.   Charles J. Eastman, who attended Mr. Eddy just before his death, agreed with Mrs. Eddy that the symptoms were those of arsenical poisoning, and she doubtless thought that the autopsy would corroborate this opinion.   After the autopsy she still clung to her conviction, and, although Dr. Noyes actually took Mr. Eddy's heart into the room where she was and pointed out to her its defects, she still maintained that her husband had died from mental arsenic.   On Monday she gave out the following interview: [4]

My husband's death was caused by malicious mesmerism. Dr. C. J. Eastman, who attended the case after it had taken an alarming turn, declares the symptoms to be the same as those of arsenical poisoning. On the other hand, Dr. Rufus K. Noyes, late of the City Hospital, who held an autopsy over the body to-day, affirms that the corpse is free from all material poison, although Dr. Eastman still holds to his original belief. I know it was poison that killed him, not material poison, but mesmeric poison. My husband was in uniform health, and but seldom complained of any kind of ailment. During his brief illness, just preceding his death, his continual cry was, "Only relieve me of this continual suggestion, through the mind, of poison, and I will recover." It is well known that by constantly dwelling upon any subject in thought finally comes the poison of belief through the whole system. . . . I never saw a more self-possessed man than dear Dr. Eddy was. He said to Dr. Eastman, when he was finally called to attend him: "My case is nothing that I cannot attend to myself, although to me it acts the same as poison and seems to pervade my whole system just as that would."

This is not the first case known of where death has occurred from what appeared to be poison, and was so declared by the attending

[4] Boston *Post,* June 5, 1882.

physician, but in which the body, on being thoroughly examined by an autopsy, was shown to possess no signs of material poison. There was such a case in New York. Every one at first declared poison to have been the cause of death, as the symptoms were all there; but an autopsy contradicted the belief, and it was shown that the victim had had no opportunity for procuring poison. I afterwards learned that she had been very active in advocating the merits of our college. Oh, isn't it terrible, that this fiend of malpractice is in the land! The only remedy that is effectual in meeting this terrible power possessed by the evil-minded is to counteract it by the same method that I use in counteracting poison. They require the same remedy. Circumstances debarred me from taking hold of my husband's case. He declared himself perfectly capable of carrying himself through, and I was so entirely absorbed in business that I permitted him to try, and when I awakened to the danger it was too late. I have cured worse cases before, but took hold of them in time. I don't think that Dr. Carpenter [5] had anything to do with my husband's death, but I do believe it was the rejected students [6]—students who were turned away from our college because of their unworthiness and immorality. To-day I sent for one of the students whom my husband had helped liberally, and given money, not knowing how unworthy he was. I wished him to come, that I might prove to him how, by metaphysics, I could show the cause of my husband's death. He was as pale as a ghost when he came to the door, and refused to enter, or to believe that I knew what caused his death. Within half an hour after he left, I felt the same attack that my husband felt—the same that caused his death. I instantly gave myself the same treatment that I would use in a case of arsenical poisoning, and so I recovered, just the same as I could have caused my husband to recover had I taken the case in time. After a certain amount of mesmeric poison has been administered it cannot be averted. No power of mind can resist it. It must be met with resistive action of the mind at the start, which will counteract it. We all know that disease of any kind cannot reach the body except through the mind, and that if the mind is cured the disease is soon relieved. Only a few days ago I disposed of a tumour in twenty-four hours that the doctors had said must be removed by the knife. I changed the course of the mind to counteract the effect of the disease. This proves the myth of matter. Mesmerism will make an apple burn the hand so that the child will cry. My husband never spoke of death as something we were to meet, but only as a phase of mortal belief. . . . I do believe in God's supremacy over error, and this gives me peace. I do believe, and have

---

[5] Dr. Carpenter was a well-known mesmerist who used to give public exhibitions in Boston.

[6] Although Mrs. Eddy usually attributed her husband's death to Mr. Arens' mesmeric influence, she sometimes mentioned Richard Kennedy as his accomplice.

been told, that there is a price set upon my head. One of my students, a malpractitioner, has been heard to say that he would follow us to the grave. He has already reached my husband. While my husband and I were in Washington and Philadelphia last winter, we were obliged to guard against poison, the same symptoms apparent at my husband's death constantly attending us. And yet the one who was planning the evil against us was in Boston the whole time. To-day a lady, active in forwarding the good of our college, told me that she had been troubled almost constantly with arsenical poison symptoms, and is now treating them constantly as I directed her. Three days ago one of my patients died, and the doctor said he died from arsenic, and yet there were no material symptoms of poison.

The " Doctor " Eastman whom Mrs. Eddy quotes as corroborating her theory that Mr. Eddy died from arsenic was not a graduate of any medical school, nor is there any evidence that he had ever studied at one, though the then lax medical laws of Massachusetts did not prevent him from writing M.D. after his name. He was a director of Mrs. Eddy's college, and his name appeared in her curriculum as an authority to be consulted on instrumental surgery, which was not taught in her classes. He was also dean of the so-called " Bellevue Medical College," which was chartered under the same undiscriminating act under which Mrs. Eddy's college was chartered, and which was later reported as a fraudulent institution and closed.

In the *Christian Science Journal*, June, 1885, Mrs. Eddy thus explains Mr. Eastman's connection with her college, but neglects to say that he was one of the original directors:

Charles J. Eastman, M.D., was never a student of mine, and, to my knowledge, never claimed to be a Christian Scientist. At the time Mr. Rice [1] alludes to he was a homeopathic physician and dean of the Bellevue

_____
[1] The Rev. Mr. Rice, a former member of the Massachusetts legislature, had written some newspaper articles against the issue of medical diplomas by Mrs. Eddy's college.

Medical College. His name appeared in my curriculum as surgeon to be consulted outside, instrumental surgery not being taught in my college. His name has been removed from my curriculum. Such are the facts wherewith Rev. Mr. Rice would slander a religious sect.

MARY B. G. EDDY,

Prest. Massachusetts Metaphysical College.

Although a genial enough fellow personally, and a frequent caller at Mrs. Eddy's house, Eastman's " professional " record is almost incredibly sinister. His private practice was largely of a criminal nature, and at the time when Mrs. Eddy made him a director of her college he had already been indicted on a charge of performing a criminal operation. In 1890 he was again before the Grand Jury on a similar charge; and in 1893, upon a third charge (the patient having died from the effects of the operation), he was sentenced to five years in the State prison. Eastman served out his term, and died a few years after his release.

Eastman's assertion that he found traces of arsenic in Mr. Eddy's body was absolutely valueless as a medical opinion.

Mr. Eddy's funeral services were held at the house in Columbus Avenue, after which his remains were taken to Tilton, N. H., by Mr. George D. Choate, and interred in the Baker family lot, Mrs. Eddy herself remaining in Boston. On the following Sunday, Mrs. Clara Choate preached a eulogistic funeral sermon before the Christian Science congregation—still a small body of less than fifty members. Mr. Eddy, indeed, died upon the eve of the determining epoch in his wife's career, and could have had no conception of the ultimate influence and extent of the movement which bears his name.

Some time after Mr. Eddy's death, his wife wrote a colloquy in verse, which she called " Meeting of my Departed Mother and Husband," in which she expressed confidence in their blessed state and in her own future.

In this dialogue the mother, Abigail Baker, asks of Mr. Eddy:

> Bearest thou no tidings from our loved on earth,
> The toiler tireless for Truth's new birth,
>> All unbeguiled?
> Our joy is gathered from her parting sigh:
> This hour looks on her heart with pitying eye,—
>> What of my child?

To this Mr. Eddy replies:

> When severed by death's dream, I woke to life:
> She deemed I died, and could not hear my strife
>> At first to fill
> That waking with a love that steady turns
> To God; a hope that ever upward yearns,
>> Bowed to his will.
>
> Years had passed o'er thy broken household band
> When angels beckoned me to this bright land,
>> With thee to meet.
> She that has wept o'er me, kissed thy cold brow,
> Rears the sad marble to our memory now
>> In lone retreat.
>
> By the remembrance of her earthly life,
> And parting prayer, I only know my wife,
>> Thy child, shall come,—
> Where farewells cloud not o'er our ransomed rest,—
> Hither to reap, with all the crowned and blest,
>> Of bliss the sum.

Many of Mrs. Eddy's students, as well as Mrs. Eddy herself, disregarded the evidence of the autopsy, and believed that Mr. Eddy had died from mesmeric poison rather than from a disease of the heart. Every new movement has its extremists, and

Christian Science was then so young that all sorts of extravagant hopes were cherished among its enthusiasts. More than one dreamer fervently believed that the grave was at last to be cheated of its victory. In any case, Mr. Eddy's death was regarded as a blow to the movement, but, since they believed that the bodily organs were impotent to contribute to either health or disease except as they were influenced by the belief of the patient, it was much less discouraging to feel that Mr. Eddy had died from the shafts of the enemy than from a simple defect of the heart-valves. In the one case, his death was a stimulus, a call to action; in the other, it was an impeachment of Mr. Eddy's growth in Science, an indication that he had not entirely got beyond the belief in the efficacy of the organs of the body. Explained as the work of animal magnetism, Mr. Eddy's death, which might otherwise have been a blow to his wife professionally, was made to confirm one of her favourite doctrines. It was upon the subject of malicious mesmerism that many of her students had differed from her and fallen away, and even the loyal found it the most difficult of her doctrines to accept. Here, in Mr. Eddy's death, was absolute evidence of what mesmerism might accomplish.

The hour had come when Mrs. Eddy needed all her friends about her. Arthur T. Buswell was still in Cincinnati, where he had been sent as a path-finder two years before. After Mrs. Eddy's tart reply when he wrote to her asking financial aid, their correspondence practically ceased until Mr. Eddy's illness, when she sent him a request to give her husband absent treatments. One day he received a telegram which said merely: "Come to 569 Columbus Avenue immediately." He accordingly gave up his position as Superintendent of Public Charities, and started at once for Boston. When he arrived at 569 Columbus Avenue, he found Mr. Eddy dead in the house, and Mrs. Eddy surrounded by half a dozen faithful students, and almost frantic from fear. She declared that mesmerism had broken down her every defence, that her students were powerless to treat against it, and that she herself was at last prostrated. Twice, she said, she had resuscitated her husband from the power which was strangling him, but the third time her strength was exhausted. Mesmerism was submerging them, and she felt that she was barely keeping her own head above water. She was afraid to go out of the house, and afraid to stay in it. This was the end, she told her faithful women; undoubtedly she would speedily follow her husband. The light of truth was to be put out, and the world would begin again its dreary vigil of centuries.

But, although beset by grief and fear, Mrs. Eddy did not abandon herself to lamentation. On the contrary, she sat almost constantly at her desk, writing press notices and newspaper interviews upon the subject of her husband's death. Mrs. Eddy, indeed, is never so commanding a figure as when she bestirs herself in the face of calamity. She gave way to fear and dread only in the short intervals when she laid aside her driven pen for rest, and her best energies were concentrated upon how she should present to the public this misfortune which, if wrongly understood, might be used as an effective argument against Christian Science, and might retard her advancement in a new field.

Soon after her husband's death, Mrs. Eddy, attended by

Mr. Buswell and Miss Alice Sibley, went to Mr. Buswell's old home at Barton, Vt., to spend the remainder of the summer. Mr. Buswell asserts that Mrs. Eddy was in an excessively nervous and exhausted condition, approaching nervous prostration, and that he was called up night after night to treat her for those hysterical attacks from which she was never entirely free. But, however ill she might have been the night before, each day found her planning for the future of her church and college, arranging for lectures to be given by her students, looking about for new practitioners, and tirelessly devising means to extend the movement. She knew that a practical reconstruction of her household would now be necessary, and began casting about in her mind for such of her students as could be counted upon to devote themselves unreservedly to her service. In one of her selections, certainly, she was not mistaken. On the day they started back to Boston, Mrs. Eddy asked Mr. Buswell to telegraph Calvin A. Frye, a young machinist of Lawrence, Mass., who had lately studied with her, to meet them at Plymouth, N. H. One is tempted to wonder what Mr. Frye would have done, when this message reached him, had he known of what it was to be the beginning. From the day he joined Mrs. Eddy at Plymouth, and returned to Boston with her, he has never left her. Having entered Mrs. Eddy's service at the age of thirty-seven, he is now a man of sixty-four, and is still at his post.

For twenty-seven years Mr. Frye has occupied an anomalous position in Mrs. Eddy's household. He has been her house-steward, bookkeeper, and secretary. When he attends her upon her ceremonial drives in Concord, he wears the livery of a footman. In a letter to her son, George Glover, written April 27, 1898, Mrs. Eddy describes Mr. Frye as her " man-of-all-work." Since Mrs. Eddy's retirement to Concord eighteen years ago, Calvin Frye has lived in an isolation almost as complete as her own, the object of surmises and insinuations. He has no personal friends outside of the walls of Pleasant View, and the oft-repeated assertion that in twenty-seven years he has not been beyond Mrs. Eddy's call for twenty-four hours is perhaps literally true. Although her treatment of him has often been contemptuous in the extreme, his fidelity has been invaluable to Mrs. Eddy; but the actual donning of livery by a middle-aged man of some education and of sturdy, independent New England ancestry, is a difficult thing to understand. Whether he feels the grave charges which have recently been brought against him, or the ridicule of which he has long been the object, it is not likely that any one will ever learn from Mr. Frye. Whatever his motives and experiences, they are securely hidden behind an impassive countenance and a long-confirmed habit of silence.

Calvin A. Frye was born August 24, 1845, in Frye Village, which is now a part of Andover, Mass., and which was formerly called Frye's Mills, as it was a settlement which had grown up about the saw-mill and grist-mill of Enoch Frye II., Calvin Frye's grandfather. The Fryes were an old American family, and their ancestors had taken part in the War of the Revolution and the War of 1812. Calvin Frye's father, Enoch Frye III., was born in the last year of the eighteenth century. After preparing himself in the Phillips Andover Academy, he entered Harvard University, and was graduated in 1821, with that

CALVIN A. FRYE
From a photograph taken about 1882

famous class to which belonged Ralph Waldo Emerson, Samuel
Hatch, Edward Loring, and Francis Cabot. The members
of this class, before their graduation, agreed to hold a reunion
every year for fifty years, and Enoch Frye was present at
the fiftieth and last reunion of his class at Cambridge in
1871.

After leaving college, Enoch Frye taught for a short time
as assistant master in one of the Boston schools. In 1823
he returned to Andover. While still a young man he had a
long illness which left him incurably lame and partially incapacitated him. After his recovery he kept a small grocery-
store. He married Lydia Barnard, and they had four children, of whom Calvin was the third. While the children were
still very young, the mother became insane, and, with the exception of lucid intervals of short duration, she was insane
until her death at an advanced age. She was twice placed in an
asylum, but, upon her return from her second stay there, she
begged her family not to send her away again, and for twelve
years thereafter she was the charge of her widowed daughter,
Lydia Roaf.

Each of Enoch Frye's children learned a trade, and Calvin,
after attending the public school in Andover, was apprenticed
as a machinist in Davis & Furber's machine-shops in North Andover. He worked there until he joined Mrs. Eddy in 1882.
He was a good machinist, and left a steady and fairly remunerative employment to follow her. When he was twenty-
six years old, Calvin married Miss Ada E. Brush of Lowell,
who was visiting in Lawrence, and who attended the same church.
She lived but one year, and after her death Calvin went back

to his father's house—the family had moved to Lawrence in the early '60's.

The Fryes were all calm, slow, and inarticulate. They kept to themselves, both in Andover and in Lawrence, and never went anywhere except to the Congregational Church, of which they all were members. In their church relations they were as quiet and unassertive as in their secular life. They went to service regularly, but evinced no special interest in the church. Indeed, their solitary manner of life seemed to come about from a general lack of interest in people and affairs, and they stayed at home not so much because of an absorbing family life as because they felt no impulse to stir about the world. The men were all good mechanics, regular and steady in their habits; Lydia, the daughter, was patient, industrious, and self-sacrificing. As a family, the Fryes were long-lived. Enoch III. lived from 1799 to 1886. His brother Andrew, now living, is between ninety-five and ninety-six years old, and a sister also lived to a great age. Careful, regular living and a systematic avoidance of any excitement long preserved the Fryes in health of mind and body. Certainly the forbears of Calvin Frye had done their best to sheathe his nerves for the uneasy office to which he was to be called and chosen.

Calvin and Lydia Frye first became interested in Christian Science through their sister-in-law, Mrs. Oscar Frye. Mrs. Clara Choate, a prominent healer in the Boston church, was called to treat the insane mother, whom the family believed was benefited by the treatments. Calvin took a course of instruction under Mrs. Eddy, after which both he and Lydia practised a little. After Calvin joined Mrs. Eddy in Boston, Lydia followed him, and for some time did Mrs. Eddy's housework. Returning ill to Lawrence, she underwent a severe surgical operation, and at last died in reduced circumstances at the home of a relative. Lydia was an ardent Christian Scientist, and almost until the day she died stoutly declared that she " did not believe in death."

From the day Calvin Frye entered the service of Mrs. Eddy, he lived in literal accordance with the suggestion of that passage in *Science and Health* [8] where Mrs. Eddy reminds us that Jesus acknowledged no family ties and bade us call no man father. Mrs. Eddy demanded of her followers all that they had to give, and Mr. Frye, certainly, complied with her demand. When his father, Enoch Frye III., died, on April 22, 1886, four years after the son had entered Mrs. Eddy's service, Calvin went down to Lawrence to attend the funeral, but his precipitate haste indicated a short leave of absence. On the way to the cemetery he stopped the carriage and boarded a street-car bound for the railway-station, in order to catch the next train back to Boston. By the time his sister Lydia died, four years later, Calvin had become so completely absorbed in his new life and duties that he did not acknowledge the notification of her death, did not go to her funeral, and did not respond to a request for a small amount of money to help defray the burial expenses. For him family ties no longer existed, and death had become merely a belief.

---

[8] *Science and Health* (1906), page 31.

CHAPTER XVI

THE Massachusetts Metaphysical College, in Boston, was
first at 569 Columbus Avenue, and later at 571, the house
next-door. The houses, which are still standing, were then
exactly alike, narrow three-and-a-half-story dwellings with gray
stone fronts and slate roofs, a type of house very common in
Boston. When Mrs. Eddy returned to the city in the fall of
1882, attended by Mr. Buswell and Mr. Frye, she at once
resumed her classes; this, of course, meant that the college had
reopened, for Mrs. Eddy was still the president and entire
faculty. Half a dozen or more of her students now made their
home in Mrs. Eddy's house, or, as they expressed it, "lived at
the college." Among these were Calvin Frye, Arthur Buswell,
Julia Bartlett, Hanover P. Smith, E. H. Hammond, and Mrs.
Whiting. (Luther M. Marston and Mrs. Emma Hopkins came
later.) They lived on a coöperative plan, each contributing
his share toward the household expenses, while Mr. Frye did the
marketing, engaged the servants, kept the accounts, and super-
intended the housekeeping. Mrs. Eddy fitted up an office on
the first floor, where most of her resident students saw their
patients. They observed a system of rotation, and each had

his fixed office hours, so that the one room met the needs of several practitioners. These practitioners, in one way and another, helped to arouse an interest in Christian Science, and Mrs. Eddy's classes began to grow larger. Her teaching was not so much of a tax upon her strength as might be imagined, for the twelve lectures were, by this time, an old story to her and the same lecture was always given in practically the same language. The lectures dealt with but one idea, and progressed rather by figurative illustrations and repetitions than by the development of a line of reasoning. But her duties by no means ended with her lectures. She kept a sharp eye on the finances of the college and the household expenditures, more than once taking Mr. Frye to task for his mistakes in bookkeeping. Mrs. Eddy's correspondence was now very large, and she usually attended to it herself. She frequently occupied the pulpit at Hawthorne Hall on Sunday, and was constantly writing replies to attacks upon her church and college, besides press notices, which Mr. Buswell took about to the editors of the Boston papers in the hope of further advertising Mrs. Eddy and her work. What with preaching, teaching, writing, and editing, Mrs. Eddy had very little time for friendly personal intercourse. She was, as her students used proudly to declare, in the saddle day and night. She went out of the house but seldom; though she liked to take a daily drive when she had time for it. With her friends and resident students she never talked of anything but Christian Science and the business problems which confronted her. When other subjects were introduced, she grew absent-minded. She read very little except the newspapers and the *New York Ledger*, which she had read since her young womanhood, and which she still read regularly every week. In earlier times Mrs. Eddy had been very fond of Mrs. Southworth's novels, but now she discouraged the reading of fiction, and *Science and Health* was the only book she kept in her room. When she lectured before her classes, Mrs. Eddy usually had a vase of flowers upon the table at her side, and, to illustrate the non-existence of matter, she often explained that there were really no flowers there at all, and that the bouquet was merely a belief of mortal mind. She was fond of flowers in spite of the fact that she had always been totally without a sense of smell—she used, indeed, to tell her students that the absence of a physical sense meant a gain in spirituality.

There was singularly little social intercourse among the students who resided at the college. Mrs. Eddy was no idler, and she found plenty of work for all her assistants. Occasionally, in the evening, a fire was lighted in the parlour downstairs, and she joined her students for an hour or two; but this did not occur often. The two memorable festivities of the Christian Scientists in the early '80's were the reception which Mrs. Clara E. Choate gave for Mrs. Eddy upon the latter's return from a visit to Washington, April 5, 1882, and the picnic at Point of Pines, July 16, 1885, which commemorated the ninth anniversary of the founding of the Christian Science Association, and was also Mrs. Eddy's sixty-fourth birthday. At this picnic E. H. Harris, a dentist, and a new protégé of Mrs. Eddy's, gave a talk in which he mentioned the advantages of Christian Science in the practice of dentistry; Mrs. Augusta Stetson, who had recently come into the Association, and who had been a professional elocutionist before she became a Christian Scientist, recited two poems; and Mrs. Eddy gave a " spiritual interpretation " of the ocean.

The atmosphere of Mrs. Eddy's house derived its peculiar character from her belief in malicious mesmerism, which exerted a sinister influence over every one under her roof. Her students could never get away from it. Morning, noon, and night the thing had to be reckoned with, and the very domestic arrangements were ordered to elude or to combat the demoniacal power. If Mrs. Eddy had kept in her house a dangerous maniac or some horrible physical monstrosity which was always breaking from confinement and stealing about the chambers and hallways, it could scarcely have cast a more depressing anxiety over her household. Those of her students who believed in mesmerism were always on their guard with each other, filled with suspicion and distrust. Those who did not believe in it dared not admit their disbelief. If a member of that household denied the doctrine, or even showed a lack of interest in it, he was at once pronounced a mesmerist and requested to leave.

Mr. Eddy's death had given malicious animal magnetism a new vogue. Mrs. Eddy was now always discovering in herself and her students symptoms of arsenical poison or of other baleful drugs. Her nocturnal illnesses, which she had for years attributed to malicious mesmerism, were now more frequent and violent than ever.

One of the principal duties of the resident students was to treat Mrs. Eddy for these attacks. These seizures usually came on about midnight. Mrs. Eddy would first call Mr. Frye, and he, after hurrying into his clothes, would go about the house, knocking at the doors of all the students, and calling to them to dress immediately and hurry down to Mrs. Eddy's room.   After arousing the inmates of the house, he would hasten through the deserted streets, summoning one after another of the healers whom Mrs. Eddy considered most effective.   When they arrived at the college, they would find a group of sleepy men standing in the hall outside Mrs. Eddy's door, talking in low tones.   They were called, one by one, by Miss Bartlett or Mr. Frye, and admitted singly into Mrs. Eddy's chamber. Sometimes she lay in a comatose condition, and would remain thus for several hours, while each student, in his turn, sat beside the bed and silently treated her for about twenty minutes.   He then left the room by another door than the one by which he had entered, and another student took his place. Again, the students would find Mrs. Eddy sitting up in bed, with a high colour, her hair in disorder, wringing her hands and uttering unintelligible phrases.   On one occasion, when Mrs. Eddy was walking the floor with a raging toothache, metaphysical treatment was abandoned, and several of her students rushed up and down Tremont Street after midnight, trying to persuade some dentist to leave his bed and come to her relief.

In animal magnetism Mrs. Eddy found a satisfactory explanation for the seeming perversity of inanimate things. Mesmerism caused the water-pipes to freeze and the washboiler to leak.   She was convinced that all the postal clerks and telegraph operators in Boston had been mesmerised, and on one occasion, when she was sending an important telegram to Chicago, she sent Luther M. Marston, one of her students, to

West Newton to despatch it via Worcester, so that it need not go through Boston at all.

When a contagion of influenza spread about Boston in the early '80's, a number of the students in Mrs. Eddy's class were affected by it. She paused one day in the midst of a lecture to say: " I notice that a number of you are sneezing and coughing, and the cause is perfectly apparent to me. Kennedy and Spofford are treating you for hashish. Just treat yourselves against hashish, and this will pass."

Even the students under Mrs. Eddy's own roof were at times accused of resorting to malicious malpractice. On one occasion Mr. Buswell secured the Rev. Dr. Andrew P. Peabody of Cambridge to preach before the Christian Science congregation at Hawthorne Hall. It was announced by Mrs. Eddy, before the students started for the service, that Mr. Frye was to introduce Dr. Peabody to the audience. When the minister ascended the rostrum, however, he was alone, and no one introduced him. After several days had passed, Mr. Frye knocked at Mr. Buswell's door late one night, and told him that he was wanted in the parlour. Mr. Buswell rose, dressed, and went downstairs, where he found Mrs. Eddy and half a dozen resident students sitting about the room. Mr. Buswell sat down, and for a few minutes every one was silent. Then Mr. Frye rose and said, " Mr. Buswell, I charge you with having worked upon my mind last Sunday, so that I could not introduce the speaker." Mrs. Eddy listened while Mr. Buswell defended himself. Several other students spoke, and then everybody went off to bed.

In the summer of 1884 Mrs. Eddy taught her first class

in Chicago. She had now fallen out with Mrs. Clara Choate, and for several weeks before she went West Mrs. Eddy was in a state of great anxiety lest Mrs. Choate should " prostrate " her through mesmerism, as she believed that Mrs. Choate herself wished to go to Chicago to teach.   Mr. Frye had bought tickets for Mrs. Eddy and himself when, on the very night before they were to start, she fell ill.   Next day she was not able to leave the house, and many of her students were summoned to the college to treat against Mrs. Choate.

This adverse treatment, now conducted with some system, was an important feature of the daily life at the college.   A regular society was organised among Mrs. Eddy's most trusted students and was called the " P. M." (Private Meeting).[1] This society met daily after breakfast in the morning and after supper at night, gathered in Mrs. Eddy's parlour, and " took up the enemy " in thought.   Mrs. Eddy was not always present at these sittings, but she usually gave out the line of treatment. She would say, for example: " Treat Kennedy. Say to him: ' Your sins have found you out. You are affected as you wish to affect me. Your evil thought reacts upon you. You are bilious, you are consumptive, you have liver trouble, you have been poisoned by arsenic,' " etc.   Mrs. Eddy further instructed her practitioners that, when they were treating their patients, they should first take up and combat the common enemy, mesmerism, before they took up the patient's error. The adverse treatments given by the students at the college were usually conducted in perfect silence, and the participants

---

[1] The sessions of this secret society later caused a good deal of discussion and criticism. In the *Christian Science Journal* of September, 1888, Mrs. Eddy admits that she " did organise a secret society known as the P. M.," but that its workings were not " shocking or terrible."

sat with their eyes closed.[2] Miss Bartlett, a very devout woman, as she sat in this silent circle, absorbed in her task, her eyes closed, her head bowed, had a habit of idly passing a side-comb again and again through her hair. Mrs. Eddy, who, when she was there, always kept an eye on the circle, on one of these occasions suddenly broke the stillness by a sarcastic remark to the effect that better work would be done if less time were spent in hair-combing and more in combating error. Miss Bartlett blushed as if she had been caught committing a mortal sin.

But Mrs. Eddy's policy of sharp rebuke proved to be a wise one. On the whole her students liked it, and on the whole they needed it. Her business assistants and practitioners were, most of them, young men whose years had need of direction. In the nature of the case, they were generally young men without a strong purpose and without very definite aims and ambitions. Whether it was that Mrs. Eddy did not want men of determination about her, or whether such men were not drawn to her and her college, the fact remains that most of the men then in her service were of the eminently biddable sort. Some of them, before they came into Christian Science, had tried other vocations and had not been successful. Mrs. Eddy drew young men of this type about her, not only because she could offer them a good living, but because she was able to give them an impetus, to charge them with energy and endow them with a certain effectiveness which they did not have of themselves. Loyal Christian Scientists point to this or that man who once worked

---

[2] Calvin Frye, Arthur Buswell, Hanover P. Smith, Luther M. Marston, E. H. Hammond, Mrs. Whiting, and Miss Julia Bartlett were at various times members of this circle.

under Mrs. Eddy and who afterward broke with her, explaining that he was more successful and useful under her than he has ever been since he went over to the enemy.   In some instances this is true.   Many of her students never worked so well after they withdrew from her compelling leadership, and their contact with her remained the most vivid and important event in their lives.   Out of her abundant energy and determination Mrs. Eddy has been able to nerve many a weak arm and to steel many an irresolute will, and she has done much of her work with tools which were temporarily given hardness and edge by the driving personality behind them.

As the college grew and her classes increased in size, Mrs. Eddy exacted, and for the most part obtained, the same absolute obedience which she had demanded of the faithful in Lynn. She had a custom of sending telegrams to students who had left Boston, summoning them to report at the college imme- diately, and giving no explanation of the order.   When they arrived there, they sometimes found that she had merely been experimenting to see how quickly they could reach her in case of need.   If they were prompt in this sort of drill, she seemed pleased and reassured.   On the Fourth of July, especially, she demanded that all her students be subject to call, and that none of the resident students leave Boston on that day. She explained that on the Fourth " mortal mind was in ebulli- tion," and she feared animal magnetism more then than at any other time.

In 1883 Mrs. Eddy brought an action against Edward J. Arens for infringement of her copyright upon *Science and Health,* and won the suit.   Arens was forbidden to circulate his book,—to which there has already been a reference in Chapter XV,—and the copies which he had on hand were ordered by the court to be destroyed. Mr. Arens' defence was that *Science and Health* was not Mrs. Eddy's own work, but that it had been taken largely from P. P. Quimby's manuscripts. As none of Mr. Quimby's manuscripts had been published or copyrighted, and as Mr. Arens did not have them in his possession, the defendant's position was obviously untenable. Although this decision had to do merely with the validity of Mrs. Eddy's copyright, and did not touch upon the authorship of the book, Mrs. Eddy chose to construe it as being a court decision to the effect that she was the sole author of *Science and Health*, and the founder and discoverer of Christian Science; and her construction cheered and encouraged her quite as much, perhaps, as an actual decision to that effect would have done. She afterward referred to this decision as her " vindication in the United States court."

The years from 1882 to 1885 were years of rapid advancement for Mrs. Eddy and Christian Science. Although a list of the members of the Christian Scientists' Association, made June 2, 1884, shows that but sixty-one persons then belonged to the Association, many people were interested in Christian Science who had not actually allied themselves with it, and Mrs. Eddy was steadily gaining some sort of recognition for herself and her teachings. She had now a considerable number of graduate students who were in practice, and their success, as well as hers, depended upon the growth of Christian Science and of the college. They sent their patients to study under her, and canvassed widely among their friends and acquaintances. Some of these students went to distant places to practise, and did the work of missionaries, encouraging their patients to go to Boston and study under Mrs. Eddy. A degree from the Massachusetts Metaphysical College meant, in most cases, a lucrative practice. In the West especially, where Boston is regarded as the sum of all that is conservative, and where even the banks consider it an advantage to have a Bostonian among their directors, a degree from a Boston institution meant a great deal, and the " Massachusetts Metaphysical College of Boston " suggested an institution devoted to higher scholarship. A combination of Boston and metaphysics seemed to leave little to be desired in the way of learning, and many a Western student, after having " gone East to college," returned home to find that, for the purpose of making a living and commanding respect among his neighbours, a degree from the Massachusetts Metaphysical College served him quite as well as a degree from Harvard. Graduate students had lectured and practised in Chicago, and when Mrs. Eddy taught a class there in the summer of 1884, she inspired a sentiment which was ultimately to build up a strong church.

The Christian Science Church was now conspicuous enough to be the object of occasional attacks from conservative theologians. These attacks were neither frequent nor bitter,—indeed, they were usually humorous or mildly ironical,—but Mrs. Eddy made the most of them, and answered them with promptness and fire, getting her replies published in the Boston newspapers whenever it was possible to do so, and, when editors proved intractable, resorting to her own periodical, the *Christian Science Journal*. She realised the value of persecution,

Photograph by H. G. Smith

MARY BAKER G. EDDY

Taken about the year 1886, while at the head of
her college in Boston

As she looked in 1870, when she first taught Christian Science in Lynn, Mass

even when it had to be helped along a little, and in the *Journal* for April, 1885, she cries: " Must history repeat itself, and religious intolerance, arrayed against the rights of man, again deluge the earth in blood? " In the *Journal* we find that in March of the same year, Mrs. Eddy was permitted to speak at a religious meeting held at Tremont Temple, and there to reply to a letter by the Rev. A. J. Gordon denouncing Christian Science, and that she gloriously vindicated her church.

Mrs. Eddy was now president of the " Massachusetts Metaphysical College," editor of the *Christian Science Journal,* president of the Christian Scientists' Association, and pastor of the First Church of Christ (Scientist). To the latter office her students had ordained her, without the aid of the clergy, in 1881, and her official letters and press communications were now usually signed " Reverend Mary Baker G. Eddy." Her classes now numbered from fifteen to twenty-five students each. The course of instruction took only three weeks, which, with a class of twenty-five, would mean that Mrs. Eddy's fees for that period of time amounted to $7,500. It is safe to say, however, that at least one-fourth of her students were admitted at a discount and paid only $200 each. Men and women of intelligence and some experience of the world began to frequent her college. Among these were Dr. J. W. Winkley, then a Unitarian minister, who had a church at Revere; Mrs. Emma Hopkins, Mrs. Ursula Gestefeld of Chicago; Mrs. Augusta Stetson, then an elocutionist in Somerville, Boston; Mrs. Ellen Brown Linscott; Mrs. Josephine Woodbury and her husband; the Rev. J. H. Wiggin, and the Rev. Frank E. Mason.

To understand the early growth of Christian Science in Boston, one must remember, first, that Boston was then, as it is now, the stronghold of radical religious sects; secondly, that, while fundamentally Mrs. Eddy never changed at all, superficially, she was continually changing for the better, and her shrewdness, astuteness, and tact grew with every year of her life. After her removal to Boston, she constantly learned from her new associates, even to the extent of resolutely breaking herself of certain ungrammatical habits of speech—no mean achievement for a woman above sixty. But the most important thing that Mrs. Eddy learned was to admit—to herself only—her own limitations. She began to submit her editorials, pamphlets, and press communications to certain of her students for grammatical censorship. She now granted interviews to strangers and new students only when she felt at her best. She withdrew herself from her followers somewhat, and built up a ceremonial barrier which was not without its effect. In writing, she acquired more and more facility as time went on. Her style of expression remained vague, but that suited her purpose, and her excessive floridity delighted many of her readers, and was condoned by others as a survival of the old-fashioned flowery manner of writing. Her letters of this date are better spelled and punctuated, and are written in a firmer and more vigorous hand, than those written when she was forty.

Mrs. Eddy now began to limit the number of her public addresses, and she delivered her Sunday sermon before her congregation at the Hawthorne rooms only when she felt that she could rouse herself to that state of emotional exaltation which it was her aim to produce in her hearers. Often as late as Sunday morning, she would notify one of her students to fill the pulpit.   At other times, after she had appointed a substitute, she would decide at the last minute to go herself, and, after the audience at Hawthorne Hall had been waiting for perhaps half an hour, Mrs. Eddy's carriage would swing into Park Street, and she would alight amid a crowd of delighted students, sweep rapidly up the aisle, ascend the rostrum, and at once begin to deliver one of her most effective sermons; perhaps a discussion of how, in His resurrection, Christ made the highest demonstration of the healing powers of Christian Science, or perhaps a prophetic discourse upon a text of which she was particularly fond, and which she always delivered with astonishing conviction: " Upon this rock I will build my church, and the gates of hell shall not prevail against it."

CHAPTER XVII

LITERARY ACTIVITIES—MRS. EDDY AS AN EDITOR—THE REV. MR.
WIGGIN BECOMES HER LITERARY ASSISTANT—HIS PRIVATE
ESTIMATE OF MRS. EDDY AND CHRISTIAN SCIENCE

WHEN Mrs. Eddy reopened the Massachusetts Metaphysical
College after her husband's death in 1882 and, with half a
dozen of her students, settled down to her old routine of teaching, she soon began to plan for a monthly publication which
should be devoted to the interests of Christian Science. Quite
as willing to contribute to the Boston dailies as she had been
to enliven with prose and verse the columns of the more modest
weeklies of Lynn, Mrs. Eddy wrote a great many press notices
regarding her church and college, and it was Arthur Buswell's
business to take these about to the various newspaper offices
and attempt to place them. Editors, however, were often
prejudiced by Mrs. Eddy's involved style and extravagant
claims, and their unwillingness to print many of her contributions suggested to Mr. Buswell and Mrs. Eddy the convenience
of having a periodical of their own.

On April 14, 1883, the *Journal of Christian Science*, a small
eight-page monthly, made its appearance, bearing the name
of Mary B. Glover Eddy as editor. The new magazine opened
with a " prospectus " which began as follows: " The ancient
Greek looked longingly for the Olympiad. The Chaldee

watched for the appearing of a star; to him, no higher destiny dawned upon the dome of being than that foreshadowed by the signs in the heavens." Whether Mrs. Eddy meant to imply that so the modern world waited for Christian Science, the reader must conjecture, for she does not say so, nor does she say anything about the purpose or policy of her journal. The only sentence in the prospectus which could be construed as having anything to do with her magazine is the following, which would seem to indicate her intended policy as editor, though this is not very clear:

While we entertain decided views as to the best method for elevating the race physically, morally, and spiritually, and shall express these views as duty demands, we shall claim no especial gifts from our divine origin, or any supernatural power, etc.

The founding of the *Journal* was perhaps the most important step Mrs. Eddy had taken since she came to Boston, as it afterward proved one of the most effective means of extending her influence and widening the boundaries of Christian Science. In the beginning the magazine had but a handful of subscribers, and the cost of printing it was not more than thirty or forty dollars an issue. This sum was raised by voluntary subscription, nearly all the Christian Scientists contributing money except Mrs. Eddy.

Although her subscription-list was small, Mrs. Eddy knew what to do with her *Journal*. Copies found their way to remote villages in Missouri and Arkansas, to lonely places in Nebraska and Colorado, where people had much time for reflection, little excitement, and a great need to believe in miracles. The metaphor of the bread cast upon the waters is no adequate sugges-

tion of the result. Mrs. Eddy and Christian Science began
to be talked of far away in the mountains and in the prairie
villages. Lonely and discouraged people brooded over these
editorials which promised happiness to sorrow and success to
failure. The desperately ill had no quarrel with the artificial
rhetoric of these testimonials in which people declared that they
had been snatched from the brink of the grave.

Soon after the *Journal* was started, Mrs. Emma Hopkins,
an intelligent and sincere young woman, came to Boston to
assume the assistant editorship of the magazine. Mrs. Hopkins had first met Mrs. Eddy at the house of one of her friends,
where Mrs. Eddy had been engaged to give a parlour lecture
on Christian Science. Mrs. Hopkins became deeply interested
in this new doctrine, and, although after her first meeting with
Mrs. Eddy she carried away an unfavourable impression, she
soon fell completely under the spell of that remarkable personality; thought her handsome, stimulating, inspiring, and
very different from any woman she had ever known. She entered one of Mrs. Eddy's classes and went through the same
experience that sensitive students of an earlier date describe;
during the lectures she felt uplifted and carried beyond herself;
and in describing the effect of Mrs. Eddy's words upon her
hearers, Mrs. Hopkins uses the same figure that we have heard
before in Lynn—that of the wind stirring the wheat-field.
When Mrs. Hopkins became assistant editor of the *Journal*,
she went to live in Mrs. Eddy's house in Columbus Avenue,
where the editorial work was done. She remained there for
two years, until, worn out by Mrs. Eddy's tyranny and selfishness, and saddened by her own disillusionment, Mrs. Hopkins

left the house and never communicated with Mrs. Eddy again. Mrs. Eddy afterward attacked her savagely in the *Journal*, and applied to her the old terms of opprobrium.

In the fall of 1885 Mrs. Sarah H. Crosse succeeded Mrs. Hopkins as assistant editor of the *Journal*, and she, in turn, was succeeded by Frank Mason, who became both editor and publisher about the end of 1888.

In its early years the *Journal of Christian Science* was almost as much Mrs. Eddy as was the Massachusetts Metaphysical College. At sixty-two Mrs. Eddy fell to playing editor with the same zest with which she had entered upon the activities of her church and college. She wrote much of the *Journal* herself, and what she did not originate she selected and largely rewrote, keeping a sharp eye on the articles and editorials written by her assistants and revising them very thoroughly. She was especially solicitous about the articles which dealt with herself, and she was almost equally anxious that the articles should deal with little else. The *Journal of Christian Science* was then scarcely more than the monthly gazette of Mrs. Eddy's doings—the diary which chronicled her thoughts and activities, and which minutely recorded the tributes of her courtiers. She no longer had to get out a new edition of *Science and Health* to give vent to her feelings about a newly discovered mesmerist. Once a month she audited her accounts, and the *Journal* was her clearing-house. Through its columns the new favourite was exalted and the old relegated to his place among the mesmerised. In one column we find, in large type, a card of thanks for a twenty-one-pound turkey which some one had sent for Mrs. Eddy's New Year's dinner; in

another a tirade upon animal magnetism; and in still another
the following acknowledgment of Christmas gifts:

From Bradford Sherman, C. S., and his wife Mrs. Mattie Sherman, C. S.,
of Chicago,—Wild Flowers of Colorado, a large elegantly bound and
embellished book, containing twenty-two paintings of the gorgeous flowers
of the Occident.

From Mrs. Hannah A. Larminie, C. S., of Chicago,—a book with a
sweet, illustrated poem, and a very elegant pocket-handkerchief.

From Mrs. Mattie Williams, C. S.,—a large, fine photograph of her
beautiful home in Columbus, Wisconsin. On the piazza are herself and
husband; on the grounds in front, her children with their bicycles.

MARY B. G. EDDY.[1]

This annual acknowledgment of Mrs. Eddy's Christmas gifts
in the *Journal* grew more formidable as the years went by.
In 1889 Mrs. Eddy listed her presents as follows:

LIST OF INDIVIDUAL OFFERINGS

Eider-down pillow, white satin with gold embroidery. Eider-down pillow,
blue silk, hand-painted, and fringed with lace. Pastel painting of Minne-
haha Falls, with silvered easel. Silver nut-pick set. Painted Sèvres China
tea-set. Book, Beautiful Story, 576 pages, with steel engravings and
lithographs. The Doré Bible Gallery, embellished. Brussels-lace tie. Silken
sofa-scarf, inwrought with gold. Pansy bed, in water-colours, with bronze
frame. Stand for lemonade-set. Silver combination-set. Silk and lace
mat. Embroidered linen handkerchief, in silken sachet-holder. Chinese
jar. Silk-embroidered plush table-scarf. Connected reclining-pillows. Work
of art, White and Franconia Mountains. Transparent painting of Jacque-
minots. Satin and lace pin-cushion. Barometer. Cabinet photograph-
holder. Perfumery. Large variety of books and poems. Face of the
Madonna, framed in oak and ivory. Moon-mirror, with silver setting, and
" the Man in the Moon." Hand-painted blotter. Embroidered linen hand-
kerchiefs. Blue silk-embroidered shawl. Plush portemonnaie. Openwork
linen handkerchief. Charm slumber-robe. Bible Pearls of Promise. Large
white silk banner with silver fringe. Sachet bags. Two velvet table mats.
Silver holder for stereoscopic views. Two fat Kentucky turkeys. Hosts
of bouquets and Christmas cards.

The following year, 1890, her publisher, Mr. William G.

---

[1] *Christian Science Journal,* January, 1886.

Nixon, tried to persuade Mrs. Eddy to omit a detailed list of her Christmas offerings, and she wrote him:

I requested you through Mr. Frye to reinstate my notice of my Christmas gifts, for the reasons I herein name.

Students are constantly telling me how they felt the *mental* impression this year to make me *no* present, and when they overcame it were strengthened and blessed. For this reason—viz., to discourage mental malpractice and to encourage those who beat it—I want that notice published.

Many of Mrs. Eddy's contributions to the *Journal* have been collected and reprinted in the volume known as *Miscellaneous Writings*. While even in the very latest edition of *Science and Health* the flavour of Mrs. Eddy lingers on every page, like a dominating strain of blood that cannot be bred out, the book has been rearranged and retouched by so many hands that the personal element has been greatly moderated. In the old files of the *Journal*, however, we seem to get Mrs. Eddy with singular directness and to come into very intimate contact with her. When she is angry one can fairly hear the voice behind the type, and when she bestows royal favours one can see the smile at the other end of the copy. These contributions were usually written in precipitate haste, and reached the despairing printer at the last possible moment, almost unintelligible, full of inaccuracies and errors, and, except for an occasional period, innocent of all punctuation. The copyreader or assistant editor did what he could at editing it as he fed it to the compositors—and the point is that he did not do too much. In the columns of the *Journal* one gets Mrs. Eddy's pages hot from her hand, as if they had not been touched since the copyboy dashed with them out of the door of 571 Columbus Avenue. In her editorial function she is more at ease than in her more strictly sacerdotal one, and in her contributions to her paper she sounds all the stops of her instrument. As she says, she " commands and countermands " and " thunders to the sinner," but for happier occasions she has a lighter tone, and she is by turns peppery and playful. A student in Chicago offends, and Mrs. Eddy calls her a "suckling " and a " petty western editress." Her students send her a watch at Christmastide, and she thanks them for their " timely " gift. They give her a fish-pond, and she asks them to pond-er.

During the early years Mrs. Eddy opened each number of the *Journal* with a crashing editorial, and, in addition to this, she conducted, under her own name, a " Questions and Answers " column, in which she met and settled queries like the following:

Has Mrs. Eddy lost her power to heal?
Has the sun forgotten to shine and the planets to revolve around it? Who was it discovered, demonstrated and teaches Christian Science? etc.

Mrs. Eddy did not hesitate to answer personal criticism and to reply to gossip in the columns of her paper. On one occasion she replies to the old story, which was forever cropping up in Lynn, that she was addicted to the use of morphine. She says that when a mesmerist was attempting to poison her, she did take large doses of morphine to see whether she were still susceptible to poison. " Years ago, when the mental malpractice of poison was undertaken by a mesmerist, to thwart that design, I experimented by taking some large doses of morphine to watch the effect, and I say it with tearful thanks, the drug had no effect upon me whatever,—the hour had struck, ' if they drink any deadly thing, it shall not hurt them.' " [2]

---

[2] *Christian Science Journal,* April, 1885.

Several years later the *Journal* takes up some petty criticism which had been made regarding Mrs. Eddy's dress:

Such views of Christian Science are well illustrated in a little incident that happened to the author of *Science and Health* a year or two ago, when she was the active pastor of the Scientist church in Boston. She had a custom of answering from the platform, questions that were passed up in writing. On one occasion she found this inquiry, " How can a Christian Scientist afford to wear diamonds and be clad in purple velvet?" She stepped forward and answered, " This ring that I wear was given me several years ago as a thank-offering from one I had brought from death back to life; for a long time I could not wear it, but my husband induced me to accustom myself by putting it on in the night, and finally I came to see it only as a sign of recognition and gratitude of my master, and to love it as such; this purple velvet is 'purple,' but it is velveteen that I paid one dollar and fifty cents for, and I have worn it for several years, but it seems to be perpetually renewed, like the widow's cruse." [3]

But the discussion of Mrs. Eddy and her affairs did not end with her signed contributions.   During the first five years of the magazine's existence Mrs. Eddy was the theme of almost every article, testimonial, and letter.   There are poems to the " bold innovator in the realms of thought," and scattered here and there are miscellaneous extracts of which the following, signed " Lily of Israel," will illustrate the drift and character:

PROPHECY

She existed from the beginning before all ages, and will not cease to exist throughout all ages; it is she who shall create in Heaven a light which shall never be extinguished; she shall rise in the midst of her people, and she shall be blessed over all those who are blessed by God, for she shall open the doors of the East, and the Desired of Nations shall appear.[4]

The " Healing Department " of the *Journal*, which held a prominent place and was perhaps the strongest element in its

---

[3] *Christian Science Journal*, February, 1889.
[4] *Christian Science Journal*, May, 1885.

success, reports at length the alleged cures made by the practising healers and, in many instances, by the mere reading of *Science and Health*. While this department was of great value in giving publicity to the claims of Christian Science its recital of the details of illness and suffering make painful reading and seem rather too intimately personal for quotation. A few of the headings will indicate the nature of these communications: " Liver Complaint of Long Standing Cured by Half an Hour's Talk "; " Cancer on the Face, Badly Broken Out, Cured in One Week "; " Heart Trouble and Dropsy, with Great Swelling of the Limbs, of Thirty Years' Standing, Cured in Two Treatments "; " Bright's Disease and also Scrofulous Bunches on the Neck Cured in Three Weeks "; " Woman Had Twenty-nine Surgical Operations "; " Had Seventeen Physicians "; " Cancer and Lockjaw "; " Cured of Both Paralysis and Mormonism."

One amusing report states that " a girl nineteen years old who was dumb and had never spoken, commenced talking after her third treatment as if she was thinking aloud, and has talked ever since." Among these notes on healing, the following, from the *Journal* of October, 1887, deserves mention:

DOG AND RATTLESNAKE

DEAR JOURNAL: Our dog was bitten by a rattlesnake on the tongue a short time ago, and the verdict, as is usual in such cases, was death; but through the understanding of God's promise that we shall handle serpents and not be harmed, if we but believe, I was able to demonstrate over the belief in four days. The dog is now as well as ever.

MRS. M. E. DARNELL.

In the *Journal* of April, 1885, occurs an interesting paragraph regarding General Grant (then in his last illness), which asserts that his physicians " are hastening him toward the manifestations of the death symptoms they hold so definitely in mind, with all the formulating speed they are capable of."

From 1883 to 1887 the *Journal* devotes considerable space to mesmerism, although some of Mrs. Eddy's students besought her to place less emphasis upon this doctrine. In the *Journal* of October, 1885, she rebukes such conservative followers sharply:

> In my public works I lay bare the capacity, in belief, of animal magnetism, to break the Decalogue, to murder, steal, commit adultery, etc.
>
> Those who deny my right or wisdom to expose its crimes, are either participants in this evil, afraid of its supposed power or ignorant of it. Those accusing me of covering this iniquity, are zealous, who, like Peter, sleep when the Teacher bids them watch; and when the hour of trial comes would cut off somebody's ears.

In 1887 a department devoted to Malicious Animal Magnetism becomes one of the regular features of the *Journal*, and continues for some years. At the head of this department regularly occurs the following quotation from Nehemiah: "*Also they have dominion over our bodies, and over our cattle, at their pleasure, and we are in great distress.*" In this department persons who believe that they have been injured in their business or tormented in body and soul by mesmerists recount their symptoms and struggles. One woman is tortured by a hatred and distrust of Mrs. Eddy (it was by producing a distrust of Mrs. Eddy that the mesmerists most frequently harried their victims), and she suffers under this " belief " until she is treated for it and cured by a fellow-Scientist. Another is tormented by a desire to write, and the tempter whispers to her that she " can write as good a book as Mrs. Eddy's." Mrs. Carrie Snider, a prominent worker in the New York church, writes at a length of five pages to describe how malicious mesmerism killed her husband, Fremont Snider. He was, she says, under the treatment of two healers whose minds were not in accord, and the thought from one confused the thought from the other, leaving him to die in the cross-fire. She was confident that if he had left the treatment of his case with her, he would have recovered. Even after a physician had pronounced him dead and had sent for the coroner, Mrs. Snider treated her husband, with some success, she says, adding that if she had had help she could even then have saved him.[5]

The history of the growth of the belief in malicious mesmerism, as one may follow it in the early files of the *Journal*, is interesting and illuminating. Here one sees how this doctrine, which was so singularly a temperamental product, born of a personal hatred and developed to meet personal needs and to explain personal caprices, begins to control the conduct and affections of people whose natures and obligations were very different from Mrs. Eddy's. So long as the belief in demonology was a mere personal vagary of Mrs. Eddy's, explaining her quarrels, affecting her spoons and pillows and telegrams, it was as harmless as it was amusing. But as one reads the letters from persons who ascribe the estrangement of friends and even the death of children to the ill-will of their neighbours and fellow-townsmen, one begins to feel the serious side of this doctrine. The reader must possess very great hardihood indeed if he can follow without sympathy one letter from Pierre, Dak., which recounts the story of the death of two young children under the treatment of their zealous mother.

---

[5] Fremont D. Snider died of heart-disease, December 17, 1888.

The mother was the wife of a banker in Pierre, a woman of unusual force of character, who had been liberally educated in Germany. Her husband was a young man of energy and promise, and they were both extravagantly fond of their children. The wife took a course of lessons under a Christian Science practitioner in Des Moines, Ia., and returned to her home in Dakota a devout convert. One of her children, a little boy four years old, fell ill; she treated him without the aid of a physician, and he died. Some months later a second child, a baby eleven months old, began to pine. She believed that he was the victim of malicious animal magnetism, exercised by the members of the Methodist Church which she had left after becoming a Christian Scientist. She even believed that the Methodists were praying for the child's death, and fled to Des Moines with the baby, where he grew better; but when she returned home he became worse again. The father was then in New York on business, and the mother, on her own responsibility, undertook the case, telegraphing to E. J. Foster Eddy, Mrs. Eddy's adopted son, for absent treatment for the child. For ten days the misguided woman watched over her baby and treated him against malicious mesmerism, which she believed brought on the spasms and convulsions. She did not notify her husband that the baby was dangerously ill until she telegraphed word of its death, nine hours after death occurred; and for those nine hours after the child had ceased to breathe she treated and prayed over him, not permitting herself to shed a tear or to " entertain the thought of death," confidently expecting that his eyes would open again. This experience and the subsequent indignation of the townspeople seem to have been too much for a friend and fellow-citizen who was there visiting at the house, and who assisted in treating the child, for she writes Mrs. Eddy an imploring letter, asking, " Why this termination? " and declaring: " We recognised no disease, and as first symptoms would appear—beliefs of paralysis, spasms, fever, etc.—we would realise the allness of God, and they would disappear." But the letter itself must be given in full. Its account of the sufferings of the baby and the terrible fortitude of the mother sound like a passage from the earlier and harsher chapters of religious history, which so often make us wonder whether there is anything else in the world that can be quite so cruel as the service of an ideal.

PIERRE, DAKOTA, Jan. 31, 1889.

Last September Mrs. N——[6] took a course of lectures in Science in Des Moines, and returned to her home here, and was the instrument of great good. Many were healed physically who sought also the spiritual benefits.

Instead of working for the church, of which she had been a consistent and active member, she gave all her time to Science. This stirred up the error in the minds of the brothers and sisters,—and caused the fiery darts to be mentally hurled at her and they seemingly penetrated her weakest point, her darling baby, eleven months old, who seemed in December to be sinking under the blows. As Herod was seeking the young child's life they thought it best to flee for a time from this mental atmosphere, and went to Des Moines where he grew better. Mr. N—— being obliged to go to New York, and Mrs. N—— hearing that mortal mind had got hold of some of her patients—determined to return to Pierre to look after their spiritual welfare.

I returned with her, and almost all our time has been spent in reading the Bible and " Science and Health " to those who were interested. Ministers called upon us and denounced Science in the strongest terms; and one Sunday every minister in the place preached against it, not knowing they could " do nothing against the Truth." We continued working quietly and speaking only to those who came to see us.

———
[6] The name is withheld in consideration for the family most intimately concerned in this case. The interested reader, however, may refer to the files of the *Christian Science Journal*, March, 1889, pages 637-639, where this letter was originally printed and where the full name is used.

Finally little Edward seemingly succumbed to an attack, while we were holding a meeting in the parlour. To all appearance he was gone, but we knew it was animal magnetism, and treating him for it he revived. We wrestled till daybreak and though there was little seeming improvement, we realised that " God's will is done " and felt that the baby was healed.

During the ten days that followed, the wiles of the evil one appeared, but they were overcome. Mrs. N—— telegraphed Dr. Foster Eddy for help, and felt that help came. The telegraph operator here, not knowing the influence of mortal mind, divulged the telegram, and this made the battle harder. Again we telegraphed for help and again the cry went out " They've sent for help." At least six times little Edward seemed to have passed. We recognised it as another temptation, took up animal magnetism and each time he rallied. Finally about 5:30 A.M. of Friday, Jan. 25th, he passed on. I took him on my lap. Mrs. N—— and I realised it must be the last temptation, hence the greatest. We had no fear and did not admit he had passed on for several hours. We kept reading the promises " according to thy faith," etc., and did not call an undertaker until evening. When Mrs. N——'s little Philip passed on a few months ago her faith alone should have raised him. But this time her faith was coupled with understanding and did not waver for a moment. Why this termination? I wish we could have some light on the subject.

We recognised no disease, and as first symptoms would appear—beliefs of paralysis, spasms, fever, etc.—we would realise the allness of God, and they would disappear. It was a clear case of ignorant and malicious magnetism. Why was it not mastered?

We are told that some church members have been praying that " God would take the child " in order that the parents might see the error of their way, and return—not to God, but—to the M. E. followers. Now comes an unprecedented history. Saturday morning a great tumult arose. The M. E. minister gathered a crowd around him on the street and denounced this pernicious doctrine, till the people were infuriated, and threatened mob law. A meeting was called at the public hall. The conservative element succeeded, notwithstanding the excitement, in getting a respectful committee appointed, and an order was served on myself and another Scientist to meet this committee at the Court House at 4 P.M. Mrs. N—— accompanied us and on the way we met the coroner, sheriff, jury and two " Medicine men " who came to demand an inquest. All returned with us to the house. The questions and the manner of the M.D.'s were insulting in the extreme. Our answers were mostly from the Bible.

All admitted the unblemished reputation of Mr. and Mrs. N——, that Mrs. N—— was a faithful, loving mother; but they could not tolerate such a religious conviction. Then we all went to the Court House and a committee told us that the sentiment of the community was (as in Acts xiii. 50) that we leave town.

I said to the committee that I came to visit Mrs. N—— and not professionally; that she was in trouble and there was no power to drive me out.

In the same number of the *Journal* is printed an extract from a letter written by the mother herself, in which she maintains that the baby's illness was not of a bodily nature, but was clearly the effect of animal magnetism working directly upon the brain:

Little Edward slept and ate well as a rule. He had no bowel affection, as the papers have stated. All the attacks were in belief, in form of brain trouble, and plainly from animal magnetism; the prayers of church members and the whole thought of the place being expressed in the hope that "God would remove the N——s' child, so that they might come back into the church." At two o'clock on the day that he passed, I sent for Mr. N—— [the father], and in the evening of the same day I called the undertaker. We buried the little boy ourselves, quietly, without any minister present, being accompanied by a number who believe in Christian Science because it has healed them.

Our trials have been severe, but we work to stand fast. We are determined to demonstrate the nothingness of this seeming power.

This case is chosen for illustration for the reason that the parents of these children were not ignorant or colourless people; they were not mystics or dreamers or in any way " different." They were young, ambitious, warm-hearted, and affectionate; they loved each other and their children, and their home was full of cordiality and kindliness. Their children were fine children; one, now grown, has become a young scholar of promise. The woman was not a religious fanatic, but a young mother. She could combat " the last temptation " over her dead baby simply because she believed with all her heart and soul that it lay with her, as a test of her faith, whether her child lived or died. Logically there was nothing extravagant about her conduct. The martyrdoms of a thousand years have proved what men and women can do and endure under the tyranny of an idea.

Whoever studies the old files of the *Journal* from 1883 to 1887 must note the rapid growth of Mrs. Eddy's sect during those years. In the first number of the *Journal*, April, 1883, appear the professional cards of fourteen authorised healers; in April, 1885, forty-three professional healers advertise in this way; and in the *Journal* of April, 1887, are the cards of one hundred and ten Christian Science practitioners. In 1887 nineteen Christian Science " institutes " and " academies " are advertised. The graduates of these schools usually went at once into practice, although sometimes they first went to Boston to take the normal course in Mrs. Eddy's college. These preparatory schools were located in various cities in California, Nebraska, Colorado, Wisconsin, Ohio, Massachusetts, and New York. In 1886 the National Christian Scientists' Association was formed with representatives from almost every State in the Union, which will be discussed in a later chapter.

In the *Journal* of 1887 and 1888 one notices certain articles and editorials signed J. H. W., or Phare Pleigh, the initials and pen-name of the Rev. James Henry Wiggin, who, in 1885, became Mrs. Eddy's literary adviser. Mr. Wiggin was graduated from the Meadville Theological Seminary in 1861, and became a Unitarian minister. In 1875 he retired from the active ministry and devoted himself to writing and editing. An old friend of John Wilson, of the University Press, Mr. Wiggin found plenty to do in proof-reading, revising, and editing manuscripts, in annotating and making indices to theological and scholarly works.

One day in August, 1885, Calvin Frye called at Mr. Wiggin's office in the old Boston Music Hall, and introduced himself as the secretary of a lady who had written a book, the manuscript of which she wished Mr. Wiggin to revise, adding that she also wished him to prepare an index for her work. A few days later Mrs. Eddy herself came to see Mr. Wiggin,[7] bringing with her a bulky package of manuscript which proved to be a fresh version of that much-written book, *Science and Health*, which she had just rewritten from the fourth edition, 1884. She gave Mr. Wiggin to understand that, while the manuscript was practically ready for the printer, it needed the touch of a literary man. She agreed to his terms and withdrew. Mr. Wiggin, who was just about to start away on his summer vacation, put the package into his bag and took it up to the mountains with him. When he examined the manuscript later, he found that a revision of it was no holiday task. The faulty spelling and punctuation could have been corrected readily enough, as well as the incorrect historical references and the misuse of words; but the whole work was so involved, formless, and contradictory that Mr. Wiggin put the manuscript away and thought no more about it until he returned to Boston. Then he saw Mrs. Eddy and told her that he could do nothing by merely correcting her manuscript; that to improve it he would have largely to rewrite it. To his surprise, she willingly consented to this. During the autumn of 1885 Mr. Wiggin

---

[7] For a graphic account of this first interview between Mrs.. Eddy and Mr. Wiggin, the reader is referred to a pamphlet, *How Reverend Wiggin Rewrote Mrs. Eddy's Book,* by Livingston Wright.

THE REVEREND JAMES HENRY WIGGIN
Who was for four years Mrs. Eddy's literary adviser

occupied himself with this task, which Mrs. Eddy carefully supervised to see that he did not in the least modify her views and that her favourite phrases were allowed to stand.

Beginning with the first edition of the book (1875), and going through the successive editions up to 1886, one sees that what Mr. Wiggin did for *Science and Health* was to put into intelligible English the ideas which Mrs. Eddy had so befogged in the stating of them. Any one who reads a chapter, a page, or even a paragraph of the 1884 edition, and compares it with the same portion in the edition of 1886, will see the more obvious part of Mr. Wiggin's work. Take, for example, the following paragraph (1884 edition):

What is man? Brains, heart, blood, or the entire human structure? If he is one or all of the component parts of the body, when you amputate a limb, you have taken away a portion of man, and the surgeon destroys manhood, and worms are the annihilators of man. But losing a limb, or injuring structure, is sometimes the quickener of manliness; and the unfortunate cripple presents more nobility than the statuesque outline, whereby we find " a man's a man, for a' that."

Mr. Wiggin's revision of this passage reads:

What is man? Brains, heart, blood, the material structure? If he is but a material body, when you amputate a limb, you must take away a portion of the man; the surgeon can destroy manhood, and the worms annihilate it. But the loss of a limb or injury to a tissue, is sometimes the quickener of manliness, and the unfortunate cripple may present more of it than the statuesque athlete,—teaching us, by his very deprivations, that " a man's a man, for a' that."

In the above example Mr. Wiggin's changes are only with regard to composition, such as any theme-reader might suggest in the work of an untrained student. But in many instances he was able to be of even greater assistance to Mrs. Eddy by helping her to give some sort of clearness and consistency to her theology.   In her chapter on the Atonement (1884) Mrs. Eddy says:

The glorious spiritual signification of the life and not death of our Master—for he never died—was laying down all of earth to instruct his enemies the way to Heaven, showing in the most sublime and un-equivocal sense how Heaven is obtained.   The blood of Jesus was not as much offered on the cross as before those closing scenes of his earth mission. The spiritual meaning of blood is offering sacrifice, and the efficacy of his life offering was greater than that of his blood spilled upon the cross. It was the consecration of his whole being upon the altar of Love, a deathless offering to Spirit.   O, highest sense of human affections and higher spiritual conceptions of our Infinite Father and Mother, show us what *is Love!*

Mr. Wiggin's revision of this passage reads:

The material blood of Jesus was no more efficacious to cleanse from sin, when it was shed upon the "accursed tree," than when it was flowing in his veins as he went daily about his Father's business.   His spiritual flesh and blood were his Life; and they truly eat his flesh and drink his blood, who partake of that Life.   The spiritual meaning of blood is sacri-fice.   The efficacy of Jesus' spirit-offering was infinitely greater than can be expressed by our mortal sense of human life.   His mission was fulfilled. It reunited God and man by his career.   His offering was Love's deathless sacrifice; for in Jesus' experience the human element was gloriously ex-panded and absorbed into the divine.

Besides granting subjects to participles, antecedents to pro-nouns, introducing the subjunctive mode in conditions contrary to fact, and giving consistency to the tenses of the verbs, Mr. Wiggin largely rearranged the matter in each chapter and gave the book its first comprehensible paragraphing.   Out of his wide reading he introduced many illustrative quotations into the text (not always to its advantage), and used many more as chapter-headings.   He prevailed upon Mrs. Eddy to omit a very libellous chapter on "mesmerists," and here and there throughout the book expurgated some amusing absurdities. Where Mrs. Eddy represents Huxley, Tyndall, and Agassiz as Goliath, and Woman as David going forth to do battle with them, Mr. Wiggin permits Woman to go on with her sling, but suppresses the worthy professors, leaving her to encounter Goliath in the shape of Materialism. It must be remembered that Mr. Wiggin's edition was not made directly from the 1884 edition, but from a manuscript revision of it made by Mrs. Eddy herself. However, when one recalls that the 1884 edition was the result of at least a fourth rewriting, it seems improbable that Mrs. Eddy could have made much headway as to English in her fifth rewriting, the manuscript from which Mr. Wiggin worked.

This collaboration with Mr. Wiggin has sometimes been referred to as discreditable to Mrs. Eddy—chiefly from the fact, doubtless, that, even in her business letters to her publishers, she has persistently referred to *Science and Health* as " God's book." There could have been no wish on Mrs. Eddy's part to avoid labour, for she has worked at the book almost continuously for half a lifetime. Excluding the chapter called " Wayside Hints," which he wrote, Mr. Wiggin would have been the last man in the world to claim any part in the real authorship of *Science and Health*. The book has been rewritten again and again since Mr. Wiggin's work upon it stopped, and the editions which bear his revisions have been considerably improved upon, especially in the arrangement of the subject-matter. But the successive editions never began to improve at all over the first one—indeed, it may be said that they grew worse rather than better—until Mr. Wiggin took hold of the book, and many passages of the work to-day remain practically in the form into which he put them.

For four years Mr. Wiggin was employed in the capacity of literary aid to Mrs. Eddy, doing editorial work upon the *Journal*, and assisting her in the composition and proof-reading of three successive editions of *Science and Health*. Mrs. Eddy paid him well, and, in addition to his salary, he got a deal of entertainment out of his connection with Christian Science. He even wrote an amusing pamphlet [8] defending the new sect upon Biblical grounds. For Mr. Wiggin combined the qualities of a humourist and a theologian. He was a man of enormous bulk and stature and immense geniality. A slight hesitation in his gait, resulting from near-sightedness, sometimes caused his friends to liken him to Dr. Johnson. Extremely courtly and polished in manner, Mr. Wiggin was not only a scholar, but a man of fine tastes and of considerable critical ability. He was a musical critic of no mean order and an indefatigable concert-goer. He united a love of theology and theological disputations with an incongruous passion for the theatre. But, as it never occurred to Mr. Wiggin that there was anything unusual in delightedly pursuing the study of the drama and church history at the same time, so it seldom perplexed his friends or his fellow-clergymen.

For years after he had given up active pastorate duties, he often supplied the pulpit of some other minister, and occasionally went back to one of his old parishes to preach, lecture, or deliver a funeral sermon. His friendships with many of his old parishioners continued until his death, and the most cordial

---

[8] *Christian Science and the Bible,* by Phare Pleigh.

relations always existed between him and the members of the Unitarian Association. He usually attended the Monday Ministers' meeting at the Unitarian headquarters on Beacon Hill, and would often go out with one or two fellow-preachers and sit down to a lunch and a lengthy theological argument. Perhaps the same evening he would gather up several young newspaper men and go to an opening night at the theatre, pouring forth between the acts such a stream of anecdote, discriminating criticism, and reminiscence, that the young critics felt the morning's " notice " of the performance growing beneath their hands. After the last curtain Mr. Wiggin frequently went back to the dressing-rooms to exchange stories and recollections with the older performers and to give encouragement and suggestions to the younger ones. Mr. Wiggin's love of the theatre came about very naturally: his uncle had been from boyhood a friend of Charlotte Cushman's, whom the nephew himself knew and concerning whom he once wrote a delightful paper for *The Coming Age.*

Mr. Wiggin, with Edward Everett Hale, Professor William J. Rolfe, and a score more, was one of the organisers of the Playgoers' Club of Boston, before which he used often to lecture upon the old days of the Boston Museum and the remarkable stock work done there. Horace Lewis, William Warren, Mrs. John Drew, Adelaide Phillips, and Sol Smith Russell were among his many warm professional friends, and esteemed his suggestions and criticisms. He was becomingly fond of the comforts of the table, and delighted to gather a party of young writers and actors about him at supper and entertain them with stories of the great artists whom he had heard in his youth. His conversation was rich in anecdote and humour, and he belonged to the day when literary quotations were introduced unblushingly into friendly talk. Indeed, Mr. Wiggin had his Shakespeare so well upon his tongue that he could illuminate almost any question with a Shakespearean quotation. He once wrote an account of how he heard Liszt, then a newly made abbé, play at a sacred concert in Rome, and managed— quite unconsciously, it would seem—to describe pretty much the whole affair in language from Macbeth. An extraordinary man, certainly, to be concerned in the shaping of *Science and Health*. Mr. Wiggin himself never got over the humour of it.

It must not be supposed that he took his task lightly enough to slight it. He was accustomed to do his hack work well, and it became with him a genuine concern, as he often said, " to keep Mrs. Eddy from making herself ridiculous." He was glad to talk theology to any one, and he doubtless enjoyed teaching a little to Mrs. Eddy. He used to tell, with enormous glee, how Mrs. Eddy would sometimes receive his suggestions by slyly remarking, " Mr. Wiggin, do you know, I sometimes believe God speaks to me through you." It was when his venerable patroness laughed that he liked her best, and with him she sometimes enjoyed a joke in a pleasant and human fashion. Among other services which he rendered her, Mr. Wiggin once drew up for Mrs. Eddy the outline of a sermon upon the " city that lieth foursquare," described in Revelation. She delivered the sermon before her congregation January 24, 1886, with great success, though the *Journal*, in reporting the occasion, says that the Rev. Mrs. Eddy laboured under some disadvantage, as she had left her manuscript at home. Mr.

Wiggin was present in the audience, and after the service the huge man made his way up to the rostrum, where Mrs. Eddy was surrounded by a crowd of delighted women. When Mrs. Eddy saw him, her eyes began to twinkle, and, putting her hand to her lips, she shot him a stage whisper: " How did it go? "

When Mr. Wiggin persuaded her to omit the libellous portion of the chapter on Mesmerism from the 1886 edition of *Science and Health* after the plates for the edition had been made, Mrs. Eddy, at Mr. Wiggin's suggestion, cut this sermon to the required length and, by inserting it, was able to send the book to press without renumbering the remaining pages. The chapter was called " Wayside Hints (Supplementary)," and Mrs. Eddy put her seal upon it by inserting, under the subject of " squareness," a tribute to her deceased husband: " We need good square men everywhere. Such a man was my late husband, Dr. Asa G. Eddy."

By the year 1890 Mrs. Eddy had begun to lose patience with Mr. Wiggin and to charge him with not taking his work seriously enough. In a letter to her publisher, Mr. William G. Nixon, she complains that Mr. Wiggin's proof corrections have a " most shocking flippancy," and the exasperation of her letter seems to indicate that the worthy gentleman had grown tired of assisting revelation:

62 N. STATE ST., CONCORD, N. H.
Aug. 28, 1890.

MY DEAR STUDENT:

The proofs which I received Aug. 27th, and returned to printer Aug. 28th, are somewhere. I had not changed the marginal references in the copy because I had before written to Mr. Wiggin to make fewer notations and more appropriate ones. When he returned the first proofs a *belief*[9] (*but don't name this to any one*) prevented my examining them as I should otherwise have done, and, to prevent delay, the proof was sent to the printer.

The second proofs have the most shocking flippancy in notations. I have corrected them, also made fewer of them, which will involve another delay caused by Mr. Wiggin. He has before changed his own marginal references which delayed the printing. Also he took back the word "cannot" throughout the entire proofs which he had before insisted upon using thereby causing another delay. I write this to let you know how things stand.

Yours truly,

MARY B. G. EDDY.

In a letter dated three months later Mrs. Eddy again complains that Mr. Wiggin is slow about getting in his proofs, and says: "This is M.A.M. [Malicious Animal Magnetism] and it governs Wiggin as it has done once before to prevent the publishing of my work. . . . I will take the proof-reading out of Wiggin's hands."

On the whole, Mrs. Eddy seems to have got along amicably with Mr. Wiggin. She liked him, greatly respected his scholarship, and was pleased to make use of his versatile talents. He, on the other hand, assisted her with good nature, advised her, and defended her with a sort of playful gallantry that went with his generous make of mind and body. He was often aghast at her makeshifts and amused by her persistence, while he delighted in her ingenuity and admired her shrewdness. He could find lines in his favourite *Macbeth* applicable even to Mrs. Eddy, and he seems always heartily to have wished her well. In a letter to an old college friend, dated December 14, 1889, Mr. Wiggin made an interesting criticism of Christian Science and gave probably the most trenchant and suggestive

[9] An illness.

sketch of Mrs. Eddy that will ever be written. We have no other picture of her done by so capable a hand, for no one else among those closely associated with her ever studied her with such an unprejudiced and tempered mind, or judged her from a long and rich experience of books and men, enlightened by a humour as irrepressible as it was kindly. Mr. Wiggin's criticism follows:

Christian Science, on its theological side, is an ignorant revival of one form of ancient gnosticism, that Jesus is to be distinguished from the Christ, and that his earthly appearance was phantasmal, not real and fleshly.

On its moral side, it involves what must follow from the doctrine that reality is a dream, and that if a thing is right in thought, why right it is, and that sin is non-existent, because God can *behold* no evil. Not that Christian Science believers generally see this, or practise evil, but the virus is within.

Religiously, Christian Science is a revolt from orthodoxy, but unphilosophically conducted, endeavouring to ride two horses.

Physically, it leads people to trust all to nature, the great healer, and so does some good. Great virtue in imagination! . . . Where there is disease which time will not reach, Christian Science is useless.

As for the High Priestess of it, . . . she is—well I could *tell* you, but not write. An awfully (I use the word advisedly) smart woman, acute, shrewd, but not well read, nor in any way learned. What she has, as documents clearly show, she got from P. P. Quimby of Portland, Maine, whom she eulogised after death as the great leader and her special teacher. . . . She tried to answer the charge of the adoption of Quimby's ideas, and called me in to counsel her about it; but her only answer (in print!) was that if she said such things twenty years ago, she must have been under the influence of *animal magnetism,* which is *her* devil. No church can long get on without a devil, you know. Much more I could say if you were here. . . .

People beset with this delusion are thoroughly irrational. Take an instance. Dr. R—— of Roxbury is not a believer. His wife *is*. One evening I met her at a friendly house. Knowing her belief, I ventured only a mild and wary dissent, saying that I saw too much of it to feel satisfied, etc. In fact, the Doctor said the same and told me more in private. Yet, later, I learned that this slight discussion made her *ill*, nervous, and had a bad effect.

One of Mrs. Eddy's followers went so far as to say that if she *saw*

Mrs. Eddy commit a crime she should believe her own sight at fault, *not* Mrs. Eddy's conduct. An intelligent man told me in reference to lies he *knew* about, that the wrong was in *us*. "Was not Jesus accused of wrong-doing, yet guiltless?"

Only experience can teach these fanatics, *i.e.*, the real believers, not the charlatans who go into it for money. . . . As for the book, if you have any edition since December, 1885, it had my supervision. Though now she is getting out an entirely new edition, with which I had nothing to do, and occasionally she has made changes whereof I did not know. The chapter B—— told you of is rather fanciful, though, to use Mrs. Eddy's language in her last note, her "friends think it a gem." It is the one called "Wayside Hints," and was added after the work was not only in type, but cast, because she wished to take out some twenty pages of diatribe on her dissenters. . . . I do not think it will greatly edify you, the chapter. As for clearness, many Christian Science people thought her early editions much better, because they sounded more *like* Mrs. Eddy. The truth is, she does not care to have her paragraphs clear, and delights in so expressing herself that her words may have various readings and meanings. Really, that is one of the tricks of the trade. You know sibyls have always been thus oracular, to "keep the word of promise to the ear, and break it to the hope."

There is nothing really to understand in "Science and Health" except that *God is all,* and yet there is no God in matter! What they fail to explain is, the origin of the *idea* of matter, or sin. They say it comes from *mortal mind,* and that mortal mind is not divinely created, in fact, has no existence; in fact, that nothing comes of nothing, and that matter and disease are like dreams, having no existence. Quimby had definite ideas, but Mrs. Eddy has not understood them.

When I first knew Christian Science, I wrote a defensive pamphlet called "Christian Science and the Bible" (though I did not believe the doctrine). . . . I found fair game in the assaults of orthodoxy upon Mrs. Eddy, and support in the supernaturalism of the Bible; but I did not pretend to give an exposition of Christian Science, and I did not know the old lady as well as I do now.

No, Swedenborg, and all other such writers, are sealed books to her. She cannot understand such utterances, and never could, but dollars and cents she understands thoroughly.

Her influence is wonderful. Mrs. R——'s husband is anxious *not* to have her undeceived, though her tenth cancer is forming, lest she sink under the change of faith, and I can quite see that the loss of such a faith, like loss of faith in a physician, might be injurious. . . . In the summer of 1888, some thirty of her best people left Mrs. Eddy, including her *leading* people, too, her association and church officers. . . . They still believe nominally in Christian Science, yet several of them . . . are studying medicine at the College of Physicians and Surgeons, Boston; and she gave consent for at least *one* of them to study at this allopathic school. These students I often see, and *they* say the professors are coming over to *their* way of belief, which means simply that they hear the trustworthiness of the laws of nature proclaimed. As in her book, and in her class (which I went through), she says, " Call a surgeon in surgical cases."

" What if I find a breech presentation in childbirth? " asked a pupil.

" You will *not*, if you are in Christian Science," replied Mrs. Eddy.

" But if I *do?* "

" Then send for the nearest regular practitioner ! "

You see, Mrs. Eddy is nobody's fool.

CHAPTER XVIII

Mary B. G. Eddy has worked out before us as on a blackboard every point in the temptations and demonstrations—or so-called miracles—of Jesus, showing us how to meet and overcome the one and how to perform the other. *Christian Science Journal,* April, 1889.

THE first five years of Mrs. Eddy's life in Boston had been years of almost uninterrupted progress. Her college had, by 1887, grown to be a source of very considerable income. Her classes now numbered from thirty to fifty students each, and a class was instructed and graduated within three weeks' time. Although some students were received at a discount and paid only two hundred dollars for their instruction, the usual tuition fee was still three hundred dollars—a husband and wife being regarded as one student and paying but one fee. The course, which was formerly the only one taught at Mrs. Eddy's college, was now called the " primary course," and she added what she termed a " normal course " (being a review of the primary), a course in " metaphysical obstetrics," and a course in " theology," in all of which she was the sole instructor. If the student took all the courses offered, his

340

tuition fees amounted to eight hundred dollars.[1] By 1887
there was such a demand for Mrs. Eddy's instruction that
she could form as many classes a year as she felt able to
teach, and her classes netted her from five to ten thousand
dollars each. In 1883 Mrs. Eddy had founded her monthly
periodical, the *Christian Science Journal*,[2] of incalculable service in spreading her doctrines. In 1886 she had, with the
assistance of the Rev. James Henry Wiggin, got out a new
and much improved edition of *Science and Health*. Between
1880 and 1887 she had published four pamphlets: *Christian
Healing, The People's God, Defence of Christian Science,* and
a *Historical Sketch of Metaphysical Healing*. Promising
church organisations were being built up in New York, Chicago,
Denver, and in dozens of smaller cities.

Systematic efforts were now begun to raise money for a
permanent church building in Boston. The congregation had
outgrown its old quarters in Chickering Hall in Tremont Street,
and was having difficulty in obtaining a place for its services,
some of the larger halls refusing to rent to the Christian
Scientists. In the summer of 1886 the church had purchased
from Nathan Matthews a piece of land in Falmouth Street,
in a tenement district of the Back Bay, which it intended to
use for a building site. But the land was subject to a mortgage
of $8,763.50, and it was for the purpose of paying off this
mortgage that the Christian Scientists were holding fairs and

---

[1] Primary Class, twelve lessons (afterward seven lessons) $300
Normal Class, six lessons............................ 200
Class in Metaphysical Obstetrics, six lessons......... 100
Class in Theology, six lessons....................... 200

Total $800

[2] The magazine was first called *The Journal of Christian Science*, but the
title was soon changed to *The Christian Science Journal*.

concerts during the latter years of the '80's, and appealing to every member of the church and to every student at the college to set aside a weekly sum to be paid into the fund.

In the Christmas holidays of 1887 Mrs. Eddy moved from her dwelling in Columbus Avenue to a more pretentious house at 385 Commonwealth Avenue. The *Christian Science Journal*, under the head " Material Change of Base," announced her removal in the following enthusiastic language:

At Xmastide Rev. Mary B. Glover Eddy began to occupy the new house which she has purchased on Commonwealth Avenue, No. 385. The price is recorded in real estate transactions as $40,000. It is a large house in the middle of the block and contains twenty rooms. . . . The spot is very beautiful and the house has been finished and furnished under the advice of a professional decorator. The locality is excellent. For the information of friends not acquainted with Boston, it may be stated that Commonwealth Avenue is the most fashionable in the city. Through the centre of it runs a slim park with a central promenade, leaving a driveway on each side of the main thoroughfare. Within a few yards of Mrs. Eddy's mansion is the massive residence of his Excellency, Oliver Ames, the present Governor of Massachusetts. To name the dwellers on this avenue would be to name scores of Boston's wealthy and influential men. On Marlboro' Street, which is the next toward the river, are many more families of note; while everybody knows that Beacon Street, which is next in line, claims the blue blood of Boston for its inheritance, especially on the water side.

The fact that some of the members of Mrs. Eddy's own Boston church began to murmur texts about the foxes having holes and the birds of the air having nests, and that Mrs. Crosse, the editor of the *Journal*, felt it necessary to print an apologetic explanation of this notice, augured ill for the year that was just beginning. A great discontent had been growing in the Boston church, and for more than two years there had been two factions in the organisation: those who were absolutely

loyal to Mrs. Eddy, and those who merely conformed—who
believed in the principle she taught, but who, as she often put
it, " tried with one breath to credit the Message and discredit
the Messenger."

Both factions believed in the supremacy of mind over matter,
and in the healing principle which Mrs. Eddy taught. But
the loyal were those who believed:

In the Fall in Lynn and its subsequent revelation.

That the Bible and *Science and Health* are one book—the
Sacred Scriptures.

That sin, disease, and death are non-existent and will finally
disappear under demonstration.

That Malicious Animal Magnetism can cause sickness, sin,
and death.

That Mrs. Eddy has interpreted the Motherhood, or feminine
idea of God, as Jesus Christ interpreted the masculine idea.

That the feminine idea of God is essentially higher than the
masculine.

The loyal disciples did not hesitate to make the claim that
Christian Science was the offspring of Mrs. Eddy's direct
communion with God, just as Jesus was the offspring of Mary's
communion, and that the result of this second immaculate conception was a book rather than a man, because this age was
" more mental " than that in which Jesus Christ lived and
taught. An article entitled " Immaculate Conception," in the
Journal of November, 1888, elaborates this idea at great
length:

Let us come in thought to another day, a day when woman shall commune
with God, the eternal Principle and only Creator, and bring forth the

spiritual idea. And what of *her* child? Man is spiritual, man is mental. Woman was the first in this day to recognise this and the other facts it includes. As a result of her communion we have Christian Science.

You may ask why this child did not come in human form, as did the child of old. Because that was not necessary. . . . As this age is more mental than former ages, so the appearance of the idea of Truth is more mental.

From the first year of its establishment, the *Christian Science Journal* insisted, as indeed Mrs. Eddy's own writings insist, upon making for her a place among the characters of sacred history. In November, 1885, we find the following outburst:

What a triumphant career is this for a woman! Can it be anything less than the " tabernacle of God with men "—the fulfilment of the vision of the lonely seer on the Isle of Patmos—the " wonder in heaven," delivering the child which shall rule all nations? How dare we say to the contrary, that she is God-sent to the world, as much as any character of Sacred Writ?

Mrs. Eddy herself wrote that the following verse from the Apocalypse " has special reference to the present age ": [3]

" And there appeared a great wonder in heaven; a woman clothed with the sun, and the moon under her feet, and upon her head a crown of twelve stars." Mrs. Eddy says that the child which this woman bore was Christian Science. In the Mother Church at Boston there is a resplendent window representing this star-crowned woman.

These comparisons did not stop with the Virgin Mary and the star-crowned woman. Throughout the first ten years of the *Journal* there is a running parallel between Mrs. Eddy and Jesus Christ. This comparison was continually heard from the pulpits of Christian Science churches. The Rev. George B. Day, " M.A., C.S.B.," in a sermon delivered before the

[3] *Science and Health* (1906), p. 560.

Chicago church and afterward approvingly printed in the *Journal*, declared that " Christian Science is the Gospel according to Woman." He went on to say:

We are witnessing the transfer of the gospel from male to female trust. . . . Eighteen hundred years ago Paul declared that man was the head of the woman; but now, in " Science and Health," it is asserted that " woman is the highest form of man."

Mr. Day called his sermon " Sheep, Shepherd, and Shepherdess," and he considered, in turn, the disciples, Christ, and Mrs. Eddy.

The Christian Scientist held that Jesus, the man, was merely a man; that " the Christ " which dwelt within him was Divine Mind, dwelling more or less in all of us, but manifested in a superlative degree in Jesus and in Mrs. Eddy. In an unsigned editorial in the *Journal* of April, 1889, called " Christian Science and its Revelator," we are told that Jesus demonstrated over sickness, sin, and death, but that his disciples did not comprehend the principle of his miracles, since neither the Gospels nor the Epistles explain them. It was left for Mrs. Eddy, in *Science and Health*, to supplement the New Testament and to furnish this explanation. " The Christ is only the name for that state of consciousness which is the goal, the inevitable, ultimate state of every mortal," and Mrs. Eddy has shown mankind how to reach that state of consciousness. The writer continues: " To-day Truth has come through the person of a New England girl. . . . From the cradle she gave indications of a divine mission and power which caused *her* mother to ' ponder them in her heart.' " The writer further says of Mrs. Eddy that she has done good to them that hated her, blessed them that cursed her, and prayed for them that despitefully used her; that she has been led as a sheep to the slaughter, and as a lamb before his shearers is dumb, so she has opened not her mouth.

It is because Eve was the first to admit her fault in the garden of Eden, Mrs. Eddy says,[4] that a woman was permitted to give birth to Jesus Christ, and that a woman was permitted to write *Science and Health* and to reveal the spiritual origin of man. It is because woman is more spiritual than man, the Christian Science writers in the *Journal* explain, that a woman perceived the nothingness of matter, though Jesus did not, and that she was able to interpret the feminine idea of God, which is essentially higher than the masculine. In answer to an inquiry concerning the edition of the Bible upon which *Science and Health* is based, the editor of the *Journal* replied:

Would it not be too material a view to speak of " Science and Health " being *based* upon any edition of the Bible? . . . The Chosen One, always with God in the Mount, speaks face to face. In other words, " Science and Health " is a first-hand revelation. When this statement by the editor, Mr. Bailey, was criticised, he replied that he meant no disparagement of the Bible, but that he considered ' the Bible and " Science and Health " as one book—the Sacred Scriptures.'

When Mrs. Eddy's following consisted of but a handful of students, her divine assumption passed unnoticed; but, as time went on, less credulous critics were heard from. She had created a wide and lively interest in mind-healing, and many people began to look into the subject. In 1882 Julius Dresser, her old fellow-patient and pupil under Phineas Parkhurst

---

[4] *Science and Health* (1906), pages 533, 534.

Quimby, returned from California, and began to practise Quimby's method of mental healing in Boston.

With Mr. Dresser's return the " Quimby controversy " [5] began. In a letter to the Boston *Post*, February 24, 1883, Mr. Dresser presented evidence which went a great way toward proving that Mrs. Eddy got her principle of mind-healing from his old teacher. He published the laudatory article upon Quimby which Mrs. Eddy had written and printed in the Portland *Courier* twenty-five years before. He republished Mrs. Eddy's poem, " Lines upon the Death of Dr. P. P. Quimby, who Healed with the Truth that Christ Taught," as well as the letter which Mrs. Eddy wrote him after her memorable fall in Lynn.

To these unguarded utterances of that long-forgotten woman, Mary M. Patterson, Mrs. Eddy replied by repudiating her own effusions, prose and verse, and saying that if she ever wrote them at all she was " mesmerised " when she did it; that Quimby was an ignorant mesmerist, etc.

In 1887 Mr. Dresser published his pamphlet, *The True History of Mental Science*, in which he repeated his statements in the Boston *Post*, and related his own experience with Mrs. Eddy when she was a patient and he was a student of Dr. Quimby in Portland. This pamphlet brought out comment that was unfavourable to Mrs. Eddy, and stirred up her disaffected students. Although Mrs. Eddy responded with fire and spirit to her critics,[6] her controversy with Mr. Dresser

---

[5] For a full account of this controversy see Chapters III, IV, and V.
[6] Mr. Dresser, she says in her *Journal*, " has loosed from the leash his pet poodle to alternately whine and bark at my heels," and she refers to a former student who has endorsed Mr. Dresser's book, as " that suckling litterateur, Mr. Marston, whom I taught and whose life I saved three years ago, but who now squeaks out an echo of Mr. Dresser's abuse."

set her less infatuate students to thinking. Many of them
decided to investigate the Quimby claim, and bought the works
of the Rev. Warren F. Evans,[7] who had been treated by Quimby
a year after Mrs. Eddy's first visit to Portland, who had
practised Quimby's method of healing both in New Hampshire
and in Massachusetts, and who had published two books upon
mental healing before the first edition of *Science and Health*
appeared—*The Mental Cure* (1869) and *Mental Medicine*
(1872).

Dr. Evans' early works had a mildness of tone which strongly
appealed to such of Mrs. Eddy's students as were interested
in the principle of mental healing alone, and were somewhat
repelled by the garnishings which she had added to it. Evans
did not deny the existence of disease, much less of matter;
he simply affirmed the power of mind. His work *The Mental
Cure* is little more than a study of the reactions of mental
states upon the organs of the body. After reading Dr. Evans,

---

[7] The Rev. Warren Felt Evans, M.D., was born in Rockingham, Vt., December
23, 1817.   He was educated at Chester Academy, Middlebury College, and Dartmouth College. Later he was granted a diploma from a chartered board of
physicians of the Eclectic School, which entitled him to the degree M.D.   Mr.
Evans left Dartmouth in the middle of his junior year and entered the ministry
of the Methodist Episcopal Church. For about twenty years he remained in
the ministry, holding charges in various towns in New Hampshire and Massachusetts. He had been frail since his youth, and during the later years of
his ministry was ill much of the time. It was in those years of broken health
that he began to study the works of Emanuel Swedenborg, and came to believe
in the possibility of curing physical disease through "the power of a living
faith." About the year 1863 Dr. Evans went to Mr. Quimby for treatment.
He was able to grasp Quimby's theories almost immediately, and became so
much interested in Quimby's work that he soon returned to Portland upon a
second visit. Dr. Evans then told Mr. Quimby that he felt he could himself
practice Quimby's method of mind cure. Receiving cordial encouragement, he
returned to his home at Claremont, New Hampshire, and at once began to
practise. He later conducted a kind of mind-cure sanatorium, known as the
"Evans Home," at Salisbury, Mass. The later years of his life were chiefly
devoted to his literary work, and he published a number of books upon mental
healing. They were *The Mental Cure* (1869), *Mental Medicine* (1872), *Soul
and Body* (1875), *The Divine Law of Cure* (1881), *The Primitive Mind Cure*
(1885), and *Esoteric Christianity* (1886).
    Dr. Evans died September 4, 1889. Personally he was devout and modest,
a thinker, and a reader, rather than a propagandist. His endeavour was to
prove that mind cure is one of the old rectifying forces of the world, and he
made no claim to discovery or to especial enlightenment. His great desire was
to arouse other people to thinking and writing upon the subject of metaphysical
healing.

CHRISTIAN SCIENTISTS' PICNIC

At Point of Pines, July 16, 1885. Mrs. Woodbury is shown in the top row, and Mrs. Stetson is the third figure from the left in the third row

a number of Mrs. Eddy's strongest students quietly dropped out of her Christian Scientists' Association and began to investigate the subject of mental healing from another side, helping to form the nucleus of what was later to become the " New Thought " movement.

Mrs. Eddy at once saw the danger of liberal study and investigation on the part of her students. As a direct rebuke to those who had become interested in the writings of Dr. Evans, she issued instructions to the members of the Christian Scientists' Association that they should read no other works upon mental healing than those written by herself, and she printed in the *Journal* a set of rules to the effect that all teachers of Christian Science should require that their students read no literature upon the subject of mind cure but her own. To prevent liberal discussion and possible " conspiracy," she introduced a by-law that no two of the members of the Association should meet to discuss Christian Science or mental healing without inviting all other members of the Association to be present at their discussion. Her idea apparently was that one of her personal representatives should always be on hand to direct the discourse into safe channels. These restrictions cost her the allegiance of thoughtful students like Dr. J. W. Winkley and his wife.

Mrs. Eddy was now facing the gravest problem which had confronted her since the founding of her church. How was she to keep Christian Science from having a literature? How was she to prevent all these people whom she had stirred and had interested in metaphysical healing from writing books upon it which might prove as satisfactory and become as popular

as her own? Mrs. Ursula Gestefeld of Chicago, who had been
a student in the class Mrs. Eddy taught in that city in April,
1884, and who was one of the most intelligent and able persons
ever associated with the Christian Science movement, in 1888
wrote a book which she called *A Statement of Christian Science*,
adding upon the title-page that it was " An Explanation of
Science and Health," and giving Mrs. Eddy all possible credit
as the originator of the basic ideas of her book. Mrs. Gestefeld's work was an intelligent and intelligible presentation of
the fundamental ideas contained in *Science and Health*, without
Mrs. Eddy's disregard of logic and order, and free from her
confusing and tawdry rhetoric. Any natural scientist would
have welcomed such a clear and careful statement of his ideas.
But Mrs. Eddy branded Mrs. Gestefeld as a " mesmerist " of
the most dangerous variety, and had her expelled from the
Chicago church. The *Journal* declared that the " metaphysics " of Mrs. Gestefeld's book " crawled on its belly instead
of soaring in the upper air," and bade her beware, as " only
the pure in heart should see God." Mrs. Gestefeld then published a pamphlet, *Jesuitism in Christian Science*, in which she
explained her position and said that if *Science and Health*
merely contained Mrs. Eddy's personal impressions, if it were
a work of the fancy or imagination, then she had a right to
object to its being used as the basis of another book. But if
Mrs. Eddy's work announced the discovery of a principle and
a universal truth, she could no more keep other people from
writing and thinking upon it than she could keep people from
affirming that twice two are four. But, with Mrs. Eddy,
obtaining recognition for her truth was always secondary to

keeping it hers. Since she first began to teach her " Science," the story of her public life is simply the story of how she kept her hold on it. The very way in which she had come by her discovery made her always afraid of losing it, and she was forever detecting some student in the act of making off with it. Even in Lynn, she slept, as it were, with her hand on the cradle.

Later, when a Christian Science periodical was being printed in German, Mrs. Eddy would not permit *Science and Health* to be translated into that language, or into any other. She was not a linguist, and, knowing that she would be unable to pass upon the text of a translation, she feared to trust her gospel to the shadings of a foreign tongue. How she has done it let him declare who can, but she has absolutely sterilised every source that might have produced Christian Science literature, and to-day a loyal Christian Scientist would be as likely to think of dynamiting the Mother Church as of writing a book upon the theory or practice of Christian Science.

Dr. Evans' school—if it is not misleading to call his patients and sympathisers by so formal a name—was a rival which caused Mrs. Eddy a good deal of alarm. It drew from her her more thoughtful students, and, though they were seldom her most loyal and tractable followers, she realised their value in giving her sect a certain standing in Boston. The Evans following had hitherto been entirely without organisation; they were simply a group of people who were interested in the metaphysical treatment of disease, each thinking in his own way and working out his own problem. Now, however, they began to meet together more systematically, to organise in groups here and there, and to publish books and periodicals, encouraging liberal discussion and investigation. In their new activity they were doubtless influenced by Mrs. Eddy's stimulating example. Whatever the more conservative school of mental healers might have to say for themselves, or even for Mr. Quimby, it was Mrs. Eddy who had brought mental healing out of comparative obscurity, who had built up a strong organisation to advertise and push it, and who had sent out scores of missionaries and healers to establish it. It was as a religion, not as a way of thinking or a manner of living, that the new idea could be made to take hold, and Mrs. Eddy had seen this when the mental scientists had not. Indeed, had they realised this fact, it is doubtful whether they would have taken any earlier action, since they believed more in untrammelled individual development than in organised effort.

Although Mrs. Eddy viewed with alarm this growing body of independent writers and investigators, she had really very little to fear from an unorganised body of theorists who, however they might worst her in argument or distance her in reasoning, were certainly not her equals in generalship. Mrs. Eddy was a good fighter, and she knew it. In 1897 she wrote from her peaceful retirement at Concord: " With tender tread, thought sometimes walks in memory, through the dim corridors of years, on to old battle-grounds, there sadly to survey the fields of the slain and the enemy's losses." This from solitude and the peace of age; but there was no tender treading in the years when the battle was on. As soon as she saw signs of activity and consolidation among the people who had been influenced by Dr. Evans, Mrs. Eddy began vigorously to attack them, realising that such an organisation as theirs must inevitably draw recruits from the disssatisfied element in her own church.   By the beginning of 1888 there was discord even in that inner circle of students who shared Mrs. Eddy's councils and who were in daily attendance upon her at her new house in Commonwealth Avenue.   This growing unrest she attributed solely to the mesmeric influence of the mental scientists.   In reality it arose from several causes.

Some of the students were disappointed in Mrs. Eddy personally; some, like Mrs. Sarah Crosse (for several years editor of the *Journal*), had lost faith in Mrs. Eddy after long service; some, like Mr. and Mrs. Charles A. Troupe, were displeased with the arbitrary way in which she conducted the Christian Scientists' Association; others were dissatisfied with her instruction in the obstetrical course which she had recently introduced into her college.   The first class in obstetrics was a large one, and each member had paid one hundred dollars tuition.   Of the six lectures which Mrs. Eddy gave them, five were devoted almost exclusively to a discussion of Malicious Animal Magnetism, and in the sixth she merely instructed them to " deny " premature birth, abnormal presentation, hemorrhage, etc.[8]

At the same time Mrs. Eddy fanned the fire of discontent by announcing that she would no longer receive students for the " normal " course who had not passed through her own

---

[8] This course in obstetrics, as taken down by a student of that first class from Mrs. Eddy's dictation, covers less than a page of letter-paper, and consists of the " denials " that the practitioner is to use at the bedside of his patient.

The practitioner is first to take up in thought the subject of premature birth, and to deny the possibility of such an occurrence in the case he is then treating.

He is to deny one by one some of the dangerous symptoms which may attend childbirth. Mrs. Eddy takes these symptoms up at random and with no consideration for their relation to each other.

It was her exceedingly informal and unsystematic treatment of her subject in her obstetrical course, as well as the fact that most of the lectures were devoted to the subject of Demonology, that caused dissatisfaction among Mrs. Eddy's students.

primary class. As many of her normal graduates were now teaching primary classes in Christian Science, but not normal classes, this ruling would have the effect of debarring students, who wished to take more than a primary course, from any institution but Mrs. Eddy's. Mrs. Eddy's primary classes would be filled at the expense of the classes of her followers. So generally was this order criticised, that Mrs. Eddy felt obliged to modify it.

Mrs. Eddy, having faithfully taught her students how to detect malicious animal magnetism in others, was now openly charged with teaching and practising it herself. In *Science and Health*,[9] and in her classes, she had taught her students how to make a vigorous defence against the black art of the malpractitioners, but she had always indignantly denied the charge of being a mesmerist herself. The very accusation, the *Journal* said, was due to the malicious work of Kennedy and Arens.[10]

It seems, however, to have been Mrs. Eddy's action in the Corner case which brought all this dissatisfaction to a head. In the spring of 1888 Mrs. Abby H. Corner of West Medford, Mass., a student of Mrs. Eddy's and a member of the Christian Scientists' Association, attended her own daughter in childbirth, with the result that the mother and baby died. Mrs. Corner

---

[9] " They (the malpractitioners) know," she writes in *Science and Health*, Vol. I, page 244, 1885 edition, " as well as we, it is morally impossible for science to produce sickness, *but science makes sin punish itself. They should have fear for their own lives* in their attempts to kill us. God is Supreme, and the penalties of their sins they cannot escape. Turning the attention of the sick to us for the benefit they may receive from us, is another milder species of malpractice *that is not safe,* for if we feel their sufferings, not knowing the individual, we shall defend ourself, and *the result is dangerous to the intruder.*"

In *Science and Health*, page 174, 1884 edition, this warning is given : " In warfare with error we attack with intent to kill, as the wounded or cornered beast turns on its assailant."

[10] " I never touched in thought personalities, though well aware that K. and A. (Kennedy and Arens) of Boston, and some of their co-adjutors do mentally attack people in this way, making them believe that she who exposes their crimes (Mrs. Eddy) is doing it."—*Christian Science Journal*, July, 1885.

was prosecuted, but was finally acquitted on the ground that her daughter's death had occurred from a hemorrhage which might have been fatal even had a physician been present. The case was widely discussed in the newspapers, and aroused a great deal of indignation and animosity toward Christian Science. It seemed the time of all times for Christian Scientists to stand together, and for the students of Mrs. Eddy's college to meet the issue squarely. They did so—all except Mrs. Eddy and those whom she directly controlled. Hundreds of Mrs. Eddy's students were then practising who knew no more about obstetrics than the babes they helped into the world. Mrs. Eddy's obstetrical course, which was a recent innovation, consisted of instructions to "deny" everything except the child itself. Fifteen years before, students had gone out from her classes in Lynn and had taken confinement cases, in which they were said to be particularly successful. Mrs. Eddy had never hinted, until she introduced her obstetrical course, that any special preparation was needed in that branch of metaphysical treatment. Mrs. Corner had acted not only according to the custom of Mrs. Eddy's students, but according to Mrs. Eddy's instructions for fifteen years past. Nevertheless, now that there was actually a question of Christian Science and the law, Mrs. Eddy completely withdrew her support from Mrs. Corner, and had a statement denouncing her printed in the Boston *Herald*. This article intimated that Mrs. Corner had received no authority from the Metaphysical College to attend confinement cases.

To THE EDITOR OF THE HERALD: The lamentable case reported from West Medford of the death of a mother and her infant at childbirth should forever put a stop to quackery. There has been but one side of this case presented by the newspapers. We wait to hear from the other side, trusting that attenuating circumstances will be brought to light. Mrs. Abby H. Corner never entered the obstetrics class at the Massachusetts Metaphysical College. She was not fitted at this institute for an accoucheur, had attended but one term, and four terms, including three years of successful practice by the student, are required to complete the college course.[11]

The members of the Christian Scientists' Association, in the main, felt that Christian Science practice itself was being tried before the courts in the person of Mrs. Corner, and lent her their cordial support. Mrs. Corner had incurred an expense of two hundred dollars in defending her case, and the members of the Association wished to pay this out of the Association funds, thus distributing the burden among the flock. Mrs. Eddy objected to this, ruling that if the members wished to aid Mrs. Corner financially, they could do so by personal contribution. In the end, however, Mrs. Corner's lawyer was paid from the Association treasury.

Mrs. Eddy's action, if not just, was politic. By repudiating Mrs. Corner she averted any reproach which, as a result of the scandal, might have attached to Christian Science practice, and left Mrs. Corner to meet as best she could the consequences of the method she had been taught. But her students regarded it as traitorous, and complained bitterly. They remembered that while their teacher advocated the practice of Christian Science in all cases, and taught them to believe they were persecuted if interfered with by the law, she took ample care to protect herself, by refusing to take patients for treat-

[11] Boston *Herald,* April 29, 1888. This notice was signed "Committee on Publication, Christian Scientists' Association," but it was published without the knowledge of the Association and has many of Mrs. Eddy's turns of phrase.

ment, or even to be consulted on diseases. "We stand the brunt and burden of Christian Science," they said, "and Mrs. Eddy gets the money and the glory."

On June 6, 1888, the Christian Scientists' Association held a stormy meeting in the old Tremont Temple. At this meeting William B. Johnson was elected secretary of the Association, Charles A. Troupe having refused to hold the office any longer —because, he said, attempts had been made to make him change the records. At this meeting Mrs. Eddy's conduct in regard to Mrs. Corner was severely criticised. Indeed, the discussion became very personal, one of the members rising to state that Mrs. Eddy had been seen in the act of pulling Mr. Frye about by the hair of his head. Mrs. Eddy, who was present, re-marked: "There is Calvin Frye. He has a good head of hair; let him speak for himself." Mr. Frye, however, sitting in his usual imperturbable silence, made no reply. Five weeks later he sent out the following explanation in a stylograph letter, dated July 14:

A student and a Free Mason gives out this report of the widow of a Free Mason and his hitherto much honoured Teacher, Rev. Mary B. G. Eddy, that in a fit of temper she pulled a handful of hair out of my head.

About two years ago, I was having much to contend with from the attacks of malicious mesmerism, by which the attempt was made to de-moralise me and through me to afflict Mrs. Eddy. While under one of these attacks, my mind became almost a total blank. Mrs. Eddy was alone with me at the time, and, calling to me loudly without a response, she saw the necessity for prompt action and lifted my head by the forelock, and called aloud to rouse me from the paralysed state into which I had fallen, this had the desired effect, and I wakened to a sense of where I was, my mind wandering, but I saw the danger from which she had delivered me and which can never be produced again. This malpractice, alias demonology, I have found out, and know that God is my refuge. "When ye shall see the abomination of desolation spoken of by Daniel the prophet, stand in the holy place, (whoso readeth, let him understand) then let them which be in Judea, flee to the mountain," where I have found my refuge.

Fraternally yours,

C. A. FRYE.

At that meeting at Tremont Temple, Mrs. Eddy saw trouble enough ahead.   She caused the new secretary, Mr. Johnson, to send out a general call to the Association to meet her at the college June 14; but, meaning to have matters well arranged before that, she sent telegrams to a few of her most zealous partisans, asking them to meet at her house on June 9, five days before the day set for the general meeting.   The telegram which she sent to New York read: " Come to the college Saturday, June 9th.   I will be there.   I have a message from God that will do you good."   When Mrs. Eddy learned that word of this first meeting had got out among the members of the Association, she sent another telegram to New York, saying: " The message will be delivered in Chicago.   Go there."   (The annual convention of the National Association was to convene in Chicago June 13, and Mrs. Eddy went there with Mr. Johnson, Mr. Frye, and a number of her faithful students from Boston.)

What the rebellious students wanted to do was simply to leave the Christian Scientists' Association, but that was not so easy as it might seem.   There were two by-laws of the Association which were very formidable obstacles to withdrawal.   They read:

Resolved, That every one who wishes to withdraw without reason shall be considered to have broken his oath.

Resolved, That breaking the Christian Scientists' oath is immorality.

From time to time members had asked to have their names withdrawn from the roll of membership, and for that reason had been expelled for " immorality." This dissenting faction had no mind to risk such dismissal, and, in the absence of Mrs. Eddy, and of Mr. Johnson, the secretary, they resorted to high-handed measures. Calling at Mr. Johnson's house, they persuaded his wife to give them the Association books. These they put in the hands of an attorney, and then told Mrs. Eddy that the books would not be returned to Mr. Johnson until she directed him to give them a letter of honourable dismissal from the Association. Mrs. Eddy attempted to patch matters up, and had Mr. Johnson send out to all the members a circular letter, in which she asked them to meet her and state their grievances. This letter reads, in part:

Our self-sacrificing Teacher, Mrs. Eddy, says: " . . . After learning a little, even, of the good I have achieved and which has been demanded and been associated with all of my movements since God commissioned me to bring Christian Science into this world of iniquity, they will learn how to estimate their [her movements] wisdom instead of traducing them. . . . At the first special meeting called in behalf of Mrs. Corner I was absent, not because unready or unwilling to *help her,* but that she needed no help, and I knew it. I was not at the second special meeting, because it was impossible, if I got ready for the trip to Chicago; also I wanted this conspiracy to come to the surface, and it has, and now is the only time for us to meet in Christian love and adjust this great wrong done to one [Mrs. Eddy] who has given all the best of her years to heal and bless the whole human family."

The dissenters, however, stood firm; refused to go to the Association meetings or to surrender the books. The matter dragged on for about a year, until they finally received their letters of dismissal, signed by Mrs. Eddy as president of the Association, and William B. Johnson as clerk. Thirty-six members withdrew at this time, at least a score of whom had been among Mrs. Eddy's most promising practitioners and efficient workers.   As the entire membership of the Boston church was considerably less than two hundred even before these thirty-six withdrew, their going made a perceptible decrease in the size of Mrs. Eddy's congregation.

CHAPTER XIX

MRS. EDDY RALLIES HER FORCES—GROWTH OF CHRISTIAN SCIENCE
IN THE WEST—THE MAKING OF A HEALER—THE APOTHEO-
SIS OF MRS. EDDY

MRS. EDDY, publicly, made little of the fact that she was
losing support in Boston. " The late much ado about nothing," she writes in the *Journal* of September, 1888, " arose
solely from mental malicious practice, and the audible falsehood
designed to stir up strife between brethren, for the purpose
of placing Christian Science in the hands of aspirants for place
and power." In practice, however, she heeded the warning.
She braced up the course in " Metaphysical Obstetrics " in her
college by engaging the services of Ebenezer J. Foster,[1] who
held a degree of Doctor of Medicine, and who had taken a
course in Christian Science the previous autumn. Dr. Foster
was to act as Mrs. Eddy's " assistant in obstetrics." The course
was made longer and the tuition fee was doubled. " Doctor
Foster," read Mrs. Eddy's announcement in the *Journal,* " will
teach the anatomy and surgery of obstetrics, and I, its metaphysics. The combination of his knowledge of Christian Science
with his anatomical skill, renders him a desirable teacher in
this department of my college. In twenty years' practice he
has not had a single case of mortality at childbirth. . . . Stu-

---

[1] Who later became her adopted son. See Chapter XX.

dents will receive the combined instruction of Mrs. Eddy and Dr. Foster for $200 tuition." In every direction she strove to strengthen her position, to regain her lost ground, and to gather new followers. She reiterated her divine right of supremacy, she asserted with greater emphasis her command of the situation, and she declared with no uncertainty the duties of Christian Scientists toward her, giving the Bible as her authority. " Students will do well," says the *Journal* (October, 1888) under the head, " Who Hath Ears to Hear, let Him Hear," " to bear in mind the Master's warning: ' except ye be converted and become as little children, ye shall not enter the Kingdom of Heaven.' This Scripture means practically to each individual to-day all that it implies in its relative bearing towards the Truth as Divine Science, and towards its rightful Discoverer."

Christian Scientists were held even more rigidly than before to the rule forbidding them to read any but Mrs. Eddy's writings on mental healing. This war against heresy was carried on too zealously at last, and when the *Journal* (October, 1890) admonished beginning students to lay aside the Bible for *Science and Health*,[2] it was felt even by Scientists that this was going too far. The *Journal* also instructed Mrs. Eddy's loyal students to burn all forbidden literature. " Burn every scrap of ' Christian Science literature,' so-called," it said, " except *Science and Health*, and the publications bearing

---

[2] " A student," says the Journal, " —in the tongue of the world called a patient—who says to a Scientist, ' I take so much comfort in reading my Bible,' if guided wisely, will be answered, ' Let your Bible alone for three months or more. Don't open it even, nor think of it, but dig night and day at *Science and Health.*' "

In response to public criticism concerning these utterances, the Christian Science publication committee met and unanimously voted that this sentiment was " unauthorised, unwise, and not the thought of our committee."

the imprint of the Christian Science Publishing Society of Boston."

This red-hot exhortation was brought out by the fact that the dissenters of 1888 were now publishing periodicals, bringing out books, and carrying on their work of healing and teaching under the name of Christian Science, exactly as if Mrs. Eddy did not exist. Most of them had adopted the policy of non-resistance. They kept a neutral attitude toward Mrs. Eddy, refused to discuss her or her church, and in their work and public utterances they adhered to the rule of excluding personalities and keeping close to principle. They no longer recognised Mrs. Eddy's favourite doctrine of Malicious Animal Magnetism, but dwelt much upon the affirmative principle of Good. But they must have missed the inspiring presence and influence of their old leader, for after a few years their publications lagged and most of these " independents " either dropped Christian Science definitely or joined the New Thought movement.

But, whether Mrs. Eddy realised it or not, sedition among the Boston students no longer meant jeopardy to her or to her cause. If there was disloyalty in Boston, hundreds of converts in New England, the middle West, and the far West waited but the word to rally to her support. Christian Science was an established faith, and was no longer at the mercy of any group of people. It had been established by those indefatigable missionaries, the healers; with Mrs. Eddy always behind them, and their devotion to her holding them together, inspiring them with one purpose, and enabling them to work for one end.

After Mrs. Eddy herself, the most remarkable thing about

Christian Science is its rapid growth. When the National Christian Science Association, formed at Mrs. Eddy's house in Boston, January 29, 1886, was little more than a year old, one hundred and eleven professional healers advertised in the pages of the *Christian Science Journal* and twenty-one academies and institutes taught Mrs. Eddy's doctrines.

In April, 1890, the *Journal* contained the professional cards of two hundred and fifty healers, men and women who were practising in all parts of the country, and nearly all of whom were depending entirely upon their practice for a livelihood. Thirty-three academies and institutes were then teaching Christian Science. These " academies " were very unpretentious— simply a room in which the teacher met her classes. In some institutes there were two teachers; usually there was but one. The " graduates " of these institutions sometimes went on to Boston to take a normal course under Mrs. Eddy, but oftener they went immediately into practice. By 1890 there were twenty incorporated Christian Science churches which announced their weekly services in the *Journal* and which met in public halls and schoolhouses, while ninety societies not yet organised into churches were holding their weekly meetings. The first Christian Science church building was dedicated at Oconto, Wis., in 1887.

When Mrs. Eddy established herself in Boston in 1882, there was but one Christian Science Church, a feeble society of less than fifty members, which had been already shattered by dissensions and quarrels. It is certainly very evident that such an astonishing growth in the space of eight years can be accounted for only by the fact that Mrs. Eddy's religion gave the people something they wanted, and that it was presented to them in a direct and effective way. " Demonstrate, demonstrate," was Mrs. Eddy's watchword. " Heal the sick, raise the dead, cleanse the lepers, cast out demons." Thus read the seal of Mrs. Eddy's college, and such were the instructions she gave her students when she sent them out into the field. She never took cases herself, but she made her students understand that they were to be proved by works, and by works alone, and that if they were children of the new birth at all, they must heal.

To appreciate the work of the healers, one must understand something about their preparation. Many of the students who left Mrs. Eddy's Metaphysical College and went out to practise knew much less about physiology, anatomy, and hygiene than the average grammar-school boy knows to-day. They had not been taught how to tie an artery or to set a broken bone, how to take a patient's temperature or how to administer the simple antidotes for poisons. Spinsters who had never even been present at a confinement went bravely out to attend women in childbirth. The healers' instruction had been after this manner:

Tumors, ulcers, tubercles, inflammation, pain, deformed joints, are all dream shadows, dark images of mortal thought which will flee before the light.[3]

Have no fears that matter can ache, swell, and be inflamed. . . . Your body would suffer no more from tension or wounds than would the trunk of a tree which you gash, were it not for mortal mind.[4]

A child can have worms if you say so,—or any other malady, timorously hidden in the beliefs, relative to his body, of those about him.[5]

The treatment of insanity is especially interesting. . . . The argu-

[3] *Science and Health* (1906), p. 418.
[4] *Science and Health* (1906), p. 393.
[5] *Science and Health* (1906), p. 413.

ments to be used in curing insanity are the same as in other diseases: namely, the impossibility that matter, brain, can control or derange the mind, can suffer or cause suffering.[6]

If a crisis occurs in your treatment, you must treat the patient less for the disease and more for the mental fermentation.[7]

When the unthinking lobster loses his claw, it grows again. If the Science of Life were understood, it would be found that the senses of Mind are never lost, and that matter has no sensation. Then the human limb would be replaced as readily as the lobster's claw.[8]

The healers were recruited from every walk of life—school-teachers, milliners, dressmakers, music-teachers, elocutionists, mothers of families, and young women who had been trained to no vocation at all. Among the male practitioners—they were greatly in the minority—there were even a few converts from the regular schools of medicine, but their contributions to the *Journal* are so disorderly and inexact, and in some cases so illiterate, as to indicate that their success in the practice of medicine was very questionable. In the first years of her college, Mrs. Eddy's consulting physician in instrumental surgery was, the reader will remember, Charles J. Eastman, afterward imprisoned for criminal practice. There were, however, among her early practitioners, honest and worthy men. One of the most successful of these was Captain Joseph S. Eastaman, for many years a leading Christian Science practitioner in Boston, and who is still practising in Cambridge.

When he went to Mrs. Eddy to lay before her the case of his sick wife, Mr. Eastaman had been a sea-captain for twenty-one years, having begun his apprenticeship to the sea when he was thirteen, as cabin-boy on board an English brig. If the old seaman soon became docile like the other men about

[6] *Science and Health* (1906), p. 414.
[7] *Science and Health* (1906), p. 421.
[8] *Science and Health* (1906), p. 489.

Mrs. Eddy he had, at least, learned obedience in a hard and manly school. The story of his life at sea, which he contributed in several articles to the *Christian Science Journal,* is a vigorous and sturdy piece of narrative-writing, full of wrecks and typhoons and adventures with cannibal tribes, which make his subsequent career seem all the more remarkable. Concerning his first meeting with Mrs. Eddy in 1884, and his conversion to Christian Science, he writes at length. His last voyage, from Peru home to Boston, was made for the purpose of joining his invalid wife.

Upon my arrival [he says], I found her much lower than I had supposed, and the consultation of physicians immediately secured only made it evident that she could not live long. In anxiety and distress, I then added my own knowledge of medicine—of necessity considerable to have enabled me for so many years to care properly for both passengers and crew. . . . One evening, as I was sitting hopeless at my wife's bedside, a friend called and asked, " Captain, why don't you get a Christian Scientist to treat your wife? "

The captain visited a healer, and learned for the first time of the existence of Mrs. Eddy. He thought, " If the healer can do so much, his teacher must heal instantly." In his narrative the captain says:

So, like a drowning man grasping at a straw, with alternating hopes and fears besieging me on the way, I went to the college. In answer to my request for a personal interview, Mrs. Eddy kindly granted me an extended audience, though to my appeal for help she made the gentle announcement that she herself did not now take patients. At this my heart failed utterly, for I felt that none less than the founder was equal to the healing necessary in my case. As I was about to leave, she turned to me and said with much earnestness, " Captain, why don't you heal your wife yourself? " I stood spellbound. I did not know what to say or think. Finally I stammered out, " How can I heal my wife? Have I not procured the best medical aid? What more can I do? " Gently she said, " Learn how to heal." Without hesitation I returned to the parlour for particulars. It seemed to me that it must require years of studying to learn Christian Science—and she whom I was trying to save would not long be here. But when I heard that the entire term required but three weeks, I gathered courage. In twenty minutes more I had arranged to enter a class.

The captain's wife was averse to his new plan. She was unwilling that he should add this tuition fee of several hundred dollars to the already heavy expenses of her long illness. Moreover, she was afraid that this Christian Science was some new kind of Spiritualism. But the captain never committed himself half-way. In that first interview Mrs. Eddy had won him completely. He had escaped typhoons and coral reefs and cannibal kings, only to arrive at an adventure of the mind which was vastly stranger. Into the class he went. He says:

The class included many highly cultured people, all more or less conversant with the rudiments of Christian Science; while I, a sailor, with only a seaman's knowledge of the world, and not the faintest inkling of the field to be opened up before me, felt very much out of place there. To that first and last and most important question "What is God?" the students replied variously. When the question came to me, I stammered out, "God is all, with all and in all. Everything that is good and pure." The teacher smiled encouragingly as my answers followed one another, and I was encouraged to go on. Every day during the term questions were asked and answers were made that puzzled me not a little. But to all my own simple earnest queries the patient teacher replied clearly and satisfactorily. The many laughs enjoyed by the class at my expense did not trouble me, therefore, for my teacher knew that I would not profess to understand when I did not. The simpler my questions, the more pains she took to explain clearly.

How much was due to my own changed thought I cannot tell, but after Christian Science was recognised in our home, even before I entered the college, my wife began to recover. As soon as I understood the rudiments, I began to treat her, and so quickly did she respond to the treatment that she was able to avail herself of the kind invitation of the teacher to accompany me to the final session.

The captain's conversion was a thorough one. He gave up

his little bit of grog—to which he had never been much addicted—and his Havana cigars, of which he had been very fond. He began to practise a little among his old friends—shipowners and sailors. After his wife had fully recovered he began to look about for work, and decided to accept an offer which had been made him by the Panama Railway Company.

I accordingly engaged passage to Aspinwall, but on the last day I was reminded of a promise made my teacher. I at once wrote her of my plans, asking if they were wise, and received immediate counsel not to go. Packed and passage taken, here was a dilemma. Still, I was ready to be rightly guided, and wrote again asking what I should do. The reply came, "Take an office." This certainly was the last thing I should have thought of doing, for I could see no way to clear my personal expenses, much less meet the added rent of a central location. However, the time had come, and the birthright in Christian Science required obedience, even though it looked like throwing away time and means. I could not disobey, so I set about office-hunting. At first I wished to take a place on trial, but a voice kept telling me that I would do better to take a lease for at least a year. And it was well I did, for mortal mind soon tried to drive me away, and at times apparently only the obligation of the lease held me firm.

Whatever unfortunate examples of the professional healer one may have seen, one believes Captain Eastaman when he says that in his practice of twenty-two years he has worked harder than he ever did at stowing cargoes in the West India service. His account of his cures is as straightforward and convincing in its style as is his story of his life at sea. No one who reads it can doubt that the captain actually believes he cured a woman of five tumours on the neck, and a workingman of cataract of both eyes.

The businesslike methods which have always been so conspicuous in the operations of the Christian Science Church had their effect in its early proselyting.

The healer had no Board of Missions back of him; he was thrown entirely upon his own resources. His income and his usefulness to Christian Science alike depended upon the number of patients he could attract, interest, influence, and heal. While this condition must have had its temptation for the healer of not very rugged integrity, it was wonderfully advantageous to the cause as a whole. Never, since religions were propagated by the sword, was a new faith advertised and spread in such a systematic and effective manner. When the healer went to a new town, he had first to create a demand for Christian Science treatments, and, if he could demonstrate successfully enough to make that demand, not only was his career assured, but he had laid the foundation of a future Christian Science church. The files of the *Journal* abound in letters from healers which show exactly how this demand was created.

Take the case of Mrs. Ann M. Otis, a healer at Stanton, Mich. She was called to Marquette to treat a young man who was suffering from a heavy cold on his lungs. As his father and brother had both died from " quick " consumption, his mother and sisters were in frantic alarm and his friends had already consigned him to go the way of his family. Under Mrs. Otis' treatment he recovered. The cure was noised about the town by his grateful relatives, and so many patients poured in upon the healer that she had to remain there for weeks.

Wherever the new religion went, it had the advantage of novelty. It was much talked about, was discussed at social gatherings and in women's clubs. Josephine Tyter, a healer at Richmond, Ind., writes in the *Journal*, September, 1888:

" It is one year next month since I came to Richmond. I

knew no one here, and no one knew me. Christian Science they knew nothing of. People thought they did not want it. I knew they did, but they could not see in darkness. The physicians paid but little attention to me at first, but now they are thoroughly aroused. At the regular meeting of the Tuesday Evening Literary Club, to which all the high order of minds of Richmond are supposed to belong, one of the physicians of this city read a paper on Christian Science." Miss Tyter then relates her own success, enumerating among her cures cases of the delusions of pregnancy, nervous prostration, lung and brain fever. She says, " Have had some fine cases of spinal curvature," and tells how she brought one man " out of a plaster cast into Truth."

Mrs. A. M. Rigby, a school-teacher at Bloomington, Ill., writes that her health, broken down by many years of service in the schoolroom, was restored by Christian Science, and that she then began to practise. When she had eighty cases, she resigned from her school, and for two years she has had from twenty-five to fifty new cases a month.

Emma A. Estes, a healer at Grandledge, Mich., writes exultantly of her trip to Newark: " My stay of three days lengthened into one of three weeks, and I was kept busy every day. Had forty-nine patients, and found my work greatly blessed. . . . Mother joins me in sending love, and adds, ' May God bless dear Mrs. Eddy for her kindness to my own little girl.' "

Mrs. Harriet N. Cordwell, Berlin Falls, N. H., writes that she has but recently become a healer, has healed one case of spinal trouble in sixteen absent treatments, a case of scrofula in thirteen treatments, case of lame back (fifteen years' standing), one treatment, etc.

L. W. P. writes from Piqua, Ohio, that over three hundred cases were treated within five months by an incoming healer, that four classes were organised for the study of *Science and Health*, and a Christian Science Sunday-school organised (July, 1890).

Ella B. Fluno, a healer then in Lexington, Ky., writes that she was painlessly delivered of a child, got up the next day and did her housework, carried water from the well and walked on the icy sidewalk in low slippers. She did not have the blinds in her bedroom lowered, and the sun shone daily in the baby's eyes, with no ill effects.

Some of these communications from healers are extremely entertaining, attesting to the efficacy of Christian Science in increasing the patient's worldly prosperity, and giving examples of how " demonstration " may be made useful in despatching housework. One woman writes:

My husband came from the stable one morning with word that a valued four-year-old colt had got into the oats-bin, had been eating all night, and was as "tight as a drum." I met the error's claim with an emphatic mental denial. . . . As soon as possible, though not immediately, I went to the barn-yard, laid my hand on the horse's head, and said in an audible voice: "You are God's horse; for all that is He made and pronounced perfect. You cannot overeat, have colic, or be foundered, for there is no power in material food to obstruct or interfere with the perfect health, activity, and freedom of all that is real and spiritual." . . . Previous to my treatment he stood with head down and short, rapid breathing. At noon he was all right, and I am delighted to know how to realise for the good of animals.

In the healer's effort to arouse interest and get business in a new field there can be no doubt that he was sometimes overzealous and disregarded those uninspiring facts of which mortal mind must still take account. The more conservative and honest workers felt the bad effects of these extreme methods, and in the *Journal* of June, 1892, one healer writes:

All healers have some instantaneous cures, but if we mention only these, does it not imply that we have no lingering cases? I call to mind a lady Scientist who wanted to make an impression in a new field where she hoped to get business. After talking of the many wonderful cures which she had effected, she added that she herself was cured in three treatments of a lifelong malady. Now, while that was substantially correct, the shadows of her belief [symptoms of her illness] were not wholly effaced for over two years, and this was known to others in Science. Would it not have been better had the Scientist qualified her statement as to the time required?

Do not Scientists make a mistake in conveying the impression, or, what is the same thing, letting an impression go uncorrected, that those in Science are never sick, that they never have any ailments or troubles to contend with? There is no Scientist who at all times is wholly exempt from aches and pains or from trials of some kind. Neither pride of knowledge nor practice nor the good of the cause require that Scientists disguise or withhold these facts.

The question of the compensation which it was proper for the healer and teacher to receive was, from time to time, discussed in the *Journal*. At the various institutes and academies where Christian Science was taught, the charge for a term of lessons was from one to two hundred dollars. The healer's usual charge was a dollar a treatment, or daily treatments at five dollars a week.

One healer writes, May, 1890: " To allow the patient to decide the price would certainly be unselfish on the part of the healer. But such laxity might allow selfishness with the patient."

Another practitioner protests that the customary fee is too little: " It is a low plane of thought," he says, " that goes through the community and *itself* erects a barrier against generosity or even fair compensation. The Science is lowered in the public estimation, the healer humiliated, if not weakened, and the chances of success in doing good greatly lessened. Selfishness still remains to imprison the patient unless his thought, in this, as in other directions, be changed."

Mrs. Buswell, a healer at Beatrice, Neb., was once summoned before the court under charge of practising medicine unlawfully. She objected that her treatments were in the nature of a religious exercise and did not come under the jurisdiction of the medical laws of the state. When, upon question, she admitted that she accepted money for these treatments, the judge cited to her the reply of Peter to Simon the sorcerer: " Thy money perish with thee, because thou hast thought that the gift of God may be purchased with money." But the Christian Scientist's God is not at all the God of Christian theology. He is, as Mrs. Eddy ceaselessly reiterates, Principle. There was really no more irreverence in Mrs. Buswell's realising the Allness of God for money than there would have been in her realising the truth of a proposition of Euclid.

Every patient healed was practically a new Christian Scientist made. If he were to keep well he must do so by studying *Science and Health*. The new converts always became immediately estranged from their old church associates, and very often from their oldest friends. They met together at one another's houses to discuss Christian Science and to hold services. These circles were, indeed, very much like that first one which used to meet in Mrs. Damon's parlour in Lynn. As soon as such groups of believers were able to do so, they formed a society and held regular Sunday services in a schoolhouse or public hall. If this society grew and prospered, which it was almost sure to do, it became an incorporated church. A Christion Science reading-room was often established, where Mrs. Eddy's works and copies of the *Journal* might be obtained. If a community happened to be slow in taking up the new faith, the missionaries sometimes attributed public disasters to the prevalence of Error over Truth. One worker in an untoward field writes in the *Journal* of November, 1890:

The result of their closed eyes and ears has been demonstrated in a startling railroad accident and sudden deaths in our midst. On the night of the fourteenth a cloudburst caused a deluge of destruction of property in the lower streets of this village and imperilled many lives. Just now is a favourable time for work.

While the growth of Christian Science must be attributed primarily to its stimulating influence upon the sick and discontented, the low vitality of the orthodox churches undoubtedly facilitated its advance. Mrs. Eddy's teachings brought the promise of material benefits to a practical people, and the appeal of seeming newness to a people whose mental recreation was a feverish pursuit of novelty. In the West, especially, where every one was absorbed in a new and hard-won material prosperity, the healer and teacher met with an immediate response. This religion had a message of cheer for the rugged materialist as well as for the morbid invalid. It exalted health and self-satisfaction and material prosperity high among the moral virtues—indeed, they were the evidences of right living, the manifestations of a man's " at-oneness " with God. Christian Science had no rebuke for riches; it bade man think always of life, of his own worthiness and security, just as the old religions had bidden him remember death and be mindful of his unworthiness and insecurity. It contributed to the general sense of self-satisfaction and well-being which already characterised a new and thrifty society.

Probably Mrs. Eddy herself was not aware of the headway which her sect had made until she attended the third annual convention of the National Christian Scientists' Association, held at Chicago in June, 1888. Mrs. Eddy went on from Boston, personally attended by Mr. Frye and Ebenezer J. Foster, who was soon to become her son by adoption. Crowds of Mrs. Eddy's Western followers here for the first time beheld her, as they put it, " face to face," and she achieved a most gratifying personal triumph.

This was the first and last annual convention Mrs. Eddy ever attended, and a *coup de théâtre* could scarcely have been better planned. On the morning of June 13, Mrs. Eddy delivered an address to an audience of more than three thousand people, eight hundred of whom were Christian Science delegates. When she stepped upon the platform the entire audience rose and cheered her.

Her address, which is said to have thrilled every listener and which was termed " pentecostal," seems, at this distance, rather below Mrs. Eddy's average. She closed with the following tribute to her church militant:

Christian Science and Christian Scientists will, must, have a history; and if I could write the history in poor parody on Tennyson's grand verse, it would read thus:

> " Traitors to right of them,
> M.D.'s to left of them,
> Priestcraft in front of them,
> Volleyed and thundered:

> Into the jaws of hate,
> Out through the door of love,
> On—to the blest above—
> Marched the one hundred."

Such sentiments as these wrought her audience to a feverish pitch of excitement. A letter to the Boston *Traveller*, afterward reprinted in the *Christian Science Journal*, thus described the outburst of feeling which followed Mrs. Eddy's address:

The scenes that followed when she had ceased speaking will long be remembered by those who witnessed them. The people were in the presence of the woman whose book had healed them, and they knew it. Up they came in crowds to her side, begging one hand-clasp, one look, one memorial from her whose name was a power and a sacred thing in their homes. Those whom she had never seen before—invalids raised up by her book, " Science and Health "—attempted to hurriedly tell the wonderful story.

A mother who failed to get near her held high her babe to look on their helper. Others touched the dress of their benefactor, not so much as asking for more.

An aged woman, trembling with palsy, lifted her shaking hands at Mrs. Eddy's feet, crying, " Help, help! " and the cry was answered. Many such people were known to go away healed. Strong men turned aside to hide tears, as the people thronged to Mrs. Eddy with blessings and thanks.

Meekly and almost silently, she received all this homage from the multitude, until she was led away from the place, the throng blocking her passage from the door to the carriage.

What wonder if the thoughts of those present went back to eighteen hundred years ago, when the healing power was manifested through the personal Jesus?

Can the cold critic, harsh opposer, or disbeliever in Christian Science call up any other like picture through all these centuries?

What was the Pentecostal hour but this same dawning of God's allness and oneness, and His supremacy manifested in gifts of healing and speaking, " with tongues "? Let history declare of Mary Eddy what were the blessings and power which she brought.

It was while Mrs. Eddy was thus making material for legend in Chicago that " conspiracy " was afoot in Boston, and the enthusiastic writer just quoted was forced to take this into account, and to add: " Is there no similarity between the past and present records of Christ, Truth, entering into Jerusalem, and the betrayal? Is the bloodthirsty tyranny of animal magnetism the Veil of the Temple, which is to be rent from top to bottom? "

CHAPTER XX

In 1888 George Washington Glover, Mrs. Eddy's long-absent son, the child of her first marriage, came to spend a winter in Boston. He brought with him from the West his wife and four children, and took a house in Chelsea. Although his relations with his mother at that time seem to have been amicable, they were certainly not of a very close or confidential nature. While Mr. Glover was in Boston his mother's business affairs were still conducted by Mr. Frye, and the son was a far from conspicuous figure in her daily life. He was not a member of her household or of her church, and took no part in her great religious enterprise. Mr. Glover and his family were first publicly introduced to Mrs. Eddy's followers in December, at a fair given by the Christian Scientists. On this occasion the Glovers were cordially welcomed by Mrs. Eddy's friends, and the resemblance of the daughter Mary Baker Glover, to her grandmother was the subject of general comment throughout the evening. At a late hour Mrs. Eddy herself appeared to grace the fair, and when she entered the hall the orchestra began to play Mendelssohn's wedding march, to symbolise, so the *Journal* explains, Mrs. Eddy's " indissoluble union with Truth."

Mr. Glover's prolonged stay in Chelsea seems not to have brought him and his mother any closer together, for, almost immediately after his return to the West, Mrs. Eddy adopted a son who was presumably more to her liking.

Ebenezer Johnson Foster was a man of forty-one when Mrs. Eddy adopted him, and she herself was then in her sixty-eighth year. Dr. Foster was a homœopathic physician who had been practising his profession at Waterbury Center, a little mountain town in Vermont. Like most of Mrs. Eddy's disciples, he had led a quiet, uneventful life until he came under her influence. As a boy of fifteen he had enlisted in the Union Army and had served for three years. Later he was graduated from the Hahnemann Medical College in Philadelphia.

Dr. Foster first heard of Christian Science through William Clark, an old army comrade who believed that his health had been restored through his study of Mrs. Eddy's book. Dr. Foster decided to investigate this new system of healing, and, in the autumn of 1887, when he went to Boston to pay a visit to an old aunt, he called at Mrs. Eddy's house in Columbus Avenue and an interview was granted. The first impressions on both sides were very agreeable. Mrs. Eddy was more than eager to enlist the sympathies of " the M.D.'s," as she termed physicians, and she saw in Dr. Foster the tractable kind of man she was always looking for. She lavished her most gracious manner upon him, and he was led away captive in the first interview. It seemed to Dr. Foster that Mrs. Eddy was very like his own mother; that she was full of gentleness and sympathy and affection. She told him that she wished him to become her student, and he entered her class the following day.

After completing his course at Mrs. Eddy's Metaphysical College, Dr. Foster returned to Waterbury Center and resumed the practice of homœopathy, experimenting more or less with the Christian Science method of healing, and industriously reading *Science and Health.* In the following May he received an urgent letter from Mrs. Eddy requesting him to attend the National Convention of the Christian Scientists' Association, which was to meet at Chicago in June. Because of division and discord in the Boston church, Mrs. Eddy, foreseeing serious trouble, was strengthening her position by every possible means, and was ascertaining, in one way and another, which of her students could be depended upon in case of an emergency. Dr. Foster was easily persuaded to go to Chicago. After the convention adjourned and Mrs. Eddy returned to Boston, he went to visit his brother in Wisconsin. There he soon received a telegram from his teacher, bidding him come at once to Boston. Before he could start, another telegram from her told him not to come. Soon afterward he received a letter urging him to come at once.

When Dr. Foster arrived at Mrs. Eddy's new house in Commonwealth Avenue, July 4, 1888, he was at a loss to know just why she had sent for him, except that the recent schism in the Boston church, resulting in the withdrawal of thirty-six members, had left her short of active workers.

Mrs. Eddy soon made it known to him, however, that he was to be a teacher in her college, and she duly installed him as professor of obstetrics.[1] She took great comfort in Dr. Foster's presence in the house and began to feel that from

[1] See Chapter XIX.

him she might hope for the unquestioning obedience and perpetual adoration she was always seeking. She loved to amaze and astonish; when her students ceased to " wonder," she was usually through with them. Each of her favourites gave her, as it were, a new lease of life; with each one her interest in everything quickened. The great outside audience meant very little as compared with the pliant neophyte beside her chair or across the table from her. It was when Mrs. Eddy was weaving her spell about a new favourite that she was at her best, and it was then that she most believed in herself. But she could never stop with enchanting, merely. She must altogether absorb the new candidate; he must have nothing left in him which was not from her. If she came upon one insoluble atom hidden away anywhere in the marrow of his bones, she experienced a revulsion and flung him contemptuously aside.

Dr. Foster had been in the house but a little while when Mrs. Eddy told him she foresaw that the relation between them must be a very close one. This announcement somewhat disconcerted him, until she explained that it was her intention to adopt him as her son. In her petition to the Court, Mrs. Eddy stated that " said Foster is now associated with your petitioner in business, home life, and life work, and she needs such interested care and relationship." On the 5th of November, 1888, accordingly, Dr. Foster's legal name became Ebenezer J. Foster Eddy.

The new son was a small man with an affectionate disposition, gentle, affable manners, and very small, well-kept hands. He had certain qualities which Mrs. Eddy had always found desirable in those who were closely associated with her. He never offered Mrs. Eddy advice, never interfered with her wishes, never questioned her wisdom or demurred to her projects—as even Mr. Frye was sometimes known to do. He says to-day that he cannot remember ever having crossed his adopted mother in anything. If he had planned to go up to Waterbury Center to visit his father, for instance, and Mrs. Eddy told him to unpack his bag and stay at home, he did so without so much as a question, and preserved a cheerful countenance.

When Foster Eddy settled himself in his new home at 385 Commonwealth Avenue, he found that not all of Mrs. Eddy's friends were so kindly disposed toward him as was his mother. At this time Miss Julia Bartlett, Captain Eastaman, Josephine Woodbury, William B. Johnson, Mrs. Augusta Stetson, Frank Mason, and Marcellus Munroe constituted a kind of executive staff for Mrs. Eddy, and the new son felt confident that several of these persons had attempted to prevent his adoption from motives of self-interest. If Mrs. Eddy were going to adopt any one, why not one of her trusted and tried rather than a comparative stranger? From the day of his installation as the son of the house, Foster Eddy felt that Mrs. Eddy's cabinet was jealous of his influence over her, of her affection for him, of his musical accomplishments and his winning manners, and of his efforts to bring sunshine into his new home.

Mr. Frye went his silent, inscrutable way, keeping a wary eye upon the new favourite. Frye was little about the house in those days. When he was not doing his marketing he was usually to be found in his own room, waiting for orders and working at his accounts. Although he seems to have been scrupulously honest, he was a poor bookkeeper. Mrs. Eddy often took him to task harshly for this fault, and it was the cause of many a scene between them. She now threatened to take the accounts altogether out of his hands and give them to her new son, but as often as she decided upon this step she as often changed her mind, and in the end the books remained in the keeping of Mr. Frye. He probably knew that Mrs. Eddy trusted him in so far as she could trust any one, but that it was necessary for her to have grievances and to break into thunder-storms about them. Every one had to take his turn at standing up under these cataclysms of nerves; if it were not Mr. Frye, then it was some one else, and the new son was soon having his occasional bad day like the rest.

Mrs. Lydia Roaf, Mr. Frye's sister, was Mrs. Eddy's cook at this time, but she and her brother had little to say to each other. Miss Martha Morgan acted as housekeeper. She had come from Maine to study under Mrs. Eddy and had stayed to help with the housework. Foster Eddy's duties were manifold, but were chiefly in the nature of personal services to Mrs. Eddy. He went about town on errands to her publishers and printers; addressed meetings which she could not attend; wrote some of her letters for her; saw visitors when she was indisposed; sometimes took a drive with her; kept her desk in order; played and sang for her when she was in a pensive mood. Mrs. Eddy liked her son to appear with some distinction when he went out to represent her. In winter he usually wore a long fur-lined coat, and Mrs. Eddy later bought him a diamond solitaire for his little finger. Since he had to speak occasionally in public, Mrs. Eddy sent him to the Boston School

EBENEZER J. FOSTER EDDY

The adopted son of Mrs. Eddy

GEORGE WASHINGTON GLOVER

Mrs. Eddy's only child

of Oratory to learn the use of the voice. She called him
" Bennie " and he addressed her as " mother."

Dr. Foster Eddy was sometimes called upon to attend Mrs.
Eddy in her illnesses, and he, like the other members of the
household, spent his spare moments in treating her against
that old foe, malicious animal magnetism, which was always
infesting the house. He also made himself useful about the
house, and sometimes helped Miss Morgan with the dishes.

When Mrs. Eddy had a bad day, Dr. Foster's new home was
a difficult place to live in, but the storms were usually forgotten in the smiles and calm which followed. Mrs. Eddy
could be the most agreeable of hostesses and of mothers when
she chose, and from the days when she told a young man of
Swampscott that if she could put on canvas her ideal of Jesus
Christ the face would look like his, she never underestimated
the human appetite for flattery. She could unblushingly refer
to the " touch of fairy fingers " or the " music of footfalls,"
and could deliver the most threadbare euphuisms with a smile
that warmed the heart of the recipient and covered him with
foolish happiness. After having fretted herself to sleep the
night before, she would sometimes arise in a mood almost beatific,
and would greet the object of yesterday's invective with a
benediction and a smile. In such a humour she would promise
the pardoned offender a larger place in her life and a greater
control of her affairs, telling him that he, more than any one
else, had understood the true meaning of her teachings and
the real significance of her life, and that she must perforce
look to him to carry on her great work after her. It was the
same old story that Mrs. Eddy had breathed to Spofford,

Arens, and Buswell, each in his turn, but to the eager listener it was always new.

By the spring of 1889 Mrs. Eddy had come to a crisis in her affairs. In spite of the brave fight she was making against those who had gone out from the church, and whom she chose to consider her enemies, she began to show the wear and strain of the eight preceding years. She had now reached the age of sixty-eight, the trembling palsy which affected her head and hands was growing more pronounced, and her fear of mesmerism amounted to a mania. Yet now, more than ever before, there was work for her to do. It was a critical moment in the history of her church. The movement was spreading rapidly, and new problems, incident to the growth of Christian Science, were presenting themselves for solution. In nearly every state the healers were coming into conflict with the law and public opinion, and her followers everywhere needed advice and direction. The " conspiracy " which had come to light the year before had shown her that the Boston church was not so completely under her control as she had believed, and she determined that something should be done to insure her domination of it in the future.

Mrs. Eddy had decided, too, to revise *Science and Health*, and to get out a new edition. In Boston her work was subject to continual interruption, and she was often irritated beyond endurance by the people about her. Mrs. Woodbury and Mrs. Stetson, in particular, had begun to wear upon her. Although Mrs. Stetson's success in building up the church organisation in New York made her indispensable, Mrs. Eddy distrusted her and was annoyed as well as pleased at her progress. Soon after Mrs. Eddy adopted Dr. Foster, Mrs. Stetson took a young man from Maine, Carol Norton, to occupy a somewhat similar position in her household, although she did not legally adopt him. When Mrs. Eddy heard of this, she exclaimed with vexation, " See how Stetson apes me!" She also made a new by-law forbidding " illegal adoption." [2]

This was the situation when Mrs. Eddy suddenly left Boston, driven from home, so she declared, by malicious mesmerism. The fear of it had for a long time completely dominated her, and it was now interfering seriously with her work in the college and church. She spent her time in talking about it; in treating and fighting against it, and in discovering and thwarting imaginary plots. She felt it reaching out to her, not only from her enemies, but from her most trusted students and friends. She believed she could see it in their faces. As she once bitterly remarked to Mrs. Hopkins, " You are so full of mesmerism that your eyes stick out like a boiled codfish's."

She had never loved any one so well that she could not, in a moment of irritation, believe him guilty, not only of disloyalty, but of theft, knavery, blackmail, or abominable corruption. She could never feel sure of even the ordinary decencies of conduct in her friends. All the suspicion, envy, and incontinent distrust which so often blazed in Mrs. Eddy's eyes seemed to have found a concrete and corporeal expression in this thing, Mesmerism.

The delusion of persecution grew upon her, and she believed that she was watched and spied upon. Her mail, her clothes,

---

[2] Illegal Adoption. Sect. 3. No person shall be a member of this church who claims a spiritually adopted child; or a spiritually adopted husband or wife. There must be legal adoption or legal marriage, which can be verified according to the laws of our land.—*Church Manual*, 1904.

her house, her friends, and even inanimate objects she thought were infected with mesmerism and made hostile to her. Throughout the winter and spring she complained continually to her adopted son that Boston was so full of mesmerism that it was choking her, and that she must escape from it. Her one thought now was " flight "—to get away from the Boston Christian Scientists and to a place where she could prosecute her work and carry out her plans without interference or interruption. She talked of going to Cincinnati or Pittsburgh, but at last she threw deliberation to the winds and announced one morning that she must go immediately—somewhere, anywhere.

Foster Eddy knew of a furnished house which was to be let in Barre, Vt., and thither he conducted Mrs. Eddy, with Mr. Frye and the women of the household—Lydia Roaf was no longer one of them, having fallen ill and gone home to die. When Mrs. Eddy arrived at Barre, new troubles awaited her. The town band customarily played of an evening in the square before her house, and although she sent Mr. Frye out to request the band boys to desist, they refused to do so. Consequently Mrs. Eddy packed up and returned to Boston. A few months later she was up and away again, this time moving into a furnished house at 62 State Street, Concord, N. H. She found no peace here, and sent Dr. Foster out to look for some place that should be a certain distance from the post-office, telegraph-office, express-office, etc. She wanted to be well out of reach of these, and yet be not too far from Boston. Dr. Foster canvassed the suburbs of that city and found a desirable house and garden for sale in Roslindale. The owner asked a price considerably above the market value, but Mrs. Eddy paid it, declaring that mesmerism was again at work, trying to keep her out of her own, and that she would have the property at any price. Dr. Foster was sent back to Commonwealth Avenue to pack her furniture and move it out to Roslindale. The new house was scarcely settled when Mrs. Eddy, believing that her neighbours were mesmerised, went back to Concord. Here she lived again at No. 62 State Street, until she moved into the house which she named Pleasant View, and in which she lived until January, 1908.

In retiring to Concord, Mrs. Eddy had no idea of loosing her hold upon Christian Science, or of resigning her leadership. It is very doubtful if, when she went away in the spring of 1889, she meant to leave Boston for good. After that date she made alterations in her Commonwealth Avenue house, and the fact that she had the walls of her own room there pulled out and interlined with a substance which would deaden sound and make the room absolutely quiet, seems to indicate that she intended to return there to live. But in going from Boston, Mrs. Eddy was acting, as always, upon the urgent need of the moment. For the present it was imperative that she should be free from the hot-bed of mesmerism in Boston, both for her own peace of mind, and in order to do what was before her; and although her retirement to Concord proved most fortunate in its general results, Mrs. Eddy, in going, was probably not concerned at the moment with anything but her own security and convenience. It was apparently not until she had left the city and had become more inaccessible to her students and followers, that she realised how greatly her administrative life in Boston had taxed her strength.   For years she had complained of the anguish of meeting people; she believed that her students, and even strangers, left the burden of their ills and sorrows with her when they went out from her presence, and she suffered excruciatingly from the nervous excitement produced by even the most casual social intercourse.   From this time on her dread of crowds and her distress at meeting people increased and she became gradually more and more inaccessible.

CHAPTER XXI

THE NEW POLICY—MRS. EDDY RESIGNS FROM PULPIT AND JOURNAL
AND CLOSES HER COLLEGE—DISORGANISATION OF THE
CHURCH AND ASSOCIATION—RECONSTRUCTION ON A NEW
BASIS—MRS. EDDY IN ABSOLUTE CONTROL AND POSSESSION

MRS. EDDY's retreat from the centre of Christian Science
activities was the first step, as will be seen, in the new policy
toward which she was slowly feeling her way. From her point
of view it was wise to let Christian Science in Boston lie fallow
for a time; to allow the plots and counterplots of the factions
composing the remnant of her church to die out; and to secure
for herself peace, and time to decide what next should be done.
There is no doubt that during her visit to Chicago the year
before, her eyes were opened to the strength of the general
movement of Christian Science, and that it was in the larger
field, and not in the local Boston church, that Mrs. Eddy now
saw her opportunity.

Mrs. Eddy retired from the editorship of the *Christian Science Journal*, May, 1889.

In announcing Mrs. Eddy's retirement, the *Journal* of that
date says:

. . . As our dear mother in God withdraws herself from our
midst, and goes up into the Mount for higher communings, to show us
and the generations to come the way to our true consciousness in God,

let us honour Him and keep silence; let us keep from her and settle among ourselves or with God for ourselves, the small concerns for which we have looked to her.

At about this time, Mrs. Eddy also gave up teaching. It was with great reluctance that she closed her college, and here again she felt her way to a final decision. The first plan was that she merely give up active teaching, and remain president of the institution, while her adopted son succeeded her as instructor. She gave this arrangement a trial, but soon announced that, as the demand was for her own instruction exclusively, she would close the college altogether. In the late summer of 1889 Mrs. Eddy again reconsidered, and announced that General Erastus N. Bates of Cleveland would reopen the college and conduct the classes. General Bates, who was a healer and preacher in his own city, gave up his practice there and came on to Boston to take up Mrs. Eddy's work. No sooner had he begun than Mrs. Eddy again changed her mind, and in less than a month after General Bates arrived she closed the college, despite his earnest protest.

Mrs. Eddy next disorganised the Association. At her request it was voted " to set aside the official organisation and the constitution and by-laws of the Massachusetts Metaphysical College Association, and to meet in the future as a voluntary association of Christians to promote growth in spirituality." The *Journal*, in its announcement, continues: " What was embraced under the name of ' business ' was thus dispensed with. Nothing valuable of the purposes of the organisation had been lost and a new realisation that all is mind and of union in love had been gained." The effect of this disorganisation, the *Journal* said, would be " to lift them from the material sensual plane to that of voluntary association or love," and to eliminate " rivalry, jealousy, envy, and stir of personality."

While she was moving about and experimenting, Mrs. Eddy was also engaged in preparing the new edition of *Science and Health,* which appeared in 1891; and her chief difficulty in getting the book on the market was, as always, mesmerism. She had fled from Boston to escape it, but it was ever on her track and it throve in Concord as well as in Boston and Vermont and Roslindale.   The ordinary delays which occur in the best-regulated of pressrooms and binderies, she attributed directly to the results of malicious animal magnetism, and that eminently reliable and decorous establishment, the University Press, was supposed to have been given over to the riotous disorders of demonology.   Mrs. Eddy set half a dozen of her students to treating the pressmen and binders against errors and delays, and wrote out an argument for them to use in their treatments.   The veteran printer, Mr. John Wilson himself, she assigned, for especial treatment, to her son, E. J. Foster Eddy.   The letter in which Mrs. Eddy issued instructions that the treatments upon the press were to begin, was written to Dr. Foster Eddy, and reads as follows:

Jan. 13, 385 Commonwealth Avenue.

My Dearest One: Please to go at once to Miss Bartlett and give her the directions inclosed. See Capt. Eastaman and give him the same. After writing out sufficient copies, distribute them as follows:

To Capt. Eastaman, Miss Bartlett; for Mrs. Munroe; Press and Bindery, for Mr. Johnson, Mr. Knapp, Mrs. Knapp.

You keep Mr. Wilson, the printer of Cambridge, under your care alone. Also the Mr. Wilson, or proprietor, whoever he is, in Boston, who manages the bindery, under your care only. You know they cannot be made sick for printing and binding God's book, and you must show your faith by works in this instance.

Attached to this letter is a sheet of manuscript in Mrs. Eddy's handwriting, which reads:

Argument

Nothing can hinder the book, Science and Health, from being published immediately. The press and machinery that publish this book and all who work on it in the press and bindery are safe in God's hands, they cannot be and are not governed by hatred. They are governed, upheld and prospered by Love and the book is coming out rapidly. When the book goes to the bindery then stop the press aid and turn all their force there.

Tell each one that I say by no means take up the mesmerists or any personality, but to have faith in God and this will do it all—just as the prayer asks.

Your personal work for the Wilsons must be done as I have taught you, to help them, and not touch others.

If I or Mr. Frye write or telegraph to you then you must stop at once the student's argument. You understand this, do you not?

The last sentence in Mrs. Eddy's instructions seems to imply that it was possible to over-treat the pressroom, and that it might be necessary to stop the treatments at any time. Just what the results of over-treatment might be, it is difficult to conjecture, but from another letter to Dr. Foster it is evident that Mrs. Eddy thought the treatments had been too vigorous and had thrown everything into confusion:

DEAREST:

I have just found what did (but did not) [1] produce a temporary tempest here. It was the help you procured on the Press! Never, never put " new wine into old bottles."

Those persons named are utterly incapable of handling the Red Dragon. [2] They can command serpents but not the last species.

At once dismiss your help and confine your treatment to the Proprietor Mr. W—— and electricity take no other personality into thought but the ones employed at the Press.

All is God, Good there is no evil.

---

[1] Mrs. Eddy's contradictory statement means that the confusion was not *real* because all is God and discord has no part in God. A " tempest " was produced in " belief " but not in reality. The sentence is peculiarly illustrative of her philosophy. One is (but is not) ill, exhausted, melancholy, etc., etc.

[2] Mesmerism.

It was in the early autumn of 1889 that Mrs. Eddy conceived the idea that malicious animal magnetism was interfering
with the proper conduct of the *Christian Science Journal*.
She sent one morning for Mr. William G. Nixon, publisher of
the *Journal*, and directed him to take the magazine and flee
with it at once into some other city; if he stayed in Boston
a month longer, she declared, mesmerism would wreck the
periodical.   Mr. Nixon tried to explain to her the difficulties
of picking up a periodical and " fleeing " with it between publication days, when no preparatory arrangements had been
made and no new location selected.   But Mrs. Eddy was immovable.   In business disputes Mrs. Eddy had always one
argument which none of her associates could hope to equal: she
would draw up her shoulders, look her opponent in the eye,
and say, very slowly, " God has directed me in this matter.
Have you anything further to say? "   Mr. Nixon naturally
wished to remain in Boston; he had brought his family there
from Dakota, and his contract with his printer was unex-
pired.   But there was nothing to be gained by arguing with
Mrs. Eddy; and there was no time to be lost if he was to find
a new location for his business in time to get out the next
month's *Journal*.   He went to Philadelphia, where he at length
found a suitable office and a printer who would undertake to
get the magazine out on time.   Just as he was about to close
the contract, he received a telegram from Mrs. Eddy telling
him to bring the *Journal* back to Boston at once.

In directing the *Journal's* policy, Mrs. Eddy was never afraid
to change her mind, and often repudiated to-day what she had
yesterday advanced as divine revelation.   On one occasion

she wrote to Mr. Nixon that God had directed her to recommend a certain candidate for the editorship of the *Journal:*

385 Commonwealth Ave.
BOSTON, Sept. 30 1889

MY DEAR STUDENT

God our God has just told me who to recommend to you for the Editor of C. S. Jour. but you are not to name me in this transaction. It is Rev. Charles Macomber Smith D.D. 164 Summer St Somerville Mass. He was healed by reading Science and Health and left a large salary to preach Christian Science and then left that position for the hope J. F. Bailey had held out to him of preaching for my Church but I objected to taking him solely because his church had not been consulted before giving him a call.

Get *him sure* but be very reticent let it not be known until he is engaged or you will have a fuss about it.

Lovingly,

M. B. G. EDDY.

Mr. Nixon had not had time to act upon this letter when he received another in which Mrs. Eddy explained that her recommendation of Mr. Smith had been the result of mesmerism, and not of divine inspiration:

CONCORD, N. H.
62 State St.

To MR. NIXON

MY DEAR STUDENT

I regret having named the one I did to you for Editor It is a mistake he is not fit It was not God evidently that suggested that thought but the person who suggests many things mentally but I have before been able to discriminate I wrote too soon after it came to my thought He has not been taught C. S. and I hear refuses to be taught by any one but me. Love to wife

Ever Affectionately

M. B. G. EDDY.

In another letter she reprimands her publisher for not affixing the author's name whenever he refers to *Science and Health* in the columns of the *Journal*, and for not printing the name of that book always in small capitals.   Mr. Nixon felt that the *Journal* should be the magazine of Christian Science rather than Mrs. Eddy's personal organ, and had rashly attempted to persuade her that it would be more dignified in her to keep her own name a little more in the background, especially when so many of her enemies were asserting that Christian Science was nothing but a glorification of Mrs. Eddy's " personality." On this point she says to Mr. Nixon, in a letter dated June 30, 1890:

Those who are trying to frighten you over using my name at suitable intervals and who are crying out personality are the very ones that persist in their purpose to keep my personality before the public through abusing it and to harness it to all the faults of other personalities and make it responsible for them.   But neither of these efforts disposes of personality nor handle it on the rule our Master taught nor deal with mortal personality scientifically.

In the same letter she reproves him for having omitted her appellation of " Reverend " when referring to her in the *Journal*.

Among Mrs. Eddy's letters to her publisher, Mr. Nixon, is this rather amusing one:

July 14 1890.
385 Commonwealth Ave.

MY DEAR STUDENT

Many thanks for your copy of Brotherham's translation of the New Testament But I cannot see the merit in it that Mr. Bailey attaches to it in his long notice in the *Journal*.   The language is decaying as fast as that of Irving's Pickwick Papers   I prefer the common version for all scriptural quotations to that.

Most truly and affectionately,

M. B. G. EDDY.

Having divested herself of her responsibilities as editor and teacher, Mrs. Eddy further protected herself from the importunities of her students by the publication in the *Journal* of seven fixed rules, which announced that she was not to be consulted regarding the personal or church difficulties of her followers.[3] Her next step was to disorganise the Boston church. Upon this action the *Journal* of February, 1890, comments as follows:

> The dissolution of the visible organisation of the church is the sequence and complement of that of the college corporation and association. The college disappeared that the spirit of Christ might have freer course among its students and all who come into the understanding of Divine Science, the bonds of the church were thrown away so that its members might assemble themselves together to " provoke one another to good works " in the bond only of love.

After Mrs. Eddy disorganised it, the church continued to hold regular services and, to all intents and purposes, went on just as before—with the one important exception that it held no more business meetings and transacted no business. The real reason for this disorganisation seems to have been just that, for the time, Mrs. Eddy wanted no business transacted. Her explanation that organisation was a detriment to spirituality could scarcely have been more than a convenient pretext, for at the same time that she put this check upon the Boston

---

[3] NOTICE.

SEVEN FIXED RULES.

1. I shall not be consulted verbally, or through letters, as to whose advertisement shall or shall not appear in the *Christian Science Journal.*

2. I shall not be consulted verbally, or through letters, as to the matter that should be published in the *Journal* and *Christian Science Series.*

3. I shall not be consulted verbally, or through letters, on marriage, divorce, or family affairs of any kind.

4. I shall not be consulted verbally, or through letters, on the choice of pastors for churches.

5. I shall not be consulted verbally, or through letters, on disaffections, if there should be any between the students of Christian Scientists.

6. I shall not be consulted verbally, or through letters, on who shall be admitted as members, or dropped from the membership of the Christian Science Churches or Associations.

7. I am not to be consulted verbally, or through letters, on disease and the treatment of the sick; but I shall love all mankind—and work for their welfare.

MARY B. G. EDDY.

church, her messages to the workers in the field continually urged them to organise churches. It would seem that what was hurtful to spirituality in Boston would be hurtful elsewhere; but the fact was that ever since the schism of 1888 Mrs. Eddy had been dissatisfied with her Boston church, and she had decided to take it to pieces and make it over. A plan was forming in her mind, and putting a stop to all the business transactions of the church gave her time to feel her way toward its accomplishment.

The Boston church was still homeless and held its meetings in public halls. In 1886 its members had purchased a lot on Falmouth Street—where the original Mother Church now stands —with the intention of erecting upon it a church building. They paid two thousand dollars down upon the date of purchase and assumed a mortgage for the balance due. By December, 1888, the church had paid $5,800 upon the property, and had reduced the mortgage to $4,963.50. Mrs. Eddy then stepped in and, through her lawyer, secured an assignment of the mortgage for the amount due upon it. Eight months later she foreclosed and bought in the property herself through her lawyer's brother.[4]

In other words, Mrs. Eddy sold to herself the land upon

---

[4] The exact steps of this transaction were as follows:
In 1886 the Boston church, through its treasurer, William H. Bradley, had purchased from Nathan Matthews the plot of ground upon which the Christian Science church now stands, paying down $2,000 and assuming a mortgage for $8,763.50. By December, 1888, the church had paid upon this land, in all, $5,800, reducing the mortgage to $4,963.50. At this date Mrs. Eddy, through her lawyer, Baxter E. Perry, later disbarred, secured an assignment of the mortgage from Mr. Matthews for exactly the sum due upon the land. Although this assignment occurred December 6, 1888, it was not recorded until August 6, 1889, this date being also the date of the recording of Mrs. Eddy's foreclosure of the mortgage. The Suffolk County Register of Deeds shows that Baxter E. Perry sold the Falmouth Street lot at a mortgage foreclosure sale held on August 3, 1889, to his brother and law partner, George H. Perry, for the sum of $5,000. George H. Perry then deeded the land to Ira O. Knapp, for the sum of $5,100, the additional $100 apparently forming Mr. Perry's fee for his part in the transaction.

which she now held the mortgage, securing for $5,000 a piece of real estate which three years before had sold for $10,763.50, —and which since then had almost doubled in value,—and the members of the Boston church had lost all equity in the property upon which they had paid $5,800.

Since Mrs. Eddy intended ultimately to give this land back to the church, why, the reader may ask, did she not come forward when the payments ran behind, and satisfy the mortgage, leaving the property unincumbered in the hands of the organisation which had already paid on it more than half the purchase price? The reason seems to have been that there were still in that body persons of whom Mrs. Eddy did not feel sure; members who might be elected to office, might have too active a part in the church government, and might even incite a new rebellion like that of 1888. Her plan now was to give this building-site to the Boston church directors under such conditions as would forever do away with congregational self-government, and would place the church wholly under the control of such trustees as she should appoint.

Mrs. Eddy was aiming at (1) the entire personal ownership of the site of the Boston church, (2) perpetual personal control of the church which should be reared upon it, (3) making the Boston church not merely a local church and the home of the Boston congregation, but a church universal, the " Mother Church " of Christian Science the world over, with Mrs. Eddy installed as its visible head. And a seemingly insignificant real-estate transaction was actually the means of accomplishing this important end.

Up to this time Mrs. Eddy's name had been kept out of the

various conveyances on the Falmouth Street property, and she desired that it should not directly appear in future transactions. She now had the land deeded to her student, Ira O. Knapp. Mr. Knapp then conveyed the property to three trustees, Alfred Lang, Marcellus Munroe, and William G. Nixon, who were to hold it for the purpose of building a church thereon. The trust deed by which the conveyance was made was of such an unusual character that Mr. Nixon insisted upon having the title examined before the trustees should place on the lot a building paid for by Christian Scientists residing in all parts of the United States. After examining it, the Massachusetts Title Insurance Company refused to insure the title, and, in spite of Mrs. Eddy's argument that " the title was from God, and that no material title could affect God's temple," the three trustees returned all the donations to the building fund which they had received, and resigned. The property was now conveyed by Mr. Knapp to Mrs. Eddy (who had in reality been its owner all the while) for a consideration of one dollar, and Mrs. Eddy began all over again.

On September 1, 1892, Mrs. Eddy conveyed this much-bandied-about plot of ground to four new trustees: Ira O. Knapp, William B. Johnson, Joseph S. Eastaman, and Stephen A. Chase, who were pledged to erect upon the site, within five years, a church building costing not less than $50,000. Among the provisos of the trust deed were the following:

That in this church there should be no services " which shall not be in strict harmony with the doctrines and practice of Christian Science as taught and explained by Mary Baker G. Eddy in the seventy-first edition of her book, entitled *Science and Health,* which is soon to be issued, *and in any subsequent edition thereof."*

That these trustees should be called the Board of Directors and should constitute a perpetual body or corporation, filling any vacancy in their body by election, and filling it only with such an one as should be " a firm and consistent believer in the doctrines of Christian Science as taught in a book entitled *Science and Health* by Mary Baker G. Eddy, beginning with," etc.

That this board should elect the pastor, speaker, or reader, maintain public worship, and was " fully empowered to make all necessary rules and regulations " for this purpose.

That " the omission or neglect on the part of said directors to comply with any of the conditions herein named, shall constitute a breach thereof, and the title shall revert to the grantor, Mary Baker G. Eddy, her heirs and assigns," etc.

That " Whenever said directors shall determine that it is inexpedient to maintain preaching, reading or speaking in said church in accordance with the terms of this deed, they are authorised and required to reconvey forthwith said lot of land *with the building thereon,* to Mary Baker G. Eddy, her heirs and assigns forever, by a proper deed of conveyance."

At last, then, Mrs. Eddy had the Boston church where she wanted it; an institution without congregational government, controlled by four directors whom she should appoint and who should elect their successors at her suggestion; who were pledged to see that the church taught only what was in the seventy-first edition of *Science and Health,* and whatever Mrs. Eddy might please to put into any subsequent edition; and who, if they did not comply with all these instructions, were bound to give back the lot, and the building upon it, to Mrs. Eddy and to her heirs forever. A Mother Church thus constructed would have great possibilities.

But here an objection arose. A corporation must be formed, and when Mrs. Eddy asked the State to grant her a new charter for a new church body, the Commissioner of Corporations refused. His reason was that the original charter, granted in 1879, had never been annulled and was still in force. But Mrs. Eddy had no intention of recognising the old church or its charter; if her new directors merely held the property in trust for a church organisation, her end would be defeated. As the deed of trust read, the directors were virtually to hold the property in trust for Mrs. Eddy herself, to the end of executing her wishes. There must be a way, Mrs. Eddy insisted, in which her trustees could hold the property without recognising the existence of the chartered church body, so she set her lawyers to work. " Guided by Divine Love," she said, her attorneys found in the laws of Massachusetts a statute whereby a body of donees might be considered a corporate body for the purpose of taking and holding grants and donations without the formal organisation of a church.[5] This old statute once unearthed, Mrs. Eddy's plan was entirely worked out: the Mother Church was now controlled absolutely by her four directors; the corporation consisted of her directors and

[5] In Section 1, Chapter 39. of the *Massachusetts Public Statutes*, it is provided that:
" The deacons, church wardens, or other similar officers of Church or religious societies, and the trustees of the Methodist Episcopal churches appointed according to the discipline and usages thereof, shall, if citizens of this Commonwealth, be deemed bodies corporate for the purpose of taking and holding in succession all grants and donations, whether of real or personal estate, made either to them or their successors, or to their respective churches, or to the poor of their churches."

not of the church body; and the congregation had no more voice in the management of the church than has the audience in the management of a theatre.

The members of the Boston church were dazzled by Mrs. Eddy's lavish gift, and very few of them had followed the legerdemain by which the church had gone into Mrs. Eddy's hands a free body and had come out a close corporation. Mrs. Eddy announced her victory in a long communication to the *Journal*, asserting, " He giveth his angels charge over thee, to keep thee in all thy ways."

In reviewing this real-estate transaction in the *Journal*, Mrs. Eddy said:

I had this desirable site transferred in a circuitous, novel way. . . . I knew that to God's gift, foundation and superstructure, no one could hold a wholly material title. The land and the church standing on it must be conveyed through a type representing the true nature of the gift; a type morally and spiritually inalienable, but materially questionable —even after the manner that all spiritual good comes to Christian Scientists to the end of taxing their faith in God and their adherence to the superiority of the claims of spirit over matter or merely legal titles. . . . Our title to God's acres here will be safe and sound " when we can read our titles clear " to heavenly mansions.

Mrs. Eddy now for the first time came out in the *Journal* and made a personal appeal for money to build her church, requesting that the contributions which Mr. Nixon and his associates had returned to the donors be doubled and forwarded to Boston. Her request had scarcely been printed when money began to pour in upon the trustees; the old contributions were doubled and in many instances were increased threefold.

The official organisation of the Mother Church was made September 23, 1892, but no mention is made in the *Journal* of such an occurrence until a year later.   Then, on October 3, 1893, the first annual meeting of the Mother Church was held in Chickering Hall.   The clerk announced in his report that " Since the meeting in which the church was formed, there have been held seven special and four quarterly meetings.   *It is in the records of those meetings that the history of the church is contained, but its doings could not be profitably set forth in a report of this kind.*"

This was the first open official meeting.   Up to this time few Christian Scientists knew that a meeting for the selection of church officers had been held in the fall of 1892, but supposed that there was still no formal organisation of the body other than the " voluntary association " which Mrs. Eddy had advocated as a means to spiritual grace, and under which the Massachusetts law allowed the trustees to receive funds.

Boston Christian Scientists had supposed that Mrs. Eddy did not wish to organise her new church under the old charter because, as she had stated, she felt that material organisation was a hindrance to spiritual growth.   But when her new church began its operations, they were confronted by a solid formal organisation which had been effected without the knowledge or consent of the church body as a whole.   In addition to the usual church officers, Mrs. Eddy had chosen twelve charter members, whose duty it was to ballot upon every candidate for admission to the church—and these twelve were the only persons permitted to vote upon such candidates.   All the original members, some of whom had been identified with the church for twelve years, were considered as " candidates " for admission to the new church, and were balloted upon by the twelve just

as were the new applicants.   In this way Mrs. Eddy was enabled carefully to select the personnel of her new church, and
to keep out of it such members of the old organisation as had
not been agreeable to her.   Every candidate for admission to
the Mother Church is still balloted upon in this way.

The Boston church, built by the contributions of Christian
Scientists throughout the country, had now lost its local character.   With a membership of 1,502 drawn almost entirely
from the branch churches, it was now the head of all the churches
in the field, and at the head of the Boston church was Mrs.
Eddy, installed under the title of " Pastor Emeritus," and governing through a subservient Board of Directors.   No more was
heard now concerning the spiritual disadvantages of organisation.   Every one realised that in unity under Mrs. Eddy, and
in obedience, lay the road of progress.   The old watchword,
" Mrs. Eddy and God make a majority," was revived.

" What," asked the Rev. D. A. Easton, pastor of the Mother
Church, in his Easter sermon, 1893, " what does membership
in the Mother Church mean?   It signifies obedience.   Mrs.
Eddy has invited Scientists everywhere to unite with the Mother
Church.   To obey cheerfully and loyally marks a growth in
Science.

> " Theirs not to reason why,
> Theirs but to do and die."

" Brethren," wrote Dr. Foster Eddy in the *Journal*, " this
is an epoch in the history of Christian Science.   The year has
been a marked one to us.   The chaff has been separated from
the wheat in a most marvellous manner."   " We have come,"
he told Christian Scientists at the first annual meeting, " to

the time when all should listen to the voice of Love, and hearing it, we should follow implicitly whether we understand or not, and the way will be made plain."

" Experience, and above all, obedience, are the tests of growth and understanding in Science," Mrs. Eddy wrote to her students through the *Journal.*

Members of all the Christian Science churches in the field began to apply for admission to the Mother Church; it was an expression of zeal and loyalty which all earnest believers were eager to make. Mrs. Eddy's direct personal control of the Boston church soon meant the direct personal control of a membership reaching from Maine to California.

The Boston congregation, which had been meeting in public halls for fifteen years, was at last to have a home, and the building of the Mother Church was about to begin. It was to be a memorial, as Mrs. Eddy said, " for her through whom was revealed to you God's all-power, all-presence, and all-science." An inscription across the front of the building was to proclaim, as it does to-day, the name of Mrs. Eddy and the title of her book.[6]

The financial distress of 1894 caused a temporary check in the growth of the building fund, and, to give the work a fresh impetus, Mrs. Eddy made a personal appeal to fifty prominent Christian Scientists, asking them to contribute $1,000 each. Her request was instantly complied with. On May 21, 1894, the corner-stone of the Mother Church was laid.

[6] This inscription reads:
"The First Church of Christ, Scientist, erected Anno Domini, 1894. A testimonial to our beloved teacher, the Rev. Mary Baker G. Eddy, discoverer and founder of Christian Science; author of *Science and Health with Key to the Scriptures;* president of the Massachusetts Metaphysical College, and the first pastor of this denomination."

During the eighteen months that the Mother Church was building, its membership, recruited from the churches in the field, continued to increase. At the second annual business meeting, held in Copley Hall, October 2, 1894, the clerk reported a total membership of 2,978—1,476 having been admitted during the year.

The original Mother Church [7] is a solidly built structure of gray granite, with a seating capacity of 1,100. In its equipment it is very like any other modern church of its size. Its one unique feature is the " Mother Room," since 1903 called the " room of our Pastor Emeritus." This room, consecrated to Mrs. Eddy's personal use, is finished in rare woods, marble, and onyx, and contains a superfluity of white-and-gold furniture. In the alcove are a stationary wash-stand and a folding-bed—in which Mrs. Eddy has slept once. All the plumbing in this alcove is gold plated. A stained-glass window represents Mrs. Eddy seated at her table in the old skylight room at Lynn, engaged in searching the Scriptures; through the open skylight shines the star of Bethlehem, enveloping her in its rays. Before this window hangs the Athenian lamp which was formerly kept burning night and day.

This room was fitted up for Mrs. Eddy by the children of Christian Scientists, who were organised into a society called the " Busy Bees " and who maintained a fund for the purpose of furnishing and caring for the Mother Room. After the fittings of the room had been paid for, the children wished to continue to express their affection for Mrs. Eddy, and their

---

[7] The original Mother Church now forms the front of an entirely new building, dedicated in 1906. The old church is still called the Mother Church, while the new structure, although many times larger than the old, is called the Annex.

offerings were used to keep the room supplied with fresh flowers
and to maintain the Athenian lamp. Mrs. Eddy showed her
appreciation by dedicating to the " Busy Bees " her next book,
Pulpit and Press, a thin volume made up of newspaper articles
upon the Mother Church and interviews with Mrs. Eddy. This
book sold at $1.06 a copy, but Mrs. Eddy announced that each
of the 2,600 children who had contributed to her room should
have one copy each at half price, fifty cents, postage extra.
By this means the author secured an additional sale of 2,600
books, and the children had the advantage of the reduction
in price. With the possible exception of the dedication there
is certainly very little in this book of press clippings to tempt
a youthful reader.

Dedicatory services were held in the Mother Church, January
6, 1895. Four times the service was repeated to audiences
that filled the assembly-room, and an address from Mrs. Eddy
was read. When her little congregation used to meet in Hawthorne Hall, Mrs. Eddy had usually been on hand to remind
them that the gates of hell should not prevail against her;
but at the dedication of her memorial church, with its membership of nearly three thousand, she was not present. Her absence must be considered as an indication of her failing strength.
Afterward, indeed, she upon two occasions spoke from the
pulpit of her new church, but the days on which she could be
sure of herself were fewer than they used to be.

From this time on Mrs. Eddy was a name rather than a
person in Boston. Her presence there was no longer necessary
to her best interests. In obtaining absolute personal control
of the Mother Church, with its national membership, she had

ended her long struggle for possession.   Before the reorganisation of the Mother Church, Mrs. Eddy had still to bring
questions of church government before the church body; she
had to conciliate, to persuade, to make concessions, and sometimes to explain and justify her own conduct.   In 1888 her
seceding students had even considered a plan to expel Mrs.
Eddy from her own church, and only by constant exertion had
she kept the organisation under her control.   But from the
time the Boston church was reorganised, Mrs. Eddy's power
over it was absolute.   She was the church.   She wrote its by-
laws, appointed its officers, selected its membership, and virtually owned the church property.   Its doctrines were her books
—the church was committed to teach as the everlasting truth
what she had written and *whatever she might write in the future.*
Mrs. Eddy was never again called upon to explain or to modify
her commands, and never again was there dissension or division
in her church.   She had completely conquered her spiritual
kingdom.   She had now but to go on revealing the alleged will
of God, and her church had but to go on obeying her.

CHAPTER XXII

LIFE AT PLEASANT VIEW——MRS. EDDY PRODUCES MORE CHRISTIAN
SCIENCE LITERATURE——FOSTER EDDY IS MADE PUBLISHER
OF THE TEXT-BOOK——THE STORY OF HIS FALL FROM FAVOUR
——RULE OF SERVICE

WHEN Mrs. Eddy retired to Concord, N. H., in the latter
part of 1889, her coming there was little noticed by the towns-
folk. Her name, which was well enough known in Boston,
Chicago, and Denver, as yet meant almost nothing in the
capital of her native state, though her birthplace was scarcely
six miles from Concord. Mrs. Eddy lived quietly at 62 State
Street for nearly three years. She kept no horses then; she
occasionally went about the town on foot, but did not mingle
with the townspeople. There was a general impression in the
neighbourhood that she was a broken-down Boston spiritualist
who had " lost her power." Because, when the chill autumn
weather came on, she had her front piazza inclosed in heavy
sail-cloth and took her exercise there, it was supposed that she
was an invalid. Not until after the dedication of the Mother
Church, in Boston, 1895, did Concord people begin to feel an
interest in Mrs. Eddy and to speak of her as a public personage.

It was while Mrs. Eddy was living in State Street that she
bought the property now known as Pleasant View, and had
the modest farmhouse which stood there remodelled into the

cheerful, jaunty structure which it is to-day. She added bow-windows and verandas, built a porte-cochère at the front of the house and a tower at the southeast corner. Pleasant View is in Pleasant Street, about a mile and a half west of the centre of the city.

The traditions of mystery and seclusion which of late years have grown up about the place are hard to reconcile with its cheerful aspect. The house stands upon a little knoll, very near the road; the drives and gateway are wide; there are no high fences or shaded walks; the trees are kept closely trimmed, the turf neatly shaven, and the flower-beds are tidy and gay. There is a fountain, and a boat-house, and a fish-pond with a fine clump of willows. The tower rooms, which were occupied by Mrs. Eddy, have large windows looking southward down a narrow valley, at the end of which rise gentle green hills, one above another, their sides covered with fields and woodland which admirably distribute light and shadow. These hills, besides being peaceful and pleasant to the eye, must have had many associations for Mrs. Eddy, for among them lies the farm upon which she was born and where she spent her childhood. Every day for seventeen years Mrs. Eddy could look off toward Bow and measure the distance she had travelled. Whatever an architect or gardener might find to quarrel with at Pleasant View, it was certainly a cheerful place for an old lady to live in, and looked out over the gentlest and friendliest of landscapes.

After she moved into Pleasant View, Mrs. Eddy gradually added more land to the estate, enlarged the stables, and built a house for the gardener. She continued to live as simply and methodically as before. She rose early, and after breakfast usually walked about the fish-pond or paced the back veranda. She invariably took a nap before dinner, which she had in the middle of the day. Promptly at two o'clock she started upon her daily drive. Mr. Frye still acted as her secretary and companion, and Martha Morgan attended largely to the house-keeping. Later Mrs. Eddy sent for Miss Kate Shannon, a music-teacher in Montreal; for Mrs. Laura Sargent, who is still in attendance upon her, and for Mrs. Pamelia Leonard, who died at her home in Brooklyn, January 8, 1908, under the care of a physician.[1]

All the members of her household lived as if they were exactly as old and as much enfeebled as Mrs. Eddy. They rose early, retired early; never went out of the house except upon her commissions; never dined out, received visits, or went to Boston for a holiday. And why should they, when they believed that the most important things that had happened in the world for at least eighteen hundred years were daily going on at Pleasant View? They had built their hope upon the fundamental proposition that Mrs. Eddy was the inspired revelator of God; that, as the *Journal* expressed it, she had retired to Pleasant View to " commune always with God in the mount." To be in the house with Mrs. Eddy was the ultimate experience, and it left them nothing more to wish for. Mrs. Eddy filled their lives. Her breakfast, her nap, her correspondence, her visitors, her clothes, even, were matters of the greatest importance. Her faithful women especially delighted in dressing her hair,

---

[1] A Christian Scientist of Brooklyn who knew the circumstances of the death of Mrs. Leonard, has written to the author, since the appearance of this history in McClure's Magazine, to say, that although a physician was called to see Mrs. Leonard before her death, this was done in order to comply with the law requiring the signature of an attending physician to be attached to the death certificate upon which the burial permit is issued; and that Mrs. Leonard never lost faith in Christian Science.

which since she left Boston she had ceased to colour, and which was now soft and white.   They used to talk among themselves about her " final demonstration " in those days, the idea being that she was husbanding her strength to perform some one final wonder which would convince the world.   Sometimes, in their fireside speculations, they encouraged one another in the hope that, when the time came, Mrs. Eddy would even demonstrate over death.   They seem to have expected that this last triumph would come, not as a mere prolongation of life, but as a sort of definite combat, a struggle from which she would rise trans-figured.[2]   While Mrs. Eddy's triumph over death was never an openly avowed belief of the church, it was the fearful hope of many a devoted creature.   These credulous and fervent souls used to go upon pilgrimages to Concord, see the venerable Mother through their tears when she addressed them briefly from her balcony, and go away saying that she had the figure of a girl, that her face was as full and smooth as the face of a young woman.

As soon as Mrs. Eddy withdrew from secular life and became inaccessible to the majority of her followers, legends began to grow up about her.   She realised this well enough, and, at her request, her adopted son bought a notebook and set down in it some of her wonderful sayings and doings.   One of the

---

[2] We may here print a letter to the New York *Evening Journal*, July 1, 1904, signed by Mrs. Augusta E. Stetson, who organised the first Christian Science church in New York:

" Any suggestion or question of a successor to Mrs. Eddy as the Leader of the Christian Science movement is one that could not be entertained nor con-sidered by any loyal Christian Scientist.   Mrs. Eddy is and ever will be the only Leader of the Christian Science movement.   There is no question among loyal Christian Scientists as to her continuing to lead them on to the demonstra-tion of eternal life, through faith in God and the understanding of the law of the spirit life in Christ Jesus, which sets us free from the law of sin and death."

Whatever Mrs. Stetson may have meant by " eternal life," such declarations were interpreted literally by simple-minded believers.

PLEASANT VIEW, MRS. EDDY'S HOME IN CONCORD. N. H.

stories he wrote down was that which Mrs. Eddy often used to tell her household concerning the state of ecstasy in which her own mother lived before Mrs. Eddy's birth. Mrs. Baker, so the legend went, felt as if all the vital forces of the world had united in her, and she knew that she was to bring forth a prodigy. This story, of course, does not agree with the one which Mrs. Eddy used to tell her early students in Lynn, of how she had been born into the world an unwelcome child, and how every man's hand had been against her, etc.

Although Mrs. Eddy was now a wealthy woman, she was still prudent in the use of her money. Her home at Pleasant View was comfortable but not luxurious. There was nothing ostentatious about her manner of living, and she never spent money lavishly, even upon herself. Her laces and jewels, even the diamond cross which is conspicuous in many of her photographs, were given to her by devoted students. The writer has an amusing letter in which Mrs. Eddy thanks one of her students for a piano, referring to the instrument as a " memento."

Mrs. Eddy's little economies are always interesting and characteristic. On one occasion she summoned Dr. Foster's old friend, William Clark of Barre, Vt., to come to Pleasant View as gardener. She wearied of Clark in a little while, decided that he ought to be a teacher of Christian Science instead of a gardener, and sent him away. While Clark had worked on her place Mrs. Eddy had paid him gardener's wages, but she felt that he ought to be reimbursed for the expense he had incurred in moving to Concord and in quitting his former occupation. Accordingly, she called Dr. Foster into her study and handed him three hundred dollars, telling him to offer the money to Clark, but adding grimly, "It will prove a curse to him if he takes it." Dr. Foster warned Clark to that effect, and Clark, rather reluctantly, refused the money. Mrs. Eddy had for some time been promising Dr. Foster a diamond ring for his little finger, and then had looked over jewellers' catalogues and discussed the sizes and prices of stones. In the end Mrs. Eddy had decided upon a smaller stone than the one Dr. Foster selected. He now took a hundred dollars of the money which had been offered to Clark in such a forbidding fashion, added it to the appropriation made for his ring, and got the diamond he wanted. The rest of the money Mrs. Eddy put into a stained-glass window for the "Mother Room" in the Boston church—the window which represents Mrs. Eddy sitting in the skylight room at Lynn and searching the Scriptures beneath the rays of a star.

Mrs. Eddy's retirement did, as she had anticipated, give her more time for literary pursuits. She was still busily writing and rewriting *Science and Health*, as she had been doing for twenty years. New editions of the book came out in 1891, 1894, and 1896. Loyal Scientists were then, as now, expected to purchase each new edition (at $3.18 a volume), although Mrs. Eddy refused to buy back their old editions at any price. Since her followers lived by one book, it behooved them to have the best edition of it, and Mrs. Eddy always pronounced the new one the best. Often a new edition contained important changes (such as permission to use morphia in cases of violent pain), and after the 1891 edition was out, a Christian Scientist who still regulated his life by the 1886 edition was living, spiritually, in the Dark Ages. As Foster Eddy wrote concerning the 1891 edition:

Mother has never had time, until the last two years, to take the numerous gems she has found in the deep mines of truth and polish them on Heaven's emery wheel, arrange them in order, and give them a setting so that *all* could behold and see their perfect purity. Now here they all are in this new revised " Science and Health."

By the time the 1891 edition was exhausted, about one hundred and fifty thousand copies of *Science and Health* had been sold since the book was first published in 1875. This did not mean that one hundred and fifty thousand persons owned copies of the book,—there are not half that many Christian Scientists in the world to-day,—but that every Christian Scientist owned several copies. The *Journal* told them that they could not own too many.

Mrs. Eddy always displayed great ingenuity in stimulating the demand for her books. In 1897, when she first published her book *Miscellaneous Writings*,—a volume of her collected editorials from the *Journal*,—she issued the following pronunciamento:

Christian Scientists in the United States and Canada are hereby enjoined not to teach a student of Christian Science for one year, commencing March 14, 1897. " Miscellaneous Writings " is calculated to prepare the minds of all true thinkers to understand the Christian Science text book more correctly than a student can. The Bible, Science and Health with Key to the Scriptures, and my other published works are the only proper instructors for this hour. It shall be the duty of all Christian Scientists to circulate and to sell as many of these books as they can.

If a member of the First Church of Christ Scientist shall fail to obey this injunction it shall render him liable to lose his membership in this church.   MARY BAKER EDDY.[3]

[3] *Christian Science Journal*, March, 1897.

There were at this time about fifty Christian Science academies in operation, and hundreds of Mrs. Eddy's followers made
their living by teaching Christian Science.   They were, without warning, directed to give up their means of support for
one year in order to increase the sale of Mrs. Eddy's new book,
and to sell the book, without commission, under penalty of
expulsion from the church.   It is scarcely necessary to say
that they obeyed without a murmur.

Loyal Christian Scientists made an endeavour to buy not
only a copy of every new edition of *Science and Health*, but
of every book that Mrs. Eddy wrote.   Mrs. Eddy discourages
general reading, and particularly the perusal of fiction.[4]   She
has no tolerance for low-priced books.   They "lower the intellectual standard to accommodate the purse" and "meet a
frivolous demand for amusement instead of instruction."[5]   For
her own books Mrs. Eddy has always demanded very high prices.
With her own audience she was, of course, without a rival.
Many of her followers read no books at all but hers.

In 1893 Mrs. Eddy published *Christ and Christmas*, an
illustrated poem which she afterward temporarily suppressed
because the pictures were displeasing to many people.   One
picture represents Jesus Christ standing beside a big, black,
upholstered coffin, raising to life an emaciated woman.   Another represents a woman, strangely like Mrs. Eddy's authorised photographs in appearance, standing at a bedside and
raising a prostrate form, while a great star burns above her

[4] It is the tangled barbarisms of learning which we deplore,—the mere
dogma, the speculative theory, the nauseous fiction. Novels, remarkable only
for their exaggerated pictures, impossible ideals, and specimens of depravity,
fill our young readers with wrong tastes and sentiments, etc.—*Science and
Health* (1898), p. 91.
[5] *Ibid,*

head.   In another, Christ is represented as hand in hand with
a woman who bears a tablet inscribed " Christian Science."
Mrs. Eddy wrote the text of this grim gift-book, and a fly-leaf
accredits the pictures to " Mary Baker G. Eddy and James F.
Gilman, artists."

In 1891 Mrs. Eddy published *Retrospection and Introspection,* a volume of autobiographical sketches in which many of
the events of the author's life are highly idealised.

At Pleasant View the members of Mrs. Eddy's household led
a life vastly more peaceful than ever they had known in
Columbus or Commonwealth Avenues.   But discipline was by no
means relaxed.   Mr. Frye still had his bad quarter of an
hour when it was good for him.   Mrs. Eddy " turned against "
the faithful Martha Morgan and packed her back to Maine.
She tired of Mrs. Anne M. Otis, whom she had called to build
up a Christian Science church in Concord, and sent her back
to the West.   Eventually even her adopted son went the way
of all her favourites.   There is no doubt that Mrs. Eddy
was fond of Foster, and that his personality was extremely
agreeable to her.   She may even have dropped a tear upon
his death-warrant, but she signed it none the less.   The story
of Foster's rise and decline is as follows:

At the close of 1892 Mr. William G. Nixon resigned his post
as Mrs. Eddy's publisher, and was succeeded by E. J. Foster
Eddy.   Dr. Foster had had no experience whatever in publishing, but the position was a lucrative one and Mrs. Eddy desired
her son to have it.   She saw, too, a way to increase her own
profits.   *Science and Health* sold for $3.18 a copy.[6]   The man-

---

[6] The eighteen cents paid the postage. The book was, of course, usually
ordered by mail.

ufacture of each book cost just forty-seven and a half cents. Mrs. Eddy had been getting one dollar royalty upon every copy sold and the publisher got the rest. When her adopted son began to publish *Science and Health*, Mrs. Eddy worked her royalty up to a dollar and a half a copy, since Dr. Foster was readily persuaded that it was all in the family.

The sale of Mrs. Eddy's works was exceedingly profitable to her and even more profitable to her publisher, since the market for them was ready-made and there was never a dollar spent in general advertising. Dr. Foster's accounts show that in the year 1893 he paid Mrs. Eddy $11,692.79 in royalties; in 1894 her royalties amounted to $14,834.12; and in 1895 she received from Dr. Foster $18,481.97, making a total profit of $45,008.88 for the three years. Needless to say, her annual royalties have greatly increased since 1895, and have now reached a figure which puts all other American authors to financial shame.

But from the day that Mrs. Eddy installed Dr. Foster as her publisher, his years were numbered. The position was the most remunerative she had to offer, and this new and substantial mark of her favour only increased the existing prejudice against her son. Ever since Foster's adoption, jealousy had rankled in the household. Mr. Frye had always watched him with a stony and distrustful eye. Each had accused the other of " mesmerising " Mrs. Eddy against him, and of using her affection for his own advantage.

There was jealousy in Boston, as well as at Pleasant View. Some of the workers there complained that Dr. Foster had been made too prominent, and that he had more personal influence than any one except Mrs. Eddy herself should have; others asserted that he over-represented and misrepresented Mrs. Eddy.

After he became his mother's publisher, Dr. Foster had to be in Boston much of the time, and stayed, when he was there, at the Commonwealth Avenue house. In his absence from Concord, one charge after another was made against him to Mrs. Eddy. Pressure was brought to bear upon her from this quarter and from that, and she seems to have realised that her favourite was marked for sacrifice. Dr. Foster relates that, upon one occasion when they were alone together, his mother drew him to the sofa and took his hand, saying despairingly, " Bennie, if I ever ask you to go away from me, do not leave me." She told him that she wanted him always near her, but that " mesmerism " had come between them. Undoubtedly, Mrs. Eddy herself had become somewhat alarmed when she realised what authority she had placed in Dr. Foster's hands; it was quite possible for her to trust him and to doubt him, to want him and to plan his downfall at the same time. The letters which she wrote him after she sent him away have not a candid tone.

Stories kept coming to Mrs. Eddy to the effect that Dr. Foster was short in his accounts, that he had conducted himself improperly with a married woman who had done some work in the publication-office, etc., etc. Finally, in the spring of 1896, Mrs. Eddy took the publishing business away from her son and transferred it to Joseph Armstrong, a Christian Scientist who had formerly been a banker in Kansas. Foster Eddy was now instructed to go to Philadelphia and build up a church. There was already a Christian Science church in Philadelphia, and when Dr. Foster arrived there he found that he had been discredited with the Philadelphia following by letters from Boston. It was his mother's way not to tell him frankly that she was through with him, though, after he reached his destination, she dropped the old endearing appellations, and no longer signed herself " Mother," but wrote to him in the following tone:

DEAR DOCTOR, I have silenced every word of the slander started in Boston about that woman by saying that I had not the least idea of any wrong conduct between you and her, for I know you are chaste. . . . This silly stuff is dead. Always kindly yours.

MARY BAKER EDDY.

Dr. Foster left Boston by water, and on the day he sailed away Mrs. Eddy sent flowers to the boat, and a crowd of Christian Scientists were at the wharf to see him off. But as the adopted son stood by the deck-rail with his bouquet in his hands, and watched the water widen between him and Boston, he realised the import of this cordiality, and knew that, through the crowd on the shore, his mother had waved him a blithe and long adieu.

After Dr. Foster reached Philadelphia and found that Christian Scientists there had been warned to have nothing to do with him, he went back to Concord to lay his wrongs before Mrs. Eddy. She granted him an audience in the house in which, a few months before, he had been master, but cut short the interview and went upstairs while he was speaking.[7] Dr. Foster

---

[7] After this interview Mrs. Eddy wrote Dr. Foster the following letter, in which she accuses him of " keeping his mind on her " and weakening her, as she used to charge Spofford and Arens with doing:

" PLEASANT VIEW,
" Concord, N. H., March 17, 1897.
" DR. FOSTER EDDY—My dear Benny: I was not 'falsely' referring to your mind on me. I am not or cannot be mistaken now in whose mind is on me. My letter was dated the 8th of March. I shall not soon forget that time. When you went to Phila. at my request I made everything ready for your

knew his mother well enough to realise that she was through with him. He made no attempt to push his case or further to practise Christian Science. He received no opportunity to refute the charges made against him.

As Mrs. Eddy's son and personal representative, Dr. Foster had been regarded as a sort of crown prince by Christian Scientists. He had been the first president of the Mother Church, had held Mrs. Eddy's highest offices, and had been listened to as her mouthpiece. Ever since she had become inaccessible at Pleasant View, Dr. Foster had been the natural recipient of the adulation that had formerly been hers. His arrival at a Christian Science convention caused almost as much excitement as if Mrs. Eddy herself had come. Wherever the Doctor went in Boston, he was pretty sure to meet people who greeted him with the greatest deference and an eager, anxious smile. Even those who did not like him tried to please him,

success, even in the Church rules, Art. 8, Sec. 14, that nothing should impede you. One of your first acts was to consult ———— in your movements and not to consult me before doing it.

"This laid the foundation of what followed. Had my letter that I sent by you to that church been read in the Church of Philadelphia on March 14, as I told you to have it, it would have saved you being kicked out of the readership. You never named to me you intended to stop till Monday in Boston. You conceal from me all you should tell—and which I would save you from doing—and then when you get into difficulty come to me for help. You had everything in your power whereby to control the situation. See *Church Manual*, pp. 13, Secs. 3 and 16. Sec. 10, edition 5.

"But you were governed by hypnotism to work against me and yourself and take me as your authority for so doing. Then turn all your papers of the fight and the burden of its settlement on to me and yourself go on a pleasure trip to Washington, and after all this tell me that you cared not for yourself in the case but for me!

"The church has written me a loving letter with regrets [regrets] that they had to do by you as they did.

"You say those with whom you now are love you. I hope this will continue to be so. As ever, lovingly,   MOTHER.

"N. B.—I open this letter to speak briefly of the apochryphal gospel. I read till disgusted and stopped. 'Hermas' is an imaginary character, and the 'old woman' has no more relation to me than Pilate's wife; both are depicted as good representative characters for that time and under those circumstances. They may or may not have been human beings.

"Such reading tends to foster the disease of moral insanity or idiocy that the magic of Mohammedism and the hypnotism of our time are engendering.

"The ethics of the dialogues in that spurious book are excellent and that makes the book dangerous lest they cause the stuff that accompanies them to take form in thought as veritable characters and history, and even prophetic —which it is not.   M. B. E."

because they believed that he could influence Mrs. Eddy for or against any one.

Mrs. Eddy's word had made Foster, and her word unmade him. From the moment the Christian Scientists understood that he was no longer in favour with his mother, Dr. Foster was ostracised. The people who had once crowded about him whenever he appeared in public no longer recognised him when they passed him in the street. When he approached a group of Christian Scientists, they melted away. Legally, of course, he was still Mrs. Eddy's adopted son, but she did not trouble herself about that, apparently. She made no charge against him, demanded no explanation, but erased him from her consciousness as if he were a coachman whom she had hired and discharged. Dr. Foster travelled in the West and in Alaska for a time, and then settled down at his old home at Waterbury Center, Vt., where he now lives. Like the rest of Mrs. Eddy's outworn favourites, he has been content to live very quietly since his fall, and he has not even resumed the practice of medicine, for fear of further angering his adopted mother.

Mrs. Eddy's retirement in Concord meant no relaxation of her vigilance over her church. Scarcely a day passed that one of her executives did not board the train at Boston, take the two hours' ride up the Merrimac, and present himself at Pleasant View. The affairs of the Mother Church ran much more smoothly with Mrs. Eddy out of the city. The hundred little annoyances which had so often led her into indiscretions were now kept from her. She planted and pulled up, built and tore down,—or, as she says, armed with pen and pruning-hook, she commanded and countermanded,—as tirelessly as ever;

but now that she worked through other people, her plans were not executed so rapidly, and she had time to change her mind before her first decision was made public. It was now possible for her executives to present questions to her with some care. They kept Mrs. Eddy informed upon the affairs of the Boston church and upon what went on in the field, but petty annoyances they kept from her. Her inability to interfere hourly gave her assistants an opportunity to execute her wishes temperately and successfully. Mrs. Eddy, the " Discoverer and Founder of Christian Science," was still in the field, through her executives, as active and powerful as ever; while Mrs. Eddy, the woman, with her disturbing personal idiosyncrasies, was safely housed at Pleasant View, surrounded by devoted and sympathetic persons whose constant care it was to calm and soothe her.

After she first took up her residence at Pleasant View, Mrs. Eddy visited Boston four times, and on each occasion remained in the city only a few hours.[8] In her retirement she has not been cut off from such of her followers as she has wished to see. By a by-law of the church, Mrs. Eddy is empowered to send for any Christian Scientist, wherever he may be, and to bring him to Pleasant View, to serve her for as long as twelve months, if need be, in whatever capacity she may designate; his recompense

---

[8] The first of these was on April 1, 1895, when she came unannounced, bringing the members of her Concord household with her, and inspected, for the first time, the newly completed Mother Church. She spent the night in the building, occupying the folding-bed in the Mother Room, while her attendants slept all night in the pews. The next month, on Sunday, May 26, Mrs. Eddy went again to the Mother Church and spoke from the pulpit for twenty minutes. Again, in February, 1896, she preached in the Mother Church, returning to Concord in a private car the same afternoon. She made her fourth visit to Boston on Monday, June 5, 1899. She spent the night in her Commonwealth Avenue house, then occupied by Septimus J. Hanna, the reader of the Mother Church, and on Tuesday afternoon she appeared at the annual meeting of the church, held in Tremont Temple. Mrs. Eddy addressed the meeting briefly, and returned to Concord the same afternoon.

being twelve hundred dollars a year and his expenses.[9]   Under this rule, a bank president whose time is worth $50,000 a year might be summoned to Pleasant View to serve for a hundred dollars a month.   But Mrs. Eddy is the last woman in the world to make unreasonable demands of her influential followers, and no greater honour can befall a Christian Scientist than to be thus summoned by his Leader.   Such a call is looked upon as a recognition of the recipient's progress in " Science," and as a rare opportunity for spiritual growth.   Concerning this service at Pleasant View, Mrs. Eddy wrote in the *Christian Science Sentinel* of April 25, 1903.

SIGNIFICANT QUESTIONS

MARY BAKER G. EDDY

Who shall be greatest?
The great Master said: " He that is least in the kingdom of heaven "—that is, he who hath in his heart in the least the kingdom of heaven, the reign of holiness, shall be greatest.
Who shall inherit the earth?
The meek who sit at the feet of Truth, bathing the human understanding with tears of repentance, and washing it clean from the taints of self-righteousness, hypocrisy, envy—shall inherit the earth—for wisdom is justified of her children.
Who shall dwell in Thy Holy Hill?
He that walketh uprightly, and worketh righteousness, and speaketh the truth in his heart.
Who shall be called to Pleasant View?
He who strives and attains—who has the divine presumption to say: " For I know whom I have believed, and am persuaded that he is able to keep that which I have committed unto him against that day " (St. Paul).

---

[9] The church by-law in regard to this rule of service reads as follows : " At the written request of our Pastor Emeritus, Mrs. Eddy, for assistance, the Board of Directors shall immediately notify the member of this church whom she selects, to go within ten days to her and to remain if needed twelve months consecutively, and it shall be the duty of this member to comply therewith.   Members who leave her in less time and when she needs them, are liable to have their names dropped from the church." *Church Manual*, Art. 22, Sec. 10.

It goes without saying that such a one was never called to Pleasant View for penance or reformation; and I call none others, unless I mistake their calling. No mesmerist, nor disloyal Christian Scientist is fit to come hither, I have no use for such, and there cannot be found at Pleasant View one of *this sort*. "For all that do these things are an abomination unto the Lord, and because of these abominations the Lord thy God doth drive them out from before thee." (Deuteronomy, 18.)

It is true that loyal Christian Scientists called to the home of the Discoverer and Founder of Christian Science, can acquire in one year the Science that otherwise might cost them a half century. But this should not be the incentive for going thither. Better far that Christian Scientists go to help their helper, and thus lose all selfishness as she has lost it, and thereby help themselves and the whole world, as she has done according to this saying of Christ Jesus: "And whosoever doth not bear his cross and come after me, cannot be my disciple."

CHAPTER XXIII

JOSEPHINE CURTIS WOODBURY AND THE ROMANTIC SCHOOL—
BIRTH OF THE PRINCE OF PEACE—MRS. EDDY WITHDRAWS
HER SUPPORT—" WAR IN HEAVEN "

MRS. EDDY's absence from Boston made it possible for some
of her ambitious leaders there to exercise a stronger personal
influence than they could ever have done had she been at her
old headquarters in Commonwealth Avenue. This opportunity
was seized, and abused, so Mrs. Eddy thought, by one of her
most prominent aids, Josephine Curtis Woodbury.

Mrs. Woodbury had been associated with Mrs. Eddy since
1879, and had been one of her foremost healers and teachers.
She had written a great deal for the *Journal*, had preached
and lectured as far west as Denver, had organised classes and
church societies, and had conducted a Christian Science " academy " at the Hotel Berkshire, in Boston.

Mrs. Woodbury was clever, self-confident, given to theatrical
display, ready with her tongue and pen, and she possessed an
amazing personal influence over her adherents. In short, she
was the only Christian Scientist in Boston who ever bade fair
to rival Mrs. Eddy in personal prominence. Like Mrs. Eddy,
she was ambitious, and delighted in leadership. She, too, could
send her students hither and yon, and keep them dancing
attendance upon her telegrams. Some of them lived in her

house and went to Maine with her in the summer; they sat spellbound at her lectures, and put their time and goods at her disposal.

Mrs. Woodbury's group of students and followers were, on the whole, very different from the simple, rule-abiding Christian Scientists who had been taught directly under Mrs. Eddy's personal supervision. Mrs. Eddy's own people never got very far away from her hard-and-fast business principles, while Mrs. Woodbury's students were distinctly fanciful and sentimental, and strove to add all manner of ornamentation to Mrs. Eddy's stout homespun. There were two or three musicians among them, and a young illustrator and his handsome wife, and most of them wrote verses. Some of Mrs. Woodbury's students went abroad with her, and acquired the habit of interlarding the regular Christian Science phraseology with a little French. Mrs. Woodbury and her students lived in a kind of miracle-play of their own; had inspirations and revelations and premonitions; kept mental trysts; saw portents and mystic meanings in everything; and spoke of God as coming and going, agreeing and disagreeing with them. Some of them affected cell-like sleeping-chambers, with white walls, bare except for a picture of Christ. They longed for martyrdom, and made adventures out of the most commonplace occurrences. Mrs. Woodbury herself had this marvel-loving temperament. Her room was lined with pictures of the Madonna. When she went to Denver to lecture on Christian Science in 1887, her train was caught in a blizzard; in relating this experience, she describes herself as " face to face with death." Her two children fell into the water on the Nantasket coast; Mrs.

Woodbury " treated " them, and they recovered.   She writes upon this incident a dramatic article entitled " Drowning Overcome."

Mrs. Woodbury and her students thus succeeded in giving to Mrs. Eddy's homely " Science "—pieced together in dull New England shoe towns and first taught to people who worked with their hands—an emotional colouring which was very distasteful to Mrs. Eddy herself.   Never was any woman less the *religieuse*.   " Discovering and founding " Christian Science had been her business, performed, in spite of all her flightiness, in a businesslike manner, and her success was eminently a businesslike success.   With yearnings and questings and raptures, Mrs. Eddy had little patience, and Mrs. Woodbury's romantic school, with its spiritual alliances, annoyed her beyond expression.

Meanwhile, Mrs. Woodbury's students inevitably found their miracle.   In June, 1890, Mrs. Woodbury gave birth to a son whom her followers believed was the result of an " immaculate conception," and an exemplification of Mrs. Eddy's theory of " mental generation."   Mrs. Woodbury named her child " The Prince of Peace," and baptised him at Ocean Point, Me., in a pool which she called " Bethsada."   " While there," writes Mrs. Woodbury, " occurred the thought of baptising little Prince in a singularly beautiful salt pool, whose rocky bottom was dry at low tide and overflowing at high tide, but especially attractive at mid-tide, with its two feet of crystal water.   A crowd of people had assembled on the neighbouring bluffs, when I brought him from our cottage not far away, and laid him three times prayerfully in the pool and when he was lifted therefrom, they joined in a spontaneously appropriate hymn of praise."

Mrs. Woodbury would not permit the child, who was called Prince for short, to address her husband as " father," but insisted that he address Mr. Woodbury as " Frank " and herself as " Birdie." The fact that he was a fine, healthy baby, and was never ill, seemed to Mrs. Woodbury's disciples conclusive evidence that he was the Divine principle of Christian Science made manifest in the flesh. It was their pleasure to bring gifts to Prince; to discover in his behaviour indications of his spiritual nature; and they professed to believe that when he grew to manhood he would enter upon his Divine ministry.

Six months before the birth of Prince, Mrs. Woodbury paid a visit to Mrs. Eddy, and she seems to imply that the venerable leader oracularly foretold the coming of her child. " In January," writes Mrs. Woodbury, " I enjoyed a visit with my ever-beloved Teacher, who gave comfort in these words, though at the moment they were not received in their deeper import: ' Go home and be happy. Commit thy ways unto the Lord. Trust him, and he will bring it to pass.' " This may have suggested to the faithful the visit of Mary to Elizabeth; but if there was any miracle-play of this sort in progress, Mrs. Eddy had certainly no intention of playing Elizabeth to Mrs. Woodbury's Mary. When word was brought her of the birth of Mrs. Woodbury's " little Immanuel," as he was often called, she was far from being convinced. " Child of light! " she exclaimed indignantly. " She knows it is an imp of Satan." In the libel suit which Mrs. Woodbury later brought against her Teacher, a letter to her from Mrs. Eddy was read in court, in which Mrs. Eddy said: " Those awful reports about you, namely that your last child was illegitimate, etc.   I again and again tried to suppress that report; also for what you tried to make people believe; namely, that that child was an immaculate conception, . . . and you replied that it was incarnated with the Devil."

Mrs. Eddy was the more vexed with Mrs. Woodbury because she herself had undoubtedly taught that in the future, when the world had attained a larger growth in Christian Science, children would be conceived by communion with the Divine mind; but she probably had no idea that any one of her students, ambitious to " demonstrate over material claims," would actually attempt to put this theory into practice.   She was wise enough, moreover, to see that such extravagant claims would bring Christian Science into disrepute, and she vigorously denounced Mrs. Woodbury's zeal.

Besides her school in Boston, Mrs. Woodbury had a large following in Maine, where she usually spent the summer.   In 1896 Fred D. Chamberlain began a suit against her for the alienation of his wife's affections—his wife being a pupil of Mrs. Woodbury's.   At this time, the Boston *Traveller*, in discussing Mr. Chamberlain's charge, took up the question of the claims that were made for Mrs. Woodbury's son, Prince.   The *Traveller* asserted that some of Mrs. Woodbury's students had been induced against their will to buy stock in an " air-engine " which Mr. Woodbury was exploiting, and published interviews with George Macomber and H. E. Jones, both of Augusta, Me., who stated that their wives had believed that Mrs. Woodbury's child was immaculately conceived, had desired to make presents to it, and had urged their husbands to buy stock in the air-engine. The *Traveller* also made the statement that Evelyn I. Rowe of Augusta had applied for a divorce from her husband upon the ground of non-support, saying that he gave all his earnings toward the education and support of Mrs. Woodbury's son, Prince, whom Mr. Rowe believed to have been immaculately conceived. After the publication of this, Mrs. Woodbury promptly sued the *Traveller* for criminal libel, and lost her case.

All this notoriety brought matters to a crisis between Mrs. Woodbury and Mrs. Eddy. Although Mrs. Eddy had found Mrs. Woodbury very useful, she had long distrusted her discretion, and had endeavoured in various ways to put a check upon her. Mrs. Woodbury had first become a member of Mrs. Eddy's church in 1886. When the Mother Church was reorganised, it was necessary, in order that Mrs. Eddy might cull out such persons as were distasteful to her, for all the old members to apply for admission and be voted upon, just as were the new candidates. Mrs. Woodbury was admitted only upon the condition that she would undergo a two years' probation, and she had some difficulty in getting back even upon those terms. Several months before her admission on probation, she wrote to Mrs. Eddy, begging her to use her personal influence in her behalf. To this petition Mrs. Eddy replied:

MRS. WOODBURY   February 27, 1895.
  DEAR STUDENT:

I have your letter asking my assistance in getting admission to the church. I have made a rule, which has been published in our Journal that I shall not be consulted on the applications for membership to this church or dismissals from it. This responsibility must rest on the First Members according to the rules of the church. Hence I return your letter to you and the church.

May the love that must govern you and the church influence your motives, is my fervent wish; But remember, dear student, that malicious hypnotism is no excuse for sin. But God's grace is sufficient to govern our lives and lead us to moral ends.

With love
MARY BAKER G. EDDY.

On April 8 Mrs. Eddy wrote to Mrs. Woodbury:

Now, dear student try one year not to tell a single falsehood, or to practise one cheat, or to break the decalogue, and if you do this to the best of your ability at the end of that year God will give you a place in our church as sure as you are fit for it. This I know. Don't return evil for evil, and you will have your reward.

April 17 Mrs. Eddy again wrote Mrs. Woodbury a warning letter:

MY DEAR STUDENT: I am willing you should let them read my letter. I forgot to mention this, hence my second line to you. Now mark what I say. This is your last chance, and you will succeed in getting back, and should. But this I warn you, to stop falsifying, and living unpurely in thought, in vile schemes, in fraudulent money-getting, etc. I speak plainly even as the need is.

I am not ignorant of your sins, and I am trying to have you in the church for protection from those temptations, and to effect your full reformation. Remember, the M. A. M., which you say in your letter causes you to sin, is not idle, and will cause you to repeat them, and so turn you again from the church, unless you pray God to keep you from falling into the foul snare. In the consciousness that you and your students are mentally speaking to me, I warn you this is forbidden by a strict rule of the by-laws as well as by conscience.

MARY B. EDDY.

After her admission to the Mother Church, Mrs. Woodbury did not go through her two years' probation. Her name was dropped from the church roll in the fall of the first year, and in the following spring (March 24, 1896) she was reinstated. Ten days later she was, in the language of the directors, " forever excommunicated."

What Mrs. Eddy wished was that Mrs. Woodbury should cease to identify herself in any way with Christian Science. "How dare you," she wrote to Mrs. Woodbury in the spring of 1896, "how dare you in the sight of God, and with your character behind the curtain, and your students ready to lift it on you, pursue the path perilous?" But Mrs. Woodbury was not made of such yielding stuff as the men who had aforetime obliterated themselves at Mrs. Eddy's bidding. She insisted upon going to Mrs. Eddy's church even after the directors refused to let her a pew, and after the little Prince of Peace had been taken up by his jacket and put bodily out of the Sunday-school.

Disgruntled Christian Scientists usually went off and started a church of their own, and there were by this time almost as many "reformed" varieties of Christian Science as there were dissenters. Mrs. Gestefeld taught one kind in Chicago, Mrs. Crosse another kind in Boston, Frank Mason another in Brooklyn, Captain Sabin was soon to teach another in Washington, while nearly all the students who had quarrelled with Mrs. Eddy or broken away from her were teaching or practising some variety of mind-cure. Mrs. Woodbury, accordingly, hired a hall—this seemed to be the only necessary preliminary in those days—and started a church of her own, to which her little flock followed her. In the Legion of Honour rooms she conducted services every Sunday morning. Sometimes she preached, sometimes she lectured, and sometimes she read a poem. When it was impossible for her to be there, her daughter, Gwendolyn, supplied her pulpit.

In 1897 Mrs. Woodbury published a veiled account of her

differences with Mrs. Eddy in a pamphlet modestly entitled *War in Heaven*. In this book her criticism of Mrs. Eddy is courteous and respectful enough to suggest that she may still have hoped for reinstatement. But Mrs. Eddy had by this time become convinced that never, since the days of Kennedy, had there been such a mesmerist as Mrs. Woodbury. Indeed, Mrs. Eddy was not alone in accrediting Mrs. Woodbury with a strange hypnotic power. Some of Mrs. Woodbury's own students were confident that if they displeased her she had power to bring upon them sickness, insanity, and disaster. They whispered tales about Robert W. Rowe of Augusta, Me., who had disobeyed and died. Whether Mrs. Eddy really believed that the woman was possessed of some diabolical power, or whether she saw that Mrs. Woodbury's adventurous temperament would bring ridicule upon Christian Science, Mrs. Eddy was determined to be rid of her, and lost no opportunity to discredit her. The two women had it back and forth for several years, and in April, 1899, Mrs. Woodbury published in the *American Register*, Paris, a poem which attacked Christian Science and which ended with these significant lines:

> Is the Dame that seemed august
> A Doll stuffed with sawdust,
> And must we believe that the Doll stuffed herself?

Mrs. Woodbury finally crossed the Rubicon by publishing in the *Arena*, May, 1899, an exposure of Mrs. Eddy and her methods.

In this attack Mrs. Woodbury satirically touched upon Mrs. Eddy's conviction that she is the star-crowned woman of the Apocalypse, and then took up the Quimby controversy, producing Mrs. Eddy's early letters and newspaper contributions as evidence that she got her theory of mind-cure from Mr. Quimby. She criticised the English of *Science and Health;* ridiculed the Mother Room; insinuated that Mrs. Eddy had illegally conferred degrees, and had been compelled to close her college for that reason; accused her of an inordinate greed for money and of " trafficking in the temple." She declared that Mrs. Eddy had been a medium, and that she was the victim of demonophobia—the fear of witchcraft. Mrs. Woodbury stated that Mrs. Eddy claimed that she had cured the Prince of Wales, now King Edward VII., of his serious illness in 1871, and that to do so she had treated him through his royal mother, as the Prince's life had been such that she could not approach him directly. According to Mrs. Woodbury, Mrs. Eddy said that she treated President Garfield after he was shot, and would have succeeded in saving his life had not Kennedy and Arens maliciously interfered to prevent her from making this convincing demonstration.

It seems that in this article Mrs. Woodbury wished to explain how she had been led to make such extraordinary claims regarding the birth of her son, Prince. She asserts that Mrs. Eddy taught her women students that they might become mothers by a supreme effort of their own minds, and that girls were terrified by the doctrine that they might be made pregnant through the influence of demons. Mrs. Woodbury had probably repented her own efforts to give a concrete example of Mrs. Eddy's theory of " mental generation," and she attacks her on this point with peculiar bitterness. She quotes the following passage from *Science and Health:*

The propagation of their species without the male element, by butterfly, bee, and moth is a discovery corroborative of the Science of Mind, because it shows that the origin and continuance of these insects rest on Principle, apart from material conditions.[1] An egg never was the origin of a man, and no seed ever produced a plant. . . . The belief that life can be in matter, or soul in body, and that man springs from dust or from an egg, is the brief record of mortal error. . . . The plant grows not because of seed or soil.

Commenting upon this passage, Mrs. Woodbury says:

To what diabolical conclusions do such deductions lead? One may well hesitate to touch this delicate topic in print, yet only thus can the immoral possibilities and the utter lack of Divine inspiration in " Christian Science " be shown.

The substance of certain instructions given by Mrs. Eddy in private is as follows:

If Jesus was divinely conceived by the Holy Ghost or Spirit, without a human father, Mary not having known her husband,—then women may become mothers by a supreme effort of their own minds, or through the influence upon them of an Unholy Ghost, a malign spirit. Women of unquestioned integrity, who have been Mrs. Eddy's students, testify that she has so taught, and that by this teaching families have been broken up; that thus maidens have been terrified out of their wits, and stimulated into a frenzy resembling that of deluded French nuns, who believed themselves brought into marital relations with the glorified Jesus, as veritably the bridegroom of his church. Whatever her denials may be, such was Mrs. Eddy's teaching while in her college; to which she added the oracular declaration that it lay within her power to dissolve such motherhood by a wave of her celestial rod.

The selfish celibacy of nuns and clergy, Christian or heathen, with consequent ecclesiastical interference in family life, have been, and are, mischief-breeding blunders, fatal alike to morals and health. One result of this interference on the part of Mrs. Eddy is that Christian Science families are notably childless.

Very tenacious is she of the paradoxical title carved on her Boston church, " The Discoverer and Founder of Christian Science." Surely a " Discoverer " cannot be the " Founder " of that which he has been under the necessity of discovering; while a " Founder " would have no need of discovering her own foundation. What she has really " discovered " are ways and means of perverting and prostituting the science of healing to her own ecclesiastical aggrandisement, and to the moral and physical

---

[1] *Science and Health* (1886), page 472.

depravity of her dupes. As she received this science from Dr. Quimby it meant simply the healing of bodily ills through a lively reliance on the wholeness and order of the Infinite Mind, as clearly perceived and practically demonstrated by a simple and modest love of one's kind. What she has " founded " is a commercial system, monumental in its proportions, but already tottering to its fall.

This certainly was strong language from one who had taught Christian Science for ten years, who had often been compared to John, the beloved disciple, and who had leaned upon the bosom of her Teacher. Mrs. Woodbury's article appeared the 1st of May, and during that same month her husband, Frank Woodbury, died. This, to many of Mrs. Eddy's faithful retainers, seemed like a direct judgment upon the apostate.

Mrs. Woodbury might have known that Mrs. Eddy would have the last word, and that it would be no gentle one. In her annual message to the Mother Church, read before the congregation at the June communion service, a few weeks after Mr. Woodbury's death, Mrs. Eddy indulged in certain vivid rhetoric which Mrs. Woodbury and her friends believed referred directly to Mrs. Woodbury; to her efforts to get back into the church; to her alleged practice of malicious animal magnetism; and to her widowhood. The address was not only read aloud in the church, but was published in the *Christian Science Sentinel* and in the Boston *Herald*. Mrs. Woodbury, accordingly, brought a suit for criminal libel against Mrs. Eddy.

The case came to trial in the following June, when Boston was full of Christian Scientists who had come to attend the June communion. Mrs. Woodbury lost her suit because such Christian Scientists as were summoned as witnesses testified that they had not understood Mrs. Eddy's denunciation to refer to Mrs. Woodbury in particular.   One of the witnesses, however, Mr. William G. Nixon, Mrs. Eddy's former publisher, stated that he had understood that Mrs. Eddy meant Josephine Woodbury.

During the trial the courtroom was crowded with Christian Scientists, and Mrs. Woodbury decided that they had effected the outcome of the suit by concentrating their minds upon the judge and witnesses, and by " treating " them in Mrs. Eddy's behalf.   She, accordingly, would not permit an appeal, but abjured Christian Science and retired into private life; and with Mrs. Woodbury's defeat perished the romantic movement in Christian Science.

CHAPTER XXIV

MRS. EDDY ADOPTS THE TITLE OF " MOTHER "—BEGINNING OF
THE CONCORD PILGRIMAGES—MRS. EDDY HINTS AT HER
POLITICAL INFLUENCE—THE BUILDING OF THE MOTHER
CHURCH EXTENSION

> A Lady with a Lamp shall stand
> In the great history of our land,
> A noble type of good,
> Heroic womanhood.[1]
> —Motto upon the cover of the *Christian Science Sentinel.*

AFTER the opening of the Mother Church in Boston, Christian Science was generally recognised as an established religion. The church had now a general membership of 1,500 and a substantial house of worship; and although the very foundation and fabric of the church was a denial of the visible and material, nothing served to give it recognition and standing like this actual sign of its existence. At the World's Congress of Religions in Chicago in 1893, Septimus J. Hanna, who was then pastor of the Mother Church, read an address, composed of selections from Mrs. Eddy's books, which attracted favourable attention, and Mrs. Eddy, as the founder of the church, became

---

[1] This verse is taken from Longfellow's *Filomena,* which was written as a tribute to Florence Nightingale's work in the hospital at Scutari. In St. Thomas' hospital in London there is a statuette of Florence Nightingale in nurse's dress, holding in her hands a night lamp such as she used in making her rounds in Scutari. Upon this statuette, which is called The Lady with the Lamp, is inscribed Longfellow's verse.

The cover design of the *Christian Science Sentinel* contains a conventionalised figure of a woman holding a Greek lamp. Under it is inscribed the motto quoted above.

an object of public curiosity and interest. In 1895 she adopted the title " Mother," [2] and instituted the Concord " pilgrimages " which later became so conspicuous. By this time the church membership had so increased that most of Mrs. Eddy's followers had never seen their leader, and as Mrs. Eddy did not attend the annual communion [3] of the general membership in the Mother Church, she telegraphed an invitation, after the June communion in 1895, to the congregation, to call upon her at Pleasant View. Accordingly, one hundred and eighty Christian Scientists boarded the train at Boston and went up to Concord. Mrs. Eddy threw her house open to them, received them in person, shook hands with each delegate, and conversed with many.

After the communion in 1897, twenty-five hundred enthusiastic pilgrims crowded into the little New Hampshire capital. Although the Scientists hired every available conveyance in Concord, there were not enough carriages to accommodate their numbers, so hundreds of the pilgrims walked out Pleasant Street to Mrs. Eddy's home.

Mrs. Eddy again received her votaries, greeted them cordially, and made a long address. The *Journal* says that her manner

[2] The Title of Mother. In the year 1895 loyal Scientists had given to the author of their textbook, the Founder of Christian Science, the individual, endearing term of Mother. Therefore, if a student of Christian Science shall apply this title, either to herself or to others except as the term for kinship according to the flesh, it shall be regarded by the church as an indication of disrespect for their Pastor Emeritus, and unfitness to be a member of the Mother Church.—*Church Manual*, Article XXII, Section 1.

In 1903 Mrs. Eddy issued a new by-law, which stated that " owing to the public misunderstanding of this name, it is the duty of Christian Scientists to drop the word *mother*, and to substitute Leader." This action was taken not long after Mark Twain, in the *North American Review*, had called attention to the title, cleverly ridiculing it. Mrs. Eddy and other Christian Scientists replied to Twain's articles, but the shaft had touched a vulnerable point and the title was dropped.

[3] This communion was originally observed once each quarter and then twice a year. Since 1899 it has been observed but once a year, on the second Sunday in June. No " material " emblems, such as bread and wine, are offered, and the communion is one of silent thought. On Monday the directors meet and transact the business of the year, and on Tuesday the officers' reports are read. As most members of the branch churches are also members of the Mother Church, thousands of Christian Scientists from all over the United States visit Boston at this time.

upon this occasion was peculiar for its "utter freedom from sensationalism or the Mesmeric effect that so many speakers seem to exert," and adds that she was " calm and unimpassioned, but strong and convincing." The *Journal* also states that upon this occasion Mrs. Eddy wore " a royal purple silk dress covered with black lace " and a " dainty bonnet." She wore her diamond cross and the badge of the Daughters of the Revolution in diamonds and rubies.

In 1901 [4] three thousand of the June communicants went from Boston to Concord on three special trains. They were not admitted to the house, but Mrs. Eddy appeared upon her balcony for a moment and spoke to them, saying that they had already heard from her in her message to the Mother Church, and that she would pause but a moment to look into their dear faces and then return to her " studio." The *Journal* comments upon her " erect form and sprightly step," and says that she wore " what might have been silk or satin, figured, and cut *en traine*. Upon her white hair rested a bonnet with fluttering blue and old gold trimmings."

The last of these pilgrimages occurred in 1904, when Mrs. Eddy invited the pilgrims to come, not to Pleasant View but to the new Christian Science church in Concord. Fifteen hundred of them gathered in front of the church and stood in reverent silence as Mrs. Eddy's carriage approached. The horses were stopped in front of the assemblage, and Mrs. Eddy signalled the President of the Mother Church to approach

---

[4] At the 1898 communion there was no invitation from Mrs. Eddy, but a number of communicants went up to Concord to see her house and to see her start out upon her daily drive. In June, 1899, Mrs. Eddy came to Boston and briefly addressed the annual business meeting of the church. In 1902 and 1903 there were no formal pilgrimages, although hundreds of Christian Scientists went to Concord to catch a glimpse of Mrs. Eddy upon her drive.

her carriage. To him, as representing the church body, she spoke her greeting. Her voice was very weak and she had aged visibly since her last official appearance. This was her last meeting with the general congregation of her church.

The yearning which these people felt toward Mrs. Eddy, and their rapture at beholding her, can only be described by one of the pilgrims. In the *Journal*, June, 1899, Miss Martha Sutton Thompson writes to describe a visit which she made in January of that year to the meeting of the Christian Science Board of Education in Boston. She says:

When I decided to attend I also hoped to see our Mother. . . . I saw that if I allowed the thought that I must see her personally to transcend the desire to obey and grow into the likeness of her teachings, this mistake would obscure my understanding of both the Revelator and the Revelation. After the members of the Board had retired they reappeared upon the rostrum and my heart beat quickly with the thought "perhaps *she* has come." But no, it was to read her message. . . . She said God was with us and to give her love to all the class. It was so precious to get it directly from her.

The following day five of us made the journey to Concord, drove out to Pleasant View, and met her face to face on her daily drive. She seemed watching to greet us, for when she caught sight of our faces she instantly half rose with expectant face, bowing, smiling, and waving her hand to each of us. Then as she went out of our sight, kissed her hand to all.

I will not attempt to describe the Leader, nor can I say what this brief glimpse was and is to me. I can only say I wept and the tears start every time I think of it. Why do I weep? I think it is because I want to be like her and they are tears of repentance. I realise better now what it was that made Mary Magdalen weep when she came into the presence of the Nazarene.

After the pilgrimages were discouraged, there was no way in which her devoted disciples could ever see Mrs. Eddy. They used, indeed, like Miss Thompson, to go to Concord and linger about the highways to catch a glimpse of her as she drove by,

until she rebuked them in a new by-law in the Church Manual:
" *Thou Shalt not Steal.*   Sect. 15.   Neither a Christian Scientist, his student or his patient, nor a member of the Mother Church shall daily and continuously haunt Mrs. Eddy's drive by meeting her once or more every day when she goes out—on penalty of being disciplined and dealt with justly by her church," etc.

Mrs. Eddy did her last public teaching in the Christian Science Hall in Concord, November 21 and 22, 1898.   There were sixty-one persons in this class,—several from Canada, one from England, and one from Scotland,—and Mrs. Eddy refused to accept any remuneration for her instruction.   The first lesson lasted about two hours, the second nearly four.   " Only two lessons," says the *Journal*, " but such lessons!   Only those who have sat under this wondrous teaching can form a conjecture of what these classes were."   " We mention," the *Journal* continues, " a sweet incident and one which deeply touched the Mother's heart.   Upon her return from class she found beside her plate at dinner table a lovely white rose with the card of a young lady student accompanying on which she chastely referred to the last couplet of the fourth stanza of that sweet poem from the Mother's pen, ' Love.'

> " Thou to whose power our hope we give
>   Free us from human strife.
>   Fed by Thy love divine we live
>   For Love alone is Life," etc.

Mrs. Eddy now achieved publicity in a good many ways, and to such publications as afforded her space and appreciation she was able to grant reciprocal favours.   The *Granite*

Monthly, a little magazine published at Concord, N. H., printed
Mrs. Eddy's poem, " Easter Morn," and a highly laudatory
article upon her.   Mrs. Eddy responded in the *Christian Science
Journal* with a request that all Christian Scientists subscribe
to the *Granite Monthly*, which they promptly did.   Colonel
Oliver C. Sabin, a politician in Washington, D. C., was editor
of a purely political publication, the Washington *News Letter*.
A Congressman one day attacked Christian Science in a speech.
Colonel Sabin, whose paper was just then making things unpleasant for that particular Congressman, wrote an editorial
in defence of Christian Science.   Mrs. Eddy inserted a card
in the *Journal* requesting all Christian Scientists to subscribe
to the *News Letter*.   This brought Colonel Sabin such a revenue
that he dropped politics altogether and turned his political
paper into a religious periodical.[5]   Mr. James T. White, publisher of the *National Encyclopædia of American Biography*,
gave Mrs. Eddy a generous place in his encyclopædia and wrote
a poem to her.   Mrs. Eddy requested, through the *Journal*,
that all Christian Scientists buy Mr. White's volume of verse
for Christmas presents, and the Christian Science Publication
Society marketed Mr. White's verses.   Mrs. Eddy made a point
of being on good terms with the Concord papers ; she furnished
them with many columns of copy, and the editors came to
realise that her presence in Concord brought a great deal of
money into the town.   From 1898 to 1901 the files of the
Journal echo increasing material prosperity, and show that
both Mrs. Eddy and her church were much more taken account

---

[5] Colonel Sabin's popularity with Mrs. Eddy and her followers was short-
lived.   Some months later, Sabin repudiated Mrs. Eddy's leadership and started
an independent healing movement, and Mrs. Eddy at once withdrew her
support and that of all Christian Scientists.

of than formerly. Articles by Mrs. Eddy are quoted from various newspapers whose editors had requested her to express her views upon the war with Spain, the Puritan Thanksgiving, etc.

In the autumn of 1901 Mrs. Eddy wrote an article on the death of President McKinley. Commenting upon this article, *Harper's Weekly* said: "Among others who have spoken [on President McKinley's death] was Mrs. Eddy, the Mother of Christian Science. She issued two utterances which were read in her churches. . . . Both of these discourses are seemly and kind, but they are materially different from the writings of any one else. Reciting the praises of the dead President, Mrs. Eddy says: ' May his history waken a tone of truth that shall reverberate, renew euphony, emphasise human power and bear its banner into the vast forever.' No one else said anything like that. Mother Eddy's style is a personal asset. Her sentences usually have the considerable literary merit of being unexpected."

Of this editorial the *Journal* says, with a candour almost incredible: "We take pleasure in republishing from that old-established and valuable publication, *Harper's Weekly*, the following merited tribute to Mrs. Eddy's utterances," etc. Then follows the editorial quoted above.

In the winter of 1898 Christian Science received great publicity through the death, under Christian Science treatment, of the American journalist and novelist, Harold Frederic, in England. Mr. Frederic's readers were not, as a rule, people who knew much about Christian Science, and his taking off brought the new cult to the attention of thousands of people for the first time.

In December, 1898, the Earl of Dunmore, a peer of the Scottish Realm, and his Countess, came to Boston to study Christian Science. They were received by Mrs. Eddy at Pleasant View, and Lady Dunmore was present at the June communion, 1899. According to the *Journal*, Lady Dunmore's son, Lord Fincastle, left his regiment in India and came to Boston to join his mother in this service, and then returned immediately to his military duties. Lady Mildred Murray, daughter of the Countess, also came to America to attend the annual communion. A pew was reserved upon the first floor of the church for this titled family, although the *Journal* explains that " the reservation of a pew for the Countess of Dunmore and her family was wholly a matter of international courtesy, and not in any sense a tribute to their rank."

In these prosperous years the Rev. Irving C. Tomlinson, in commenting in the *Journal* upon Brander Matthews' statement that English seemed destined to become the world-language, says: " It may be that Prof. Matthews has written better than he knew. *Science and Health* is fast reaching all parts of the world; and as our text-book may never be translated into a foreign tongue, may it not be expected to fulfil the prophet's hope, ' Then will I turn to the people a pure language,' " etc.

In January, 1901, Mrs. Eddy called her directors together and charged them to send expressions of sympathy to the British government and to King Edward upon the death of the Queen.

Truly the days of the Lynn shoemakers and the little Broad Street tenement were far gone by, and it must have seemed to Mrs. Eddy that she was living in one of those *New York*

Ledger romances which had so delighted her in those humbler times. Even a less spirited woman than she would have expanded under all this notoriety, and Mrs. Eddy, as always, caught the spirit of the play. A letter written to her son, George Glover, April 27, 1898, conveys some idea of how Mrs. Eddy appeared to herself at this time:

PLEASANT VIEW, CONCORD, N. H., April 27, 1898.

DEAR SON: Yours of latest date came duly. That which you cannot write I understand, and will say, I am reported as dying, wholly decriped and useless, etc. Now one of these reports is just as true as the others are. My life is as pure as that of the angels. God has lifted me up to my work, and if it was not pure it would not bring forth good fruits. The Bible says the tree is known by its fruit.

But I need not say this to a Christian Scientist, who knows it. I thank you for any interest you may feel in your mother. I am alone in the world, more lone than a solitary star. Although it is duly estimated by business characters and learned scholars that I lead and am obeyed by 300,000 people at this date. The most distinguished newspapers ask me to write on the most important subjects. Lords and ladies, earles, princes and marquises and marchionesses from abroad write to me in the most complimentary manner. Hoke Smith declares I am the most illustrious woman on the continent—those are his exact words. Our senators and members of Congress call on me for counsel. But what of all this? I am not made the least proud by it or a particle happier for it. I am working for a higher purpose.

Now what of my circumstances? I name first my home, which of all places on earth is the one in which to find peace and enjoyment. But my home is simply a house and a beautiful landscape. There is not one in it that I love only as I love everybody. I have no congeniality with my help inside of my house; they are no companions and scarcely fit to be my help.

I adopted a son hoping he would take Mr. Frye's place as my bookkeeper and man of all work that belongs to man. But my trial of him has proved another disappointment. His books could not be audited they were so incorrect, etc., etc. Mr. Frye is the most disagreeable man that can be found, but this he is, namely (if there is one on earth), an honest man, as all will tell you who deal with him. At first mesmerism swayed him, but he learned through my forbearance to govern himself. He is a man that would not steal, commit adultery, or fornication, or break one of the Ten Commandments. I have now done, but I could write a volume on what I have touched upon.

One thing is the severest wound of all, namely, the want of education among those nearest to me in kin. I would gladly give every dollar I possess to have one or two and three that are nearest to me on earth possess a thorough education. If you had been educated as I intend to have you, to-day you could, would, be made President of the United States. Mary's letters to me are so mis-spelled that I blush to read them.

You pronounce your words so wrongly and then she spells them accordingly. I am even yet too proud to have you come among my society and alas! mispronounce your words as you do; but for this thing I should be honoured by your good manners and I love you. With love to all

MARY BAKER EDDY.

P. S.—My letter is so short I add a postscript. I have tried about one dozen bookkeepers and had to give them all up, either for dishonesty, or incapacity. I have not had my books audited for five years, and Mr. Ladd, who is famous for this, audited them last week, and gives me his certificate that they are all right except in some places not quite plain, and he showed Frye how to correct that. Then he, Frye gave me a check for that amount before I knew about it.

The slight mistake occurred four years ago and he could not remember about the things. But Mr. Ladd told me that he knew it was only not set down in a coherent way for in other parts of the book he could trace where it was put down in all probability, but not orderly. When I can get a Christian, as I know he is, and a woman that can fill his place I shall do it. But I have no time to receive company, to call on others, or to go out of my house only to drive. Am always driven with work for others, but nobody to help me even to get help such as I would choose.

Again,

MOTHER.

The idea of her own possible political power was evidently rather pleasing to Mrs. Eddy, for in a letter to the editor of the Concord *Monitor*, October 2, 1897, she had already suggested it. " It would seem," she writes, " as if Christian Science were engirdling the earth. London lords and ladies throng to learn its teachings, it is in the White House of our national capital, in Windsor Castle, England, and the leading minds in almost every Christian land are adopting its essential theo-

THE FIRST CHURCH OF CHRIST, SCIENTIST, BOSTON

The Mother Church

logical points. . . . As it is, if you were a candidate for the Presidency, mayhap I could give you one hundred thousand votes for the chair in Washington, D. C." While Mrs. Eddy was working out her larger policy she did not forget the little things. The manufacture of Christian Science jewelry was at one time a thriving business, conducted by the J. C. Derby Company of Concord. Christian Science emblems and Mrs. Eddy's " favourite flower " were made up into cuff-buttons, rings, brooches, watches, and pendants, varying in price from $325 to $2.50. The sale of the Christian Science teaspoons was especially profitable. The " Mother spoon," an ordinary silver spoon, sold for $5.00. Mrs. Eddy's portrait was embossed upon it, a picture of Pleasant View, Mrs. Eddy's signature, and the motto, " Not Matter but Mind Satisfieth." Mrs. Eddy stimulated the sale of this spoon by inserting the following request in the *Journal*: [6]

On each of these most beautiful spoons is a motto in bas relief that every person on earth needs to hold in thought. Mother requests that Christian Scientists shall not ask to be informed what this motto is, but each Scientist shall purchase at least one spoon, and those who can afford it, one dozen spoons, that their families may read this motto at every meal, and their guests be made partakers of its simple truth.

MARY BAKER G. EDDY.

The above-named spoons are sold by the Christian Science Souvenir Company, Concord, N. H., and will soon be on sale at the Christian Science reading rooms throughout the country.

Mrs. Eddy's picture was another fruitful source of revenue. The copyright for this is still owned by the Derby Company. This portrait is known as the " authorised " photograph of Mrs. Eddy. It was sold for years as a genuine photograph of Mrs.

---

[6] February, 1899.

Eddy, but it is admitted now at Christian Science salesrooms
that this picture is a " composite." The cheapest sells for one
dollar. When they were ready for sale, in May, 1899, Mrs.
Eddy, in the *Journal* of that date, announced:

It is with pleasure I certify that after months of incessant toil and
at great expense Mr. Henry P. Moore, and Mr. J. C. Derby of Concord,
N. H., have brought out a likeness of me far superior to the one they
offered for sale last November. The portrait they have now perfected
I cordially endorse. Also I declare their sole right to the making and
exclusive sale of the duplicates of said portrait.

I simply ask that those who love me purchase this portrait.

MARY BAKER EDDY.

The material prosperity of the Mother Church continued and
the congregation soon outgrew the original building. At the
June communion in 1902 ten thousand Christian Scientists were
present. In the business meeting which followed they pledged
themselves, " with startling grace," as Mrs. Eddy put it, to
raise two million dollars, or any part of that sum which should
be needed, to build an annex.

In the late spring of 1906 the enormous addition to the
Mother Church—the " excelsior extension," as Mrs. Eddy calls
it—was completed, and it was dedicated at the annual communion, June 10, of that year. The original building was in
the form of a cross, so Mrs. Eddy had the new addition built
with a dome to represent a crown. The auditorium is capable
of holding five thousand people; the walls are decorated with
texts signed " Jesus, the Christ " and " Mary Baker G. Eddy "
these names standing side by side.

CHAPTER XXV

GEORGE WASHINGTON GLOVER—MRS. EDDY'S SON BRINGS AN
ACTION AGAINST LEADING CHRISTIAN SCIENTISTS—WITH-
DRAWAL OF THE SUIT—MRS. EDDY MOVES FROM CONCORD,
N. H., TO NEWTON, MASS.

AMONG the mistakes of Mrs. Eddy's early life must be
accounted her indifference to her only child, George Washington Glover. Mrs. Eddy's first husband died six months after
their marriage, and the son was not born until three months
after his father's death. When he was a baby, living with
Mrs. Glover in his aunt's house, his mother's indifference to
him was such as to cause comment in her family and indignation
on the part of her father, Mark Baker.[1] The symptoms of
serious nervous disorder so conspicuous in Mrs. Eddy's young
womanhood—the exaggerated hysteria, the anæsthesia, the
mania for being rocked and swung—are sometimes accompa-
ned by a lack of maternal feeling, and the absence of it in Mrs.
Eddy must be considered, like her lack of the sense of smell,
a defect of constitution rather than a vice of character.

After he went West with the Cheneys in 1857, George Glover
did not see his mother again until 1879. He was then living
in Minnesota, a man of thirty-five, when he received a telegram
from Mrs. Eddy, dated from Lynn, and asking him to meet

---

[1] For a full account of Mrs. Eddy's separation from her son, see Chapter II.

her immediately in Cincinnati. This was the time when Mrs. Eddy believed that mesmerism was overwhelming her in Lynn; that every stranger she met in the streets, and even inanimate objects, were hostile to her, and that she must " flee " from the hypnotists (Kennedy and Spofford) to save her cause and her life. Unable to find any trace of his mother in Cincinnati, George Glover telegraphed to the Chief of Police in Lynn. Some days later he received another telegram from his mother, directing him to meet her in Boston. He went to Boston, and found that Mrs. Eddy and her husband, Asa G. Eddy, had left Lynn for a time and were staying in Boston at the house of Mrs. Clara Choate. Glover remained in Boston for some time and then returned to his home in the West.

George Glover's longest stay in Boston was in 1888, when he brought his family and spent the winter in Chelsea. His relations with his mother were then of a friendly but very formal nature. In the autumn, when he first proposed going to Boston, his plan was to spend a few months with his mother. Mrs. Eddy, however, wrote him that she had no room for him in her house and positively forbade him to come. Mrs. Eddy's letter reads as follows:

> Massachusetts Metaphysical College.
> Rev. Mary B. G. Eddy, President.
> No. 571 Columbus ave.
> Boston, Oct. 31, 1887

DEAR GEORGE: Yours received. I am surprised that you think of coming to visit me when I live in a schoolhouse and have no room that I can let even a boarder into.

I use the whole of my rooms and am at work in them more or less all the time.

Besides this I have all I can meet without receiving company. I must have quiet in my house, and it will not be pleasant for you in Boston the Choates are doing all they can by falsehood, and public shames, such as advertising a college of her own within a few doors of mine when she is a disgraceful woman and known to be, I am going to give up my lease when this class is over, and cannot pay your board nor give you a single dollar now. I am alone, and you never would come to me when I called for you, and now I cannot have you come.

I want quiet and Christian life alone with God, when I can find intervals for a little rest. You are not what I had hoped to find you, and I am changed. The world, the flesh and evil I am at war with, and if any one comes to me it must be to help me and not to hinder me in this warfare. If you will stay away from me until I get through with my public labour then I will send for you and hope to then have a home to take you to.

As it now is, I have none, and you will injure me by coming to Boston at this time more than I have room to state in a letter. I asked you to come to me when my husband died and I so much needed some one to help me. You refused to come then in my great needs, and I then gave up ever thinking of you in that line. Now I have a clerk [2] who is a pure-minded Christian, and two girls to assist me in the college. These are all that I can have under this roof.

If you come after getting this letter I shall feel you have no regard for my interest or feelings, which I hope not to be obliged to feel.

Boston is the last place in the world for you or your family. When I retire from business and into private life, then I can receive you if you are reformed, but not otherwise. I say this to you, not to any one else. I would not injure you any more than myself. As ever sincerely,

M. B. G. Eddy.

After Mrs. Eddy retired to Pleasant View, neither her son nor his family were permitted to visit her, and, when they came East, they experienced a good deal of difficulty in seeing her at all. Mr. Glover believed that his letters to his mother were sometimes answered by Mr. Frye, and that some of his letters never reached his mother at all. Mr. Glover states that he finally sent his mother a letter by express, with instructions to the Concord agent that it was to be delivered to her in person, and to no one else. He was notified that Mrs. Eddy could not receive the letter except through her secretary, Calvin Frye.

---

[2] Calvin Frye.

January 2, 1907, Mr. Glover and his daughter, Mary Baker Glover, were permitted to have a brief interview with Mrs. Eddy at Pleasant View. Mr. Glover states that he was shocked at his mother's physical condition and alarmed by the rambling incoherent nature of her conversation. In talking to him she made the old charges and the old complaints: " people " had been stealing her " things " (as she used to say they did in Lynn); people wanted to kill her; two carriage horses had been presented to her which, had she driven behind them, would have run away and injured her—they had been sent, she thought, for that especial purpose.

After this interview Mr. Glover and his daughter went to Washington, D. C., to ask legal advice from ex-Senator William E. Chandler. While there Mr. Glover received the following letter from his mother:

PLEASANT VIEW, CONCORD, N. H., Jan. 11, 1907.

MY DEAR SON: The enemy to Christian Science is by the wickedest powers of hypnotism trying to do me all the harm possible by acting on the minds of people to make them lie about me and my family. In view of all this I herein and hereby ask this favour of you. I have done for you what I could, and never to my recollection have I asked but once before this a favour of my only child. Will you send to me by express all the letters of mine that I have written to you? This will be a great comfort to your mother if you do it. Send all—ALL of them. Be sure of that. If you will do this for me I will make you and Mary some presents of value, I assure you. Let no one but Mary and your lawyer, Mr. Wilson, know what I herein write to Mary and you. With love,

MOTHER, M. B. G. EDDY.

Mr. Glover refused to give up his letters, and on March 1, 1907, he began, by himself and others as next friends, an action in Mrs. Eddy's behalf against ten prominent Christian Scientists, among whom were Calvin Frye, Alfred Farlow, and the officers of the Mother Church in Boston. This action was brought in the Superior Court of New Hampshire. Mr. Glover asked for an adjudication that Mrs. Eddy was incompetent, through age and failing faculties, to manage her estate; that a receiver of her property be appointed; and that the various defendants named be required to account for alleged misuse of her property. Six days later Mrs. Eddy met this action by declaring a trusteeship for the control of her estate. The trustees named were responsible men, gave bond for $500,000, and their trusteeship was to last during Mrs. Eddy's lifetime. In August Mr. Glover withdrew his suit.

This action brought by her son, which undoubtedly caused Mrs. Eddy a great deal of annoyance, was another result of those indirect methods to which she has always clung so persistently. When her son appealed to her for financial aid, she chose, instead of meeting him with a candid refusal, to tell him that she was not allowed to use her own money as she wished, that Mr. Frye made her account for every penny, etc., etc. Mr. Glover made the mistake of taking his mother at her word. He brought his suit upon the supposition that his mother was the victim of designing persons who controlled her affairs—without consulting her, against her wish, and to their own advantage—a hypothesis which his attorneys entirely failed to establish.

This lawsuit disclosed one interesting fact, namely, that while in 1893 securities of Mrs. Eddy amounting to $100,000 were brought to Concord, and in January, 1899, she had $236,-200, and while in 1907 she had about a million dollars' worth of taxable property, Mrs. Eddy in 1901 returned a signed statement to the assessors at Concord that the value of her taxable property amounted to about $19,000. This statement was sworn to year after year by Mr. Frye.

About a month after Mr. Glover's suit was withdrawn, Mrs. Eddy purchased, through Robert Walker, a Christian Scientist real-estate agent in Chicago, the old Lawrence mansion in Newton, a suburb of Boston. The house was remodelled and enlarged in great haste and at a cost which must almost have equalled the original purchase price, $100,000. All the arrangements were conducted with secrecy, and very few Christian Scientists knew that it was Mrs. Eddy's intention to occupy this house until she was there in person.

On Sunday, January 26, 1908, at two o'clock in the afternoon, Mrs. Eddy, attended by nearly a score of her followers, boarded a special train at Concord. Extraordinary precautions were taken to prevent accidents. A pilot-engine preceded the locomotive which drew Mrs. Eddy's special train, and the train was followed by a third engine to prevent the possibility of a rear-end collision. Dr. Alpheus B. Morrill, a second cousin of Mrs. Eddy and a practising physician of Concord, was of her party. Mrs. Eddy's face was heavily veiled when she took the train at Concord and when she alighted at Chestnut Hill station. Her carriage arrived at the Lawrence house late in the afternoon, and she was lifted out and carried into the house by one of her male attendants.

Mrs. Eddy's new residence is a fine old stone mansion which has been enlarged without injury to its original dignity. The grounds cover an area of about twelve acres and are well wooded. The house now contains about twenty-five rooms.

There is an electric elevator adjoining Mrs. Eddy's private apartments and two large vaults have been built into the house. Since her arrival at Chestnut Hill, Mrs. Eddy, upon one of her daily drives, saw for the first time the new building which completes the Mother Church and which, like the original modest structure, is a memorial to her.

There are many reasons why Mrs. Eddy may have decided to leave Concord. But the extreme haste with which her new residence was got ready for her—a body of several hundred labourers was kept busy upon it all day, and another shift, equally large, worked all night by the aid of arc-lights—suggests that, even if practical considerations brought about Mrs. Eddy's change of residence, her extreme impatience may have resulted from a more personal motive. It is very probable that Mrs. Eddy left Concord for the same reason that she left Boston years ago: because she felt that malicious animal magnetism was becoming too strong for her there. The action brought by her son in Concord the previous summer she attributed entirely to the work of mesmerists who were supposed to be in control of her son's mind. Mrs. Eddy always believed that this strange miasma of evil had a curious tendency to become localised: that certain streets, mail-boxes, telegraph-offices, vehicles, could be totally suborned by these invisible currents of hatred and ill-will that had their source in the minds of her enemies and continually encircled her. She believed that in this way an entire neighbourhood could·be made inimical to her, and it is quite possible that, after the recent litigation in Concord, she felt that the place had become saturated with mesmerism and that she would never again find peace there.

CHAPTER XXVI

TRAINING THE VINE—HOW MRS. EDDY HAS ORGANISED HER CHURCH — HER MANAGEMENT AND DISCIPLINE — THE CHURCH MANUAL—RECENT MODIFICATIONS IN CHRISTIAN SCIENCE PRACTICE—MEMBERSHIP OF THE CHURCH—PRACTICAL RESULTS OF MRS. EDDY'S LIFE-WORK

THE years since 1892 Mrs. Eddy has spent in training her church in the way she desires it to go, in making it more and more her own, and in issuing by-law after by-law to restrict her followers in their church privileges and to guide them in their daily walk. Mrs. Eddy, one must remember, was fifty years of age before she knew what she wanted to do; sixty when she bethought herself of the most effective way to do it,— by founding a church,—and seventy when she achieved her greatest triumph—the reorganisation and personal control of the Mother Church. But she did not stop there. Between her seventieth and eightieth year, and even up to the present time, she has displayed remarkable ingenuity in disciplining her church and its leaders, and resourcefulness and energy in the prosecution of her plans.

Mrs. Eddy's system of church government was not devised in a month or a year, but grew, by-law on by-law, to meet new emergencies and situations. To attain the end she desired it was necessary to keep fifty or sixty thousand people working as if the church were the first object in their lives ; to encourage hundreds of these to adopt church-work as their profession and make it their only chance of worldly success ; and yet to hold all this devotion and energy in subservience to Mrs. Eddy herself and to prevent any one of these healers, or preachers, or teachers from attaining any marked personal prominence and from acquiring a personal following.   The church was to have all the vigour of spontaneous growth, but was to grow only as Mrs. Eddy permitted and to confine itself to the trellis she had built for it.

Naturally, the first danger lay in the pastors of her branch churches.   Mrs. Stetson and Mrs. Laura Lathrop had built up strong churches in New York ; Mrs. Ewing was pastor of a flourishing church in Chicago ; Mrs. Leonard of another in Brooklyn ; Mrs. Williams in Buffalo ; Mrs. Steward in Toronto ; Mr. Norcross in Denver.   These pastors naturally became leaders among the Christian Scientists in their respective communities, and came to be regarded as persons authorised to expound *Science and Health* and the doctrines of Christian Science.   Such a state of things Mrs. Eddy considered dangerous, not only because of the personal influence the pastor might acquire over his flock, but because a pastor might, even without intending to do so, give a personal colour to his interpretation of her words.   In his sermon he might expand her texts and improvise upon her themes until gradually his hearers would come to accept his own opinions for Mrs. Eddy's.   The church in Toronto might come to emphasise doctrines which the church in Denver did not ; here was a possible beginning of differing denominations.

So, as Mrs. Eddy splendidly puts it, " In 1895 I ordained the Bible and *Science and Health* with *Key to the Scriptures,* as the Pastor, on this planet, of all the churches of the Christian Science Denomination." In the *Journal* of April, 1895, she announced, without previous warning, that there were to be no more preachers; that each church should have, instead, a First and a Second Reader, and that the Sunday sermon was to consist of extracts from the Bible and from *Science and Health,* read to the congregation. In the beginning the First Reader read from the Bible and the Second Reader from Mrs. Eddy's book. But this Mrs. Eddy soon changed. The First Reader now reads from *Science and Health,* and the Second reads those passages of the Bible which Mrs. Eddy selects as correlative. This service, Mrs. Eddy declares, was " authorised by Christ." [1]

When Mrs. Eddy issued this injunction, every Christian Science preacher promptly and silently obeyed it. Many of them kissed the rod. L. P. Norcross, one of the deposed pastors, wrote humbly in the August *Journal:*

Did any one expect such a revelation, such a new departure would be given? No, not in the way it came. . . . . A former pastor of the Mother Church once remarked that the day would dawn when the current methods of preaching and worship would disappear, but he could not discern how. . . . Such disclosures are too high for us to perceive. *To One alone did the message come.*

Mrs. Eddy had no grudge against her pastors, and many of

---

[1] In a notice to the churches, 1897, Mrs. Eddy says:
" The Bible and the Christian Science text-book are our only preachers. We shall now read scriptural texts and their co-relative passages from our text-book—these comprise our sermon. The canonical writings, together with the word of our text-book, corroborating and explaining the Bible texts in their denominational, spiritual import and application to all ages, past, present, and future, constitute a sermon undivorced from truth, uncontaminated or fettered by human hypotheses and authorised by Christ."

them were made Readers in the churches which they had built and in which they had formerly preached.

The " Reader " is well hedged in with by-laws and his duties and limitations are clearly defined:

He is to read parts of *Science and Health* aloud at every service.

He cannot read from a manuscript or from a transcribed copy, but must read from the book itself.

He is, Mrs. Eddy says, to be " well read and well educated," but he shall at no time make any remarks explanatory of the passages which he reads.

Before commencing to read from Mrs. Eddy's book " he shall distinctly announce its full title and give the author's name."

A Reader must not be a leader in the church.   Besides these restrictions there is a by-law which provides that Mrs. Eddy can, without explanation, remove any reader at any time that she sees fit to do so.[2]

In the same number of the *Journal* in which she dismissed her pastors and substituted Readers, Mrs. Eddy stated, in an open letter, that her students would find in that issue " the completion, as I now think, of the Divine directions sent out to the churches."   But it was not the completion.   By the summer of 1902 Septimus J. Hanna, First Reader of the Mother Church in Boston, had become, without the liberty to preach or to " make remarks," so influential that Mrs. Eddy made a new ruling that the Reader's term of office should be limited

---

[2] For the text of these by-laws see *Christian Science Manual* (1904), Articles IV and XXIII.

to three years,[3] and, Mr. Hanna's term then being up, he was put into the lecture field. The highest dignity, then, that any Christian Scientist could hope for was to be chosen as Reader for three years at a comfortable salary.

Why, it has often been asked, did the more influential pastors —people with a large personal following, like Mrs. Stetson— consent to resign their pulpits in the first place and afterward to be stripped of privilege after privilege? Some of them, of course, submitted because they believed that Mrs. Eddy possessed " Divine Wisdom " ; others because they remembered what had happened to dissenters before them. Of all those who had broken away from Mrs. Eddy's authority, not one had attained to anything like her success or material prosperity, while many had followed wandering fires and had come to nothing. Christian Science leaders had staked their fortunes upon the hypothesis that Mrs. Eddy possessed " divine wisdom " ; it was as expounders of this wisdom that they had obtained their influence and built up their churches. To rebel against the authority of Mrs. Eddy's wisdom would be to discredit themselves ; to discredit Mrs. Eddy's wisdom would have been to destroy their whole foundation. To claim an understanding and an inspiration equal to Mrs. Eddy's would have been to cheapen and invalidate everything that gave Christian Science an advantage over other religions. Had they once denied the Revelation and the Revelator upon which their church was founded, the whole structure would have fallen in upon them. If Mrs. Eddy's

---

[3] Mrs. Eddy stated in regard to this ruling that it was to have immediate effect only in the Mother Church, adding: "Doubtless the churches adopting this by-law will discriminate its adaptability to their conditions. But if now is not the time the branch churches can wait for the favoured moment to act on this subject."

intelligence were not divine in one case, who would be able to say that it was in another? If they could not accept Mrs. Eddy's wisdom when she said " there shall be no pastors," how could they persuade other people to accept it when she said " there is no matter "? It was clear, even to those who writhed under the restrictions imposed upon them, that they must stand or fall with Mrs. Eddy's Wisdom, and that to disobey it was to compromise their own careers. Even in the matter of getting on in the world, it was better to be a doorkeeper in the Mother Church than to dwell in the tents of the " mental healers. "

Probably it was harder for Mrs. Stetson to retire from the pastorship than for any one else. Mrs. Stetson had gone to New York when Christian Science was practically unknown there, and from poor and small beginnings had built up a rich and powerful church. But, when the command came, she stepped out of the pulpit she had built. She is to-day probably the most influential person, after Mrs. Eddy, in the Christian Science body. In 1907 the New York *World* published several interviews with persons who asserted that they believed Mrs. Eddy to be controlled by a clique of Christian Scientists who were acting for Mrs. Stetson's interests. In June Mrs. Stetson wrote Mrs. Eddy a letter which was printed in the *Christian Science Sentinel* and which read in part:

BOSTON, Mass., June 9, 1907.

MY PRECIOUS LEADER:—I am glad I know that I am in the hands of God, not of men. These reports are only the revival of a lie which I have not heard for a long time. It is a renewed attack upon me and my loyal students, to turn me from following in the footsteps of Christ by making another attempt to dishearten me and make me weary of the struggle to demonstrate my trust in God to deliver me from the "accuser of our brethren." It is a diabolical attempt to separate me from you, as my Leader and Teacher. . . .

Oh, Dearest, it is such a lie! No one who knows us can believe this. It is vicarious atonement. Has the enemy no more argument to use, that it has to go back to this? It is exhausting its resources and I hope the end is near. You know my love for you, beloved; and my students love you as their Leader and Teacher; they follow your teachings and lean on the "sustaining infinite." They who refuse to accept you as God's messenger, or ignore the message which you bring, will not get up by some other way, but will come short of salvation. . . .

Dearly beloved, we are not ascending out of sense as fast as we desire, but we are trusting in God to put off the false and put on the Christ. This lie cannot disturb you nor me. I love you and my students love you, and we never touch you with such a thought as is mentioned.

Lovingly your child,

AUGUSTA E. STETSON.

But Mrs. Stetson's protestations of loyalty availed her nothing. She was more than ever kept under surveillance by Mrs. Eddy's directors, and when at last, in December, 1908, it became known that Mrs. Stetson had formed elaborate plans to extend her church system in New York, Mrs. Eddy was acutely alarmed. Mrs. Stetson, with her church behind her, had, without consulting Mrs. Eddy it would seem, completed her plans for building a magnificent new church on Riverside Drive, New York. This church, so it was announced, was to "rival in beauty of architecture any other religious structure in America," and it was to be built by Mrs. Stetson, and managed by her and an advisory board. Although Mrs. Stetson explained that the proposed new church would be organised regularly as a branch of the Mother Church in Boston and in accordance with the regulations laid down by Mrs. Eddy in the *Church Manual*, it was evident that Mrs. Eddy regarded the plan as a scheme of Mrs. Stetson's to rival the great Boston temple and to build up a church system of her own.

Mrs. Eddy lost not a moment in condemning the project. Her daily newspaper, the *Christian Science Monitor* of Boston, and her church organ, the *Christian Science Sentinel*, which reach the entire Christian Science membership, announced editorially that Mrs. Eddy was not pleased " with what purport to be plans of First Church of Christ Scientist of New York City, for she learned of this proposed rival to the Mother Church for the first time, from the daily press." " Three leading facts," continued the editorial, " remain immortal in the history of Christian Science, namely:

1. This Science is already established, and it has the support of all true Christian Scientists throughout the world.

2. Any competition or any rivalry in Christian Science is abnormal, and will expose and explode itself.

3. Any attempt at rivalry or superiority in Christian Science is unchristian; therefore it is unscientific. The great Teacher said: " As ye would that men should do to you, do ye."

Thoughtful Christian Scientists are profoundly grateful to their beloved Leader, Mrs. Eddy, because in her far-seeing wisdom she has ordained The First Church of Christ, Scientist, in Boston, Mass., already famous for originating reforms, as The Mother Church of Christian Science, and all other churches in the denomination as branches of the parent Vine. Says the *Church Manual*: " In its relation to other Christian Science churches, in its by-laws and self-government, The Mother Church stands alone; it occupies a postion that no other church can fill " (Art. xxiii., Sec. 3). It is a fact of general observation that in proportion as branch churches adhere loyally to The Mother Church, and obey implicitly its by-laws, they bear abundant fruit in healing the sick and sinful.

Machinery was set in motion at headquarters to restrain and repress Mrs. Stetson's activities. In the summer of 1909 a new by-law was issued. It provided that teachers and practitioners could no longer maintain offices or rooms in the churches, in the reading-rooms, or in rooms connected therewith. It was known by those who understood the situation that this ruling was aimed directly at Mrs. Stetson. With other healers of her congregation she had maintained handsome offices in the First Church in New York, where she healed patients, instructed classes and individuals, and daily met her friends and co-workers. Mrs. Stetson obeyed this by-law. She merely retreated to her house, which adjoins her church and is connected with it by a covered passage, and conducted her work as before.

Mrs. Eddy, however, was not to be thus easily defeated. She was determined that Mrs. Stetson, whom she considered as an open rival, should be removed as such, and that her circle should be broken up. During the summer and early autumn of 1909 Mrs. Stetson was brought before the Mother Church directors in Boston and closely questioned, and many of her students were also examined before this court-martial. It was decided that Mrs. Stetson must be disciplined, and she was officially deprived of her rank as a healer and as a teacher. She was forbidden to teach or practise Christian Science until she had proved her fitness for such work. She was, therefore, placed on a three years' probation, at the conclusion of which, if her conduct has been exemplary and if she has met Mrs. Eddy's requirements as to loyalty, she may, if Mrs. Eddy sees fit, again be permitted to teach and practise. The reasons given by the directors for reducing Mrs. Stetson were: erroneous teaching of Christian Science; the exercise of undue influence over her students, which tended to hinder their moral and spiritual growth; turning the attention of her students to herself and away from Divine principle; teaching and practising contrary to *Science and Health;* and finally, that " Mrs. Stetson attempts to control and to injure persons by mental means, this being utterly contrary to the teachings of Christian Science."

It is interesting to note that, in dealing with the case of Mrs. Stetson, Mrs. Eddy once again resorted to the faithful weapon which had never failed her in all her executions of the past— the time-worn charge of mental malpractice.

Her pastors having been satisfactorily dealt with, the next danger Mrs. Eddy saw lay in her teachers and " academies." Mrs. Eddy had found, of course, that a great many Christian Scientists wished to make their living out of their new religion; that possibility, indeed, was one of the most effective advantages which Christian Science had to offer over other religions. In the early days of the church, while Mrs. Eddy was still instructing classes in Christian Science at her " college," teaching was a much more remunerative business than healing. Mrs. Eddy charged each student $300 for a primary course of seven lessons, and the various Christian Science " institutes " and " academies " about the country charged from $100 to $200 per student. So long as Mrs. Eddy was herself teaching and never took patients, she could not well forbid other teachers to do likewise. But after she retired to Concord, she took the teachers in hand. Mrs. Eddy knew that Christian Science was propagated and that converts were made, not through doctrine, but through cures. She had found that out in the beginning, when Richard Kennedy's cures brought her her first success. She knew, too, that teaching Christian Science was a much easier profession than healing by it, and that the teacher risked no encounter with the law. Since teaching was both easier and more remunerative it would be natural for teachers to multiply at the sacrifice of the healers, and Mrs. Eddy discouraged this by cutting down the teacher's fee, and limiting the number of pupils which one teacher might instruct in a year. By 1904 Mrs. Eddy had got the teacher's fee down to fifty dollars per student, and a teacher was not permitted to teach more than thirty students a year. From 1903 to 1906 all teaching was suspended under the by-law " Healing better than teaching."

In the fall of 1895 Mrs. Eddy issued her instructions to the churches in the form of a volume entitled the *Church Manual of the First Church of Christ, Scientist, in Boston, Mass.* The by-laws herein contained, she says, " were impelled by a power not one's own, were written at different dates, as occasion required." This book is among Mrs. Eddy's copyrighted works, and has now been through more than forty editions. Some of the by-laws in the earlier editions are perplexing.

We find that " Careless comparison or irreverent reference to Christ Jesus, is abnormal in a Christian Scientist and prohibited." [4] It is probable that no Christian church had ever before found it necessary to make such a prohibition.

The Manual, however, is chiefly interesting as an exposition of Mrs. Eddy's method of church government and as an inventory of her personal prerogatives. Never was a title more misleadingly modest than Mrs. Eddy's title of " Pastor Emeritus " of the Mother Church.

Next to Mrs. Eddy in authority is the Board of Directors, who were chosen by Mrs. Eddy and who are subject to her in

[4] *Church Manual* (11th ed.), Article XXXII.

all their official acts. Any one of these directors can at any time be dismissed upon Mrs. Eddy's request, and the vacancy can be filled only by a candidate whom she has approved. All the church business is transacted by these directors,—no other members of the church may be present at the business meetings, —and at any time Mrs. Eddy's request will remove them. The members of this board are pledged to secrecy; they " shall neither report the discussions of this Board, nor those with Mrs. Eddy." [5]

These directors are Mrs. Eddy's executive self, created by her and committed to silence. Their chief duties are to elect to office whomsoever Mrs. Eddy appoints, and to hold their peace.

The President of the church is annually elected by the directors, the election being subject to Mrs. Eddy's approval. [6]

The First and Second Readers are elected every third year by the directors, subject to Mrs. Eddy's approval, but she can remove a Reader either from the Mother Church or from any of the branch churches whenever she sees fit and without explanation. [7]

The Clerk and Treasurer of the church are elected once a year by the directors, subject to Mrs. Eddy's approval. [8]

Executive Members: Prior to 1903 these were known as First Members. They shall not be less than fifty in number, nor more than one hundred. They must have certain qualifications (such as residing within five hundred miles of Boston), and they must hold a meeting once a year and special meetings at

---

[5] *Church Manual* (43d ed.), Article I, Sec. 5.
[6] *Ibid.* (43d ed.), Article I, Sec. 2.
[7] *Ibid.* (43d ed.), Article I, Sec. 4. *Ibid.* (11th ed.), Article XXIII, Sec. 2.
[8] *Ibid.* (43d ed.), Article I, Sec. 3.

Mrs. Eddy's call. They have no powers and no duties [9] and they are not allowed to be present at the business meetings of the church. The manner of their election is unusual. The by-laws state that a member can be made an Executive Member only after a letter is received by the directors from Mrs. Eddy requesting them to make said persons Executive Members; and then, " they shall be elected by the unanimous vote of the Board of Directors." [10]

This " executive " board is a form only, and membership on it is merely a mark of Mrs. Eddy's personal favour. To her followers, however, this is sufficient reason for its existence, and they are proud to be called members of it.

Although Mrs. Eddy has made a by-law which says that the branch churches shall have " local self-government," she gives special instructions in the Manual as to what the branch churches may or may not do. The *Church Manual* is closely followed by all the branch churches, and as practically all the members of the branch churches are also members of the Mother Church, it is the duty of each to obey all the requirements of the Manual.

A branch church can only be organised by a member of the Mother Church. [11]

A branch church may not use the article " the " in its title. Only the Mother Church may employ it. [12]

No conference of branch churches shall be held except the annual conference at the Mother Church. [13]

---

[9] Formerly the Executive Members were permitted to fix the salaries of the Readers, but in the last edition of the *Manual* this privilege has been withdrawn.
[10] *Church Manual* (43d ed.), Article VI.
[11] *Ibid.* (1904), Article XXVIII.
[12] *Ibid.* (1904), Article XXVIII.
[13] *Ibid.* (1904), Article XXVIII.

A branch church may not have other church branches, nor shall it be organised with Executive Members.[14]

Communion time for the branch churches is fixed by the Manual.[15]

In laying its corner-stone, a branch church must not permit a " large gathering of people." [16]

The services of the branch churches are definitely prescribed; they are to consist of music, Mrs. Eddy's prayer, and oral readings from *Science and Health* and the Bible.

Mrs. Eddy may appoint or remove—without explanation—the Readers of the branch churches at any time.[17]

The branch churches may never have comments or remarks made by their Readers, either upon passages from *Science and Health* or from the Bible.[18]

The branch churches may have lectures only by lecturers whom Mrs. Eddy has appointed in the usual way—through the " vote " of her Board of Directors.[19]   And the lecture must have passed censorship.[20]

After listening to such a lecture, the members of the branch churches are not permitted to give a reception or to meet for social intercourse.   Mrs. Eddy tells them to " depart in quiet thought." [21]   It seems probable that this by-law was devised for the spiritual good of the lecturer.   If fêted or made much of after his discourse he might easily become puffed up with pride of place.

---

[14] *Church Manual* (1904), Article XXVIII.
[15] *Ibid.* (1904), Article XXVIII.
[16] *Ibid.* (1904), Article XXVIII.
[17] *Ibid.* (11th ed.), Article XXIII.
[18] *Ibid.* (43d ed.), Article IV.
[19] *Ibid.* (43d ed.), Article XXXIV.
[20] *Ibid.* (43d ed.), Article XXXIV.
[21] *Ibid.* (43d ed.), Article XXXIV.

Services in the branch churches, as in the Mother Church, are limited to the Sunday morning and evening readings from the Bible and *Science and Health,* the Wednesday evening experience meetings, and to the communion service. (In the Mother Church this occurs but once a year, in the branch churches twice.) There is no baptismal service,[22] no marriage or burial service, and weddings and funerals are never conducted in any of the Christian Science churches.

Included in the Mother Church organisation are the Publication Committee, the Christian Science Publishing Society, the Board of Lectureship, the Board of Missionaries, and the Board of Education, all under Mrs. Eddy's personal control.

The manager of the Publication Committee, at present Mr. Alfred Farlow, is " elected " annually by the Board of Directors under Mrs. Eddy's instructions. His salary is to be not less than $5,000 a year. This Publication Committee is a press bureau, consisting of a manager with headquarters in Boston and of various branch committees throughout the field. It is the duty of a member of this committee, wherever he resides, to reply promptly through the press to any criticism of Christian Science or of Mrs. Eddy which may be made in his part of the country, and to insert in the newspapers of his territory as much matter favourable to Christian Science as they will print. In replying to criticism this bureau will, if necessary, pay the regular advertising rate for the publication of their statements. The members of this committee, after having written and published their articles in defence of Christian Science, are also

---

[22] When the Boston church was holding its services in Chickering Hall, Mrs. Eddy baptised a class of children. No water was used in the ceremony. This was the only baptismal service ever held in a Christian Science church.

responsible, says the Manual, " for having the papers containing these articles circulated in large quantities." This press agency has been extremely effective in pushing the interests of Christian Science, in keeping it before the public, and in building up a desirable legendry around Mrs. Eddy.

The Christian Science Publishing Society is conducted for the purpose of publishing and marketing Mrs. Eddy's works and the three Christian Science periodicals, the *Christian Science Journal*, the *Christian Science Sentinel*, and *Der Christian Science Herold*. It is managed and controlled by a Board of Trustees appointed by Mrs. Eddy, and the net profits of the business are turned over semi-annually to the treasurer of the Mother Church. The manager and editors are appointed for one year only, and must be elected or reëlected by a vote of the directors *and* " the consent of the Pastor Emeritus, given in her own handwriting." The Manual also states that a person who is not accepted by Mrs. Eddy as suitable shall in no manner be connected with publishing her books or editing her periodicals.

Until 1898 any Christian Scientist could give public talks or lectures upon the doctrines of his faith, but in January of that year Mrs. Eddy withdrew this privilege. She appointed a Board of Lectureship, carefully selecting each member and assigning each to a certain district. In this work she placed several of her most influential men, among whom was Septimus J. Hanna. As itinerant lecturers these men could not very well build up a dangerously strong personal following, and they could very ably set forth the Christian Science doctrines. These lecturers are elected annually, subject to Mrs. Eddy's approval.

Their representative lectures must be censored by the clerk of the Mother Church. The Manual stipulates that these lectures must " bear testimony to the facts pertaining to the life of the Pastor Emeritus."

Seven missionaries are elected annually by the Board of Directors, and their duties are to fill vacancies in pulpits and to " correctly propagate " Christian Science wherever it is most needed.

The Board of Education consists of three members, the President, Vice-President, and a teacher. Mrs. Eddy is the permanent President—unless, says the Manual, she sees fit to " resign over her own signature." The Vice-President and teacher are elected from time to time, " subject to the approval of the Pastor Emeritus."

It is not easy to become a member of the Mother Church. The applicant for admission must read nothing upon metaphysics or religion except Mrs. Eddy's books and the Bible, and his application must be countersigned by one of Mrs. Eddy's loyal students, who is made responsible for the candidate's sincerity. There are many things for which the new member may be expelled after he is once admitted into the church. He may not haunt the roads upon which Mrs. Eddy drives. He may not discuss, lecture upon, or debate upon Christian Science in public without permission from one of her representatives. He must not be a " leader " in the church and must never be called one. He may read only the Bible and Mrs. Eddy's books for religious instruction. He shall not " vilify " the Pastor Emeritus. He must go to Mrs. Eddy's home and serve her in person for one year if she requires it of him. He may not permit his children to believe in Santa Claus—Mrs. Eddy abolished Santa Claus by proclamation in 1904. He may not read or quote from Mrs. Eddy's books without first naming the author. Mrs. Eddy says, in explanation of this by-law: " To pour into the ears of listeners the sacred revelations of Christian Science indiscriminately, or without characterising their origin and thus distinguishing them from the writings of authors who think at random on this subject, is to lose some weight in the scale of right thinking." [23]

A Christian Scientist " shall neither buy, sell nor circulate Christian Science literature which is not correct in its statement," etc., Mrs. Eddy, of course, determining whether or not the statement is correct. He " shall not patronise a publishing house or bookstore that has for sale obnoxious books."

A Christian Scientist may not belong to any club or society, which excludes either sex, Free Masons excepted, outside the Mother Church. Mrs. Eddy says that church organisations are ample for him.[24]

It is indicative of Mrs. Eddy's influence over her followers that when this by-law was issued, less than twenty inquiries (so her secretary announced) were received at Pleasant View. Men resigned from their political, business, and social clubs, women from their literary and patriotic organisations, without a murmur and without a question.

No hymns may be sung in the Mother Church unless they have been approved by Mrs. Eddy, and Mrs. Eddy's hymns must be sung at stated intervals. " If a solo singer in the

---

[23] *Church Manual* (11th ed.), Article XV.
[24] *Ibid.* (43d ed.), Article XXVI.

Mother Church shall either neglect or refuse to sing alone a hymn written by our Leader and Pastor Emeritus, as often as once each month, and oftener if the Directors so direct, a meeting shall be called and the salary of this singer shall be stopped."

Above all these lesser by-laws Mrs. Eddy holds one in which her supreme authority rests. A mesmerist or " mental malpractitioner " is to be excommunicated, and " if the author of *Science and Health* shall bear witness to the offence of mental malpractice, it shall be considered sufficient evidence thereof." [25] The accused can make no defence, and has no appeal. In the matter of hypnotism, Mrs. Eddy's mere word is enough. She has, she says, an unerring instinct by which she can detect hypnotism in any creature:

I possess a spiritual sense of what the malicious mental practitioner is mentally arguing which cannot be deceived; I can discern in the human mind thoughts, motives, and purposes; and neither mental arguments nor psychic power can affect this spiritual insight.[26]

Of late years Mrs. Eddy has shown a disposition to so modify the practice of Christian Science healing as not to conflict with the laws. Christian Scientists formerly treated all diseases, without regard to legal restrictions. But experience has shown Mrs. Eddy that an evasion of the law is regarded by the public as a defiance of the law, and forms a serious obstacle to the spread of Christian Science. It also has involved Christian Scientists constantly in lawsuits.

In March, 1901, Mrs. Eddy announced in the *Journal* that

[25] *Church Manual* (43d ed.), Article XXII, Sec. 4.
[26] *Christian Science History,* by Mary B. G. Eddy (1st ed.), p. 16.

thereafter Christian Scientists must submit to vaccination, and report cases of contagion as required by law.

A year later the teaching and practice of obstetrics was dropped by order of Mrs. Eddy, who gave as the reason, " Obstetrics is not Science, and will not be taught." This was after obstetrics had been taught and practised as " Science " for thirty-two years.

An important change of practice was instituted when, in December, 1902, the *Journal* announced: " Mrs. Eddy advises, until the public thought becomes better acquainted with Christian Science, that Christian Scientists decline to doctor infectious or contagious diseases." On the same subject Mrs. Eddy wrote: " Christian Scientists should be influenced by their own judgment in the taking of a case of malignant disease, they should consider well their ability to cope with the case—and not overlook the fact that there are those lying in wait to catch them in their sayings; neither should they forget that in their practice, whether successful or not, they are not especially protected by law."

Christian Scientists are now permitted to consult with medical practitioners in certain cases. A by-law provides that, " if a member of this church has a patient that he does not heal; and whose case he cannot lawfully diagnose, he may consult with an M.D. on the anatomy involved. And it shall be the privilege of a Christian Scientist to confer with an M.D. on ontology, or the Science of Being."

Christian Scientists are no longer allowed to use the titles, " Reverend," or " Doctor," unless they have received these titles under the laws of the state.

A practitioner is not permitted to sue a patient to recover payment for his services, and he is required to " reasonably reduce " his fee in chronic cases, and in cases where he has not effected a cure.

The result of Mrs. Eddy's planning and training and pruning is that she has built up the largest and most powerful organisation ever founded by any woman in America. Probably no other woman so handicapped—so limited in intellect, so uncertain in conduct, so tortured by hatred and hampered by petty animosities—has ever risen from a state of helplessness and dependence to a position of such power and authority. All that Christian Science comprises to-day—the Mother Church, branch churches, healers, teachers, Readers, boards, committees, societies—are as completely under Mrs. Eddy's control as if she were their temporal as well as their spiritual ruler. The growth of her power has been extensive as well as intensive.

In June, 1907, the membership of the Mother Church, according to the Secretary's report, was 43,876. The membership of the branch churches amounted to 42,846. As members of the branch churches are almost invariably members of the Mother Church as well, there cannot be more than 60,000 Christian Scientists in the world to-day, and the number is probably nearer 50,000.

In June, 1907, there were in all 710 branch churches. Fifty-eight of these are in foreign countries: twenty-five in the Dominion of Canada, fourteen in Great Britain, two in Ireland, four in Australia, one in South Africa, eight in Mexico, two in Germany, one in Holland, and one in France. There are also 295 Christian Science societies, not yet incorporated into churches, thirty of which are in foreign countries.[27]

In reading these figures one must bear in mind the fact that thirty years ago the only Christian Science church in the world was struggling to pay its rent in Boston.

An effective element in the growth of the church is the fact that a considerable proportion of Christian Scientists make their living by their religion, and their worldly fortunes as well as their spiritual comfort are in their church; they must prosper or decline with Christian Science, and they prosecute the cause of their church with all their energies and with entire singleness of purpose. The perfect system under which the church is organised provides for the constant advertising, by the Publication Committee, of the religion, of the church, and of Mrs. Eddy; and this has been perhaps the greatest factor in the growth of the church. There is an impression to-day that the Christian Science church numbers its members by hundreds of thousands; and this impression was created and is continued by the exaggerated statements of Mrs. Eddy herself, and of her leading church officers, and by the insistent work of the Publication Committees.

Christian Science itself presents, superficially, an old and well-worn truth, besides much that is fallacious and absurd; and the secret of its popularity lies in the fact, not that it has played tricks with metaphysical platitudes, but that it has adapted them to the buoyant spirit of the times.

---

[27] In June, 1907, there were 3,515 authorised Christian Science "healers" in the world, 3,268, of whom are practising in the United States, 1 in Alaska, 63 in the Dominion of Canada, 5 in Mexico, 1 in Cuba, 1 in South Africa, 18 in Australia, 1 in China, 105 in England, 5 in Ireland, 9 in Scotland, 7 in France, 15 in Germany, 4 in Holland, 1 in India, 1 in Italy, 1 in the Philippine Islands, 1 in Russia, 1 in South America, 7 in Switzerland.

What Mrs. Eddy has accomplished has been due solely to her own compelling personality. She has never been a dreamer of dreams or a seer of visions, and she has not the mind for deep and searching investigation into any problem. Her genius has been of the eminently practical kind, which can meet and overcome unfavourable conditions by sheer force of energy, and in Mrs. Eddy's case this potency has been accompanied by a remarkable shrewdness, which has had its part in determining her career. Her problem has been, not to work out the theory of mental healing, but to popularise it, and having popularised it, to maintain a personal monopoly of its principle; and the history of Christian Science shows how near she has come to doing this.

Not until Mrs. Eddy met Quimby had she ever known any serious purpose, and although she was superbly equipped by nature to blaze the way for new and bizarre ideas, and was always the first to take up with such irregular and passing notions as mesmerism, clairvoyance, writing-mediumship, etc., she had never produced an original idea on her own account. With Quimby came her opportunity, and once given an actual purpose, Mrs. Eddy, with her unequalled zeal for not letting go of a thing, was at once upon the highroad to success.

For herself, she has won what has always seemed to her most valuable, and what has been from the beginning a crying necessity of her nature: personal ease, an exalted position, and the right to exact homage from the multitude.

For Quimby, she has, and mainly by reason of her ingratitude toward her old benefactor, secured public attention to his theory of mental healing.   Through Dr. Warren F. Evans and Mr. and Mrs. Julius A. Dresser the Quimby idea,[28] previous to the Christian Science interpretation of it, had been slowly and laboriously coming into a limited practice; but with the entrance of Mrs. Eddy into the field, with her extravagant claims of miraculous revelation and her violent methods of procedure, the whole movement received a tremendous impetus; and unconsciously and very much against her will, she has been the most effective agent in promoting Quimbyism as well as Eddyism. For, although it has been one of Mrs. Eddy's chief cares to stem the progress of the rival school, and to raise an impassable barrier between her own cult and that of all other mental healers, it has not disturbed the fact that for practical purposes, Eddyism is simply Quimbyism, overlaid with superstition and ignorance; and the future of Mrs. Eddy's school depends largely upon the willingness of her followers to continue their self-deception on this point, which is the chief requirement of her religion.

Whatever there is of value to the world in Mrs. Eddy's system, lies in the practicality of its healing methods, and the foregoing chapters have shown that Mrs. Eddy realises this,

[28] The reader who is interested in Quimby's teaching and healing is referred to *The True History of Mental Science*, by Julius A. Dresser, published by George H. Ellis, 272 Congress Street, Boston.

Dr. Warren F. Evans, in his book, *Mental Medicine*, published three years before the first edition of *Science and Health*, said: Disease being in its root a *wrong belief*, change that belief and we cure the disease.   By faith we are thus made whole.   There is a law here which the world will sometime understand and use in the cure of the diseases that afflict mankind.   The late Dr. Quimby, of Portland, one of the most successful healers of this or any age, embraced this view of the nature of disease, and by a long succession of the most remarkable cures, effected by psychopathic remedies, at the same time proved the truth of the theory and the efficiency of that mode of treatment. Had he lived in a remote age or country, the wonderful facts which occurred in his practice would now have been deemed either mythical or miraculous.   He seemed to reproduce the wonders of Gospel history.   But all this was only an exhibition of the force of suggestion, or the action of the law of faith, over a patient in the impressible condition."

for she has not only constantly stimulated the healing department of her church, but, year by year, she has restrained and
modified its practice, until to-day Christian Science is scarcely
more radical in its methods than are the regular schools of
her best hated enemy, *materia medica*.   Physicians have been
forced to take into account, more and more, in their dealings
with the sick, the condition of the patient's mind, and to use
it as a co-operative force with their medical treatment; and
in America this is largely owing to the stir made by Mrs. Eddy's
healers in the sick world.   In Europe this result has been obtained, not through mystery and revelation and quackery, but
in the course of regular scientific study and experiment, and
in the schools of the foremost European neurologists, psychical
treatment for certain disorders has been for many years a
recognised and established method.

There is now in America a benevolent attempt on the part
of certain churches to introduce a kind of reformed Christian
Science, and to establish " clinics " where sick cases may be
diagnosed by regular school physicians, while the pastors in
charge of the clinics administer the psychical treatment in an
effort to aid in the cure.   They aim, at these clinics, to conduct
the treatment on as scientific a basis as is possible, and their
failures as well as their successful cures are honestly recorded.
These church movements are an indirect outcome of Mrs. Eddy's
activities.   Her own congregations are built up at the expense
of those of the orthodox churches, and it is largely as a means
of self-preservation, as well as owing to a laudable desire to
increase the benefits of mental healing, that these churches are
taking up the practical side of Christian Science, and are

trying to make it " regular " and to conform to what is known of psychological causes and effects.

These various efforts to investigate the source and workings of an elusive healing principle are not without their value, even if the actual practice is more often based upon enthusiasm than upon any exact knowledge. They serve to emphasise both the benefits of psychical treatment and the harm which may rise from its ignorant or exclusive application in radical cases. But, from the nature of the subject, it is certain that the permanent value of suggestive therapeutics will ultimately be determined, not by the inexperienced or the overzealous in any walk of life, but through the slow and patient experiments of medical science; and this, too, will be the final test of the value of Mrs. Eddy's life-work.

APPENDIX A

IN Mrs. Eddy's autobiography, *Retrospection and Introspection*, she gives the following story of her ancestry:

> My ancestors, according to the flesh, were from both Scotland and England, my great-grandfather on my father's side being John McNeil of Edinburgh. His wife, my great-grandmother, was Marion Moor, and her family is said to have been in some way related to Hannah More, the pious and popular authoress of a century ago. John and Marion Moor McNeil had a daughter who perpetuated her mother's name. This second Marion McNeil was married to an Englishman named Joseph Baker, and so became my paternal grandmother. Joseph Baker and his wife, Marion McNeil, came to America seeking freedom to worship God, though they could scarcely have crossed the Atlantic more than a score of years prior to the Revolutionary period. A relative of my grandfather Baker was General Henry Knox, of Revolutionary fame. In the line of my grandmother Baker's family was the late Sir John McNeil, a Scotch knight who was prominent in British politics and at one time held the position of ambassador to Persia.

The statements made by Mrs. Eddy concerning her connection with the McNeil family of Scotland having been published in a way that brought them to the attention of that family in Scotland, drew a denial from the granddaughter of the real Sir John MacNeill. In the *Ladies' Home Journal* for November, 1903, there appeared an article entitled " Mrs. Eddy as She Really Is," introduced by an editorial note which stated: " The writing of this article and the making of illustrations on the opposite page were done with the special permission of Mrs. Eddy, and both pages having been seen by her in proof, received her full approval." In the course of this article, it is said: " Among Mrs. Eddy's ancestors was Sir John McNeill, a Scotch knight prominent in British politics, and ambassador to Persia. Her great-grandfather was the Right Honourable Sir John McNeill of Edinburgh, Scotland. Mrs. Eddy is the only survivor of her father's family, which bore the coat-of-arms of the ancient McNeills. The motto is *Vincere aut mori* (conquer or die). Surrounding the shield and enclosed in a heavy wreath is the motto of the Order of the Bath, *tria juncta in uno* (three joined in one)." Soon after this was published it was challenged by a granddaughter of Sir John MacNeill, Mrs. Florence Macalister of Aberdeen, Scotland, who wrote to Mrs. Eddy correcting her statement, and caused a correction to be published in London *Truth.* She says:

I am the only married grandchild of the late Right Honourable Sir John MacNeill, G.C.B., of Edinburgh, "who was prominent in British politics and Ambassador to Persia," and Mrs. Eddy is certainly not my daughter.

My mother, Margaret Ferooza MacNeill, was the only child of his who reached maturity, though he was three times married; she married my father, Duncan Stewart, R.N., now captain, retired, and died in 1871. Of her six children, one died unmarried, three years ago; five survive, of whom four are unmarried.

I am the wife of Commander N. G. Macalister, R.N., who is at present inspecting officer of coast guard for Aberdeen division.

I wrote to the editor of the *Ladies' Home Journal* who published Mrs. Eddy's statement, asking him to publish a correction, and I sent a copy of the letter to Mrs. Eddy herself. She did not reply at all, and he excused himself from publishing it on the ground that the correction could not appear for five months.

In March, 1904, after the publication of Mrs. Macalister's correction had been copied widely in American papers, Mrs. Eddy caused a paragraph to be inserted in the *Christian Science Sentinel*, saying that writers of her genealogy had been accustomed to connect her with the Sir John MacNeill family, and it was supposed she had a right to use the MacNeill coat-of-arms. She notified genealogical writers not to do so thereafter. Mrs. Eddy, however, continues to use the MacNeill coat-of-arms, which is engraved upon her stationery and impressed upon her seal. She defended her continued use of the coat-of-arms in a widely-published statement, issued in January, 1907, as follows:

The facts regarding the McNeill coat-of-arms are as follows: Fannie McNeill, President Pierce's niece, afterward Mrs. Judge Potter, presented to me my coat-of-arms, saying that it was taken in connection with her own family coat-of-arms. I never doubted the veracity of the gift.

Mrs. Macalister, in a recent letter, writes: " I have been amused to find that Mrs. Eddy still uses my grandfather's coat-of-arms on her notepaper, including the motto of the Bath, which even his son, had he left one, would have had no right to use, as the G.C.B. was for life only."

APPENDIX B

ANDREW JACKSON DAVIS was born August 11, 1826, in Blooming Grove, Orange County, N. Y. He grew up in poverty and ignorance, and at seventeen he had received about five months' schooling and had learned to read, write, and do simple sums in arithmetic. He was of average intelligence and had no tastes or ambitions out of the ordinary. In the year 1843, he first heard of animal magnetism, and he was himself magnetised repeatedly by William Levingston, a tailor in Poughkeepsie, where Davis then lived. Davis showed surprising clairvoyant powers while in the magnetic state, and soon he, with Levingston as magnetiser, was using his clairvoyant ability to diagnose cases of sickness and to prescribe remedies. By degrees what he called his " scientific " insight was developed, and soon, his biographer says, " there was no science the general principles and much of minutiæ of which he did not seem to comprehend while in his abnormal state."

On March 7, 1844, Davis fell into a magnetic or " superior " condition without the assistance of the magnetic process, and for two days he was " insensible to external things." He wandered in the Catskill Mountains, and while there he received, " interiorly," information of his future mission.

The following year he went to New York and commenced to lecture, while in the clairvoyant state, Dr. S. S. Lyon of

Bridgeport, Conn., acting as his magnetiser.   The last of these
lectures was delivered on January 25, 1847.   The lectures were
published in a book entitled, *The Principles of Nature, Her
Divine Revelations, and a Voice to Mankind.*   Davis continued
to lecture, and to write voluminously.   His written works consist of thirty-six volumes, nearly all of which, it is claimed,
were produced while the author was in a state of clairvoyance.
The chief of these are his first books, the *Divine Revelations*
(1847), and *The Great Harmonia* (1850).   In these Davis
gives a history of the universe, the formation of the earth, the
origin of man, and the gradual development of present civilisa-
tion.   In his first volume he gives a " Key " to the principles
of nature, and relates the " true " version of sacred history, correcting and explaining the Old and New Testaments as he
goes along.   He gives his interior impressions of the real
scheme of the material universe and of the spiritual world, and
the relations between the two.

Davis called this " revealed " system " The Harmonial Philosophy," and developed it at length in the six volumes of *The
Great Harmonia.*   In many points Davis's philosophy of life
and his theory of disease resemble Quimby's, and much of the
terminology is the same.   (When Davis began to lecture and
to write, Quimby had for several years been practising and
teaching but, so far as known, Davis had never met Quimby.)
For example, Davis states: " There is but one Principle, one
united attribute of Goodness and Truth."   This he calls the
" unchangeable, eternal Positive Mind," which " fills all negative substances.   Worlds, their forces, their physical existences,
with their life and forces, are all *negative* to this Positive Mind.

This is the great Positive Power." He compares his system to a wheel, the centre of which " is a Focus for the universal diffusion of knowledge, Truth, and the one unchangeable Principle." " Truth," he states, " is positive Principle; error is a negative principle, and as Truth is positive and eternal, it must subdue error, which is only temporal and artificial."

This Positive Mind he also calls Divine Intelligence, the First Cause, etc. He says: " Power, Wisdom, Goodness, Justice, Mercy, Truth, are the gradual developments of an eternal and internal Principle, constituting the Divine, original Essence!"

Disease, in the Davis philosophy, is not a part of the " Great Harmonia." His conclusions as to disease are:

" That *disease* is *discord;* and that this disease originates in a want of equilibrium in the circulation of the spiritual Principle throughout the organism.

" That the spiritual Principle is an organisation of refined and sublimated materials; consequently, being material, it is susceptible to material influences.

" That those physical developments which are called *diseases*, are simply evidences of constitutional or spiritual disturbances; and consequently, that there is but one ' disease,' having innumerable symptoms."

The mission of the physician, Davis says, is not to the body, " for the body is but a subordinate portion of the individual." " Disease is an effect, not a cause." " Disease is an evil to be prevented; it is an effect to be overcome. Physicians are designed to minister to the spiritual principle." " Man is a Unit," he says again. " It is not true that he has a *body* to be cured of disease separate from his *mind*."

To dispel disease and to promote individual health and happiness, Davis says, the Divine Principle working through Nature has provided certain remedial agents. These agents are " Dress, Food, Water, Air, Light, Electricity, and Magnetism." " Vital magnetism and electricity," he writes, " are the divine elements of spiritual nourishment, and are the mediums through which the spirit acts upon the body; and to restore harmony or health, the *prime-moving* principle in the body must be addressed by and through identical mediums or elements."

He also says: " By self-magnetisation, or by the magnetic or spiritual action of the influence of one individual upon another . . . the human soul can rise superior to every species of discord, and thus subdue and expel disease."

Davis believed that Christ employed animal magnetism in making cures. " It is clear, at least to the interiorly-enlightened mind, that Christ cast out diseases, Satans, or devils, by the exercise of that spiritual power, which, in our century, has unfortunately been termed ' Animal Magnetism.' "

In applying his principle practically to the care of the sick, he recommends a cheerful, hopeful spirit on the part of the patient, strict attention to diet and temperature, and regular, simple habits. Occasionally, as for rheumatism, he prescribes a kind of beverage and gives instructions how to prepare it. " The patient is requested to remember," he writes, " that I recommend a reconciliation with Nature, and not medicines, to accomplish his cure."

Like Mrs. Eddy, Davis had not much respect for learning. " Book-learning," he writes, " is mainly ephemeral and useless; but Wisdom which unfolds from out the depths of intuition, is everlasting and more valuable than seas of diamonds." He taught that true wisdom comes only through spiritual or interior vision, and that the evidence of the senses is not always trustworthy.

Some time after the publication of his first books, Davis joined the Spiritualistic movement and became well known as a leader in that sect, travelling and lecturing extensively.

APPENDIX C

THERE is no fundamental similarity between Christian Science and Shakerism, but there are significant resemblances. Ann Lee's main contribution to religious theories or pretensions was the idea that God is both masculine and feminine. She, herself, claimed to be the " female principle of God," and the Shakers believed and taught that she was the " female Christ." Mrs. Eddy also teaches the femininity of God, and Christian Scientists have claimed that she is the " feminine principle of Deity." The Shakers asserted for Ann Lee that she was greater than Christ. Mrs. Eddy has said that her revelation of Christian Science was " higher, clearer, and more permanent," [1] than that given eighteen centuries ago. The Shakers prayed always to " Our Father and Mother which are in Heaven," while Mrs. Eddy has " spiritually interpreted " the Lord's Prayer, making it read: " Our Father-Mother God." The Shakers proclaimed Ann Lee to be the woman of the Apocalypse, calling her the " God-anointed Woman," and the " Holy Comforter." In *Science and Health*, Mrs. Eddy has called the attention of her followers to the significance of the chapter in Revelation on the woman of the Apocalypse and its " relation to the present age," suggesting that the woman represents the founder of Christian Science. Christian Science, Mrs. Eddy teaches, is the " Holy Comforter." In the original

---

[1] A statement in a personal letter.

494

Mother Church in Boston is a stained-glass window, showing the woman of the Apocalypse clothed in the sun and crowned with twelve stars. It is titled " The Woman God Crowned," and above it is a representation of the book *Science and Health.* Shakers always called Ann Lee " Mother "; Christian Scientists formerly thus addressed Mrs. Eddy. Mother Ann, like Mother Eddy, declared that she had the gift of healing. She also believed that she took upon herself the sins and sufferings of others; in the early days, Mrs. Eddy had the same idea. The Shakers believed that Mother Ann had spiritual illumination— the mind that saw things as they were; that the rest of the world was deceived; that the evidence of the senses, used against her, might mislead; this is a prevailing idea in regard to Mrs. Eddy among Christian Scientists. Ann Lee governed largely through fear; her followers believed that, with her mental powers, she could inflict torment upon them in this world. In the early Christian Science days, if not now, " malicious animal magnetism "—as Mrs. Eddy named this power of mentally working evil on others—was an orthodox doctrine. The Shakers called their establishment " The Church of Christ "; Mrs. Eddy used the same name, adding the word " Scientist." They called the original foundation the " Mother Church "; Mrs. Eddy so designated her first Boston building. Ann Lee forbade audible prayer, teaching that it " exposed the desires "; Mrs. Eddy opposes audible prayer, which may " utter desires which are not real." Finally, Ann Lee enjoined celibacy. Mrs. Eddy teaches that celibacy is a more spiritual state than marriage; she permits the marriage relation merely as " expedient,"—" suffer it to be so now."

AFTERWORD

Mary Baker Eddy died of pneumonia 3 December 1910; she was in her ninetieth year. Following a simple service attended by fifty or so mourners, she was buried December eighth in Mount Auburn Cemetery near Boston. The church she had founded was taken over by the board of five directors that she had personally appointed and continues to be governed in the same way today. Membership in the Christian Science church has grown during the twentieth century; although the majority of its adherents are in the United States, there are significant numbers in all countries of the world with large Protestant populations. No membership figures have been published since 1936, but estimates range between three and five hundred thousand members worldwide. In recent years the relatively high profile of Christian Science has had less to do with its system of therapy and metaphysics than with its well-respected news media, especially *The Christian Science Monitor*. Its broad international scope, its objective standards of reporting, and its freedom from sensationalism have distinguished this publication from the outset and have brought a high degree of public respect for the Christian Science movement.

The "Georgine Milmine" biography of Mrs. Eddy, however, was treated by her followers in a different spirit. To Christian Scientists in 1909 the book had the same heretical status as Salman Rushdie's *Satanic Verses* does to many Muslims today. Numerous stories surround its publication. Witter Bynner, then assistant editor at McClure's, recalled that three spokesmen for the Christian Science church visited the McClure's office and tried to suppress publication of the magazine series.[1] Christian Scientists were said to have later bought and destroyed most copies of the book, and library copies were said to be kept out of general circulation through constant borrowings by church members.[2] In *Mrs. Eddy*, Edwin Franden Dakin writes that "according to reliable sources" the copyright for the Milmine book was purchased by a friend of Christian Science, the plates from which the book was printed were destroyed, and the original manuscript also acquired.[3] That this happened is supported by the fact that manuscripts for the "Milmine" book are held in the Archives and Library of The First Church of Christ, Scientist, in Boston.[4]

There were very few reviews of the book when it was published and again rumor has it that newspaper and magazine editors did not want to offend their Christian Science readers and advertisers by continuing to bring this controversial work to public attention. Three reviews located, however, are all very positive. An unnamed reviewer for *The Nation* (19 February 1910) describes the book as "an historical record of high value and of fascinating interest" (138) and tactfully argues that if Mrs. Eddy is sometimes handled roughly, the metaphysical truth she stumbled on remains unimperiled. For the true believer, the reviewer argues, "*Science and Health with Key to the Scriptures* retains its efficacy, whatever happens to Mrs. Eddy or her reputation" (139). An unidentified reviewer for the *New York Times Book Review*. (26 February 1910), describes the book as a "remarkable" volume, the product of "highly intelligent labor" and claims that if the subject were of more importance it would "rank among the really great biographies" (105).

A more scholarly estimate, signed by I. Woodbridge Riley, appeared in the *American Historical Review* (Vol. 15, July 1910). The reviewer, a student of nervous disorders, feels that "Milmine" does not do enough to explain the abnormal psychology of the founder of Christian Science—the record of hysteria, hypochondria, and the delusion of persecution. However, he deems this an important collection of materials and a "lively" and respectable account of Christian Science. His concluding paragraph gives what still seems like a fresh and astute estimate of what Willa Cather achieved in writing this peculiarly American life:

In fine, this book . . . offers a strangely interesting human document.
Mrs. Eddy is more than a personality, she is a type. Given the free
field of a democracy she illustrates the possibilities of a shrewd combination of religion, mental medicine, and money. Neurotic yet of in-
domitable will, illiterate yet of high imaginative power, illogical yet
of great business ability, there is here presented the extraordinary
spectacle of a career progressing from mean surroundings, through
painful invalidism, to successful supremacy. (900)

After the book came into the public domain, it was reprinted
in 1971 by Baker House Books of Grand Rapids, Michigan, with
an introduction by Stewart Hudson. While Hudson did not know
the extent of Cather's work on the biography, he nonetheless
perceived some significant connections between the biography
and Cather's fiction, focusing particularly on the question of evil
and on the eccentricities of numerous Cather characters. His es-
say makes an important start in viewing *The Life of Mary Baker
G. Eddy* as part of the Cather canon.

The reception of the "Milmine" biography, beyond the three
reviews cited above, has rested almost entirely with historians
writing in support of Mrs. Eddy and Christian Science. Early biographers of Mary Baker Eddy, such as Sibyl Wilbur and Lyman
P. Powell, essentially ignore the existence of the "Milmine" volume.[5] Only Edwin F. Dakin's sharply critical *Mrs. Eddy* gives
the "Milmine" study any prominence. However, in his monumental, three-volume biography of Mary Baker Eddy, Robert J.
Peel treats "Milmine's" biography with scholarly equanimity.
Although he has written a biography that is wholly sympathetic
to its subject, and identifies the "Milmine" book as the most hostile work written about Mrs. Eddy, he nonetheless refers frequently to "Milmine's" research, modifying her judgments when
new evidence allows, and using some of her information to give
as full a portrait of his subject as possible. Now, however, the
fate of the "Milmine" biography will also be determined by students of Willa Cather, for readers will find nascent, in this pivo-
tal apprentice work, the narratives, the themes, and the language of the future novelist.

NOTES

1. Bynner's recollections are recorded in Peter Lyon's *Success Story: The Life and Times of S. S. McClure* (New York: Scribner's, 1963), 299–302.

2. In *Willa Cather: A Memoir* (rept., Lincoln: Nebraska, 1963) Elizabeth Shepley Sergeant writes: "The book that followed the magazine serial disappeared almost immediately from circulation—the Christian Scientists are said to have bought the copies. It is hard to find one nowadays, even in a big library, and the reader is likely to have to borrow the only copy from the chief librarian's safe, and be watched by a detective while reading it" (56). Sergeant's report is corroborated by an account of church members similarly trying to suppress circulation of the first edition of *Science and Health*. Edwin Anderson of the New York Public Library told Willa Cather in a letter that the Library made a number of photographic facsimiles of the first edition for patrons, but the book was still protected by copyright so that when Trustees of Mrs. Eddy's estate learned about the library's practice they called on the library to destroy the negatives from which copies had been made and forced the library to recall those that had been sold. Edwin Anderson to Willa Cather, 28 November 1922, Anderson Papers, Manuscripts and Archives Division, New York Public Library.

3. See Edwin Franden Dakin, *Mrs. Eddy: The Biography of a Virginal Mind* (New York: Scribner's, 1929), p. 541.

4. The manuscript belongs to the "Milmine collection." References to this repository of materials appear in the notes for volume three of Robert J. Peel's biography of Mrs. Eddy. Volume three is titled *Mary Baker Eddy: The Years of Authority* (New York: Holt, Rinehart and Winston, 1977).

5. In *Life of Mary Baker Eddy* (Concord Publishing Company, 1909), Sibyl Wilbur makes no mention of the *McClure's* series at all, while Lyman P. Powell in *Mary Baker Eddy: A Life Size Portrait* (New York: Macmillan, 1930) makes only a passing reference to the series in his introduction and gives three footnotes to information he has culled from the "Milmine" book.

Acknowledgments: L. Brent Bohlke's discovery of the confidential letter from Willa Cather to Edwin H. Anderson initiated the identification of *The Life of Mary Baker G. Eddy and the History of Christian Science* as part of the Cather canon. This reissue of the book stems from the late Professor Bohlke's extensive research into religion in Willa Cather's fiction.

I have been assisted in preparing both the introduction and afterword for this edition by several individuals who have provided both research materials and advice in relation to this project. These include Professor Susan Rosowski, University of Nebraska–Lincoln; Helen Cather Southwick, Pittsburgh; Professor Blanche Gelfant, Dartmouth College; Janet Giltrow, Simon Fraser University; Beverley Bohlke, Lincoln; Laura K. O'Keefe, Manuscripts Specialist, The New York Public Library.

I especially thank Kevin Synnott, Russell Sage College, Troy, New York, who examined the "Milmine Collection" in the Archives and Library of The First Church of Christ, Scientist, and determined without doubt that Willa Cather had participated editorially in preparing the magazine articles for book publication.